IDEAS IN CONTEXT

PHILOSOPHY IN HISTORY

IDEAS IN CONTEXT

Edited by Richard Rorty, J. B. Schneewind and Quentin Skinner

The books in this series will discuss the emergence of intellectual traditions and of related new disciplines. The procedures, aims and vocabularies that were generated will be set in the context of the alternatives available within the contemporary frameworks of ideas and institutions. Through detailed studies of the evolution of such traditions, and their modification by different audiences, it is hoped that a new picture will form of the development of ideas in their concrete contexts. By this means, artificial distinctions between the history of philosophy, of the various sciences, of society and politics, and of literature, may be seen to dissolve.

This is the first volume in the series. Forthcoming titles include:

J. G. A. Pocock, *Virtue, Commerce and History*
David Lieberman, *The Province of Legislation Determined*
Noel Malcolm, *Hobbes and Voluntarism*
Quentin Skinner, *Studies in Early Modern Intellectual History*
Edmund Leites (ed.), *Conscience and Casuistry in Early Modern Europe*
Lynn S. Joy, *Gassendi the Atomist: Advocate of History in an Age of Science*
Mark Goldie, *The Tory Ideology: Politics and Ideas in Restoration England*

This series is published with the support of the Exxon Education Foundation.

PHILOSOPHY IN HISTORY

Essays on
the historiography of philosophy

EDITED BY

RICHARD RORTY
J. B. SCHNEEWIND
QUENTIN SKINNER

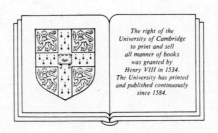

The right of the
University of Cambridge
to print and sell
all manner of books
was granted by
Henry VIII in 1534.
The University has printed
and published continuously
since 1584.

CAMBRIDGE UNIVERSITY PRESS

CAMBRIDGE

LONDON   NEW YORK   NEW ROCHELLE
MELBOURNE   SYDNEY

Published by the Press Syndicate of the University of Cambridge
The Pitt Building, Trumpington Street, Cambridge CB2 1RP
32 East 57th Street, New York, NY 10022, USA
296 Beaconsfield Parade, Middle Park, Melbourne 3206, Australia

© Cambridge University Press 1984

First published 1984

Printed in Great Britain at
The Pitman Press, Bath

Library of Congress catalogue card number: 84–9524

British Library cataloguing in publication data
Philosophy in history. – (Ideas in context)
1. Philosophy – Historiography
I. Rorty, Richard II. Schneewind, J.B.
III. Skinner, Quentin IV. Series
107'.22   B51.4

ISBN 0 521 25352 7 hard covers
ISBN 0 521 27330 7 paperback

CONTENTS

v

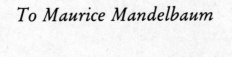

To Maurice Mandelbaum

PREFACE

The lectures published here were delivered as a series with the general title 'Philosophy in history' at the Johns Hopkins University during 1982–3. The series was made possible by a grant from the Exxon Education Foundation, whose president, Dr Robert Payton, did everything a patient and generous friend could do in assisting us at every stage of our venture. His encouragement and faith in the project remained cheering and constant through all the changes in our plans. For his confidence, and for the graciousness of the Foundation, we are deeply grateful.

We wish to thank the Johns Hopkins University for donating the use of its accounting offices and for providing us with facilities for holding the lectures. The practical burdens of arrangements were largely carried by Ms Nancy Thompson of the Johns Hopkins University Philosophy Department, who handled transatlantic complexities and local emergencies with equal skill and patience. We offer her our warmest thanks. We also wish to thank Mr T. Cleveland for his assistance, and to express our deep gratitude to Jonathan Sinclair-Wilson, our Editor at the Cambridge University Press, and to Elizabeth O'Beirne-Ranelagh, who sub-edited our type-script, for the care and efficiency they have displayed at every stage in the production of this book.

In commissioning the essays that follow, we had in mind the desirability of including particular case-studies as well as more general reflections on the relationship between philosophy and its history. We have organized the volume in such a way as to reflect both these interests. Although the division is not a hard-and-fast one, Part I consists mainly of more general essays, while Part II consists of examples taken from ancient, early-modern and more recent philosophy.

While the editors do not think with one mind or speak with one voice, the selection of lecturers and the general ideas expressed in the Introduction are the work of all three of us.

Richard Rorty
J. B. Schneewind
Quentin Skinner

CONTRIBUTORS

M. R. Ayers is Tutorial Fellow in Philosophy at Wadham College, Oxford. His publications include a number of papers on the history and historiography of philosophy, and he is at present completing a study of Locke's philosophy.

Thomas Baldwin is a Lecturer in Philosophy at the University of Cambridge. He has published several articles on ethics and the philosophy of language and is at present engaged on a study of G. E. Moore.

Myles Burnyeat is Laurence Professor of Ancient Philosophy in the University of Cambridge and a Fellow of Robinson College. He is the editor of *The Skeptical Tradition* (1983) and two volumes of his essays, *Philosophical Explorations in Ancient Thought*, are forthcoming from Cambridge University Press.

John Dunn is Reader in Politics at the University of Cambridge and a Fellow of King's College. His books include *The Political Thought of John Locke* (1969), *Political Obligation in its Historical Context* (1980), *Locke* (1984), and *Rethinking Modern Political Theory* (forthcoming from Cambridge University Press).

Michael Frede is Professor of Philosophy at Princeton University. His publications include monographs on Plato's *Sophist* and on Stoic logic, as well as articles on Greek philosophy, Greek grammarians and Greek medicine.

Ian Hacking is Professor of the History and Philosophy of Science and Technology at the University of Toronto. His books include *The Emergence of Probability* (1975) and *Representing and Intervening: Introductory Topics in the Philosophy of Natural Science* (1984).

Peter Hylton is Assistant Professor of Philosophy at the University of California at Santa Barbara. He has published articles on the philosophy of language and the origins of analytical philosophy, on which he is at present writing a book.

Lorenz Krüger is Professor of Philosophy at The Free University of Berlin. His publications include articles on the philosophy of science and the history of modern philosophy and two books, *Rationalismus und Entwurf einer universalen Logik bei Leibniz* (1969), and *Der Begriff des Empirismus: Erkenntnistheorische Studien am Beispiel John Lockes* (1973).

Bruce Kuklick is Professor of History at the University of Pennsylvania. His books include *Josiah Royce: An Intellectual Biography* (1972), *The Rise of American Philosophy: Cambridge Massachusetts 1860–1930* (1977) and a forthcoming study, *Churchmen and Philosophers: From Jonathan Edwards to John Dewey 1746–1934*.

Wolf Lepenies is Professor of Sociology at The Free University of Berlin, and currently a member of The School of Social Science at the Institute for Advanced Study, Princeton. His books include *Melancholie und Gesellschaft* (1969), *Soziologische Anthropologie* (1971) and *Das Ende der Naturgeschichte* (1976).

Alasdair MacIntyre is Professor of Philosophy at Vanderbilt University. His books include *A Short History of Ethics* (1966) and *After Virtue* (1981).

Richard Rorty is Kenan Professor of the Humanities at the University of Virginia. His books include *Philosophy and the Mirror of Nature* (1979) and *The Consequences of Pragmatism* (1982).

J. B. Schneewind is Professor of Philosophy at The Johns Hopkins University. His books include *Backgrounds of English Victorian Literature* (1970) and *Sidgwick's Ethics and Victorian Moral Philosophy* (1977).

Quentin Skinner is Professor of Political Science in the University of Cambridge and a Fellow of Christ's College. His publications include *The Foundations of Modern Political Thought* (1978) and *Machiavelli* (1981).

Hans Sluga is Professor of Philosophy at the University of California at Berkeley. He has published articles on Frege and Wittgenstein and is the author of *Gottlob Frege* (1980).

Charles Taylor is Professor of Philosophy at McGill University. His books include *The Explanation of Behaviour* (1964), *Hegel* (1975), *Hegel and Modern Society* (1979), and two volumes of his *Philosophical Papers* are forthcoming from Cambridge University Press.

Introduction

Imagine a thousand-volume work entitled *The Intellectual History of Europe*. Imagine also a great convocation of resurrected thinkers, at which every person mentioned in the pages of this work is given a copy and invited to begin by reading the passages concerning himself or herself, and then to read alternately backwards and forwards until he has mastered the full thousand volumes. An ideal work of this title would fulfil the following conditions:

1. The person whose activities and writings are being described finds the description intelligible, except for the parenthetical remarks which say things like 'This was later to be known as . . .' and 'Since the distinction between X and Y was yet to be drawn, A's use of "Z" cannot be interpreted as . . .', and he comes to understand even these remarks as he reads on.

2. On finishing the book, everyone described endorses the description of himself as, though of course insufficiently detailed, at least reasonably accurate and sympathetic.

3. The entire assemblage of the resurrected, at the point at which they have all read through the book, are in as good a position to exchange views, to argue, to engage in collaborative inquiry on subjects of common interest, as secondary sources for their colleagues' works can make them.

This seems a plausible ideal for intellectual history because we hope that such history will give us a sense of Europe as (in the phrase which Gadamer has adapted from Hölderlin) 'the conversation which we are'. We hope that intellectual history will weave a thick enough rope of overlapping beliefs and desires so that we can read our way back through the centuries without ever having to ask 'How could rational men and women have thought (or done) that?' So we think that an ideal *Intellectual History of Europe* should let, e.g., Paracelsus get in touch with Archimedes on the one hand and Boyle on the other. It should put Cicero, Marsilius of Padua, and Bentham in a position to engage in debate. To give up on such hopes, to believe that overlap will fail at crucial points and that 'incommensurability' in some sense strong enough to frustrate conversation will occur, is to give up the idea of intellectual progress. Such pessimism must resign itself to regarding 'the history of European thought' as a misleading description of what is in fact a miscellany of self-contained traditions. On this view, we should not attempt intellectual history, for what is needed is something more like a series of ethnographic reports. Such pessimism is characteristic of those who are impressed with how very strange some ways of speaking and acting in the European past have been, and with how very anachronistic (i.e., un-intelligible to the figures being described) much intellectual history is.

There has been much debate among both philosophers of science and historians about whether such pessimism is justified – about whether discontinuities, intellectual revolutions, and epistemological ruptures are to be seen merely as places where communication becomes difficult, or as places where it becomes genuinely impossible. We believe that it is not justified, that there are always what have been called 'rational bridgeheads' – not high-level criteria, but rather low-level platitudes – which have made conversation possible across chasms. But for our present purposes we need not insist on this optimism. For we wish to discuss not the question of whether *The Intellectual History of Europe* can be written, but rather the question: supposing it were written, what would be its relation to the history of philosophy?

Such a question would be equally in point if one substituted 'economics' or 'law' or 'morality' or 'the novel' for 'philosophy'. For the lines which demarcate topics or genres or disciplines are not drawn in *The Intellectual History of Europe*. Indeed, the ideal book of this title could not be written unless the issue of whether a certain question was philosophical or scientific or theological, or whether a given problem was one of morals or of manners, had been bracketed. More generally, such a history would have to bracket most questions of reference and of truth. The author of such a history does not care, for purposes of her work, whether Paracelsus was right about sulphur, or Cicero about republics. She only cares about knowing what each would have said in reply to various different sorts of contemporaries, and about facilitating communication between all of them and their ancestors and descendants. Her thousand volumes never take up the question 'What are these people talking about?', much less 'Which ones got it right?' That is why she must write a chronicle rather than a treatise. She is like the literary executrix of an extraordinarily imaginative and productive writer of fantasy – one who has spun an enormously long, rambling, story which must be reconstructed from the writer's letters to friends, memoirs by those friends, jotting on old envelopes, and rejection letters from publishers, as well as from the surviving manuscripts. She must enter the world of the texts, determined to paste together the ideally complete version of the fantasy. She must not allow herself to wonder which parts of it were based on real-life characters, nor whether she approves of its moral tone. She does not view herself as writing a story of progress nor of decline, because, for the purposes of her work, she has no views about how the story should come out.

For her readers, however, things are different. They typically read her book as a story of progress – progress in the field of their special interest, or in matters of particular concern to them. (Some, of course, may read it as a story of decline, but they too see the story as having a direction. They care about how it comes out.) Her readers automatically gloss various passages with such phrases as 'first recognition of the fact that *p*', 'first clear grasp of the concept *C*' and 'failure to recognize the irrelevance of *q* to *r*'. If the reader is a philosopher who is reasonably content with the present state of his discipline he will find himself saying things like 'Here philosophy separates itself from __ and begins to have a history of its own' or 'I now realize that the really important figures in the history of philosophy were. . .' All such judgments are attempts to tie his own views about what is the case into a story about the gradual discovery of these facts, and of the even more gradual discovery of a vocabulary in which one can ask the questions to which his own views are answers.

When a philosopher mines *The Intellectual History of Europe* for materials for a *History of Western Philosophy* his choices will depend not only upon the decade and the country in which he is writing, but on his special interests within philosophy. If he is interested primarily in metaphysics, epistemology, and philosophy of language he will tend to ignore the links of belief and vocabulary which, in *The Intellectual History of Europe*, connect Spinoza and Seneca. He will be more interested in those which link Spinoza with Descartes. If he is concerned primarily with philosophy of religion he will attend to links between Spinoza and Philo, and be less interested in those between Spinoza and Huygens. If he specializes in social philosophy, he will care more about Spinoza's relation to Hobbes than about his relation to Leibniz.

Spinoza was a nodal point in a web of communications and concerns which cannot easily be mapped on the present organization of intellectual life. Spinoza could not easily have answered the question whether it was his concern with God, or with the state, or with the passions, or with mathematical physics, or with what was later known as 'the theory of ideas', which was 'at the centre of his philosophy'. But the author of a *History of Western Philosophy* needs to ask such questions. He needs to see Spinoza's writing as organized around certain distinctively philosophical problems, and he needs to separate discussion of these problems from 'the transient concerns of Spinoza's day'.

The task of the author of *The Intellectual History of Europe* was lightened, and indeed made possible, by the fact that she could ignore such questions. In her book, Spinoza is not described as 'a philosopher' as opposed to 'a scientist' or 'a renegade rabbi', nor as 'a rationalist' nor as 'a panpsychist'. She mentions such terms without using them. The measure of her tact, and thus of the extent to which her work approaches the ideal, consists largely in her use of quotation marks. Her book is of no help in constructing a grid which will put him in his proper place – which will show, for example, that he was or was not a 'great philosopher'.

To construct such a grid – to construct criteria for answering such questions as 'Should we include Spinoza (or, to take more debatable cases, Montaigne or Emerson) among the philosophers?', 'among the *great* philosophers?' – is to have a view about the relation of intellectual history to the way things really are. For the idea of a 'proper place' requires a relatively closed intellectual world – a determinate lay-out of reality, and thus of the problems which reality poses to the inquiring mind. It requires that one know quite a bit about how the world (not just the world of stars and plants and mud, but that of poems and moral dilemmas and politics as well) divides up into areas and problems – solved or unsolved. The author of *The Intellectual History of Europe* has to pretend not to know the way the world is.

One might be tempted to put the difference between our ideal intellectual historian and the author of a *History of Western Philosophy* by saying that she is concerned with the meanings of past utterances whereas he is concerned with their truth and importance as well. She is concerned with the pattern of use of terms, he with the relation of that use to the way the physical and moral worlds actually are. But this way of putting the matter can be, and has been, very misleading. For it suggests that he can take her word for what a given sentence means, and then confront that meaning with the facts. But it is not clear that *The Intellectual History of Europe* tells you what the sentences of the past meant. To read through the ideal version of this book (updated through last year) would indeed put the would-be historian of philosophy in the best possible position to assign a meaning to a sentence in a text from the past. But that is like saying that years of living among, and bickering with, a tribe, puts the anthropologist in the best possible position to translate their sentences. So it does, but he may have a lot of further work to do before being able to actualize this capacity. It is one thing to fall in with another's language-game and another to translate her language into yours. Similarly, it is one thing to have mastered *The Intellectual History of Europe* and another thing to know how to put one of the sentences quoted in it in a form which allows confrontation with the way the world is.

This gap exists just insofar as the vocabulary used in the sentence strikes us moderns as an inconvenient, awkward way of describing the world, or of stating the problems to be addressed. We are then tempted to say things like 'Well, if you take it as meaning p, then it's of course true, and indeed trivial, but if you take it as meaning q, then. . .' Your reading of *The Intellectual History of Europe* does not, *by itself*, help you know which way to take it. For although that book lets you know what the original inscriber of the sentence would have said he meant, what he would have said to a whole range of questions from his contemporaries about the kind of speech-act he was performing and about its expected audience and impact, all this information is of little use in choosing between interpreting the sentence, for purposes of confrontation with reality, as p or as q. 'P' and 'q' are sentences of *our* language, convenient and elegant sentences designed to fit the contours of the world as we know it to be. The predicates they contain pick out kinds of things into which we know the world to be divided (e.g., stars and galaxies, prudence and morality). The fluency in awkward and inconvenient ways of talking given by a thorough acquaintance with *The Intellectual History of Europe* does little to let one know which of these elegant alternatives to prefer.

It is tempting to pose the question of whether the meaning, or the reference, or both, of the terms used in such a sentence have changed between its author's time and our own. But it is not clear that this question needs to be asked by either sort of historian. Recent discussion of such questions by philosophers of science and philosophers of language was, to be sure, inspired by problems encountered in the historiography of the natural sciences. But although such discussion has served to broaden and deepen the range of considerations and examples thought relevant within philosophical semantics, it has not produced results which have made historians clearer about their tasks or methods. Nor does it seem likely to do so in the future. For although it was the history of science which engendered many current disputes about meaning and reference, these disputes have now become sufficiently remote from the practice of interpretation as to make it dubious that historians should expect anything like a 'theory of interpretation' to eventuate. Neither the controversy between Gadamer and Betti about the objectivity of interpretation, nor that between Charles Taylor and Mary Hesse about the distinction between *Geistes-* and the *Naturwissenschaften*, nor that between Davidson and Dummett concerning holism in semantics, nor those concerning the viability of a causal theory of reference, seem likely to tell the would-be historian of philosophy more than he already knows about how to mine *The Intellectual History of Europe* for the raw material he needs. The thousand volumes he has read have told him all there is to know about the

changes in the *uses* of the terms in which he is interested. He may be
forgiven for saying that he does not care how, on the basis of those uses,
semantics proceeds to distribute meaning and reference.

Rather than 'philosophical foundations of the practice of interpretation',
what such an historian needs is a sense of when it is permissible to simply
filter out the sentences for which such problems of interpretation seem
insoluble and confine himself to those sentences where a translation into
the modern idiom can be hammered out, and fitted neatly together with
translations of other sentences. Such a translation will, typically, not be
word-for-word, but it may nevertheless be quite straightforward. The
anthropologist often has to say things like 'What he *said* was "The other
white god died because he quarrelled with the spirit inhabiting the *mburi*",
but what he *meant* was that Pogson-Smith died because, like an idiot, he'd
eaten some of those berries over there.' The historian of philosophy often
has to say things like 'What Kant *said* was "This thoroughgoing identity of
the apprehension of a manifold which is given in intuition contains a
synthesis of representation and is possible only through the consciousness
of this synthesis. . ." but what he *meant* was that, however primitive and
disorderly the experience is supposed to be, if it is accompanied by self-
consciousness then it will have to admit of at least that degree of intellectual
organization which is involved in one's being able to claim one's past
mental states as one's own.'* By filtering out certain sentences as irrelevant
to his concerns, and to the concerns the author himself would have had if he
had known more about how the world is, while giving a sympathetic
rendering of the remainder, the historian of philosophy helps the dead
philosopher put his act together for a new audience.

Such filtering and paraphrasing produces a history which is nothing like
a selection of passages from *The Intellectual History of Europe*. But it
obviously has to be done if one is going to have a history 'of philosophy' or
'of the mind–body problem' or 'of empiricism' or 'of secular morality'. To
say that such histories are anachronistic is true but pointless. They are
supposed to be anachronistic. The anthropologist is not doing his job if he
merely offers to teach us how to bicker with his favorite tribe, how to be
initiated into their rituals, etc. What we want to be told is whether that tribe
has anything interesting to tell us – interesting by *our* lights, answering to
our concerns, informative about what *we* know to exist. Any anthropologist who rejected this assignment on the grounds that filtering and
paraphrase would distort and betray the integrity of the tribe's culture

---

* The double-quoted sentence beginning 'This thoroughgoing identity' comes from Kant,
Critique of Pure Reason, B.113. The portion of the sentence after 'What he *meant* was' is taken
from Jonathan Bennett, *Kant's Analytic* (Cambridge: Cambridge University Press, 1966),
p. 119.

would no longer be an anthropologist, but a sort of cultist. He is, after all, working for *us*, not for *them*. Similarly, the historian of *X*, where *X* is something we know to be real and important, is working for those of us who share that knowledge, not for our unfortunate ancestors who did not.

Someone who wishes to write *A History of Western Philosophy* must, therefore, either deny that contemporary philosophy is something real and important (in which case he will write the history of philosophy as one might write the history of witchcraft), or else proceed to filter out the sentences which are not worth translating, while being conscientiously anachronistic in translating the remainder. Most such writers do a bit of both, for most of them despair of making a coherent story out of *all* the texts which one or another contemporary philosophical school calls 'philosophical'. A coherent story will be one which shows some of these texts to be central and others peripheral, some to be genuinely philosophical and others merely pseudo-philosophical (or only tangentially and momentarily philosophical). The historian of philosophy is going to have to have views about whether, for example, moral philosophy is central and epistemology relatively peripheral to the subject, or the converse. He will also have to have views about which schools or movements within contemporary philosophy count as 'genuine' or 'important' philosophy. It is because of disagreements on these matters that historians of philosophy occlude texts which are highlighted by their rivals. Each historian of philosophy is working for an 'us' which consists, primarily, of those who see the contemporary philosophical scene as he does. So each will treat in a 'witchcraft' manner what another will treat as the antecedents of something real and important in contemporary philosophy.

From the description we have given, it might seem that the intellectual historian and the historian of philosophy are doing such different jobs that they can hardly be thought of as producing two species of a single genus called 'history'. Such doubts about what his or her counterpart is doing are, indeed, voiced by both. Thus the historian of philosophy may dismiss the intellectual historian as a mere antiquarian. She, in turn, may dismiss him as a mere propagandist – someone rewriting the past for the benefit of a faction in the present. He may think of her as uninterested in philosophical truth, and she may think of him as uninterested in historical truth. Such exchanges of recriminations have led to attempts to wrest the history of philosophy out of the hands of the intellectual historians, and counter-attempts to reinstate intellectual history by arguing that the first duty of the historian is to avoid anachronism. Sometimes it is suggested that we must develop a third genre – a happy medium, more philosophical than *The Intellectual History of Europe* and more historically accurate than any known or currently imaginable *History of Western Philosophy*.

We do not wish to suggest an attempt of either sort, nor to suggest that a third genre is needed. An opposition between intellectual historians and historians of philosophy seems to us as factitious as would an opposition between scientists and engineers, or librarians and scholars, or rough-hewers and shapers. It is an appearance created by the attempt to be sententious about 'the nature of history' or 'the nature of philosophy' or both, treating 'history' and 'philosophy' as names of natural kinds – disciplines whose subject and purpose are familiar and uncontroversial. Such attempts produce red-faced snortings about how a given book 'isn't what I call history' or 'doesn't count as philosophy'. They take for granted that there is a well-known part of the world – the past – which is the domain of history, and another well-known part, usually thought of as a set of 'timeless problems', which is the domain of philosophy.

There is nothing wrong with saying that 'history gives us the truth about the past' except triviality. Pseudo-problems arise, however, when one tries to make a distinction between knowing about the relation of the past to the present and knowing about the past in itself. These are special cases of the more general pseudo-problem raised when one tries to make a distinction between knowing about the relation of reality to our minds, languages, interests and purposes and knowing about reality as it is in itself. These are pseudo-problems because there is no contrast to be drawn between knowing about X and knowing about the relations between X and Y, Z, etc. There is nothing to be known about X save how to describe it in a language which will exhibit its relations to Y, Z, etc. The idea of 'the truth about the past, uncontaminated by present perspectives or concerns' is like the idea of 'real essence, uncontaminated by the preconceptions and concerns built into any human language'. It is a romantic ideal of purity which has no relation to any actual inquiry which human beings have undertaken or could undertake.

The idea of 'sticking to the philosophical problems and eschewing anti-quarianism' is less absurd than that of 'sticking to the past and eschewing its relation to the present' only because it is possible simply to enumerate what will count as 'the philosophical problems', whereas it is not possible to point to 'the past'. One can, in other words, delimit something for 'philosophy' to name by being fairly specific about what will count and what will not, but one cannot delimit something for 'history' to name by gesturing over one's shoulder. 'Philosophy' is a sufficiently flexible term so that no one is greatly surprised when a philosopher announces that half of the previous canon of 'great philosophers' must be thrown out because the problems of philosophy have been discovered to be different than had previously been thought. Such a philosopher usually explains that the slack will be taken up by something else ('religion' or 'science' or 'literature').

But this very flexibility is the reason why it is hopeless to say something general and interesting about the relation between philosophy and history.

There is, however, something to be said about the relation between books which can most easily be seen as chunks of *The Intellectual History of Europe* and books which think of themselves as offering all, or a chunk of, the history of Western philosophy. The first thing to say is that our previous description of these two genres has been a description of two impossibly ideal types. Our intellectual historian who has no interest in how the story comes out and our historian of philosophy who knows perfectly well what philosophy is, and can tell a central philosophical problem from a peripheral one or from a non-philosophical one at a glance, are caricatures. But we have tried to make them sympathetic caricatures, for we see both as limiting cases of efforts which are altogether praise-worthy, equally indispensable to the health of the republic of letters. Each of these efforts is led, on occasion, to caricature itself – but this is the sort of self-caricature which an honest devotion to a worthy aim can easily induce.

There will never be such a book as *The Intellectual History of Europe,* not only because the ideal we have specified could never be attained in a mere thousand (or million) volumes, but because – such is the size of our brains and the span of our lives – anybody who had read or written a few of these volumes would not be able to read or write most of the others. The simple fact that any historian has got to start by being selective – by singling out some texts as central and relegating others to footnotes – is enough to disabuse us of the ideal that we have set up. The thought that descriptions of political discourse in twelfth-century France, metaphysics in nineteenth-century Germany, and painting in fifteenth-century Urbino, might some day flow together to create the seamless tapestry which would be our ideal *Intellectual History of Europe* is an elevating one. But it is the idea of a book written by no human hand.

Since every book on such topics will be conditioned by the author's sense of relevance, a sense determined by everything she knows – not just the things she knows about her period but by everything she knows about everything – no such work will fit seamlessly together with works on flanking periods or topics written a generation earlier or a generation later. No intellectual historian can avoid the kind of selectivity which automati-cally results from an awareness of present-day science, theology, philos-ophy and literature. Intellectual history cannot be written by people who are illiterate in the culture of their prospective readers, for it is one thing to bracket questions of truth and reference and another not to know when such questions arise. To put present-day readers in touch with a past figure is precisely to be able to say such things as 'This was later to be known as. . .' and 'Since the distinction between X and Y was yet to be drawn, A's use of "Z" cannot be interpreted as. . .' But knowing when to say such things – knowing what to bracket when – requires knowing what has been going on recently in all sorts of areas.

Just as the need to select means that the intellectual historian could not ignore the philosophy of her own day when writing about Spinoza even if she wanted to, so the need to write about Spinoza (rather than merely about what one would be saying were one now to utter one of Spinoza's sentences) means that the historian of philosophy cannot ignore intellectual history. Nor, of course, does he ever do so for long. The pose such historians sometimes affect – 'Well, let's see whether the old boy got anything right' – is only a pose, and always short-lived. One cannot figure out whether Spinoza got anything right before figuring out what he was talking about. Since Spinoza himself may not have known what he *was* talking about when he wrote a given sentence (because he was so confused about what the world really is like) one will not know how to map his sentence on to the world as we now know it to be without reading lots and lots of those sentences in the hermeneutic, reconstructive, charitable ways characteristic of intellectual historians. No matter how philistine the historian of philosophy may want to be, he will need translations of what Spinoza wrote which will let him get a handle on the truth-value of Spinoza's sentences. This will require him to examine present translations critically to see whether they are infected with the philosophies of some intervening epoch, and eventually to work out his own translations. He will become an historical scholar and re-translator whether he wants to or not. He will find himself driven to read the treatments of Spinoza's intellectual environment in the works of intellectual historians in order to know how to translate, just as the intellectual historian will, consciously or unconsciously, derive her sense of what is worth translating from contemporary philosophical movements.

So the result of constructing these two ideal types, and seeing that they are *merely* ideal, is the realization that there cannot be a nice clear-cut division of functions between intellectual history and the history of philosophy. Rather, each genre will continually be correcting and updating the other. Another way to put this moral is to say that we might do well to forget the bugbears of 'anachronism' and 'antiquarianism'. If to be anachronistic is to link a past X to a present Y rather than studying it in isolation, then every historian is always anachronistic. In practice, the charge of anachronism means that a past X has been related to a contemporary Y rather than, as it might better have been, to a contemporary Z. It is always a matter of selecting among contemporary concerns with which to associate X, not a matter of abjuring such concerns. Without some selecting, the historian is reduced to duplicating the texts which constitute the relevant past. But why do that? We turn to the historian because we do not understand the copy of the text we already have. Giving us a second copy will not help. To understand the text just *is* to relate it helpfully to something else. The only question is what that something else will be.

Conversely, if to be antiquarian is to study X without regard to such concerns, nobody has ever succeeded in being antiquarian. At most she has succeeded in relating X to some Y which makes X less interesting than if it had been related to Z. *Some* concern must dictate the questions we ask and the criteria of relevance we use, and contemporary concerns at least make for interesting history. Avoiding them will merely substitute the concerns of some previous generation. This can of course be done, but unless they are also our concerns there is no particular reason to do it.

There is, in our view, nothing general to be said in answer to the question 'How should the history of philosophy be written?' except 'As self-consciously as one can – in as full awareness as possible of the *variety* of contemporary concerns to which a past figure may be relevant.' However, once one comes down from the level of questions about 'the nature of the history of philosophy', there remains much to be said about contemporary trends in the historiography of philosophy. We would urge that, in Britain and America, the historiography of philosophy has recently been less self-conscious than it ought to have been. In particular, the influence of analytic philosophy has worked against self-consciousness of the desired sort. Analytic philosophers have seen no need to situate themselves within Gadamer's 'conversation which we are' because they take themselves to be the first to have understood what philosophy is, what questions are the genuinely philosophical ones.

The result of having this self-image has been an attempt to tease out the 'genuinely philosophical elements' in the work of past figures, putting aside as irrelevant their 'religious' or 'scientific' or 'literary' or 'political' or 'ideological' concerns. It has become customary to take the concerns of contemporary analytic philosophy as the focus of attention, and to leave aside present-day religious or scientific or literary or political or ideological concerns, as well as those of present-day non-analytic philosophers. This, in turn, has the result of dividing up past philosophers into those who anticipated the questions asked by contemporary analytic philosophers and those who held back the maturity of philosophy by diverting attention to other questions. Such an attitude produces a history of philosophy which eschews continuous narrative, but is more like a collection of anecdotes – anecdotes about people who stumbled upon the 'real' philosophical questions but did not realize what they had discovered. It is hard to make a sequence of such anecdotes mesh with the sort of narratives intellectual historians construct. So it is inevitable that such narratives should strike analytic philosophers as 'not getting at the *philosophical* point' and that intellectual historians should see analytic philosophers as 'anachronistically' reading current interests back into the past.

'Anachronism' is, we have said, not the right charge to make. Rather, the complaint should be that stories about people who almost stumbled upon what we now know to be philosophy are like stories about people who would have discovered America if they had just sailed a little further. A collection of such stories cannot be a *history* of anything. On the analytic philosophers' own account of the situation, indeed, there is nothing which can properly be called 'the history of philosophy', but only a history of almost-philosophy, only a pre-history of philosophy. If analytic philosophers were willing to accept this consequence – if they were willing to turn over the construction of coherent narratives to the intellectual historians, and not to worry about whether the latter saw 'the *philosophical* point', all might be well. But they are not. They would like to have it both ways.

This will not work. Analytic philosophers cannot both be the discoverers of what Descartes and Kant were really up to and be the culmination of a great tradition, participants in the final episode of a narrative of progress. They cannot construct such a narrative by leaving out, e.g., most thinkers between Ockham and Descartes, or between Kant and Frege. A gappy narrative of this sort will not explain 'how philosophy became mature' but will merely show how, on various occasions, it narrowly failed to become mature.

A preference for such a collection of anecdotes produces an impatience with the intellectual historians' attempts at continuous narrative. Analytic philosophers see such attempts as conflating philosophy with non-philosophy, as misunderstanding philosophical questions by mixing them up with religious, literary, etc., questions. This attitude is not so much the result of treating philosophy as a newly developed 'hard science' as of continuing to hold a pre-Kuhnian view of the historiography of the hard sciences. On that sort of view, questions do not change but answers do. On a Kuhnian view, by contrast, the major task of the historian of a scientific discipline is to understand when and why the questions changed. The principal defect of the kind of history of philosophy to which analytic philosophy has given rise is its lack of interest in the rise and fall of questions. For understanding why certain questions once called 'philosophical' were replaced by others, and why the old questions were then labelled 'religious', 'ideological', 'literary', 'sociological', etc., requires knowing quite a lot about religious, literary, and social developments. It requires seeing past Xs in terms of present non-philosophical Zs

as well as in terms of the *Y*s which are the topics of contemporary analytic philosophy.

It is a pity that analytic philosophers have tried to think of themselves as the culminating development of a natural kind of human activity ('philosophical reflection'), rather than simply as participants in a brilliant new intellectual initiative. This attempt has had bad effects not only on the relations between philosophers and intellectual historians (and thus to a lot of *Sprachstreit* about what is to count as 'history of philosophy'), but on philosophy itself. For the disciplinary matrix of analytic philosophy has made it increasingly difficult for those within it to recognize that questions once asked by great dead philosophers are still being asked by con-temporaries – contemporaries who count neither as 'philosophers' nor as 'scientists'. Analytic philosophy inherited from positivism the idea that the only fitting conversational partners for philosophers were scientists, and so recent history of philosophy has pursued connections between Kant and Helmholtz but not between Kant and Valéry, between Hume and G. E. Moore but not between Hume and Jefferson. The same idea has made it difficult for analytic philosophers to think about their relation to culture as a whole, and particularly easy for them to set aside, as a pointless distraction, the question of their relation to the rest of the humanities. By trying to interpret past figures as having done things which culminated in what analytic philosophy is now doing, philosophers occlude lots of the ways in which works of the past figures traditionally tagged as 'philos-ophers' lead up to a lot of other things that are going on nowadays. By limiting the range of contemporary *Y*s to which past *X*s can be related, they limit both their ability to read past philosophers and their own philosophi-cal imagination.

This problem of lack of self-consciousness concerning one's place in history was less acute before the rise of analytic philosophy, simply because training in the subject was then much more historical. In earlier periods, the reinterpretation of past philosophers so as to change the received account of 'philosophical progress' was a familiar mode of philosophical self-expression. That approach to philosophy sometimes produced the excess of historical self-consciousness which Nietzsche characterized as 'a disadvantage of history for life'. But it did have the advantage of inculcating a sense of historical contingency, a sense that 'philosophy' has meant many quite different things. It suggested that phil-osophy might not be a natural kind, something with a real essence, and that the word 'philosophy' functions as a demonstrative – marking out an area of logical space which the speaker occupies – rather than a rigid designator.

We are not suggesting that philosophy is best done in the form of historical commentary, much less that it should cease to be 'analytic'. But we do suggest that analytic philosophers will be missing a desirable form of self-consciousness as long as they ignore the attempts of intellectual historians to inculcate a sense of historical contingency. For the reasons we have rehearsed above, we think that it does no service to either philosophy or intellectual history to pretend that the two can operate in independence of one another. We do not offer any concrete suggestions about how present disciplinary matrices might be reformed in order to make the inevitable interdependence between these fields more visible, but we hope that the essays in this volume (and further volumes in the series of which this volume is a member) may make people in both fields more aware of the possibility of such reforms.

R.R.

J.B.S.

Q.S.

PART I

◁ ════════════════════════════════════ ▷

Philosophy and its history

CHARLES TAYLOR

I

There is an ideal, a goal that surfaces from time to time in philosophy. The inspiration is to sweep away the past and have an understanding of things which is entirely contemporary. The attractive idea underlying this is that of liberation from the dead weight of past errors and illusions. Thought casts off its chains. This may require a certain austere courage, because naturally we have grown comfortable, we have come to feel secure in the prison of the past. But it is also exhilarating.

One great model for this kind of thing is the Galilean break in science. Social scientists and psychologists periodically announce something of the kind, or else assure us of its imminence. But the last time this wind swept philosophy in our culture was with the surge of logical positivism almost half a century ago. As a doctrine, this rapidly fell on the defensive, and has been retreating ever since. But the *habit* of treating philosophy as an exercise which could be carried on in entirely contemporary terms has lingered on, and is still very widespread. Past authors may be read, but they are treated as if they were contemporaries. They earn a right to enter the dialogue because they happen to offer good formulations of one or another position which is worthy of a hearing. They are not explored as origins, but as atemporal resources.

The rival view of the nature of philosophy is the one so strongly articulated by Hegel. Philosophy and the history of philosophy are one. You cannot do the first without also doing the second. Otherwise put, it is essential to an adequate understanding of certain problems, questions, issues, that one understand them genetically. Without espousing Hegel's precise reasons, it is a view of this kind which I want to defend here. What I would like to do is to show how this fact about philosophy, that it is inherently historical, is a manifestation of a more general truth about human life and society, from which, I think, certain things follow about validity and argument in philosophy.

First, let me try to present the case again for the historical view.

17

Philosophy is an activity which essentially involves, among other things, the redescription of what we are doing, thinking, believing, assuming, in such a way that we bring our reasons to light more perspicuously, or else make the alternatives more apparent, or in some way or other are better enabled to take a justified stand to our action, thought, belief, assumption. Philosophy involves a great deal of articulation of what is initially inarticulated.

Now, one way of making the historical thesis about philosophy is to argue that successful articulation frequently requires – though it never simply reduces to – recovering previous articulations which have been lost. In other words, the kind of redescription we need in order to be in a better position to take a justified stand frequently requires that we recover previous formulations, precisely the ones we need to give an account of the origins of our present thoughts, beliefs, assumptions, actions.

I would like to persuade you that this is so, first of all by looking at a couple of examples. These are, of course, controversial; but then so is my main thesis.

Let us take first of all a cluster of assumptions much attacked these days (and justly attacked), which I will call the epistemological model. The underlying notions defining this are that our awareness of the world, whether in the organized, regimented form we call science, or in the looser forms of common everyday awareness, is to be understood in terms of our forming representations – be they ideas in the mind, states of the brain, sentences we accept, or whatever – of 'external' reality. A corollary of this view is that we can construe our awareness of and understanding of each other on the same representational model, so that we can, for instance, cast light on my understanding your idiolect as you speak by describing it in terms of a *theory* that I hold about you and the meanings of your words. If we look for an outstanding example of an influential philosopher cleaving to this epistemological model, Quine naturally comes to mind.

Now for those of us who are critical of this model, it seems evident that the situation is this: its proponents are impervious to the objections one might raise – e.g., they don't even see what you are driving at when you challenge the assumption that our mutual understanding in conversation can be construed in terms of *theories* which each of us holds of the other – because they do not see what an alternative to this epistemological model could conceivably look like. This is the challenge faced by the objector. To him, what seems clear is that we badly need some perspicuous redescription which will show the epistemological model as one possible construal among others, rather than as the only conceivable picture of mind-in-world.

Now, as a matter of fact, those who have made successful such redescriptions – e.g., Hegel, Heidegger, Merleau-Ponty – have had recourse to history. That is, their redescriptions have involved recovering the formulations which were at the origins of the epistemological model. And in particular the retrieval and re-interpretation of Descartes and Kant has played a big role in this critique. But, one might argue, it didn't have to be so. It was just that the critics were philosophy professors, which in those cultures (German and French) have a notorious professional deformation which makes them compulsively engage in expositions and re-interpretations of the canonical texts. The enterprise could be carried out otherwise.

I do not accept this view. I do not think it is contingent that one has recourse to history at this point. This is because some forgetting has taken place here. In the critic's eyes, the epistemologist is, as it were, imprisoned in his model because he cannot begin to see what an alternative could look like. But in this, he is in an important respect less aware than the foundational thinkers of this model. True, they may also have had the view that any other construal of knowledge was confused and incoherent, that one *had* to adopt their view. This certainly seems to have been the outlook of Descartes. And one of the striking facts about the intellectual landscape in which he moved was that the originally very different Aristotelian-scholastic model of knowledge was progressively misunderstood in the Renaissance and expounded more and more as though it were a representational theory.[1]

Nevertheless, the difference remains between a Descartes and a Quine that, however dogmatically the former may have believed that his construal was the only coherent one, he nevertheless had to arrive at it himself by one of those creative redescriptions which I am arguing are of the essence of philosophy.

In saying this, I in no way want to impugn or play down the originality of Quine. He himself has been at the origin of some striking creative redescriptions, e.g., those which open the way to a 'naturalized' epistemology. But these are firmly situated within the epistemological model, whereas Descartes' are foundational to this model. Quine's redescriptions will suffice for us if the model seems unquestionable. But if we want to challenge it, then we have to retrieve Descartes'.

In other words, if one wants to climb out of the epistemological prison, if one wants to be able to see this model no longer just as the contour map of the way things obviously are with the mind-in-world, but as one option among others, then a first step is to see it is something one could come to

[1] Cf. Gilson on Eustache de Saint Paul, probably the late scholastic figure whose works Descartes would have been exposed to at La Flèche. E. Gilson, *Études sur le role de la pensée mediévale dans la formation du système cartesien* (Paris: Vrin, 1930).

espouse out of a creative redescription, something one could give reasons for. And this you get by retrieving the foundational formulations.

But of course, even this will not be enough in this case. If we want to be able to conceive genuine alternatives to this model, then we cannot take Descartes' formulation as final either. What we need is a further reformulation of what he did which will do justice to the alternatives which he relegated to the trashcan of history, principally in this case the Aristotelian view.[2] We need to get the Aristotelian view into focus beyond the deformations of the late Renaissance which made it such easy meat for the rising epistemological view. Only in this way can we get a view of the Cartesian demarche as genuinely one of a range of alternatives; because in Descartes' own terms it comes across as the only way you can sensibly see things. If you're going to reopen the issue he foreclosed, in part by retrieving his formulations (i.e., the steps by which he foreclosed it), you have to re-interpret these steps. And this means a further retrieval, which sends us further back in history – in this case, to Aristotle and Aquinas.

So much is clear: if you do go back to Descartes in your attempt to climb out of the epistemological model, then you cannot just take him on his own estimation. You have to reinterpret his creative destruction of the past, which means retrieving this past. No retrieving Descartes for this enterprise without also retrieving Aristotle. But have I convinced you that one *must* do this by retrieving Descartes? Maybe I have given you reasons why this is *a* good way of doing things – but *the* way? Why can't one reconstruct and articulate purely contemporary reasons why epistemologists hold to their model, and in doing so point out purely contemporary alternatives, without going back in history? Isn't that in a way what, e.g., Heidegger and Merleau-Ponty have also done? For instance, Heidegger's famous analysis of being-in-the-world offers an alternative construal of mind-in-the world (if Heideggerians will excuse this expression), which seems innocent of history.

The reason the genetic account is indispensable has something to do with the nature of the forgetting here. How does a model like the epistemological one move from being an exciting conquest of creative redescription to being too obvious for words? How is the forgetting mediated? This comes about because the model becomes the organizing principle for a wide range of the practices in which we think and act and deal with the world. In this particular case, the model became embedded in our manner of doing natural science, in our technology, in some at least of the dominant ways in which we construe political life (the atomistic ones), later in various of our ways of healing, regimenting, organizing people in society, and in other spheres too numerous to mention. This is how the model could sink to the

---

[2] Though not only; there were Platonic views which should be recovered as well.

level of an unquestionable background assumption. What organizes and makes sense of so much of our lives cannot but appear unchallengeable at first, and hard even to conceive alternatives to.

One has an ironic sense of how things have changed, when one reads Descartes advising his readers to ponder the Meditations seriously, and even to spend a month thinking about the first one, so difficult did it seem to him to break the previous mind-set and grasp the dualist truth. Today, philosophers of my persuasion spend years trying to get students (and decades trying to get colleagues) to see that there is an alternative. Cartesian dualism is immediately understandable to undergraduates on day one. The idea that the only two viable alternatives might be Hobbes or Descartes is espoused by many, and is a perfectly comprehensible thesis even to those who passionately reject it. They feel its power, and the need to refute it. Such was not the situation in the 1640s.

If one tries to identify the reasons for this differential placing of the onus of proof from age to age; why certain views have to fight for credence, how they can only acquire plausibility through creative redescription while others are so to speak credible from the start, the answer is to be found in the background of practices, scientific, technological, practical, and the nature of their organizing principles. These are of course never monolithic; but in a given society at a given time, the dominant interpretations and practices may be so linked with a given model that this is, as it were, constantly projected for the members as the way things obviously are. I think this is the case – both directly, and via its connection with influential modern understandings of the individual and his freedom and dignity – with the epistemological model.

But if this is so then freeing oneself from the model cannot be done just by showing an alternative. What we need to do is get over the presumption of the unique conceivability of the embedded picture. But to do this, we have to take a new stance towards our practices. Instead of just living in them and taking their implicit construal of things as the way things are, we have to understand how they have come to be, how they came to embed a certain view of things. In other words, in order to undo the forgetting, we have to articulate for ourselves how it happened, to become aware of the way a picture slid from the status of discovery to that of inarticulate assumption, a fact too obvious to mention. But that means a genetic account; and one which retrieves the formulations through which the embedding in practice took place. Freeing ourselves from the presumption of uniqueness requires uncovering the origins. That is why philosophy is inescapably historical.

I have tried to expound this thesis in relation to the epistemological model, but a number of other examples could have been chosen. I could for instance have mentioned the atomist assumptions, or the assumptions

about individual rights, which form the starting point for much contemporary moral and political theory (think, for instance of Nozick and
Rawls). Prising ourselves free from presumptions of uniqueness here also
requires that we go back, e.g., to Kant and Locke. In each case, one has to
go back to the last perspicuous formulation, a formulation which did not
rely on a background of practices which make the picture seem
unproblematically truistic, i.e., on a background which virtually assures
that without a special effort at retrieval a great deal will not be said, or will
not seem worth saying.

But historical retrieval is not only important where you want to free
yourself from some picture. It is very important to my thesis that even in
this negative case, where you want to break loose, you need to understand
the past in order to liberate yourself. But liberation is not the only possible
motive. We may also find ourselves driven to earlier formulations in order
to *restore* a picture, or the practices it is meant to inform. This is the reason,
for instance, why some people turn to the paradigm formulations of the
civic humanist tradition. Or without seeking either outright rejection or
straight restoral, we may be looking for a perspicuous reformulation for
our time of some traditional doctrine, and this too may require that we go
back. In order to have a better look at this whole gamut of possibilities, I
would like to say something in general terms about practices and their
articulations.

II

I think it will help to understand this kind of philosophical enquiry, and the
way it sends us back to our origins, if we place it in the context of the need
we often experience to formulate the point of our practices, which need in
turn must frequently be met with an historical account.

The context in which this need arises is the fact that a basic way – I want
to argue, *the* basic way – in which we acknowledge and mark the things that
are important to us in the human context is through what we can call social
practices. By this I mean roughly: ways that we regularly behave to/before
each other, which (a) embody some understanding between us, and which
(b) allow of discrimination of right/wrong, appropriate/inappropriate.

Now, social practices can be largely inarticulate. This is not to say that
we carry them on without language. There is almost no practice one can
imagine which does not require some verbal exchange. Rather I mean that
the good, the value embodied in a practice, its point or purpose, may not be
formulated. The people engaged in the practice have to have some sense
of the good or the purpose, and this emerges, for instance, in the 'fouls'
they call on each other when they deviate (or the 'fairs' they call when

people do well). But they may have no way of *saying* what this good consists in.

Thus the practitioners of an art, be it flamenco guitar playing or philosophy, make certain judgements of excellence. They may or may not have articulated in what the excellence consists. This is likely to have happened in the latter case, because philosophers are compulsive articulators; less so in the former. They may just respond by applause and other forms of recognition; e.g., imitation, acknowledgement of mastership, etc. They may have words for the various excellences, or not even that. But even in the latter case, there are nevertheless non-arbitrary discriminations. One is inducted into a sense of them in the course of being inducted into the practice. One learns them in learning *cante jondo* itself; one learns them from one's master. The practice incorporates these discriminations, and essentially; or else it is not the practice that it is. But the norms may be quite inexplicit.

Take the example of the gentleman; or his seeming opposite, the macho male. In either case, there may be very little articulation of the norms, of how you have to act and feel in order to be a proper gentleman, or macho. But this will be carried in the way we act towards each other, towards women, etc.; and it will be carried also very much in the way we display ourselves to others; the way we present ourselves in public space. Style is extremely important here. This is another set of practices which are learned like a language, from others, with a minimum of formal articulation. Indeed, the real mark of a gentleman is to live by unwritten rules. Whoever needs to have the rules spelled out is not a gentleman.

We have a gamut of articulateness. At the bottom, there is the case where no descriptive words are used at all. We live our machismo, say, entirely in the way we stand, walk, address women and each other. It is carried in style and self-presentation entirely. We can imagine moving further up, to where virtue words are used, e.g., 'macho', 'gentleman', and also perhaps a more varied vocabulary: 'gallant', 'courageous', etc.; but still not further articulated. Or we have a language in which the fairs and fouls have names, but still it is not further formulated what makes them fairs and fouls. At the upper end, we have practices where the point of the activity, the underlying goods, or embedded purposes, are fully worked out, and an elaborate justification of them made in philosophical terms, including perhaps an underlying theory.

Now, the inarticulate end of this gamut is somehow primary. That is, we are introduced to the goods, and inducted into the purposes of our society much more and earlier through its inarticulate practices than through formulations.

This is fairly clear, ontogenetically speaking. Our language itself is woven into a range of social practices, of conversation, exchange, giving and receiving of orders, etc. We learn it only through these exchanges. We learn in particular the virtue terms and the terms for excellences, things worthy of admiration and contempt, and so on, first through their application to cases in such exchanges.

This means that our grip on these terms, however we may later develop our own peculiar outlook, insights, and interpretations, comes originally through the judgement 'calls' made by others, and then also ourselves, in the exchanges through which we learn practices. Even the vocabulary for the deeper formulations is one we can acquire in apprenticeship practices, where we learn, say, to think about and describe moral matters, learn to use scientific and metaphysical vocabularies, and so on.

This helps to explain the process I called 'historical forgetting' above. As an outlook which may first have been won by a heroic effort of hyper-articulateness comes to be the basis of widespread social practice, it may continue to inform the life of a society – indeed, it may come to seem virtually unchallengeable to common sense – even though the original formulations, and especially their background reasons, may be widely neglected, rehearsed only by specialists. Even these, carried by the common sense of their day, will fail to recognize the significance of some of the original arguments, first proffered in a world with quite different background assumptions. Something like this has happened, I want to claim, with the atomist, epistemology-centred outlook pioneered by Descartes and others in the seventeenth century.

Challenging an outlook of this kind means undoing this process of forgetting. Just presenting an alternative will not help, as long as we are captured within the terms of a certain received 'common sense'. For if this holds us in virtue of being embedded in our practices, then we have to articulate what they embody if we are to neutralize its effects. Otherwise, we remain as it were captured in the force field of a common sense which frustrates all our attempts to take a critical stance towards its basic assumptions. The field distorts the alternatives, makes them look bizarre or inconceivable. To take some distance from this, we have to formulate what is now unsaid.

This helps to explain why this process of re-articulation so often involves going back in history. We very often cannot raise a *new* issue really effectively until we have re-articulated our *actual* practices. But these frequently owe something to an outlook which was better, or fuller, or more perspicuously formulated in the past. Getting clear on them involves recovering this formulation. And this may not be easy. For even where the formulae of earlier thinkers are lovingly rehearsed by later specialists, the reasons underlying them have frequently become opaque in a later age.

Of course, recovering an earlier formula is never sufficient to re-articulate a practice. It would be a madly idealist view to see all current practices as somehow the embodiment of earlier explicit theories. But the case I am making here depends on no such outlandish claim. It suffices that, for whatever reason, some earlier formulations *have* been taken up, and have been given some kind of foundational or paradigm status in the development of a practice. Then, although social change, drift, the pressure of other practices, unsuspected success, alterations in the scale of the society, and historical forgetting will all have done their work – so that the upshot would be quite unrecognizable to the founding formulators – nevertheless, it can be that recovering their formulations is one essential condition of understanding this upshot.

Thus to take a familiar example, the modern society based on the notion of free individual agents held together by contracts helped to provide the background in which technological capitalism grew. But this growth has totally changed the context of the practice. The original theory cannot be understood by practitioners today in the same way as by their prede-cessors; the attempt to do so results in confusion and muddle. It badly needs reformulation.

But this reformulation requires that one get clear on the original form. It is not that this original formulation is somehow the true articulation of what underlies today's reality. On the contrary, a great change has patently taken place, with the rise of giant, bureaucratic, multinational corpora-tions, and contemporary state structures. But because today's reality is what has arisen through the drift, and hyper-development, of a society informed by the original model, recovering this is essential to our being able to understand what now exists. The society is out of true with the original. But that is just it. We are dealing with a society which is characterized by the fact that it is out of true with *this* original. This makes it all the more important to understand the original, if we are to understand the society.

Thus modern capitalism is out of phase with the system described and recommended by Adam Smith. But this makes it essential to be clear on what Adam Smith said. That is because (a) his was a paradigm articulation of some of the practices and self-understandings which helped to bring about modern capitalism over a good part of the globe, and (b) this articulation in turn actually was taken up and helped inform the process. Even had Adam Smith not brought out the *Wealth of Nations* in 1776, it would remain an extremely important manuscript to read today for reason (a); but we also find it extremely important for reason (b).

All this is *not* to say at all that Adam Smith gives us the theory of contemporary capitalism. Those who think this must be out of their minds, however many Nobel prizes they may win, or large states they may misgovern. But it *is* to say that a theory which thus informs a development becomes indispensable for truly understanding this development and what issues from it, however out of true the end result will be. What we need is to get clear on the theories with which our present moving reality is out of true. By this is meant not just any theories not true of them, but those which played and may still play a formative role.

So to understand ourselves today, we are pushed into the past for paradigm statements of our formative articulations. We are forced back to the last full disclosure of what we have been about, or what our practice has been woven about. I have mentioned how this necessity may arise as a result of change or development. But it may also arise because of the way articulations can distort or partly hide what is implicit in practices.

This may be the case of a formative articulation for a given period. It may be the dominant generally accepted one, and for this reason be formative; but it may block out or deny important parts of the reality implicit in our practices. It will be distortive in that these practices go on being carried out; we remain allegiant to other goods, although in a confused and half-acknowledged way.

We can have a good example of this, if we look at modern liberal democracies. There are three great formulations, or theory types, which have played an important role in the development of these societies. The crucial source was the original, medieval-based theory of men as rights-bearers, under imperium and law, whose basic telos was the defence and protection of these rights. The second was the atomist view, which sees men as individual seekers after welfare, each following an individual strategy, and coming together to live under law because of common interest and the demands of security which are felt equally by all. The third is the civic humanist model, which sees us as citizens of a republic, under a common law which gives us our identity.

These three have played various roles in the development of modern society. They have been important at different dates; and the civic humanist model has even undergone eclipse to re-appear later. But all of them have left their sediment in the practices of modern republics. However, it can happen that for a given group for a time, one of them is under eclipse. The civic humanist heritage was little recognized, not only in the academy, but in many milieux of the public, in recent decades in Anglo-Saxon democracies. As a result, an atomist interest conception tended to predominate, a notion of the political life as the adjustment of interests between individuals and groups, which was certainly accurate up to a point, but which was blind to the immense importance of citizenship for modern men, not just as an instrumental hedge against exploitation by government. It put in the shade all the practices, symbolic and transactive, whereby the sense is recreated that citizenship is part of the dignity of a free person, that one is less than fully free and adult if one lives under tutelage. This is enshrined in countless places in the fairs and fouls of our social and political life; in the demands we make to be heard, in the importance put on incorrupt voting, in the jealous guarding of the accountability of public servants; in the challengings of authority by underlings not only in the political sphere, but in universities, families, places of work, etc.

Here we have a typical case of a distortive or partial formulation acting as a screen. In order to understand what is going on in a case like this, we have to go back. We have to recover the last full-blooded formulation of the side that is being thus suppressed. Once more this will not be because we can only read the reality as the embodiment of this. On the contrary, there cannot but have been distortions in the practice as a result of this blindness and partiality in the formulation. But because this last full formulation will give us the theory with which our society is out of true, it is an indispensable part of the story.

And so, in all these ways, the fact that our practices are shaped by formulations, and that these impart a certain direction to their development, makes it the case that self-understanding and reformulation sends us back to the past: to the paradigms which have informed development, or the repressed goods which have been at work. Repression can only make the past irrelevant where it actually succeeds in totally abolishing the practices whose implicit goods it covers up. But this happens much more rarely than we might think. Our practices are in fact very resilient and long lasting. And they are, moreover, frequently linked with each other, so that suppressing some while maintaining others is virtually impossible. The interwoven practices of liberal democracy are a case in point. How to get rid of citizenship while keeping the society of rights, or of strategic individual actors? This is not easy to envisage. To have one without the other, you need societies with very different histories to ours. Perhaps some Latin American societies are of this nature: or certain other societies in the Third World.

These examples illustrate what I said at the end of the first section. We may be driven to historical retrieval not only by the need to escape from a given social form, but also because we want to recover or restore one which is under pressure and in danger of being lost. This is the spirit in which proponents of civic humanism frequently recur to history in our time. Or we may be uncertain, and want to take our bearings relative to the dominant social reality. This may motivate historical retrieval, for instance, in an attempt to generate a better theory of contemporary advanced capitalism.

What is common to all these enterprises is the need to articulate the unsaid in present practices. In all these cases, we are driven back to what we can call the last (most recent) perspicuous formulation of the good or purpose embedded in the practice. And sometimes this, in turn, may send us back even earlier, to the outlook against which this formulation was defined.

III

I want to place what I called in the first section 'creative redescriptions' against this background. The philosophical reformulations which allow us to find a better position from which to take a justified stand on some belief, assumption, cast of thought, have something of the nature of our formulations of continuing practices. They transfer what has sunk to the level of an organizing principle for present practices, and hence is beyond examination, into a view for which there can be *reasons*, either for or against. And they are genetic and historical for the same reason. In order to understand properly what we are about, we have to understand how we got where we are. We have to regress to the last perspicuous disclosure, which in the case of philosophical issues will be a formulation. That is why doing philosophy, at least if it involves such creative redescriptions, is inseparable from doing the history of philosophy.

The analysis has interesting ramifications for the question of truth and relativity in philosophical matters. In recent years the tide of criticism against the epistemological model has risen. It has been more and more widely appreciated that it is not the only conceivable picture of mind-in-world. There are alternatives. But in some cases, this discovery of alternatives has been taken for an argument in favour of a kind of philosophical relativism, or at least a view which might be labelled a species of non-realism, according to which reason cannot arbitrate between the alternatives. Professor Rorty seems to defend a view of this kind. The different pictures of mind-in-world can be defended in terms of the ways of living, feeling, etc., that they involve. We can mount a persuasive case for one or the other in the light of people's preferences in forms of life. But we cannot argue that one is truer than the other, more faithful to reality or the way things are.

To say something of this latter kind is even thought to be espousing a way of speaking which only makes sense within the representational viewpoint, on the grounds that it smacks of the correspondence model of truth which most naturally arises on this model. But a criterion which only makes sense *within* one model could hardly arbitrate *between* them.

Now, I think there is something deeply mistaken about this non-realist view. It misses the whole point of what we have learned through our challenge to the epistemological model. It is not just that the notion of truth, or faithfulness to reality, does not need to be construed on a correspondence model. More fundamentally, it is that the very nature of the discourse whereby we escape the epistemological prison, for instance, is misunderstood if we make this non-realist move.

The point is that the debate is not between two propositions which are rivals in the ordinary way that empirical hypotheses are – say, the big bang versus the steady state cosmologies. In this latter case, the truth of each is incompatible with the truth of the other, but not with its intelligibility. But here the clash is sharper. The whole strength of the epistemological model lies in the supposed unintelligibility of a rival account. It is this presumption which a less distorted account of history explodes.

Truth is involved here on two levels: the account of the history is freed from certain distortions – e.g., Aristotle is rescued from the late scholastic glosses – and is hence less untrue; and the presumption of uniqueness is shown to be false. This does not necessarily dictate a new unique answer to the conundrum of mind-in-world. We are probably never in that predicament. But it does mean that the philosophical views which were founded on that presumption of uniqueness are now indefensible in their present form. For instance, you will no longer be able just to *assume* that we have theories of each other which we apply when we converse with understanding.

To turn around and treat the issue as though having understood both sides one could be genuinely agnostic between them – as is undoubtedly the case between the two cosmologies – is to have forgotten what the nature of the issue is: that the intelligibility of one implies the falsity of the other.

To treat them as rival hypotheses which one cannot arbitrate between by reason is really to fall back into the epistemological perspective. This was the viewpoint which kept generating sceptical arguments, and which tends to make us see all knowledge claims as touching a realm of entities beyond our representations; which in turn forces the famous moves: to scepticism, or some distinction between the transcendental and the empirical, or some reduction of the issue of truth to what works, or whatever. All these moves only made sense *within* the epistemological paradigm. It is they which are out of place once one has challenged it. We continue to make them only if we are still unclear about what is involved in exploding the presumption of uniqueness.

But an even more important point arises out of this analysis concerning the limits of philosophical reason. We are not condemned to agnosticism between these two construals of mind-in-world; indeed, we cannot be undecided once we understand what is at stake, because of the relation of the two rival views, where one's truth impugns the other's intelligibility. But these two views are placed in this relation through the way they have become embedded in the history and practices of our civilization. The exclusivity of the epistemological model was an important polemic instrument in the establishing of new forms of scientific thought, and technological, political, ethical practices. The issue is whether we can give a less distorted account of the rise and continuation of these practices by abandoning this presumption of exclusivity. The issue arises within a culture and history; within a set of practices, as between rival formulations of these practices.

This means that we shall be in a quite different predicament if we oppose two philosophical views emanating from quite different cultures and histories. If someone summons you to decide between the Buddhist view of the self and Western conceptions of personality, you are going to be in trouble. I am not saying that even this kind of issue is ultimately unarbitrable; but clearly we start off without the remotest idea how even to go about arbitrating it. Imagine an extra-terrestrial being asked to award the palm to the civilization with the most plausible view of human nature. He would straightway take flight back to Sirius. Any arbitration of that kind would presuppose that we had elaborated a common language. And that means developed a common set of practices. We would have had to grow together as civilizations for us to see how to judge.

But seeing these limits of philosophical reason points to another way of identifying the error in philosophical non-realism. It is to assimilate all philosophical issues, even those like that over the epistemological model, to the kind our extra-terrestrial would face. But we could only find *all* issues like this if we were in fact at home nowhere, if we did not belong to any culture or set of practices. Pure philosophical non-realism would make sense only for a subject who was thoroughly disengaged, who was equidistant from all cultures. A picture of the subject as disengaged is, of course, another notion generated by the epistemological tradition. And this is perhaps another respect in which those who conclude from the overturning of the epistemological model to a kind of ultimate non-realism show merely that they are as yet not fully emancipated from the model.

◁ ════════════════════════════════════ ▷

2

The relationship of philosophy
to its past

ALASDAIR MACINTYRE

It is all too easy to imprison oneself within the following dilemma. *Either* we read the philosophies of the past so as to make them relevant to our contemporary problems and enterprises, transmuting them as far as possible into what they would have been if they were part of present-day philosophy, and minimizing or ignoring or even on occasion misrepresenting that which refuses such transmutation because it is inextricably bound up with that in the past which makes it radically different from present-day philosophy; *or* instead we take great care to read them in their own terms, carefully preserving their idiosyncratic and specific character, so that they cannot emerge into the present except as a set of museum pieces. The power of this dilemma can be measured by the extent to which, even although its very formulation is enough to arouse a large dissatisfaction with either alternative, we nonetheless in practice do so very often succumb to one or the other. That we do so is certainly a consequence of both the number and the importance of the different ways in which we may be separated or distanced from past stages in the history of philosophy.

Consider first of all the effect of changes in the academic division of labour. We now characteristically distinguish philosophical problems and enquiries from scientific or historical or theological problems and enquiries; but it has not always been so. Hume's ambition was to be the Newton of the moral sciences; and Descartes thought the relationship of his metaphysics to his physics was that of trunk to branches in a single tree. What we are apt to treat as the history of philosophy, properly so called, involves often enough the abstraction of what *we* now take to be the genuinely philosophical parts from larger wholes. But in so doing we cannot avoid distortion; conceptual claims on the one hand and empirical and theoretical claims on the other are to some large degree inseparable, a lesson to be learnt both from the history itself and from a consideration of the implications of Quine's critique of the analytic–synthetic distinction. The subject-matter of the moral philosophy of the seventeenth and eighteenth centuries provides a telling example. Its twentieth-century intellectual heirs and beneficiaries include not only the attenuated and impoverished discipline that modern philosophical ethics has become at the hands of most of its modern practitioners, but psychology and the other social sciences. And this has not of course simply involved a reallocation of topics and issues. The very process of reallocation has been a transforming one, and the transformations have extended beyond the academic disciplines to the idiom of everyday life. Cost-benefit analyses, psychological evaluations of personality traits and studies of political order and disorder are nowadays characteristically conducted in a way that presupposes that these are not essentially moral enterprises. The scope of morality has diminished along with that of moral philosophy.

A second dimension of historical difference is as obvious: that of change in the internal structuring of philosophy in terms of what issues are taken to be central, what peripheral, what methods fruitful, what sterile. I speak here of issues rather than of problems because rival conceptions of what is problematic may be precisely what poses an issue. And rival conceptions of what is problematic are likely to be inseparable from rival conceptions of the ends to which philosophical activity is to be directed. So what is or seems to be the same or a very similar argument occurring in two different philosophical epochs may have very different import. Augustine's use of the *cogito* is not at all the same as Descartes' use. Augustine's account of the place of ostensive definition in language learning points towards the divine illumination of the mind; Wittgenstein's very similar account – that Wittgenstein erroneously took his account to be at odds with Augustine's reinforces my central thesis – points towards the concept of a form of life.

These two kinds of difference are reinforced by a third: that of literary genre. Plato, Berkeley, Diderot and John Wisdom all wrote philosophy in the form of a dialogue. But Plato's dialogues constitute a genre of philosophy very different from anything possible in the eighteenth or twentieth centuries; and in the course of writing his dialogues Plato himself transformed the genre. Augustine and Anselm both wrote philosophy as prayer, Aquinas and Scotus as intellectual debate, Dante and Pope as poetry, Spinoza in what he took to be the form of geometry, Hegel as history, George Eliot, Dostoevsky and Sartre in novels and many of us in that most eccentric latecomer of all philosophical genre forms, the article contributed to a professional journal.

Changes in the overall academic division of labour, in the internal structuring of philosophy and in literary genre are of course all intimately related to conceptual change and related, not as three independent processes interacting with each other and with a fourth, but as aspects of one and the same complex, but unified history. The measure of conceptual change is the measure of difficulty encountered in trying to translate or to paraphrase concepts which are at home in one specific linguistic and philosophical culture by means of those that members of quite another such culture possess or can construct. I think for example of the kind of linguistic innovation that was required in George Thomson's history of early Greek philosophy in modern Irish as well as of his translations of Plato into that same language. The problems that Thomson must have encountered are illuminated by considering the outcome of the resolution of parallel problems in the translation of poetry. Take any passage in Homer, Sarpêdôn's speech to Glaukos at *Iliad* xii. 309–28, for example, and compare Chapman's sixteenth-century with Pope's eighteenth-century and Fitzgerald's twentieth-century readings. There are indeed points at which one of these misrepresents the Greek original in a way that another does not. But in many respects they are not in competition: Fitzgerald is a first-rate translator of our own time, Chapman and Pope are first-rate translators of theirs. The notion of a timelessly best translation makes no sense. And I see no reason to suppose that this is not as true of Plato as it is of Homer (the awfulness of Jowett matches splendidly the awfulness of Lang, Leaf and Myers).

It would be quite wrong to infer from any of the considerations adduced so far that any part of the past is necessarily inaccessible to us here now. But they do suggest the extent and the ingenuity of the stratagems that we shall have to employ if we are not to be, often to an unsuspected degree, prisoners of the present in our ostensible renderings of the past. In so doing they accentuate the dilemma which I framed initially. For even the argument so far suggests that in some large degree the sense of continuity that so many standard histories of philosophy provide is illusory and depends upon the adroit, although doubtless unconscious, use of a series of devices designed to mask difference, to bridge discontinuity and to conceal unintelligibility. But even this misleading sense of continuity can be disrupted if we read too many different standard histories of philosophy written in different times and places. Undertake the exercise of reading the history of philosophy from the age of Kant in German, from that of Dugald Stewart in English and from that of Victor Cousin in French up to the present and at once an additional dimension of difference presents itself. Each age, sometimes even each generation has its own canon of the great philosophical writers and indeed of the great philosophical books. Consider the different treatment in different times and places of Giordano Bruno, of Hume, of Port-Royal or of Hegel. Or consider how the relative importance assigned to different dialogues of Plato has changed at intervals ever since the Renaissance. These differences partially reflect and partially reinforce some of the others that I have already noticed. They suggest how the history of philosophy as a subdiscipline may on occasion help to reinforce the prejudices of the present by insulating us from that in the past which would most disquiet us. Once again there is nothing in the argument which suggests that any part of the past is ever *necessarily* unavailable. But the multiplication of contingent factors also suggests that we cannot rule out either of two possibilities. One is that there may be periods in the history of philosophy so mutually alien that the later cannot hope to comprehend the earlier adequately, but will inescapably misinterpret. And this seems already to have occurred in for example the eighteenth-century French Enlightenment's incomprehension of medieval thought. Yet we may well feel that this possibility does not threaten *us*, for our very success in identifying such cases of misunderstandings suggests that we can overcome barriers and circumvent obstacles that defeated our eighteenth-century predecessors. This cultural pride may well of course be misplaced. But even if it is not, a second possibility opens up, namely that our very success in interpreting socially, culturally and intellectually alien periods in the history of philosophy may make us aware of modes of philosophical thought and enquiry whose forms and presuppositions are so different from ours that we are unable to discover sufficient agreement in concepts and standards to provide grounds for deciding between the rival and incompatible claims embodied in such modes without begging the question. For whatever standard or criterion we found it rational to appeal to would be one whose employment already presupposed the rational justifiability of our own specific modes of philosophical thought and enquiry, while precisely because it belonged so securely within the context of those modes, it could never have appeared rationally justifiable, perhaps could not even have been intelligible, to those whose alien mode of philosophical thought and enquiry is the one with which we wish to engage in rational controversy. But if this were to occur, then the rationality of our own modes of philosophical thought and enquiry would be put in question. For we should be aware of the existence of another rival set of philosophical beliefs, attitudes and forms of enquiry whose implicit or explicit claims to rational hegemony were incompatible with the parallel claims embodied in our own philosophical activity, but whose claims could not be shown by rational argument – for any valid and relevant argument would turn out to presuppose what we required it to demonstrate – to be rebutted or defeated in favour of our own. (That precisely the same type of issue could obviously arise in defining our relationship to the mode of philosophical activity carried on within some alien cultural tradition has of course been noticed on occasion by anthropologists; but I am concerned here with the specific problems which arise in situations where we are concerned only with past eras within our own cultural tradition.)

It will of course be the case that in the kind of situation which I am envisaging the very same type of reason that makes it impossible for us to provide rational warrant for asserting the superiority of *our* mode of philosophical activity over that of some rival period from our past will make it impossible equally to provide rational warrant for preferring *their* claims to ours. But this should afford very small consolation. For it was in part, at least, the discovery of rival theological modes of enquiry embedded in rival forms of religious practice similarly unable, and for similar reason, to defeat each other's claims at a fundamental level by rational argument that led to the Enlightenment and post-Enlightenment discrediting of theology as a mode of rational enquiry. So the question necessarily arises: why should philosophy not suffer the same discredit?

The question has force for two distinct reasons. The first is that it is a more sophisticated version of a question that is already often posed by non-philosophers. Philosophy, so it is sometimes claimed, differs from the natural sciences in its inability to resolve fundamental disagreements; since philosophers address the world in varying and discordant voices, why should any attention be paid to them? And secondly this crude but common attempt to discredit philosophy is reinforced by the whole family of considerations that I have been adducing. Consider in a little more detail how success in the task of correcting the misinterpretation of some particular past period in philosophy may result in identifying its radical differences from us in such a way that we seem unable rationally to resolve the question of which fundamental point of view is in the right. I once again take my example from moral philosophy.

In a chapter of *Freedom and Reason* entitled 'Backsliding', Professor R. M. Hare has remarked that

There are analogies . . . between expressions like 'think good' and 'think that I ought' on the one hand and the word 'want' on the other . . . We must not however become so obsessed by the analogies between wanting and making value-judgments that we ignore their differences. Doing just this, perhaps, led Socrates into his famous troubles over the question of moral weakness. It is in their universalizability that value-judgments differ from desires . . . and nearly all the difficulties of Socrates stem from failing to notice this. (Hare 1963: 71).

Hare's footnote to this passage refers not to the original Platonic source, the *Protagoras*, but to Aristotle's discussion in Book VII of the *Nicomachean Ethics* (1145b 25). I take it that Socrates' alleged 'famous troubles' consist in his asserting that nobody acts contrary to what it is best to do except through ignorance, in a way that allows Aristotle to suggest initially that what he takes to be Socrates' thesis is plainly at odds with *ta phainomena* of *akrasia*; and that Hare's claim is that, had Socrates only recognized the type of distinction between wanting and making value-judgments upon

which Hare insists, Socrates would have understood that if I want
something so much that I pursue it, even although doing so is contrary to
the value-judgment as to how people in this particular type of situation
ought to behave to which I had hitherto professed commitment, then,
provided that it is in my power not to try to satisfy this particular desire, it
cannot be the case that I now really assent to the value-judgment. So, on
Hare's view, nobody ever does act in a way that flouts their own value-
judgments for 'It is a tautology to say that we cannot sincerely assent to a
command addressed to ourselves, and *at the same time* not perform it, if
now is the occasion for performing it and it is in our (physical and
psychological) power to do so' (Hare 1952:20, quoted in Hare 1963:79). So
had Socrates only possessed Hare's degree of insight, he would never have
got into his famous troubles.

What Plato actually represented Socrates as doing and saying has had to
undergo two successive transformations in order that it should provide
Hare with Socrates as a whipping-boy. The original context in the
Protagoras is a dialectical one in which Socrates' immediate purpose is the
refutation of the belief of *hoi polloi* that human beings may be diverted
from the pursuit of what they know to be good by being overcome by the
attraction of pleasure, in which Socrates' larger purpose concerns the place
of knowledge in the virtues. To call the context dialectical is to say that we
misunderstand Socrates if we take him in these passages to be making
assertions in the course of moving towards *conclusions*, a mistake
sometimes fostered by translators. At the end of the *Protagoras* Socrates is
represented as saying: 'it seems to me that our point of exit from the
arguments just now *hê arti exodos* is like a man accusing and jeering at
us . . .' (361a 4). Mr C. C. W. Taylor translates '*hê arti exodos*' as 'the
conclusions we have just reached', a translation which loses the dramatic
allusion – an *exodos* is among other things the finale of a play and Socrates'
use of the expression here is connected with the use of the idiom of comedy
elsewhere in the dialogue – and makes it easy to suppose falsely that
Socrates has tried to reach a conclusion and is now acknowledging his
failure. But Socrates' philosophical activity, at least as represented in these
passages of the *Protagoras*, was a very different kind of activity from that in
which most subsequent philosophers have engaged when they have
asserted promises and inferred conclusions, and the first subsequent
philosopher to misunderstand him was Aristotle.

Aristotle was not indeed and did not take himself to be pointing to any
troubles or difficulties of Socrates, famous or otherwise. For when he says
that the view which he ascribes to Socrates is at odds with *ta phainomena*,
what he means is *not* that it is at odds with 'the observed facts' (W. D. Ross'
translation) or 'the plain facts' (H. Rackham's translation), but with

received opinion (Owen 1961), something that the Socrates of the *Protagoras* already understood very well. And what Aristotle concludes – and *he* of course *is* making assertions and drawing conclusions – is explicitly (1147b 15) that Socrates was right, that someone who seems to do what is contrary to what he or she knows to be best for him or herself cannot *really* know it to be so. Of course in agreeing with Socrates Aristotle has anticipated his modern successors in ignoring the closing passages of the *Protagoras* and the dialectical nature of Socrates' philosophical activity, and has thus misrepresented Socrates. But this misrepresentation is itself further misrepresented when Aristotle's discussion of *akrasia* is treated by Hare as a discussion of the same topics that Hare discusses under the rubrics of 'backsliding' and 'weakness of will', so that Hare's account of these matters can be used – as it is by Hare – to make clear to us what was true and what was false in Socrates' (and by implication Aristotle's) account of *akrasia*.

What this ignores are crucial differences in moral and cultural context so that the place of backsliding in any modern morality has to be very different from that of *akrasia* in Athenian thought and practice. The context of Aristotle's theory – it will be clear that I think one has to be very cautious in ascribing theories to Socrates – is a teleological account of the virtues within which it is necessary to furnish explanations both of how someone may do just actions, but not be a just person, and of how someone may do unjust actions, but not be simply an unjust person. To explain this latter is at least a central function of Aristotle's account of *akrasia* (1151a 11). *Akrasia* has nothing to do with the conditions for assent to value-judgments. Its occurrence presupposes a distinction between the person who exhibits the virtues and the person who, although he has at least true opinion and perhaps knowledge as to the end which the virtues serve, lapses from them. That someone's moral beliefs stand in no need of correction with respect to *content* is a precondition of that person's exhibiting *akrasia*. What a person manifesting *akrasia* lacks is full *epistêmê* operative on this particular occasion and the full disposition of character that could sustain and embody that operation. By contrast, in any modern prescriptivist account of morality, such as Hare's, not only can there be no place for, indeed no conception of the relevant species of *epistêmê*, but there can be no logical possibility of the kind of gap between knowledge and action which *akrasia* exemplifies. Assent to principles, on a prescriptivist view, *is* acting upon them except on occasions when it is not in one's power so to do. But *akrasia* is not a matter only of particular occasions; it is a character trait.

That *akrasia* and weakness of will or backsliding are very different is unsurprising once we bear in mind the radical difference of cultural and moral contexts. A prescriptivist morality of principles is at home in an essentially post-Kantian social world where the established morality is one of moral rules which the agent prescribes to him or herself and where doing other than that which accords with one's moral professions of allegiance to specific rules is to exhibit what Hare calls backsliding. But the *akratês* is not necessarily or characteristically a backslider at all. He is someone whose moral education is as yet incomplete and imperfect, whose movement towards the *telos* that is both his true and his already recognized good – albeit one perhaps still implicitly rather than explicitly acknowledged – is diverted by his lack of control over the *pathê* that afflict him. The *akratês* thus occupies a quite different place in a very different moral order from that which the backslider is accorded both by prescriptivist moral theory and by modern moral practice. But to have understood this is to have corrected misinterpretation at the cost of having to confront just that state of affairs which I identified earlier as putting in question the rational warrant of fundamental philosophical standpoints.

At the heart of Greek moral philosophy is the figure of the educated moral agent whose desires and choices are directed by the virtues towards genuine goods and ultimately towards *the* good. At the heart of distinctively modern moral philosophy is the figure of the autonomous individual whose choices are sovereign and ultimate and whose desires are, in one version of such moral theory, to be weighted equally along with those of every other person, or, in another version of such theory, to be constrained by categorical rules which impose neutral constraints upon all desires and interests. Justice on the characteristically Greek view is a matter of desert, of allocating goods in accordance with one's contribution to that form of political community which is the moral arena. Justice on the characteristically modern view is a matter of fundamental equality. For each body of theory the key concepts are so interrelated within a complex body of beliefs, attitudes and practices that to abstract each conceptual difference in turn in an attempt to decide the issues one by one is necessarily for the most part to falsify and distort, while to view each body of theory as a whole is to discover that each carries within it its own account of the rational justification of judgments about moral practice.

This particular example of the dilemma which the relationship of the philosophy of the present to that of the past engenders exhibits every one of the dimensions of difference which I catalogued earlier. Greek thought, like Greek practice, understands morals-and-politics as a unified object of enquiry; modern moral theory distinguishes itself both from political philosophy and even more sharply from political science. So the academic division of labour allows us to pretend that our pupils can understand Aristotle's *Ethics* without reading the *Politics* and vice versa. Greek moral thought makes central to its concerns issues of the nature of human psychology which are as alien to characteristically modern moral philosophy as are some of its central issues, the fact/value distinction and the relationship of morality to utility, for example, to Plato and Aristotle. Differences that arise from differing uses of literary genres and from the canonization of specific bodies of writing scarcely need spelling out; and the difficulties of conceptual paraphrase are at the very core of the problem. So that what we see exemplified here is a vivid and telling example of what our inability to resolve the initial dilemma has produced: a consequent inability to confront the moral philosophy of the very culture inheritance from which made our own moral philosophy possible. How should we respond?

One inviting strategy is to ignore the whole situation, which is after all what most of us do already. That is to say, we shall continue to deal with our philosophical past in two quite distinct ways. As philosophers on the one hand, defining our discipline in terms of what members of the American Philosophical Association currently do, we shall admit the philosophers of the past to our debates only in our own terms, and if that involves historical distortion, so much perhaps the better. We shall have paid the past the compliment of supposing it to be as philosophically acute as we are. As historians of philosophy on the other hand we shall be genuinely scrupulous in trying to understand the past as it actually was and, if this makes the past philosophically irrelevant, we shall simply decry relevance and, where others speak of antiquarianism, we shall speak of scholarship.

So we may momentarily congratulate ourselves that what seemed to be an acute problem has in fact turned out to be an adroit solution. But this delight can be no more than momentary. For this solution carries a clear and, I hope, unacceptable implication. The past will have become the realm only of the *de facto*. The present alone will be the realm of the *de jure*. The study of the past will have been defined so as to exclude any consideration of what is true or good or rationally warranted, rather than of what they then with their peculiar concepts of truth, goodness and rationality believed to be so. Enquiries into what actually is true, good and rational will be reserved for the present. But notice that for any particular philosophical generation its occupation of the present can only be temporary; in some not too distant future it will have been transmuted into one more part of the philosophical past. Its *de jure* questions and answers will have been translated into a *de facto* frame of reference. It will turn out not to have contributed to an enquiry continuing through generations, but to have removed itself from active philosophical enquiry to become a mere subject-matter for historians. Quine has joked that there are two sorts of people interested in philosophy, those interested in philosophy and those interested in the history of philosophy. On the view that I have just sketched, the counter-joke is: the people interested in philosophy now are doomed to become those whom only those interested in the history of philosophy are going to be interested in in a hundred years' time. So the philosophical nullifying of the past by this conception of the relationship of past and present turns out to be a way of nullifying ourselves in advance. This particular division of labour between the positive historian and the philosopher ensures that in time everything is delivered over to historical positivity.

It seems then that the dilemma cannot be ignored; inaction too will have drastic negative consequences. Nothing short of a cogent account of how it is possible to confront the philosophical past philosophically as well as historically will give us what we need. But such an account will have to explain how one large-scale philosophical standpoint can engage with another in cases where each standpoint embodies its own conceptions of what rational superiority consists of in such a way that there can apparently be no appeal to any neutral and independent standard. Yet we are of course not the first to need such an account. The problems of how issues can be rationally resolved when they divide the adherents of large and comprehensive points of view whose systematic disagreements extend to disagreements about how those disagreements are to be characterized, let alone resolved, are ones which have already been confronted by historians and philosophers of natural science, under the name conferred upon them by Thomas Kuhn. They are the problems of incommensurability. It is therefore well worth asking where that debate stands – or perhaps ought to stand – to see if we can derive from it assistance with our own problem.

The characteristics of the natural sciences, identification of which led Kuhn to his initial claims about incommensurability, were of course more limited in scope than the characteristics of philosophy which generate our present problem. For one thing, even in an historian as liberal as Kuhn, the conception of natural science which informs his whole argument is one in which modern conceptions of natural science are largely allowed to determine which theories and activities in pre-modern societies are to be accounted precursors of the history of natural science. And this is of course entirely legitimate; for the very concept of our natural sciences is in an important way a distinctively modern concept, brought to birth between the sixteenth and the nineteenth centuries, whereas the concept of philosophy is not. Nonetheless the form of Kuhn's initial problem was precisely the same as that of ours: how is it possible to treat as rival claims, claims embedded in contexts so different that no neutral criterion or standard of argument is available – as, so Kuhn argued, is the case sometimes when two large-scale bodies of scientific theory, such as the physical cosmology of Aristotle and that of Galileo, confront one another? We cannot appeal in such cases to neutral and independent data afforded by observation, for how we characterize and even how we perceive the relevant data, and in addition which data we take it to be relevant to observe, will depend on which of the rival theoretical standpoints we have first adopted: 'when Aristotle and Galileo looked at swinging stones, the first saw constrained fall, the second a pendulum', wrote Kuhn in his early formulation of this point. And he later concluded that any conception of a match 'between the entities with which the theory populates nature' on the one hand and 'what is "really there"' on the other has to be rejected: 'There is, I think, no theory-independent way to reconstruct phrases like "really there" . . .' (Kuhn 1970: 121 and 206). And that is to say, each large-scale body of theory of this kind comes to us bearing with it its own conceptualization of that observable reality of which it gives an account. Hence there is no appeal away from the body of theory to the independently and neutrally observable character of that reality.

Moreover Kuhn also has arguments designed to show that the use of such apparently independent criteria as the degree of confirmation of one body of theory relative to another by observation or a comparison of the degree and kind of anomaly to be identified in each of two rival bodies of theory will not yield us the kind of rationally warranted neutral and independent criteria that we aspire to discover. For *what* we take to be significant confirming instances of a theory, and *which* anomalies in a theory or in the relationship of a theory to observation we take to be of central rather than peripheral importance, will both also in key part depend upon which of the rival theoretical standpoints we adopt. Thus, if we follow Kuhn's arguments through we shall, it seems, be compelled to conclude that in such types of theory-choice we do indeed lack any neutral and independent criterion by means of which we could evaluate the contending claims. Such bodies of theory seem to be mutually incommensurable.

The reactions of philosophers of science to Kuhn's identification of the phenomenon of incommensurability have for the most part been of two kinds. Some have argued that Kuhn is in fact mistaken and that the concept of incommensurability lacks application in the history of science. Others have accepted Kuhn's thesis and have argued in favour of inferences from it far more drastic than any that he would accept. What both parties agree on is that the following entailment holds: if and insofar as the concept of incommensurability has application to a choice between rival bodies of theory, then we can have no rational grounds for accepting any one of those rivals rather than any other. This entailment I wish to challenge. The argument which I want to deploy requires an initial emphasis upon two points to which philosophers of science have so far perhaps paid insufficient attention.

The first is that theories in the natural sciences as elsewhere have an essentially historical existence. There is no such thing as *the* kinetic theory of gases; there is only the kinetic theory as it was in 1850, the theory as it was in 1870, the theory as it is now and so on. And equally there was no such thing as medieval (Aristotelian) physical theory as such; but only such theory as it was held in early-fourteenth-century Paris or late-fifteenth-century Padua. Bodies of theory, that is to say, themselves progress or fail to progress and they do so because and insofar as they provide by their incoherences and their inadequacies – incoherences and inadequacies judged by the standards of the body of theory itself – a definition of problems, the solution of which provides direction for the formulation and reformulation of that body of theory. And that is to say, the incoherences and inadequacies of a theory are never to be regarded as merely negative aspects of that theory. They are indeed the points at which a body of theory provides itself with problems, those problems in dealing with which it shows itself still capable of growth, still scientifically fertile, or on the other hand incapable and sterile. By providing itself with problems, a body of theory provides itself with goals and with some measure of its own progress or lack of progress towards those goals. The relevance of this point to the problems of incommensurability becomes clear when we add to it another.

Particular small-scale theories come to us for the most part embedded in larger bodies of theory; and such larger bodies of theory are in turn embedded in still more comprehensive schemes of belief. It is these schemes of belief which provide the framework of continuity through time within which the transition from one incommensurable body of theory to its rival is made; and there has to be such a framework, for without the conceptual resources which it affords we could not understand the two bodies of theory as rivals which provide alternative and incompatible accounts of *one and the same subject-matter* and which offer us rival and incompatible means of achieving *one and the same set of theoretical goals*. It is a condition of the two rival bodies of theory being genuinely incommensurable that this shared specification of subject-matter and theoretical goals should not be such as to provide ground for rational choice between them; but without the common specification of subject-matter and theoretical goals at the level of the framework beliefs – at the level of *Weltanschauung* – the theories would simply lack the logical properties which warrant us in classifying them as rivals. So in physical theory the concepts of *weight*, of *mass as defined by Newton* and of *mass as defined within quantum mechanics*, concepts embodied in incommensurable bodies of theory, have all to be understood as concepts of *that property of bodies which determines their relative motion*, if we are to be able to understand what makes those bodies of theory contending rivals. And it is this shared higher order vocabulary, this stock of senses and references provided at the level of *Weltanschauung*, which makes it possible for the adherents of rival incommensurable bodies of theory to recognize themselves as moving towards what can be specified at that level as the same goals. So medieval physicists grappling with the problems internal to impetus theory, Renaissance followers of Galileo and twentieth-century contributors to quantum mechanics all had or have a more or less shared vocabulary which would enable them to recognize themselves as trying to achieve as general and complete as possible an account of moving bodies. Why does this matter?

It matters because an adequate formulation of these two points is required not only for the statement of the problems posed by the incommensurability of rival bodies of theory, but also for its solution. And this solution can now be formulated as a criterion by means of which the rational superiority of one large-scale body of theory to another can be judged. One large scale of theory – say, Newtonian mechanics – may be judged decisively superior to another – say, the mechanics of medieval impetus theory, if and only if the former body of theory enables us to give an adequate and by the best standards we have true explanation of why the latter body of theory both enjoyed the successes and victories that it did *and* suffered the defeats and frustrations that it did, where success and failure, victory and defeat are defined in terms of the standards for success and failure, victory and defeat provided by what I earlier called the internal problematic of the latter body of theory. It is not success and failure, progress or sterility as we, making our judgments from the standpoint of the rationally superior theory, identify them that provide material for that theory to explain. It is success and failure, progress and sterility in terms both of the problems and the goals that were or could have been identified by the adherents of the rationally inferior theory. So from the standpoint of Newtonian mechanics it is possible to explain why impetus theorists, lacking the concepts of inertia, could proceed only so far and no further in solving those problems which barred their movement towards the goal of formulating general equations for motion.

What I am arguing then is that one incommensurable body of scientific theory can speak to another across time, not only as providing a better set of solutions to its central problems, since of course it is on the definition of what constitutes a central problem that two incommensurable theories are likely to disagree, but as providing an historical explanation of why certain of the key experiences of its adherents in wrestling with their own problems were what they were. The application of this test of rational superiority is simplest in those cases where it is possible to supplement it with another test that is not by itself either necessary or sufficient to decide between the claims of two rival incommensurable bodies of theory. In cases where the tradition of enquiry defined by a particular body of theory has degenerated in respect of coherence or sterility or cannot accommodate new discoveries without lapsing into incoherence (this last is essentially the import of Galileo's early attempts to fit new discoveries into the old physics), then the adherents of that body of theory may themselves have good grounds for rejecting it, without having any clearly good reasons for selecting any one particular alternative as worthy of their allegiance. (I make this point as a corrective to what I wrote in MacIntyre 1977, but in general I regard this argument as a development of some points made in that paper.) It is worth noticing that we do not really need to add to the criteria that I have formulated as a further requirement that the body of theory judged rationally superior shall itself be relatively coherent (not of course *too* coherent, since, as I have already suggested, incoherence is the source of intellectual progress) and fruitful in problem-solving; for no body of theory that failed to meet this requirement could as a matter of fact furnish the kind of historical explanation, the provision of which is the test of rational superiority.

What emerges then, perhaps surprisingly, is that the history of natural science is in a certain way sovereign over the natural sciences. At least where those large-scale incommensurable bodies of theory that Kuhn first identified are concerned, the superior theory in natural science is that which affords grounds for a certain kind of historical explanation, that which gives to an historical narrative an intelligibility that it would not otherwise possess. The rational superiority of Newtonian mechanics derives in key part, so it turns out, from its ability to play a part in furnishing us with an explanation of late medieval experiences of intellectual frustration. How we judge the status of the science depends upon how we judge the quality of the history that it assists in providing. It follows also that no natural scientific theory is ever vindicated as such; it is vindicated or fails to be vindicated only relatively to those of its predecessors with whom it has competed so far. The best reasons that we have for accepting quantum mechanics are a conjunction of its account of nature and the historical account which that account of nature can assist in furnishing of the breakdown of Newtonian mechanics. Thus there is an ineliminable historical reference backwards from each scientific standpoint to its incommensurable predecessor. The natural sciences, in spite of the anti-historical cast of mind which so often informs the ways in which they are taught and transmitted, cannot escape their past. But to have recognized this is to have reached a point at which it is possible to turn back from the history of the natural sciences to that of philosophy and to enquire whether the relation of past and present in philosophy can be understood, if not in the same, at least in a closely analogous way.

A condition of being able to do this would be that the questions raised by three crucial differences between the problems posed by the natural sciences and those posed by philosophy can be answered in at least a minimally satisfactory way. First, I noticed at the outset that Kuhn was able to rely on a modern definition of the natural sciences in order to delimit what counts as their history in the past. But in philosophy, for reasons that are by now obvious, it would be fatal to our whole project to allow the philosophical present to determine what was to be counted as the philosophical past. Yet this does not mean that we are resourceless. For whereas the natural sciences derive their minimal unifying definition from the point that they have now reached, philosophy is able to derive a similar minimal unifying definition from its starting-point. Nobody is to count as a philosopher who does not have to be judged in the end against standards set by Plato. I do not say this only because Plato does already in fact to a surprisingly large degree provide philosophy both with its starting-point and with the definition of its scope and subject-matter. But Plato transcends, in just the way that I have described, the limitations of Pre-Socratic philosophy and in so doing sets a standard for all later attempts to transcend his limitations in turn. This is how he made Aristotle possible; this is indeed how he made philosophy possible. Hence all philosophers after Plato must confront a situation in which if you cannot transcend the limitations or what you take to be the limitations of Plato's fundamental positions, then you have no sufficient reason for failing to recognize yourself as a Platonist – unless, that is, you abandon philosophy altogether. Coleridge was wrong in thinking that everyone is either a Platonist or an Aristotelian, but he would have been right if he had declared instead that everyone is either a Platonist or something else – a non-trivial exhaustive disjunction, since all philosophy must have this ineliminable backward reference to Plato's dialogues. To recognize this is to provide for philosophy that minimal unity both prospectively and retrospectively which the present condition of the natural sciences provides retrospectively.

Secondly, it was an important part of my thesis about the natural sciences that the discontinuities of incommensurability occurred within a framework of continuity provided at the level of what I call *Weltanschauung*, those shared beliefs and points of reference not put in question when so much else is. And it might be suggested that, since large-scale philosophical disagreements often seem to include within their scope what I called *Weltanschauung*, the requisite continuities, the requisite shared beliefs and points of reference the characterization of which is essential to even the statements, let alone the solution of any particular incommensurability problems, may well be lacking in otherwise largely parallel episodes in the history of philosophy. I do not of course want to quarrel with the contention that large-scale philosophical disagreement has a scope far beyond that of the most radical conflicts in the natural sciences and that it often extends to what I called *Weltanschauung*. But even the most radical of philosophical conflicts occur within the context of not dissimilar continuities. The philosophical truth, and it is a truth, that not everything can be put in question simultaneously is relevant: and where for example we confront the discontinuities in the history of Aristotelian *pathe*, seventeenth-century passions, eighteenth-century sentiments and twentieth-century emotions, we do so knowing that *anger* and *fear* or their equivalents have to figure in the catalogue of each of them and that even if we have reservations about translating, say, *ira* straightforwardly as *anger* and *timor* as *fear*, our reservations have to be stated in such a way that what that translation achieves as well as what it fails to achieve emerges. And that is to say the types of discontinuity and difference catalogued at the beginning of my argument require as their counterpart an equally comprehensive catalogue of the types of continuity, resemblance and recurrence. To have noticed this earlier would in no way have removed or mitigated the problem which is created by the discontinuities and differences. But at this later point in the argument, to notice it is a pre-condition of moving from a conclusion about the history of the natural sciences to one about the history of philosophy.

Thirdly, my account of the relationship of the natural sciences to their history took it for granted that almost universally in that history the later has defeated the earlier. But although in fact this has been so, it was not and is not necessarily so. And in philosophy I see much less reason to believe that it has been so and no reason at all to proceed from the outset on the assumption that it has been so. But having uttered this warning, I face no further major barrier to reformulating the account that I gave of what it is that entitles one large-scale body of natural scientific theory to be accounted rationally superior to another, so that it becomes an account of what it is that entitles one large-scale body of philosophical theory to be accounted rationally superior to another. That reformulation will run as follows.

Philosophical arguments, debates and conflicts, we shall have to recognize, are of at least two distinct kinds. There are of course those that occur *within* a very largely shared body of assumptions about background beliefs, standards of argument, modes of characterizing counter-examples, paradigms of refutation and so on. But there are also the types of debate or conflict between rival large-scale standpoints that I noticed earlier, where disagreement is systematic in a way that apparently eliminates the possibility of any common standard for the rational resolution of disagreement. Each of the rival standpoints in such a large-scale confrontation will have its own internal problematic, its moments of incoherence, its unsolved problems, judged that is by *its own* standards of what is problematic, what is coherent, and what a satisfactory solution is. The adherents of a particular standpoint may not of course always recognize what the application of their own standards would involve; and we do not need to limit ourselves to what they do or did in fact recognize, in order to assert that what constitutes the rational superiority of one large-scale philosophical standpoint over another is its ability to transcend the limitations of that other by providing from its own point of view a better explanation and understanding of the failures, frustrations and incoherences of the other point of view (failure, frustrations and incoherences, that is, as judged by the standards internal to that other point of view) than that other point of view can give of itself, in such a way as to enable us to give a better historical account, a more adequate and intelligible true narrative of that other point of view and its successes and failures than it can provide for itself.

It thus turns out that, just as the achievements of the natural sciences are in the end to be judged in terms of achievements of the history of those sciences, so the achievements of philosophy are in the end to be judged in terms of the achievements of the history of philosophy. The history of philosophy is on this view that part of philosophy which is sovereign over the rest of the discipline. This is a conclusion which will seem paradoxical to some and unwelcome to many. But it has at least one merit: it is not original. Vico, Hegel and Collingwood all at various points come very close to theses remarkably, and indeed not at all by coincidence, similar. But each of them in urging this type of point of view allowed, as I too must, that the crucial test of such theses occurs not at all at the level of argument at which I have conducted it so far, and at which they often enough themselves conducted it. The crucial question is: can the requisite kind of history actually be written? And the only way to answer that question is by trying to write it and either failing or succeeding.

REFERENCES

Hare, R. M. 1952. *The Language of Morals.* Oxford: Oxford University Press.

Hare, R. M. 1963. *Freedom and Reason.* Oxford: Clarendon Press

Kuhn, T. S. 1970. *The Structure of Scientific Revolutions*, 2nd edition. Chicago: University of Chicago Press

MacIntyre, Alasdair. 1977. 'Epistemological crises, dramatic narrative and the philosophy of science', *The Monist* 60(4): 453–72

Owen, G. E. L. 1961. 'Tithenai ta Phainomena', in S. Mansion (ed.), *Aristote et les problèmes de methode*. Proceedings of the second Symposium Aristotelieum. Louvain

3

The historiography of philosophy:
four genres

RICHARD RORTY

I Rational and historical reconstructions

Analytic philosophers who have attempted 'rational reconstructions' of
the arguments of great dead philosophers have done so in the hope of
treating these philosophers as contemporaries, as colleagues with whom
they can exchange views. They have argued that unless one does this one
might as well turn over the history of philosophy to historians – whom
they picture as mere doxographers, rather than seekers after philosophical
truth. Such reconstructions, however, have led to charges of anachronism.
Analytic historians of philosophy are frequently accused of beating texts
into the shape of propositions currently being debated in the philosophical
journals. It is urged that we should not force Aristotle or Kant to take sides
in current debates within philosophy of language or metaethics. There
seems to be a dilemma: either we anachronistically impose enough of our
problems and vocabulary on the dead to make them conversational
partners, or we confine our interpretive activity to making their falsehoods
look less silly by placing them in the context of the benighted times in
which they were written.

Those alternatives, however, do not constitute a dilemma. We should do
both of these things, but do them separately. We should treat the history of
philosophy as we treat the history of science. In the latter field, we have no
reluctance in saying that we know better than our ancestors what they were
talking about. We do not think it anachronistic to say that Aristotle had a
false model of the heavens, or that Galen did not understand how the
circulatory system worked. We take the pardonable ignorance of great
dead scientists for granted. We should be equally willing to say that
Aristotle was unfortunately ignorant that there are no such things as real
essences, or Leibniz that God does not exist, or Descartes that the mind is
just the central nervous system under an alternative description. We
hesitate merely because we have colleagues who are themselves ignorant of
such facts, and whom we courteously describe not as 'ignorant', but as

49

'holding different philosophical views'. Historians of science have no colleagues who believe in crystalline spheres, or who doubt Harvey's account of circulation, and they are thus free from such constraints.

There is nothing wrong with self-consciously letting our own philosophical views dictate terms in which to describe the dead. But there are reasons for *also* describing them in other terms, their own terms. It is useful to recreate the intellectual scene in which the dead lived their lives – in particular, the real and imagined conversations they might have had with their contemporaries (or near-contemporaries). There are purposes for which it is useful to know how people talked who did not know as much as we do – to know this in enough detail so that we can imagine ourselves talking the same outdated language. The anthropologist wants to know how primitives talk to fellow-primitives as well as how they react to instruction from missionaries. For this purpose he tries to get inside their heads, and to think in terms which he would never dream of employing at home. Similarly, the historian of science, who can imagine what Aristotle might have said in a dialogue in heaven with Aristarchus and Ptolemy, knows something interesting which remains unknown to the Whiggish astrophysicist who sees only how Aristotle would have been crushed by Galileo's arguments. There is knowledge – historical knowledge – to be gained which one can only get by bracketing one's own better knowledge about, e.g., the movements of the heavens or the existence of God.

The pursuit of such historical knowledge must obey a constraint formulated by Quentin Skinner:

No agent can eventually be said to have meant or done something which he could never be brought to accept as a correct description of what he had meant or done.
(Skinner 1969: 28)

Skinner says that this maxim excludes 'the possibility that an acceptable account of an agent's behaviour could ever survive the demonstration that it was itself dependent on the use of criteria of description and classification not available to the agent himself'. There is an important sense of 'what the agent meant or did', as of 'account of the agent's behaviour', for which this is an ineluctable constraint. If we want an account of Aristotle's or Locke's behaviour which obeys this constraint, however, we shall have to confine ourselves to one which, at its ideal limit, tells us what they might have said in response to all the criticisms or questions which would have been aimed at them by their contemporaries (or, more precisely, by that selection of their contemporaries or near-contemporaries whose criticisms and questions they could have understood right off the bat – all the people who, roughly speaking, 'spoke the same language', not least because they were just as ignorant of what we now know as the great dead philosopher himself). We may want to go on to ask questions like 'What would Aristotle have said about the moons of Jupiter (or about Quine's anti-essentialism)?' or 'What would Locke have said about labour unions (or about Rawls)?' or 'What would Berkeley have said about Ayer's or Bennett's attempt to "linguistify" his views on sense-perception and matter?' But we shall not describe the answers we envisage them giving to such questions as descriptions of what they 'meant or did', in Skinner's sense of these terms.

The main reason we want historical knowledge of what unre-educated primitives, or dead philosophers and scientists, would have said to each other is that it helps us to recognize that there have been different forms of intellectual life than ours. As Skinner (1969:52–3) rightly says, 'the indispensable value of studying the history of ideas' is to learn 'the distinction between what is necessary and what is the product merely of our own contingent arrangements'. The latter is indeed, as he goes on to say, 'the key to self-awareness itself'. But we also want to imagine conversations between ourselves (whose contingent arrangements include general agreement that, e.g., there are no real essences, no God, etc.) and the mighty dead. We want this not simply because it is nice to feel one up on one's betters, but because we would like to be able to see the history of our race as a long conversational interchange. We want to be able to see it that way in order to assure ourselves that there has been rational progress in the course of recorded history – that we differ from our ancestors on grounds which our ancestors could be led to accept. The need for reassurance on this point is as great as the need for self-awareness. We need to imagine Aristotle studying Galileo or Quine and changing his mind, Aquinas reading Newton or Hume and changing his, etc. We need to think that, in philosophy as in science, the mighty mistaken dead look down from heaven at our recent successes, and are happy to find that their mistakes have been corrected.

This means that we are interested not only in what the Aristotle who walked the streets of Athens 'could be brought to accept as a correct description of what he had meant or done' but in what an ideally reasonable and educable Aristotle could be brought to accept as such a description. The ideal aborigine can eventually be brought to accept a description of himself as having cooperated in the continuation of a kinship system designed to facilitate the unjust economic arrangements of his tribe. An ideal Gulag guard can eventually be brought to regard himself as having betrayed his loyalty to his fellow-Russians. An ideal Aristotle can be brought to describe himself as having mistaken the preparatory taxonomic stages of biological research for the essence of all scientific inquiry. Each of these imaginary people, by the time he has been brought to accept such a new description of what he meant or did, has become 'one of us'. He is our contemporary, or our fellow-citizen, or a fellow-member of the same disciplinary matrix.

To give an example of such conversation with the re-educated dead, consider Strawson (1966) on Kant. *The Bounds of Sense* is inspired by the same motives as *Individuals* – the conviction that Humean psychological atomism is deeply misguided and artificial, and that attempts to replace the common-sense 'Aristotelian' framework of things with 'events' or 'stimuli' (in the manner common to Whitehead and Quine) are deeply misguided. Since Kant agreed with this line of thought, and since much of the 'Transcendental Analytic' is devoted to making similar points, it is natural for someone with Strawson's concerns to want to show Kant how he can make those points without saying some other, less plausible, things which he said. These are things which the progress of philosophy since Kant's day has freed us from the temptation to say. Strawson can, for example, show Kant how to get along without notions like 'in the mind' or 'created by the mind', notions from which Wittgenstein and Ryle liberated us. Strawson's conversation with Kant is the sort one has with somebody who is brilliantly and originally right about something dear to one's heart, but who exasperatingly mixes up this topic with a lot of outdated foolishness. Other examples of such conversations are Ayer's (1936) and Bennett's (1971) conversations with the British Empiricists about phenomenalism – conversations which try to filter out the pure essence of phenomenalism from questions about the physiology of perception and about the existence of God (subjects about which we are now better informed, and thus able to perceive the irrelevance). Here again we have a fulfillment of the natural desire to talk to people some of whose ideas are quite like our own, in the hope of getting them to admit that we have gotten those ideas clearer, or in the hope of getting them clearer still in the course of the conversation.[1]

---

[1] Thus I cannot agree with Michael Ayers' strictures on such attempts, nor with his claim that it is an 'illusion' that ideas in metaphysics, logic, and epistemology, share with Euclid's mathematical ideas 'an independence of the accidents of history' (Ayers 1978: 46). I agree with Jonathan Bennett's claim, quoted by Ayers at p. 54 of his essay, that 'we understand Kant only in proportion as we can say, clearly and in contemporary terms, what his problems were, which of them are still problems and what contribution Kant makes to their solution'. Ayers' reply is that 'On its natural interpretation, this statement [of Bennett's] implies that there can be no such thing as understanding a philosopher in his own terms as something distinct from, and prior to, the difficult achievement of relating his thought to what we ourselves might want to say.' I would rejoin, on Bennett's behalf, that there is indeed a sense in which we can understand what a philosopher says in his own terms before relating his thought to ours, but that this minimal sort of understanding is like being able to exchange courtesies in a foreign tongue without being able to translate what one is saying into our native language. Similarly, one might learn to prove Euclid's mathematical theorems in Greek before learning how to translate them into contemporary mathematical jargon. Translation is necessary if 'understanding' is to mean something more than engaging in rituals of which we do not see the point, and translating an utterance means fitting it into *our* practices. (See fn. 3 below.) Successful historical reconstructions can only

Such enterprises in commensuration are, of course, anachronistic. But if they are conducted in full knowledge of their anachronism, they are unobjectionable. The only problems they raise are the verbal one of whether rational reconstructions are to be viewed as 'making clear what the dead really said', and the equally verbal one of whether rational reconstructors are 'really' doing *history*. Nothing turns on the answer to either question. It is natural to describe Columbus as discovering America rather than Cathay, and not knowing that he had done so. It is almost equally natural to describe Aristotle as unwittingly describing the effects of gravity rather than of natural downward motion. It is slightly more strained, but just a further step along the same line, to describe Plato as having unconsciously believed that all words were names (or whatever other premise modern semantically minded commentators find handy in reconstructing his arguments). It is fairly clear that in Skinner's sense of 'mean' Plato meant nothing like this. When we anachronistically say that he 'really' held such doctrines we mean that, in an imagined argument with present-day philosophers about whether he should have held certain other views, he would have been driven back on a premise which he never formulated, dealing with a topic he never considered – a premise which may have to be suggested to him by a friendly rational reconstructor.

Historical reconstructions of what unre-educated dead thinkers would have said to their contemporaries – reconstructions which abide by Skinner's maxim – are, ideally, reconstructions on which all historians can agree. If the question is what Locke would be likely to have said to a Hobbes who had lived and retained his faculties for a few more decades, there is no reason why historians should not arrive at a consensus, a consensus which might be confirmed by the discovery of a manuscript of Locke's in which he imagines a conversation between himself and Hobbes.

be performed by people who have some idea of what they themselves think about the issues under discussion, even if only that they are pseudo-issues. Attempts at historical reconstruction which are selfless in this respect (e.g., Wolfson's book on Spinoza) are not so much reconstructions as assemblages of raw material for such reconstructions. So when Ayers says at p. 61 that 'Instead of holding Locke's terminology up against that of our own theories, we should try to understand his purposes in relating thought and sensation as he does', I would urge that we cannot do much of the latter until we have done quite a bit of the former. If you do not believe that there are such mental faculties as 'thought' and 'sensation' (as many of us post-Wittgensteinian philosophers of mind do not), you are going to have to spend some time figuring out acceptable equivalents to Locke's terms before reading on to see how he uses them – the same sort of thing we atheists have to do when reading works of moral theology. In general, I think that Ayers overdoes the opposition between 'our terms' and 'his terms' when he suggests that one can do historical reconstruction first and leave rational reconstruction for later. The two genres can never be *that* independent, because you will not know much about what the dead meant prior to figuring out how much truth they knew. These two topics should be seen as moments in a continuing movement around the hermeneutic circle, a circle one has to have gone round a good many times before one can begin to do *either* sort of reconstruction.

Rational reconstructions, on the other hand, are not likely to converge, and there is no reason why they should. Somebody who thinks that the question of whether all words are names, or some other semantical thesis, is the sort of question which is decisive for one's views about lots of other topics will have a quite different imaginary conversation with Plato than somebody who thinks that philosophy of language is a passing fad, irrelevant to the real issues which divide Plato from his great modern antagonists (Whitehead, Heidegger, or Popper, for example). The Fregean, the Kripkean, the Popperian, the Whiteheadian, and the Heideggerian will each re-educate Plato in a different way before starting to argue with him.

If we picture discussion of great dead philosophers as alternating between historical reconstruction, which depends on obeying Skinner's maxim, and rational reconstruction, which depends on ignoring it, there need be no conflict between the two. When we respect Skinner's maxim we shall give an account of the dead thinker 'in his own terms', ignoring the fact that we should think ill of anyone who still used those terms today. When we ignore Skinner's maxim, we give an account 'in our terms', ignoring the fact that the dead thinker, in his linguistic habits as he lived, would have repudiated these terms as foreign to his interests and intentions. The contrast between these two tasks, however, should not be phrased as that between finding out what the dead thinker meant and finding out whether what he said was true. Finding out what someone meant is a matter of finding out how his utterance fits into his general pattern of linguistic and other behaviour – roughly, finding out what he would have said in reply to questions about what he said previously. So 'what he meant' is different depending upon who is asking such questions. More generally, 'what is meant' is different depending upon how large a range of actual and possible behavior one envisages. People often say, quite reasonably, that they only found out what they meant by listening to what they said later on – when they heard themselves reacting to the consequences of their original utterance. It is perfectly reasonable to describe Locke as finding out what he really meant, what he was really getting at in the *Second Treatise*, only after conversations in heaven with, successively, Jefferson, Marx, and Rawls. It is also perfectly reasonable to set aside the question of what an ideal and immortal Locke would have decided that he meant. We do the latter if we are interested in the differences between what it was like to be a political thinker in Locke's England and in our twentieth-century trans-Atlantic culture.

We can, of course, restrict the term 'meaning' to what we are after in the latter, Skinnerian, enterprise, rather than using it in a way which permits there to be as many meanings of a text as there are dialectical contexts in which it can be placed. If we wish to so restrict it, we can adopt E. D.

Hirsch's distinction between 'meaning' and 'significance', and confine the former term to what accords with the author's intentions around the time of composition, using 'significance' for the place of the text in some other context.[2] But nothing hangs on this, unless we choose to insist that it is the task of the 'historian' to discover 'meaning' and (in the case of philosophical texts) of 'the philosopher' to inquire into 'significance' and eventually into truth. What does matter is making clear that grasping the meaning of an assertion is a matter of placing that assertion in a context – not of digging a little nugget of sense out of the mind of the assertor. Whether we privilege the context which consists of what the assertor was thinking about around the time he or she made the assertion depends upon what we want to get out of thinking about the assertion. If we want, as Skinner says, 'self-awareness', then we need to avoid anachronism as much as possible. If we want self-justification through conversation with the dead thinkers about our current problems, then we are free to indulge in as much of it as we like, as long as we realize that we are doing so.

What, then, of finding out whether what the dead thinker said was true? Just as determining meaning is a matter of placing an assertion in a context of actual and possible behavior, so determining truth is a matter of placing it in the context of assertions which we ourselves should be willing to make. Since what counts for us as an intelligible pattern of behavior is a function of what we believe to be true, truth and meaning are not to be ascertained independently of one another.[3] There will be as many rational reconstructions which purport to find significant truths, or pregnant and important falsehoods, in the work of a great dead philosopher, as there are importantly different contexts in which his works can be placed. To repeat my initial point, the appearance of difference between the history of science and the history of philosophy is little more than a reflection of the uninteresting fact that some of these differing contexts represent the differing opinions of members of the same profession. That is why we find more disagreement about how many truths are to be found in the writings of Aristotle among historians of philosophy than among historians of

---

[2] See Hirsch 1976: 2ff for this distinction. I would disagree with Hirsch's Ayers-like claim that we cannot start discovering significance unless we first discover meaning, for the same Davidsonian reasons as I disagreed with Ayers in the previous note.

[3] See Donald Davidson's articles, collected in his forthcoming *Inquiries Into Interpretation and Truth*, for a defense of my claim in the previous notes that we cannot find out what somebody means prior to finding out how his linguistic and other practices resemble and differ from ours, nor independently of the charitable assumption that *most* of his beliefs are true. Ayers' assumption that historical reconstruction is naturally prior to rational reconstruction, and Hirsch's that discovery of meaning is naturally prior to discovery of significance, both seem to me to rest on an insufficiently holistic account of interpretation – an account which I have defended elsewhere (e.g., in 'Pragmatism, Davidson and truth', forthcoming in a volume of essays on Davidson to be edited by Ernest Lepore).

biology. The resolution of these debates is a 'philosophical' rather than an 'historical' question. If similar discord obtained among historians of biology, then its resolution would be a 'biological' rather than an 'historical' matter.

II *Geistesgeschichte* as canon-formation

So far I have been suggesting that the history of philosophy differs only incidentally from the history of one of the natural sciences. In both we have a contrast between contextualist accounts which block off later developments from sight and 'Whiggish' accounts which draw on our own better knowledge. The only difference I have mentioned is that, because philosophy is more controversial than biology, anachronistic reconstructions of great dead philosophers are more various than those of great dead biologists. But my discussion so far has ignored the problem of how one picks out who counts as a great dead *philosopher*, as opposed to a great dead something else. So it has ignored the problem of how one picks out the history of *philosophy* from the history of 'thought' or 'culture'. The latter sort of problem does not arise for history of biology, because it is co-extensive with the history of writing about plants and animals. The problem arises only in a relatively trivial form for the history of chemistry, because nobody much cares whether we call Paracelsus a chemist, an alchemist, or both. Questions about whether Pliny was a biologist in the same sense as Mendel, or about whether Aristotle's *De Generatione et Corruptione* counts as chemistry, do not inspire profound passions. This is because we have, in these areas, clear stories of progress to tell. It does not make much difference at what point we start telling the story – at what point we see a 'discipline' emerging out of a chaos of speculation.

It does, however, make a difference when we come to the history of philosophy. This is because 'history of philosophy' covers a third genre, in addition to the two I have discussed so far. Besides such Skinnerian historical reconstructions as John Dunn's of Locke or J. B. Schneewind's of Sidgwick, and the sort of rational reconstructions offered by Bennett of the British Empiricists or Strawson of Kant, there are the big sweeping *geistesgeschichtlich* stories – the genre of which Hegel is paradigmatic. This genre is represented in our time by, for example, Heidegger, Reichenbach, Foucault, Blumenberg, and MacIntyre.[4] It aims at self-justification in the

---

4 I am thinking of Heidegger 1973, and of the way in which his later works fill out these sketches. I have discussed Reichenbach's *The Rise of Scientific Philosophy* (the most comprehensive version of the positivist story of how philosophy gradually emerged from prejudice and confusion) in Rorty 1982: 211ff. Foucault's *The Order of Things* is discussed as an example of *Geistesgeschichte* in section IV of this essay. My references to Blumenberg and to MacIntyre are to *The Legitimacy of the Modern Age* and *After Virtue* respectively.

same way as does rational reconstruction, but on a different scale. Rational reconstructions typically aim at saying that the great dead philosopher had some excellent ideas, but unfortunately couldn't get them straight because of 'the limitations of his time'. They usually confine themselves to a relatively small portion of the philosopher's work – e.g., Kant on the relation between appearance and reality, or Leibniz on modality, or Aristotle on the notions of essence, existence, and prediction. They are written in the light of some recent work in philosophy which can reasonably be said to be 'about the same questions' as the great dead philosopher was discussing. They are designed to show that the answers he gave to these questions, though plausible and exciting, need restatement or purification – or, perhaps, the kind of precise refutation which further work in the field has recently made possible. In contrast, *Geistesgeschichte*, works at the level of problematics rather than of solutions to problems. It spends more of its time asking 'Why should anyone have made the question of — central to his thought?' or 'Why did anyone take the problem of — seriously?' than on asking in what respect the great dead philosopher's answer or solution accords with that of contemporary philosophers. It typically describes the philosopher in terms of his entire work rather than in terms of his most celebrated arguments (e.g., Kant as the author of all three *Critiques*, the enthusiast for the French Revolution, the forerunner of Schleiermacher's theology, etc., rather than Kant as the author of the 'Transcendental analytic'). It wants to justify the historian and his friends in having the sort of philosophical concerns they have – in taking philosophy to be what they take it to be – rather than in giving the particular solutions to philosophical problems which they give. It wants to give plausibility to a certain image of philosophy, rather than to give plausibility to a particular solution of a given philosophical problem by pointing out how a great dead philosopher anticipated, or interestingly failed to anticipate, this solution.

The existence of this third, *geistesgeschichtlich*, sort of history of philosophy is an additional reason for the *prima facie* difference between history of science and history of philosophy. Historians of science feel no need to justify our physicists' concern with elementary particles or our biologists' with DNA. If you can synthesize steroids, you do not require historical legitimation. But philosophers do need to justify their concern

---

When I say that these are works of self-justification, I of course do not mean that they justify the present state of things, but rather that they justify the author's attitude towards the present state of things. Heidegger's, Foucault's, and MacIntyre's downbeat stories condemn present practices but justify the adoption of their authors' views towards those practices, thereby justifying their selection of what counts as a pressing philosophical issue – the same function as is performed by Hegel's, Reichenbach's, and Blumenberg's upbeat stories.

with semantics, or perception, or the unity of Subject and Object, or the enlargement of human freedom, or whatever the philosopher who is telling the big sweeping story is in fact concerned with. The question of which problems are 'the problems of philosophy', which questions are *philosophical* questions, are the questions to which *geistesgeschichtlich* histories of philosophy are principally devoted. By contrast, histories of biology or chemistry can dismiss such questions as verbal. They can simply take the currently uncontroversial portions of the discipline in question as that to which history leads up. The *terminus ad quem* of history-of-science-as-story-of-progress is not in dispute.

I said above that one reason for the apparent difference between the history of philosophy and the history of science stemmed from the fact that philosophers who differ about, say, the existence of God are nevertheless professional colleagues. The second reason for the apparent difference is that those who differ about whether the existence of God is an important or interesting or 'real' question are also professional colleagues. The academic discipline called 'philosophy' encompasses not only different answers to philosophical questions but total disagreement on what questions are *philosophical*. Rational reconstructions and *geistesgeschichtlich* reinterpretations are, from this point of view, different only in degree – degree of disagreement with the great dead philosopher who is being reconstructed or reinterpreted. If one disagrees with him mainly about solutions to problems, rather than about which problems need discussion, one will think of oneself as reconstructing him (as, e.g., Ayer reconstructed Berkeley). If one thinks of oneself as showing that one need not think about what he tried to think about (as in, e.g., Ayer's dismissive interpretation of Heidegger, or Heidegger's dismissive description of Kierkegaard as a 'religious writer' rather than a 'thinker') then one will think of oneself as explaining why he should not count as a fellow-philosopher. One will redefine 'philosophy' so as to read him out of the canon.

Canon-formation is not an issue for the history of science. There is no need to affiliate one's own scientific activity to that of a great dead scientist in order to make it look more respectable, nor to disparage some purportedly distinguished predecessor as a pseudo-scientist in order to justify one's own concerns. Canon-formation is important in the history of philosophy because 'philosophy' has an important honorific use, in addition to its descriptive uses. Used descriptively, the term 'philosophical question' can mean a question which is currently being debated by some contemporary 'school', or it can mean a question debated by all or many of those historical figures customarily catalogued as 'philosophers'. Used honorifically, however, it means questions which *ought* to be debated – which are so general and so important that they *should* have been on the minds of thinkers of all places and times, whether these thinkers managed to formulate these questions explicitly or not.[5]

This honorific use of 'philosophical question' is, in theory, irrelevant to rational reconstructions. A contemporary philosopher who wants to argue with Descartes about mind–body dualism or with Kant about the appearance–reality distinction or with Aristotle about meaning and reference need not, and usually does not, claim that these topics are inescapable whenever human beings reflect upon their condition and their fate. The rational reconstructor typically confines himself to saying that these are topics which have had an interesting career and on which interesting work is still being done – as an historian of science might say the same about the taxonomy of birds or the varieties of insanity. For purposes of rational reconstruction and ensuing argument, there is no need to worry about whether a topic is 'inescapable'. For *Geistesgeschichte*, the sort of intellectual history which has a moral, there is such a need. For the moral to be drawn is that we have, or have not, been on the right track in raising the philosophical questions we have recently been raising, and that the *Geisteshistoriker* is justified in adopting a certain problematic. The rational reconstructor, by contrast, feels no more need to ask whether philosophy is on the right track than the historian of science needs to ask whether contemporary biochemistry is in good shape.

The honorific use of 'philosophy' is also irrelevant, in theory, to historical reconstruction. If the *Geistesgeschichte* of the day reads Locke or Kierkegaard out of the philosophical canon, contextualist historians can continue imperturbably describing what it was like to be Locke or Kierkegaard. From the point of view of contextualist history, there is no need for great big stories, sweeping over many centuries, in which to embed an account of what it was like to be concerned with politics in seventeenth-century England or with religion in nineteenth-century Denmark. For such historians, the question of whether their chosen figure was 'really' a major philosopher, a minor philosopher, a politician, a theologian, or a belle-lettrist, is as irrelevant as the taxonomic activities of the American Ornithological Union are to the field naturalist taking notes on the mating behavior of a flicker, one which the AOU has just

---

[5] The need for an honorific use of 'philosophy', for a canon, and for self-justification seems to me to explain what John Dunn calls 'the weird tendency of much writing, in the history of political thought especially, to be made up of what propositions in what great books remind the author of what propositions in what other great books' (1980: 15). This tendency is the mark of most *Geistesgeschichte*, and does not seem to me weird. It is the tendency both historians and philosophers indulge when they doff their robes and converse about what they have found useful in their favorite great books. The nice thing about *Geistesgeschichte*, in my view – the thing that makes it indispensable – is that it meets needs which neither unphilosophical history nor unhistorical philosophy is likely to fulfill. (See section IV below for discussion of the suggestion that we repress these needs.)

reclassified behind his back. One might, in one's philosophical capacity, share the Anglo-Saxon belief that no philosophical progress occurred between Kant and Frege and still, as an historian, delight in recapturing the concerns of Schiller and Schelling.

But this theoretical independence of both historical and rational reconstructions from canon-formation is rarely lived up to in practice. Rational reconstructors do not really want to bother reconstructing, and arguing with, minor philosophers. Historical reconstructors would like to reconstruct people who were 'significant' in the development of something – if not philosophy, then perhaps 'European thought' or 'the modern'. Work in both reconstructive genres is always done with one eye out for the most recent work in canon-formation, and that is the prerogative of the *Geisteshistoriker*. For he is the person who wields terms like 'philosophy' and 'philosophical question' in their honorific senses. He is thus the person who decides what is worth thinking about – which questions are matters of the 'contingent arrangements' of our day and which are the ones which tie us together with our ancestors. As the person who decides who was 'getting at' what was really important and who was merely distracted by the epiphenomena of his times, he plays the role which, in the ancient world, was played by the sage. One difference between that world and ours is that the high culture of modern times has become aware that the questions human beings have thought inescapable have changed over the centuries. We have become aware, as the ancient world was not, that we may not know which questions are the really important ones. We fear that we may still be working with philosophical vocabularies which are to 'the real' problems as, say, Aristotle's vocabulary was to 'the real' subject-matter of astrophysics. This sense that one's choice of vocabulary matters at least as much as one's answers to the questions posed within a given vocabulary has caused the *Geisteshistoriker* to displace the philosopher (or, as with Hegel, Nietzsche and Heidegger, has caused 'philosophy' to be used as the name of a certain particularly abstract and free-wheeling kind of intellectual history).

This last point can be put more simply by saying that nowadays nobody is sure that the descriptive senses of 'philosophical question' have anything much to do with the honorific sense of this term. Nobody is quite sure whether the issues discussed by contemporary philosophy professors (of any school) are issues which are 'necessary' or merely part of our 'contingent arrangements'. Furthermore, nobody is sure whether the issues discussed by all or most of the canon of great dead philosophers offered by books called *The History of Western Philosophy* – e.g., universals, mind and body, free will, appearance and reality, fact and value, etc. – are *important* issues. Occasionally, both inside and outside of philosophy, the suspicion is voiced that some or all of these are 'merely philosophical' – a term used in the same pejorative way as a chemist uses 'alchemical', or a Marxist 'superstructural', or an aristocrat 'middle class'. The self-awareness which historical reconstructions have given us is the awareness that some people who were our intellectual and moral equals were not interested in questions which seem to us inescapable and profound. Because such historical reconstructions are a source of doubt about whether philosophy (in either of its descriptive senses) is important, the *Geisteshistoriker* now puts the philosopher in his place, rather than the converse. He does this by assembling a cast of historical characters, and a dramatic narrative, which shows how we have come to ask the questions we now think inescapable and profound. Where these characters left writings behind, those writings then form a canon, a reading-list which one must have gone through in order to justify being what one is.

I can sum up what I have been saying about the third genre of historiography of philosophy by saying that it is the genre which takes responsibility for identifying which writers are 'the gread dead philosophers'. In this role, it is parasitic upon, and synthesises, the first two genres – historical reconstructions and reconstructions. Unlike rational reconstructions, and unlike the history of science, it has to worry about anachronism, for it cannot regard the question of who counts as a philosopher as settled by the practices of those presently so described. Unlike historical reconstructions, however, it cannot stay within the vocabulary used by a past figure. It has to 'place' that vocabulary in a series of vocabularies and estimate its importance by placing it in a narrative which traces changes in vocabulary. It is self-justificatory in the way that rational reconstruction is, but it is moved by the same hope for greater self-awareness which leads people to engage in historical reconstructions. For *Geistesgeschichte* wants to keep us aware of the fact that we are still en route – that the dramatic narrative it offers us is to be continued by our descendants. When it is fully self-conscious it wonders whether *all* the issues discussed so far may not have been part of the 'contingent arrangements' of earlier times. It insists on the point that even if some of them really *were* necessary and inescapable, we have no certainty about which these were.

III Doxography

The three genres I have described so far bear little relation to the genre which comes first to mind when the term 'history of philosophy' is used. This genre, my fourth, is the most familiar and most dubious. I shall call it doxography. This is exemplified by books which start from Thales or

Descartes and wind up with some figure roughly contemporary with the author, ticking off what various figures traditionally called 'philosophers' had to say about problems traditionally called 'philosophical'. It is this genre which inspires boredom and despair. It is the one to which Gilbert Ryle (1971: x) referred when he offhandedly said, as an excuse for his own risky rational reconstructions of Plato and others, that the existence of 'our standard histories of philosophy' was 'calamity itself, and not the mere risk of it'. I suspect that most of his readers heartily agreed. Even the most honest and conscientious and exhaustive books called *A History of Philosophy* – especially these, indeed – seem to decorticate the thinkers they discuss. It is this calamity to which proponents of historical reconstruction respond by insisting on the need for spelling out the contexts in which the texts were written, and to which proponents of rational reconstruction respond by insisting that we look at the great dead philosophers in the light of 'the best work now being done on the problems they discussed'. Both are attempts to revitalize figures who have unintentionally been mummified.

The explanation of the calamity, I think, is that most historians of philosophy who try to tell 'the story of philosophy from the pre-Socratics to our own day' know in advance what most of their chapter headings are going to be. Indeed, they know their publishers would not accept their manuscripts if a substantial number of the expected headings were missing. They work, typically, with a canon which made sense in terms of nineteenth-century neo-Kantian notions of 'the central problems of philosophy', notions which few modern readers take seriously. This has resulted in desperate attempts to make Leibniz and Hegel, Mill and Nietzsche, Descartes and Carnap, talk about some common topics, whether the historian or his readers have any interest in those topics or not.

In the sense in which I shall be using the term, doxography is the attempt to impose a problematic on a canon drawn up without reference to that problematic, or, conversely, to impose a canon on a problematic constructed without reference to that canon. Diogenes Laetius gave doxography a bad name by insisting on answering the question 'What did X think the good was?' for every X in an antecedently formulated canon. Nineteenth-century historians gave it a worse one by insisting on answering the question 'What did X think the nature of knowledge was?' for every X in another such canon. Analytic philosophers are in a fair way to worsening the situation by insisting on an answer to the question 'What was X's theory of meaning?' as are Heideggerians by insisting on an answer to 'What did X think Being was?' Such awkward attempts to make a new question fit an old canon remind us, however, that new doxographies usually started off as fresh, brave, revisionist attempts to dispel the dullness of the previous doxographic tradition, attempts inspired by the conviction that the true problematic of philosophy had finally been discovered. So the real trouble with doxography is that it is a *half-hearted* attempt to tell a new story of intellectual progress by describing all texts in the light of recent discoveries. It is half-hearted because it lacks the courage to readjust the canon to suit the new discoveries.

The main reason for this recurrent half-heartedness is the idea that 'philosophy' is the name of a natural kind – the name of a discipline which, in all ages and places, has managed to dig down to the same deep, fundamental, questions. So once somebody has somehow been identified as a 'great philosopher' (as opposed to a great poet, scientist, theologian, political theorist, or whatever), he has to be described as studying those questions.[6] Since each new generation of philosophers claims to have discovered what those deep fundamental questions really are, each has to figure out how the great philosopher can be viewed as having been concerned with them. So we get brave new doxographies which look, a few generations further on, just as calamitous as their predecessors.

To get rid of this idea that philosophy is a natural kind, we need more and better contextualist historical reconstructions on the one hand, and more self-confident *Geistesgeschichte* on the other. We need to realize that the questions which the 'contingent arrangements' of the present time lead us to regard as *the* questions are questions which may be *better* than those which our ancestors asked, but need not be the *same*. They are not questions which any reflective human being must necessarily have encountered. We need to see ourselves not as responding to the same stimuli to which our ancestors responded, but as having created new and more interesting stimuli for ourselves. We should justify ourselves by claiming to be asking better questions, not by claiming to give better answers to the permanent 'deep, fundamental questions' which our ancestors answered badly. We can think of the fundamental questions of philosophy as the ones which everybody really ought to have asked, or as the ones which everybody would have asked if they could, but not as the ones which everybody *did* ask whether they knew it or not. It is one thing to say that a great dead philosopher would have been driven to have a view on a certain topic if we had had a chance to talk to him, thus enabling him to see what the fundamental questions of philosophy really were. It is

---

[6] Jonathan Rée is very informative on the development of the idea that there is a common ahistorical set of questions for philosophers to answer. In his excellent essay 'Philosophy and the history of philosophy', Rée speaks of Renouvier's conviction that 'the so-called history of philosophy was really only the story of individuals opting for different philosophical positions; the positions themselves were always there, eternally available and unchanging' (Rée 1978: 17). This is the guiding assumption of what I am calling doxography.

another thing to say that he had an 'implicit' view on that topic which we can dig out of what he wrote. What is interesting about him often is that it never crossed his mind that he had to have a view on the topic. This is just the sort of interesting information we get from contextualist historical reconstructions.

My claim that philosophy is not a natural kind can be restated with reference to the popular notion that philosophy deals with 'methodological', or 'conceptual', meta-issues thrown off by the special disciplines, or more generally by other areas of culture. Such a claim is plausible if it means that, in every period, there have been questions which arose from the clash between old ideas and new ideas (in the sciences, in art, in politics, etc.) and that these questions are the concern of the more original, dilettantish and imaginative intellectuals of the day. But it becomes implausible if it means that these questions are always about the same topics – e.g., the nature of knowledge, or reality, or truth, or meaning, or the good, or some other abstraction sufficiently fuzzy to blur the differences between historical epochs. One can parody this notion of philosophy by imagining that, at the dawn of the study of animals, a distinction became established between 'primary biology' and 'secondary biology', analogous to Aristotle's distinction between 'first philosophy' and 'physics'. On this conception, the larger, more salient, more impressive and paradigmatic animals were the concern of a special discipline. So theories were developed about the common features of the python, the bear, the lion, the eagle, the ostrich, and the whale. Such theories, formulated with the help of some suitably fuzzy abstractions, were rather clever and interesting. But people kept coming along with other things to be fitted into the canon of 'primary animals'. The giant rat of Sumatra, the giant butterflies of Brazil, and (more controversially) the unicorn had to be taken into account. Criteria for the adequacy of theories in primary biology became less clear as the canon was enlarged. Then came the bones of the moa and the mammoth. Things got still more complicated. Eventually the secondary biologists got so good at producing new forms of life in test tubes that they amused themselves by bringing their gargantuan new creations upstairs and challenging the bewildered primary biologists to make a place for them. Watching the contortions of the primary biologists as they tried to devise theories which would accommodate these new canonical items engendered a certain contempt for primary biology as an autonomous discipline.

The analogies I wish to draw are between 'primary biology' and 'history of philosophy', and between 'secondary biology' and 'intellectual history'. History of philosophy, disconnected from the wider history of the intellectuals, makes some sense if it covers only a century or two – if it is, for example, a story of the steps which led from Descartes to Kant. Hegel's story of the unfolding of Cartesian subjectivity into transcendental philosophy, or Gilson's story of the *reductio ad absurdum* of representationalist theories of knowledge, are examples of interesting narratives which can be constructed by ignoring wider contexts. These are just two among many plausible and interesting ways of noting similarities and differences between a dozen salient and impressive figures who span about 175 years (Descartes, Hobbes, Malebranche, Locke, Condillac, Leibniz, Wolff, Berkeley, Hume, and Kant – plus or minus a few names at the historian of philosophy's discretion). But when one tries to tack on Hegel himself at one end of such a story, or Bacon and Ramus at the other, things get rather tendentious. When one tries to tie in Plato and Aristotle, there seem so many ways to do so – depending upon which Platonic dialogue or Aristotelian treatise one takes as 'fundamental' – that alternative stories proliferate wildly. Further, Plato and Aristotle are *so* big and impressive that describing them in terms originally developed for use on people like Hobbes and Berkeley begins to seem a little odd. Then there is the problem of whether to treat Augustine and Aquinas and Ockham as philosophers or as theologians – not to mention the problems raised by Lao Tse, Shankara, and similar exotic specimens. To make everything worse, all the time that historians of philosophy are wondering how to get all these people in under the old rubrics, mischievous intellectuals keep concocting new intellectual compounds and daring historians of philosophy to refuse to call them 'philosophies'. Once it becomes necessary to contrive a story which connects all or most of the people previously mentioned with G. E. Moore, Saul Kripke and Gilles Deleuze, historians of philosophy are about ready to give up.

They *should* give up. We should just stop trying to write books called *A History of Philosophy* which begin with Thales and end with, say, Wittgenstein. Such books are interspersed with desperately factitious excuses for not discussing, e.g., Plotinus, Comte, or Kierkegaard. They gallantly attempt to find a few 'continuing concerns' which run through all the great philosophers who do get included. But they are continually embarrassed by the failure of even the most silent and unskippable figures to discuss some of those concerns, and by those vast arid stretches in which one or other concern seems to have escaped everybody's mind (They have to worry, for example, about the absence or the skimpiness of chapters headed 'Epistemology in the sixteenth century' or 'Moral philosophy in the twelfth century' or 'Logic in the eighteenth century'.) It is no wonder that *geistesgeschichtlich* intellectual historians – those who write the great sweeping self-justifying stories – are often contemptuous of the sort of doxography common to Windelband and Russell. Nor is it any wonder that analytic philosophers and Heideggerians should try – each in their separate ways – to find something new for the history of philosophy to be. The attempt to skim the cream off intellectual history by writing a history 'of philosophy' is as foredoomed as the attempt of my imaginary 'primary biologists' to skim the cream off the animal kingdom. Both attempts assume that certain elementary components of the miscellaneous stuff churning around at the bottom naturally float up to the top.

This cream-skimming picture assumes a contrast between the higher and purer history of something called 'philosophy' – the quest for knowledge about permanent and enduring topics by people who specialized in that sort of thing – and 'intellectual history' as the chronicle of quaint tergiversations of opinion among people who were, at best, littérateurs or political activists or clergymen. When this picture, and this implicit contrast, are challenged, offense is often taken at the suggestion that philosophy is not the pursuit of knowledge, that it is (as the freshmen like to say) 'all a matter of opinion'. Alternatively, this same offense is expressed by saying if we discard the traditional contrast we shall have reduced philosophy to 'rhetoric' (as opposed to 'logic') or 'persuasion' (as opposed to 'argument') or something else low and literary rather than high and scientific. Since the self-image of philosophy as a professional discipline still depends upon its quasi-scientific character, criticism of the assumption behind the cream-skimming picture is taken as a challenge to philosophy itself as a professional activity, not merely to one branch of it called 'history of philosophy'.

One can mitigate the offense while still avoiding the cream-skimming picture by adopting a sociological view of the distinction between knowledge and opinion. On this view, to say that something is a matter of opinion is just to say that deviance from the current consensus on that topic is compatible with membership in some relevant community. To say that it is knowledge is to say that deviance is incompatible. For example, in America the choice of whom to vote for is 'a matter of opinion' but we *know* that the press should be free from government censorship. Good-thinking Russians know that such censorship is necessary, but they regard the question of whether to send dissidents to labor camps or asylums as a matter of opinion. These two communities do not accept as members those who fail to claim as knowledge what is generally so claimed. Analogously, to say that the existence of real essences, or of God, is a 'matter of opinion' within philosophy departments is to say that people who differ on this point can still get grants from, or be employed by, the same institutions, can award degrees to the same students, etc. By contrast, those who share Ptolemy's opinions on the planets or William Jennings Bryan's on the origin of species are excluded from respectable astronomy and biology departments, for membership there requires that one know that these opinions are false. So anybody can legitimize his use of the term 'philosophical knowledge' simply by pointing to a self-conscious community of philosophers, admission to which requires agreement on certain points (e.g., that there are, or are not, real essences or inalienable human rights, or God). Within that community, we shall have agreement on known premises, and the pursuit of further knowledge, in just the sense in which we find such premises and such a pursuit in biology and astronomy departments.

The existence of such a community is, however, entirely irrelevant to the question of whether anything links that community to Aristotle, Plotinus, Descartes, Kant, Moore, Kripke, or Deleuze. Such communities should be at liberty to seek out their own intellectual ancestors, without reference to a previously established canon of great dead philosophers. They should also be free to claim to have no ancestors at all. They should feel free to pick out whatever bits of the past they like and call those 'the history of philosophy', without reference to anything anybody has previously called 'philosophy', or to ignore the past entirely. Anybody who is willing to give up the attempt to find common interests which unite him or her with all the other members of, say, the American Philosophical Association or the Mind Association or the Deutsche Philosophische Gesellschaft (and one would have to be a bit mad to be unwilling to give up *that* attempt) is thus free to give up the attempt to write *A History of Philosophy* with the usual chapter headings. He or she is free to create a new canon, as long as they respect the right of others to create alternative canons. We should welcome people who, like Reichenbach, wave Hegel aside. We should encourage people who are tempted to dismiss Aristotle as a biologist who got out of his depth, or Berkeley as an eccentric bishop, or Frege as an original logician with unjustified epistemological pretensions, or Moore as a charming amateur who never quite understood what the professionals were doing. They should be urged to try it, and to see what sort of historical story they can tell when these people are left out and some unfamiliar people are brought in. It is only with the aid of such experimental alterations of the canon that doxography can be avoided. It is just such alterations which *Geistesgeschichte* makes possible and which doxography discourages.

IV Intellectual history

So far I have distinguished four genres and suggested that one of them be allowed to wither away. The remaining three are indispensable and do not compete with one another. Rational reconstructions are necessary to help us present-day philosophers think through our problems. Historical reconstructions are needed to remind us that these problems are historical products, by demonstrating that they were invisible to our ancestors. *Geistesgeschichte* is needed to justify our belief that we are better off than those ancestors by virtue of having become aware of those problems. Any given book in the history of philosophy will, of course, be a mixture of these three genres. But usually one or another motive dominates, since there are three distinct tasks to be performed. The distinctness of these tasks is important and not to be broken down. It is precisely the tension between the brisk Whiggery of the rational reconstructors and the mediated and ironic empathy of the contextualists – between the need to get on with the task at hand and the need to see everything, including that task, as one more contingent arrangement – that produces the need for *Geistesgeschichte*, for the self-justification which this third genre provides. Each such justification, however, insures the eventual appearance of a new set of complacent doxographies, disgust with which will inspire new rational reconstructions, under the aegis of new philosophical problematics which will have arisen in the meantime. These three genres thus form a nice example of the standard Hegelian dialectical triad.

I should like to use the term 'intellectual history' for a much richer and more diffuse genre – one which falls outside this triad. In my sense, intellectual history consists of descriptions of what the intellectuals were up to at a given time, and of their interaction with the rest of society – descriptions which, for the most part, bracket the question of what activities which intellectuals were conducting. Intellectual history can ignore certain problems which must be settled in order to write the history of a discipline – questions about which people count as scientists, which as poets, which as philosophers, etc. Descriptions of the sort I have in mind may occur in treatises called something like 'Intellectual life in fifteenth-century Bologna', but they may also occur in the odd chapter or paragraph of political or social or economic or diplomatic histories, or indeed in the odd chapter or paragraph of histories of philosophy (of any of the four genres distinguished above). Such treatises, chapters and paragraphs produce, when read and pondered by someone interested in a certain spatio-temporal region, a sense of what it was like to be an intellectual in that region – what sort of books one read, what sorts of things one had to worry about, what choices one had of vocabularies, hopes, friends, enemies, and careers.

To have a sense of what it was to be a young and intellectually curious person in such a region one has to know a lot of social, political and economic history as well as a lot of disciplinary history. A book like E. P. Thompson's *Making of the English Working Class* (1963) tells one a lot about the chances and audiences open to Paine and Cobbett as well as about wages, the living conditions of miners and weavers, and the tactics of politicians. A book like Norman Fiering's *Moral Philosophy at Seventeenth-Century Harvard* (1981) tells one a lot about what kind of intellectual it was possible to be at Harvard in that period. Fiering's book flows together with passages in biographies of Harvard presidents and Massachusetts governors to produce a sense of how these possibilities changed. Passages in Thompson's flow together with passages in biographies of Bentham and of Melbourne to show how other possibilities changed. The totality of such books and passages comes together in the minds of those who read them in such a way as to produce a sense of the differences between the options open to an intellectual at different times and places.

I should want to include under 'intellectual history' books about all those enormously influential people who do not get into the canon of great dead philosophers, but who are often called 'philosophers' either because they held a chair so described, or for lack of any better idea – people like Erigena, Bruno, Ramus, Mersenne, Wolff, Diderot, Cousin, Schopenhauer, Hamilton, McCosh, Bergson and Austin. Discussion of these 'minor figures' often coalesces with thick description of institutional arrangements and disciplinary matrices, since part of the historical problem they pose is to explain why these non-great philosophers or quasi-philosophers should have been taken so much more seriously than the certifiably great philosophers of their day. Then there are the books about the thought and influence of people who are not usually called 'philosophers' but are at least borderline cases of the species. These are people who in fact did the jobs which philosophers are popularly supposed to do – impelling social reform, supplying new vocabularies for moral deliberation, deflecting the course of scientific and literary disciplines into new channels. They include, for example, Paracelsus, Montaigne, Grotius, Bayle, Lessing, Paine, Coleridge, Alexander von Humboldt, Emerson, T. H. Huxley, Mathew Arnold, Weber, Freud, Franz Boas, Walter Lippman, D. H. Lawrence, and T. S. Kuhn – not to mention all those unfamiliar people (e.g., the authors of influential treatises on the philosophical foundations of *Polizeiwissenschaft*) who turn up in the footnotes to Foucault's books. If one wants to understand what it was to be a scholar in sixteenth-century Germany or a political thinker in eighteenth-century America or a scientist in late-nineteenth-century France or a journalist in early-twentieth-century Britain – if one wants to know what sort of issues and temptations and dilemmas confronted a young person who wanted to become part of the high culture of those times and places – these are the sort of people one has to know about. If one knows enough about enough of them, one can tell a detailed and convincing story of the conversation of

Europe, a story which may mention Descartes, Hume, Kant, and Hegel only in passing.

Once we drop below the skipping-from-peak-to-peak level of *Geistesgeschichte* to the nitty-gritty of intellectual history, the distinctions between great and non-great dead philosophers, between clear and borderline cases of 'philosophy', and between philosophy, literature, politics, religion and social science, are of less and less importance. The question of whether Weber was a sociologist or a philosopher, Arnold a literary critic or a philosopher, Freud a psychologist or a philosopher, Lippman a philosopher or a journalist, like the question of whether we can include Francis Bacon as a philosopher if we exclude Robert Fludd, are obviously matters to be settled after we have written our intellectual history rather than before. Interesting filiations which connect these borderline cases with clearer cases of 'philosophy' will or will not appear, and on the basis of such filiations we shall adjust our taxonomies. Furthermore, new paradigm cases of philosophy produce new termini for such filiations. New accounts of intellectual history interact with contemporary developments to readjust continually the list of 'philosophers', and eventually these readjustments produce new canons of great dead philosophers. Like the history of anything else, history of philosophy is written by the victors. Victors get to choose their ancestors, in the sense that they decide which among their all too various ancestors to mention, write biographies of, and commend to their descendants.

As long as 'philosophy' has an honorific use it will matter which figures count as 'philosophers'. So if things go well we can expect continual revisions of the philosophical canon in order to bring it into line with the present needs of high culture. If they go badly, we can expect the stubborn perpetuation of a canon – one which will look quainter and more factitious as the decades pass. On the picture I wish to present, intellectual history is the raw material for the historiography of philosophy – or, to vary the metaphor, the ground out of which histories of philosophy grow. The Hegelian triad I have sketched becomes possible only once we have, with an eye both to contemporary needs and to the recent writings of revisionist intellectual historians, formulated a philosophical canon. Doxography, on the other hand, as the genre which pretends to find a continuous streak of philosophical ore running through all the space–time chunks which the intellectual historians describe, is relatively independent of current developments in intellectual history. Its roots are in the past – in the forgotten combination of transcended cultural needs and outdated intellectual history which produced the canon it enshrines.

This role as inspiration for the reformulation of the (philosophical and other) canons is, however, not the only use for intellectual history.

Another is to play the same dialectical role with respect to *Geistesgeschichte* as historical reconstruction plays to rational reconstruction. I have said that historical reconstructions remind us of all those quaint little controversies the big-name philosophers worried about, the ones which distracted them from the 'real' and 'enduring' problems which we moderns have managed to get in clearer focus. By so reminding us, they induce a healthy skepticism about whether we are all that clear and whether our problems are all that real. Analogously, Ong on Ramus, Yates on Lull, Fiering on Mather, Wartofsky on Feuerbach, and so on remind us that the great dead philosophers whom we spend our time reconstructing were often less influential – less central to the conversation of their own and several intervening generations – than a lot of people we have never thought about. They also make us see the people in our current canon as less original, less distinctive, than they had seemed before. They come to look like specimens reiterating an extinct type rather than mountain peaks. So intellectual history works to keep *Geistesgeschichte* honest, just as historical reconstruction operates to keep rational reconstructions honest.

Honesty here consists in keeping in mind the possibility that our self-justifying conversation is with creatures of our own phantasy rather than with historical personages, even ideally re-educated historical personages. Such a possibility needs to be acknowledged by those setting out to write *Geistesgeschichte*, because they need to worry about whether their own chapter headings may have been too much influenced by those of the doxographies. In particular, when a professor of philosophy sets out on such a self-justificatory project he usually does so only after decades of giving courses on various great dead philosophers – those whose names appear in the syllabus for examinations to be taken by his students, a syllabus he is likely to have inherited rather than composed. It is natural for him to write *Geistesgeschichte* by stringing a lot of those notes together, thus skipping between the same old peaks, passing over in silence the philosophical flatlands of, e.g., the third and fifteenth centuries. This sort of thing leads to such extreme cases as Heidegger's attempt to write 'the history of Being' by commenting upon texts mentioned in Ph.D. examinations in philosophy in German universities early in this century. In the aftermath of being enthralled by the drama Heidegger stages, one may begin to find it suspicious that Being stuck so closely to the syllabus.

Heidegger's followers changed the syllabus in order to make everything lead up to Nietzsche and Heidegger, just as Russell's changed the syllabus to make it lead up to Frege and Russell. *Geistesgeschichte* can change canons in a way that doxography does not. But such partial canon-revision highlights the fact that Nietzsche may only seem that important to people overly impressed by Kantian ethics, just as Frege may only seem that important to people overly impressed by Kantian epistemology. It still leaves us bemused by the question how Kant ever got to be that important in the first place. We tend to explain to our students that their own philosophical thinking must go through Kant rather than around him, but it is not clear that we mean more than that they will not understand our own books if they have not read Kant's. When we draw back from the philosophical canon in the way made possible by reading the detailed and thickly interwoven stories found in intellectual history, we can ask whether it is all that important for the students to understand what we contemporary philosophers are doing. That is the sort of honest self-doubt which gives people the motive and the courage to write *radically* innovative *Geistesgeschichte* – the kind exemplified by Foucault's *The Order of Things*, with its famous reference to 'the figure we call Hume'.

Foucauldians may object to my description of that book as *Geistesgeschichte*, but it is important for my argument to group it together with, e.g. Hegel's and Blumenberg's histories. For all of Foucault's insistence on materiality and contingency, his conscious opposition to the *geistlich* and dialectical character of Hegel's story, there are lots of resemblances between that story and his own. Both help to answer the question which doxography eschews: in what ways are we better and in what ways worse off than this or that set of predecessors? Both assign us a place in an epic, the epic of modern Europe, though in Foucault's case it is an epic over which no *Geschick* presides. Foucault's, like Hegel's, is a story with a moral; it is true that both Foucault and his readers have trouble formulating that moral, but we should remember that the same was true for Hegel and his readers. Foucault ties in 'the figure we call Hume' with what the doctors and the police were up to at the time, just as Hegel tied in various philosophers with what the priests and the tyrants of their times were doing. Hegel's subsumption of the material under the spiritual attempts the same task as Foucault's account of truth in terms of power. Both try to convince us intellectuals of something we badly need to believe – that the high culture of a given period is not just froth, but rather an expression of something that goes all the way down.

I insist on this point because the example of Foucault, taken together with the suspicion I have voiced about philosophy as a natural kind, and about the cream-skimming model of the relation between intellectual history and the history of philosophy, might lead one to suggest that if doxography goes it should take *Geistesgeschichte* with it. Many admirers of Foucault are inclined to think that we do not need any more accounts of how *die Gipfel sehen einander*. Indeed, one might be tempted to go further and suggest that 'the historiography of philosophy' is itself a notion which has outlived its usefulness – because, roughly, the honorific use of 'philosophy' has outlived its. If we have the sort of complicated, thick, intellectual history which is wary of canons (philosophical, literary, scientific, or other) do not we have enough? Is there any need for history of something special called 'philosophy' any more than there is a need to carry on a discipline which goes by that name? If we really believe that there is no God, no real essences, nor any surrogate for either, if we follow Foucault in being consistently materialistic and nominalist, will we not want to stir things up so that there is no way at all to distinguish the cream from the milk, the conceptual and philosophical from the empirical and historical?[7]

As a good materialist and nominalist, I am obviously sympathetic to this line of thought. But as an amateur of *Geistesgeschichte* I want to resist it. I am all for getting rid of canons which have become merely quaint, but I do not think that we can get along without canons. This is because we cannot get along without heroes. We need mountain peaks to look up towards. We need to tell ourselves detailed stories about the mighty dead in order to make our hopes of surpassing them concrete. We also need the idea that there is such a thing as 'philosophy' in the honorific sense – the idea that there are, had we but the wit to pose them, certain questions which everybody should always have been asking. We cannot give up this idea without giving up the notion that the intellectuals of the previous epochs of European history form a community, a community of which it is good to be a member. If we are to persist in this image of ourselves, then we have to have both imaginary conversations with the dead and the conviction that we have seen further than they. That means that we need *Geistesgeschichte*, self-justificatory conversations. The alternative is the attempt which Foucault once adumbrated but which he has, I hope, given up – the attempt to have no face, to transcend the community of the European intellectuals by affecting a context-less anonymity, like those characters in Beckett who have given up self-justification, conversational interchange, and hope. If one does wish to make such an attempt, of course, then *Geistesgeschichte* – even the sort of materialistic, nominalistic, *entzauberte Geistesgeschichte* I am attributing to Foucault – is one of the first things one has to get rid of. I have been writing on the assumption that we do not want to make this attempt, but rather want to make our conversation with the dead richer and fuller.

On this assumption, what we need is to see the history of philosophy as the story of the people who made splendid but largely unsuccessful

---

[7] One expression of this sceptical line of thought is Jonathan Rée's polemic against the role of 'the idea of the History of Philosophy' in presenting 'philosophy as a self-contained, eternal sector of intellectual production' and as having 'a history of its own going back like a tunnel through the centuries' (Rée 1978:32). I entirely agree with Rée, but think that one can avoid this myth, while continuing the three genres I have commended, simply by *self-consciously* using 'philosophy' as an honorific rather than a descriptive term.

attempts to ask the questions which we ought to be asking. These will be the people who are candidates for a canon – a list of authors whom one would be well advised to read before trying to figure out what questions are the philosophical ones, in the honorific sense of 'philosophy'. Obviously, any given candidate may or may not share the concerns of this or that group of contemporary philosophers. One will not be in a position to know whether this is his fault, or the fault of the group in question, until one has read all the other candidates and settled on one's own canon – told one's own *Geistesgeschichte*. The more intellectual history we can get, of the kind which does not worry about what questions are philosophical and who counts as a philosopher, the better our chances of having a suitably large list of candidates for a canon. The more various the canons we adopt – the more competing *Geistesgeschichten* we have at hand – the more likely we are to reconstruct, first rationally and then historically, interesting thinkers. As this competition grows more intense, the tendency to write doxographies will be less strong, and this will be all to the good. The competition is not likely ever to be resolved, but as long as it continues we shall not lose that sense of community which only impassioned conversation makes possible.[8]

REFERENCES

Ayer, A. J. 1936. *Language, Truth and Logic.* London: Gollancz

Ayers, Michael. 1978. 'Analytical philosophy and the history of philosophy', in Jonathan Rée, Michael Ayers and Adam Westoby, *Philosophy and its Past.* Brighton: Harvester Press

Bennett, Jonathan. 1971. *Locke, Berkeley, Hume: Central Themes.* Oxford: Oxford University Press

Dunn, John. 1980. *Political Obligation in its Historical Context.* Cambridge: Cambridge University Press

Fiering, Norman. 1981. *Moral Philosophy at Seventeenth-Century Harvard: A Discipline in Transition.* Chapel Hill: University of North Carolina Press

Heidegger, M. 1973. 'Sketches for a history of being', in *The End of Philosophy*, trans. Joan Stambaugh. New York: Harper & Row

Hirsch, E. D., Jr. 1976. *The Aims of Interpretation.* Chicago: University of Chicago Press

Rée, Jonathan. 1978. 'Philosophy and the history of philosophy', in Jonathan Rée, Michael Ayers and Adam Westoby, *Philosophy and its Past.* Brighton: Harvester Press

Rorty, Richard. 1982. *Consequences of Pragmatism.* Minneapolis: University of Minnesota Press

[8] I am grateful to David Hollinger for helpful remarks on an earlier version of this paper, and to the Center for Advanced Study in the Behavioral Sciences for providing ideal circumstances for its composition.

Ryle, Gilbert, 1971. *Collected Papers*, vol. 1. London: Hutchison

Skinner, Quentin. 1969. 'Meaning and understanding in the history of ideas', *History and Theory* 8: 3–53

Strawson, P. F. 1966. *The Bounds of Sense: An Essay on Kant's 'Critique of Pure Reason'*. London: Methuen

Thompson, E. P. 1963. *The Making of the English Working Class*. Baltimore: Penguin Books

4

Why do we study
the history of philosophy?

LORENZ KRÜGER

It is hardly disputable that nowadays the overwhelming majority of philosophers study the history of their field, at least part of the time. In this respect other disciplines behave differently, and there was a time when philosophers behaved differently, too. Are there good reasons for the change? Do we know those reasons? Do we have well-founded and agreed views on why and for what purpose we, the majority of philosophers or the profession in general, study the history of philosophy? I do not think so. I have gained this impression from many conversations and from my reading, including reading what I myself have written.

My first suspicion that there is something dubious about our apparent affinity to philosophical history arose when I read historical studies which were perfectly straightforward and interesting in themselves, and yet were prefaced by quick and vague assurances of a familiar type, assurances to the effect that these studies were undertaken from a systematic point of view or with a systematic goal in mind. It seems to be a recently adopted distinguished tone among philosophers to say some such thing, a tone which grows louder as the interests of the profession become more historical. We must ask to what extent this common strategy of reconciling historical studies with present-day tasks is convincing. Sometimes, it seems to me, such reconciliation can be better effectuated by simply probing into history as contingent individual interests may suggest, and then letting history speak for itself. Occasionally, the tone signals a bad conscience, either admitted or unconscious, arising from an awareness that urgent questions remain without an answer, a deficiency that may successfully be concealed, or at least excused, by twisted detours into the past. Frequently, of course, the tone simply signals the good sense of an author who has experienced the depths of the problem at hand and thereby been led to conclude that he cannot do better than turn to his great predecessors in order to tackle it.

However this may be, I see a discrepancy or an imbalance between the impressive amount of (frequently excellent) historical study on the one hand, and the extent of understanding and justification of this study on the other. This imbalance would be of minor importance, were it not for the fact that philosophers study the history out of some awareness of their professional needs and obligations. Yet, this awareness is far from clear and distinct; rather it is itself a philosophical problem. In short, I see a challenge to understand, if not overcome, the imbalance or discrepancy between research practices and theoretical self-assessments.

My present attempt to meet this challenge will be directed by the idea that at least one important reason, if not the most important reason, for philosophers to study the history of philosophy consists in the fact that the natural sciences, and the technology based on the natural sciences, possess an irreducible historical dimension. This is not the trivial point that science and technology did not emerge suddenly like Athena from the head of Zeus. The point is rather that they cannot adequately be understood, without being viewed as unique historical events.

It may seem fairly implausible, at first sight, to assume that philosophy receives its irreducible historicity from the *natural* sciences. For it is precisely these disciplines which are distinguished by their ability to develop successfully without bothering about their origin or their histories. They are appreciated precisely because their results reliably refer to the facts of nature which lie beyond history. Hence it would seem that if, or to the extent that, philosophy can be tied to these disciplines it should be able to overcome the contingencies of the history of reason and finally reach a persistent truth. (Kant comes to mind here, as one who wanted to reform philosophy on the model of natural science in order 'to set metaphysics upon the secure path of a science'.)[1] Conversely, one might expect that only to the extent in which philosophy is dissociated from natural science, and tied either to other academic disciplines or to social and cultural life as a whole, will it become essentially and irreducibly historical. (Here we may think of Hegel,[2] or of Dilthey's *Aufbau der geschichtlichen Welt in den Geisteswissenschaften* (Dilthey 1910), or, more recently, of Gadamer (Gadamer 1960) whose work will be examined more closely below.) So my attempt at connecting the historicity of philosophy primarily with the natural sciences will look misdirected. I think, however, that a more conventional and more plausible approach could not succeed in

---

[1] Kant 1781 and 1787, B XXIII–XXIV, translation by N. Kemp Smith, p. 26.
[2] A condensed formula reads: 'Philosophy [is] its time apprehended in thought', Hegel 1820, Vorrede. The connection between philosophy and the social sciences established by Hegel is analysed in an illuminating way by Bubner 1982, with special emphasis given to this Hegelian dictum.

demonstrating, as I wish to, that philosophy is *essentially* of an historical nature.[3]

In order to explicate and defend this implausible contention I shall proceed in several steps: (I) I shall discuss the most widely spread and most easily accepted philosophical view of the history of philosophy: the 'history of problems' view. I hope to show its insufficiency, and in particular also its fundamentally ahistorical character. (II) I shall add a few remarks concerning the relationship of modern science and philosophy, which may elucidate the motives for tying the history of philosophy to disciplines *other* than the natural sciences. (III) I shall then discuss one recent and influential version of the affinity between historically conceived philosophy and the *Geisteswissenschaften*, Hans-Georg Gadamer's hermeneutical philosophy; and I shall attempt to point out the limitations of this view. (IV) I then turn to the question of whether the natural sciences and technology are not themselves inherently historical, a conception I hope to make plausible. (V) In the last section I shall draw some consequences which argue for the historicity of philosophy itself, and relate this thesis to major figures and themes in twentieth-century German philosophy.

I

The idea of writing histories of philosophical problems (or 'problematic histories' of philosophy) gradually developed in the course of writing the more involved histories of philosophical systems. It was explicitly formulated by Windelband and later propagated by Nicolai Hartmann in Germany.[4] At present, it is almost indisputably dominant, especially in the English-speaking countries. Simplifying somewhat, the common core of several different variants of this view can be identified as the assumption that philosophy is characterized by a specific set of tasks which remain constant through history. This set, it is claimed, becomes manifest in the continued recurrence of certain typical problems as well as in the persistence of certain fundamental alternative approaches to their solution. On a sufficiently general level this view may easily be illustrated by examples: since Plato, we ask questions like 'What is knowledge?' or 'What are the foundations of moral behaviour?' etc. It is perhaps less clear how one should indicate the typology of recurring alternative attitudes in

---

[3] I take for granted that (almost) everybody would concede that there are pragmatic reasons for occasionally studying historical material in order to produce trans-historical philosophical insight. The point of this paper is to show that this position is much too weak: it does not do justice to our actual historical commitments and it does not reveal the extent and importance of our historical tasks.

[4] This strand of the history of historiography of philosophy is described in detail in Geldsetzer 1968b. Further sources are quoted in Oehler 1957, cf. esp. his n.29 on p. 521.

answering such questions. Presumably, we are to think of pairs of concepts like 'dogmatic noologism' and 'sceptical empiricism' (Kant's terminology in his history of reason),[5] or 'idealism' and 'materialism', 'freedom' and 'determinism' (Renouvier 1885–6), etc.

It is, however, not necessary to subscribe to such schematizations in order to explicate the main idea of 'problem' history. Maurice Mandelbaum (1965) has explicated this idea by distinguishing between spatio-temporally continuous 'developmental histories' on the one hand and discontinuous 'partial' or 'special histories' on the other. Cultural history is an example of the first type, the history of philosophy of the second. The internal connections of the latter sort of history consist in interrelated arguments which bridge spatio-temporal gaps and, at the same time, provide causal links. The existence of such connections also accounts for the intellectual independence or autonomy of the discipline, which, of course, need not be expectionless or absolute. This view is well known and widely accepted. Moreover, it has an undeniable basis in reality: one philosopher reads and criticizes another.

It may be more interesting to ask how or why the increasing preoccupation with problems as opposed to doctrines, theories, or systems, has come about. For a set of problems, a set of terms in which the problems can be formulated, plus a set of basic approaches to those problems – all these data are still a meagre basis for continuity, compared with what, in other cases, is taken as a prerequisite for the existence of a continuous discipline: i.e., methods and theories. One may surmise that the restriction to problems and approaches had something to do with the growing opposition to metaphysics that occurred after the decline of the great idealistic systems. Certainly, the theme of 'problems' recurs among critics of Hegel around the turn of the century. German names of problem historians can be supplemented with English names: in 1910–11 G. E. Moore gives lectures entitled *Some Main Problems of Philosophy*, and B. Russell in 1912 publishes his *The Problems of Philosophy*.[6] The new strategy of philosophical analysis (as opposed to the construction of theories and systems) leads eventually to the aphorisms in which the later Wittgenstein recommended a merely therapeutic role for philosophy, conceiving its function as restricted to the dissolution of isolated puzzles or problems. These hints are only intended to illustrate the price the problem historian has to pay: he gives up the quest for theoretical continuity in order to save continuity at the level of problems.

---

[5] Immanuel Kant 1781 and 1787, A852/B880ff.
[6] I am grateful to Ian Hacking for drawing my attention to this feature of the recent history of philosophy. To my knowledge no detailed and explanatory study of it is available so far. I am indebted to Lorraine Daston for illuminating comments.

In the nineteenth century, however, these costs were unlikely to be foreseen. On the contrary, focussing on problems may have appeared as a typically scientific move, hence a strategy that should be introduced into the social sciences, the humanities, history and philosophy as well. But then problems must have appeared as a natural, indeed the leading, topic for historiography.

A related reason for the restriction to problems can probably be found in the failure of philosophical systems to match the rapid expansion of scientific knowledge in various disciplines during the nineteenth century. Philosophers must have felt an increasing difficulty in maintaining the reputation and intellectual acceptability of their work in the scientific world. The historiographical model of problem history served, among other things, to provide room for something like progress of philosophical research. Windelband, for instance, observes that 'each of the great systems of philosophy starts solving the reformulated task *ab ovo* again as if other systems had hardly existed' (Windelband 1889: Einleitung, §2.1, p. 7), while nevertheless, through a history of previous systems, attempting to ascertain the permanent structure of human reason (Windelband 1889: Einleitung, §2.6, p. 16; cf. pp. 11–14). John Passmore's article 'Philosophy, Historiography of' in the standard English-language dictionary of philosophy codifies, as it were, the view that problem history is progressive; he says: 'the historian of philosophy, unlike the cultural historian, is particularly interested in periods of advance'.[7] Philosophy is here characterized as analogous to other disciplines, i.e., as (relatively) autonomous research. This is, of course, what renders the problem-history view so popular.[8]

I shall now turn to a critical appraisal of this view. I am far from arguing that it is always wrong to write problem history; such history is often useful, and sometimes excellent, philosophy. Yet I believe that the corresponding historiographical position, taken as a piece of philosophical theory, is seriously incomplete. Because of this incompleteness, problem history fails to confront a central part of the historical task. The leading idea of my criticism is the claim that the problem-history view replaces genuine temporal development by a spurious present. In order to explicate

[7] Passmore 1967:229. The quoted passage refers to the problem historian, as is shown by the context.

[8] Jürgen Mittelstrass has recently advocated the problem-history view as the only one which permits us to construe the history of philosophy as teaching us something (Mittelstrass 1977). He agrees with John Passmore who had claimed that 'it is *only* from problematic history that the philosopher has anything to learn' (Passmore 1965; the quotation is from p. 31). What needs clarification here is the question: teaching about or for what? Passmore and Mittelstrass appear to assume an answer to this question which is independent of historical knowledge and which determines whether or not a given historiography is conducive to learning. This assumption of independence is precisely what I want to question in this paper.

this statement I shall discuss three concatenated points: (1) The assimilation of philosophy to ordinary research is misleading; (2) philosophy is not autonomous; and (3) a view that makes philosophy similar to ordinary, autonomous, research loses the true historical dimension of philosophy.

As to (1), one may note in passing that the very assumption of the persistence of problems is at odds with the claim that philosophy advances. Advance would seem to imply the solution of problems rather than their recurrence. One might reply that basic problems recur in the history of ordinary research, e.g. physical theory, as well; say, the problem of the structure of matter. To answer this objection I must make a more substantive point; viz., that to put the problem of matter today is a different thing from putting it in antiquity or in the seventeenth century. The problem situation in natural science is not determined by competition between basic alternative views (e.g. continuous versus atomistic structure), hence is not invariant through time but is essentially transformed by antecedent theory. The modern atomist does not relate his work to that of Democritus, even though he may be said to share the basic Democritean approach, but rather to certain parts of continuum mechanics, e.g. the mechanics of waves. The progressive character of scientific research appears to depend on the existence of a series of theories, theories which may not be mutually compatible but admit of connection and gradual improvement. The problem historian, however, rests his case on the admission that this kind of theoretical continuity does not exist in philosophy.

As to (2), i.e., concerning the autonomy of philosophy, one will have to ask where the problems of philosophy come from. The problem-history view by its very nature leaves no room for a philosophical account of the origin and the (relative) weights of these problems. In the texts of problem historians I have seen, the origin of new problems always appears as an additional factual assumption, indeed as a concession which goes a long way toward granting objections against the autonomy of philosophy. I let Windelband, who is one of the most determined advocates of autonomy, speak for the position:

Philosophy receives its problems, as well as the material for their solution, from the ideas of the general consciousness of the time and from the needs of society. The great achievements and the novel questions of the particular sciences, the movement of religious consciousness, the revolutions of social and political life give sudden new impulses to philosophy and determine the directions of interest . . . no less than the changes of question and answer through time.[9]

Not only autonomy, but also the existence, or at least the relevance of

---

[9] Windelband 1889: Einleitung, §2.4, p. 11; my translation.

recurrent problems seems to be called into question here. (How Windelband tries to escape the predicament will be discussed briefly below.) If the historical context is a context of problems, not of doctrines or theories, then the selection, the weight and the interrelation of these problems cannot be explained or assessed by the help of previous philosophical theory. Instead, we shall need a continuous evaluation of the current problem situation in accordance with the perceived needs of the present. Nothing seems wrong with this, provided the perception of needs is acute enough. But, on this account, there is no indication of why the problems should be recurrent, or in any sense specific to philosophy. Moreover, the essential reference to the present will reduce the past (or more exactly, past problems as they happen to have been selected for study) to a spurious present.

Finally, as to (3), i.e., concerning a temporally invariant subject matter of philosophy, we should consider the possibility of reclaiming a specific domain of reality for philosophy. If there were such a thing, it would account for the persistence of questions even without the continuity of theories. The peculiar character of the subject-matter might account for the lack of theory. Given the fact that there is no aspect or part of reality which is not claimed also by at least one other discipline, the suggestion that there is a specific subject matter of philosophy appears awkward. We may, nevertheless, consider the most likely candidate for philosophical subject-matter. If we restrict ourselves to the modern period, this is doubtless the human intellect and conscience, the human mind, or more generally, human nature. The majority of the great modern philosophers took the study of this subject-matter to be the theoretical core of their doctrines. Kant expressed most aptly what the critique of the human cognitive faculty was intended to achieve: to turn metaphysics into a science.[10] No surprise then to rediscover the vestiges of this idea in the faithfully Kantian problem historian Windelband who says, for instance: 'The subject-matter of the history of philosophy are those cognitive formations that, being either forms of conceiving or of judging, have permanently remained alive and hence have brought the internal structure of reason to clear recognition.'[11] The self-awareness of reason reappears at the heart of the seeming historicity of problem history.[12] Richard Rorty has recently argued that the assumption of a timeless human reason or human nature is essential for the very idea of modern philosophy as an autonomous discipline and

[10] Kant 1781 and 1787, B XXIII–XXIV, translation by N. Kemp Smith, p. 26.
[11] Windelband 1889: Einleitung, §2.1, p. 7.
[12] It may be worth noting that later problem historians who did away with the transcendental remainder in Windelband's historiography no longer had a conceptual defence of philosophical autonomy and of the identity of problems. The tenability of this view is more intimately connected with traditional epistemology than is often realized.

that it was the vehicle for what he calls 'an attempt to escape from history'.[13]

I agree with Rorty on two of his major claims: (a) that the grandiose attempt of modern philosophy to establish itself as an independent and fundamental discipline was inimical to true historicity, and (b) that the attempt failed. The failure was partly due to the successful competition of the sciences which call the *a priori* character of philosophy into question, and partly, perhaps more importantly, to a consequential oversight: *ex hypothesi* the problems and the possible approaches to their solution are themselves ahistorical. They may emerge in the course of history, but only as new candidates for trans-historical philosophical concern. It is us, living now, who have our problems. We modestly and wisely decide to enlarge the circle of philosophical discussants to whom we listen to include a number of remarkable past colleagues. This is – put in somewhat sloppy terms – the attitude that is implied by the problem-history view; it corresponds largely to its actual historiographical practice, and sometimes to its theoretical self-assessment as well.[14]

To avoid misunderstanding I should emphasize that I am not objecting to treating our great predecessors, occasionally, as contemporaries; we may indeed learn directly from them. The assumption of common problems may even disclose *historical* insights. What I am puzzled about are the conditions of the possibility of this learning or these insights. The problem-history view leaves them as unexplained facts. To this limitation corresponds another: the reasons for doing historical work remain *ad hoc* and merely pragmatic. History does not appear as an essential part of philosophy, or else philosophy is not itself conceived as something historical.

In short, the result of my critique is the following: the history of philosophy as conceived by the problem historian lacks the theoretical context without which it cannot be assimilated to scientific research (which was a goal of the problem historian). The missing context may be supplied from outside, either from science or from cultural and social history in general. But the problem historian cannot, as philosopher, accept this supplementation, for it violates the autonomy of philosophy, which he values so highly. Moreover, it contradicts his basic belief in permanent problems. On the other hand, the attempt to supply the missing context of

---

[13] Rorty 1979:8–9. The contemporary problem historian appears to agree: Passmore, for instance, explains the recurrence of problems since Plato by referring to the fact that we are all human beings (1965, p. 13).

[14] A prominent example is critically reported by Michael Ayers: P. F. Strawson praises J. Bennett for treating Kant as 'a great contemporary . . . with whom we can argue', as we can with Locke, Leibniz, Berkeley and Hume no less than with Ryle, Ayer and Quine. Thus in Bennett (1968) on Kant; the report is taken from Rée, Ayers, and Westoby 1978:55.

philosophical history from inside philosophy, and thereby to establish its autonomy, relies on an evaluation of the current problem situation. Thus it leads to the contraction of the past into a spurious present; it entails the loss of history.

One consequence of all this is that the problem-history view retains the discrepancy previously mentioned between an historiographical practice and the philosophical understanding of or justification for it, *pace* the popular thesis which says that *only* this view can overcome the discrepancy.[15] Another, perhaps more important, consequence is that a philosophical justification even of the current set of philosophical problems is bound to fail. In order for it to succeed, philosophy would need a theoretical framework as well established as that of the successful sciences. Since, admittedly, there is nothing of the sort to be had, we may ask if the quest for an analogy between philosophy and the sciences was not perhaps misdirected. Perhaps the relationship of science and philosophy should be conceived in a completely different way?

II

At this point a few historical remarks concerning the relationship between philosophy and other disciplines may be in order. I hope they may prepare the way for an improved conception of the historical character of philosophy. Originally and for a long time it was difficult, if not impossible, to draw a line between philosophy and other theoretical disciplines. At least this was true for the European tradition, in particular for the great innovators of modern philosophy. Descartes' *Principia Philosophiae* or Hobbes' trilogy *De Corpore, De Homine, De Cive* illustrate very clearly what I have in mind. On the other hand it had been clear since the great days of Greek science that mathematics and the exact sciences can take care of themselves. They carry the standards for their beliefs and their actions in themselves. In short, they strive for, and are capable of, autonomy.

The term 'autonomy' is here opposed to the property of being determined by tradition or 'traditionality'. This opposition is a familiar aspect of the self-characterization of the Enlightenment, but it needs comment. Do not the exact sciences have and require their own traditions? It seems clear enough that they do; but then it should be puzzling how they can avoid resorting to tradition in order to justify themselves. An easy way out is to refer to the presence and permanent availability of the object under

---

15 Thus John Passmore identifies 'problematic history of philosophy' with 'real history of philosophy' and claims that only this kind of history can help the philosopher to become a better philosopher (Passmore 1965:30–1). In Germany Klaus Oehler has argued for the claim that 'the problem is the true and essential link between philosophy and its history' (Oehler 1957:524). Cf. also n. 8 above.

study: nature. Indeed, there appears to exist only one genuine counter-example of a science[16] which does not object to traditionality but rather makes essential use of it for its legitimation: theology. Its 'object', God, is conceived as always present and immutable (more so than nature) but lacking availability.

Now, theology provided the reliable frame of reference for all cognition and action until the rise of modern science. For the sake of my argument I shall take for granted that this reliability must have looked increasingly questionable as the autonomy of science was recognized. Philosophy, being intertwined with, and still almost inseparable from, those sciences that were affirming their autonomy, forsook its ancillary position with respect to theology and very naturally assumed the role of the single alternative source of orientation for cognition and action. Yet in one decisive respect philosophy could not assimilate itself to theology: it could not submit to traditionality. In this respect European philosophy not only started as, but also reaffirmed itself as, a worldly discipline, whatever else may distinguish it from ordinary and useful sciences.

As a result, philosophy faced the problem of how it related to the world, to an object of study with the presence and availability which could make autonomy possible. The rapid growth of the natural sciences entailed an increasing institutional and substantial distinctiveness for philosophy, and this forced philosophers to search for an independent and specifically philosophical foundation of autonomy. Philosophy developed into transcendental philosophy, i.e., into the attempt at justifying all objective claims by the self-ascertainment of the cognizing subject. Philosophy found its own object in the human intellect and the human conscience, or in reason under its two aspects: theoretical and practical, with a hope of relating the two in a unified conceptual framework. Given this, philosophical knowledge which made no appeal to traditionality seemed possible, for other sciences had become autonomous by establishing a specific reference to certain aspects or parts of (non-human) nature.

I do not propose to pursue the difficulties and the eventual failure of transcendental philosophy. (I do think that it is possible and necessary to continue to investigate transcendental questions and arguments, but not to have a transcendental theory or discipline.) We have already taken this failure for granted when we recognized the initial plausibility of the problem-history view. The failure is, of course, due not least to the recurring conflict of *a priori* philosophical claims with scientific findings.

[16] At this point I have to ask the reader's permission to use the term 'science' for any discipline with recognizable professional standards and cognitive claims which is taught at our institutions of higher learning – in short for everything that is called 'Wissenschaft' in German. This inflationary use of the term has one advantage for my present purpose: it does not prejudge a certain classification of academic disciplines.

Kant's principles of natural science are a case in question. It is, however, a failure that occurred for very good reasons, prominent among them the intertwining of philosophy and other sciences, and the orientation of philosophy toward autonomy.

These brief historical remarks are not meant to offer anything but familiar perspectives; they may, however, let us see more clearly what possibilities are open for a theoretical grasp of the deeply entrenched historicity of present-day philosophy which we observe in actual academic practice, and occasionally in the conscious self-assessment of philosophers. I see two such possibilities: (a) to sever the bonds between philosophy and the (presumably) ahistorical natural sciences and to tie philosophy to the somewhat younger but vigorously growing historical and social sciences, or (b) to show the inherent historicity of all sciences, particularly and most importantly the natural sciences. I will discuss them in this order.

Possibility (a) may be said to have been disclosed for the first time by Hegel. He remained within the framework of transcendental philosophy, but had already assumed the priority of historical insight over that of natural science and thus paved the way for the subsequent alliance of mainstream Continental philosophy with the historical *Geisteswissenschaften*. Although Hegel's transcendental claims and his idealism were heavily criticized, this new alliance took root in the minds of some of the most prominent post-Hegelian thinkers like Marx, Nietzsche, Dilthey and Heidegger. A recent stage of this development, and a particularly explicit expression of its underlying assumptions, is represented in the work of Hans-Georg Gadamer. I therefore propose to discuss his view of the inevitable historicity of philosophy in order to sketch as clear an alternative as possible to the problem-history view, a view I have claimed to be ahistorical *au fond*.

III

Since I am using Gadamer simply as an example of a certain type of historically minded philosophy, I may be excused from doing justice to this work in general. I shall restrict myself to some features of his thought that I find especially suggestive and helpful. Gadamer's principal book (Gadamer 1960, valuable clarifications and extensions in Gadamer 1967a) contains an attempt to disclose the true nature of philosophy, in particular its historicity, by relating it to art and to the *Geisteswissenschaften*. The latter are given their distinctive character to a large extent by being contrasted to the natural sciences. In all this Gadamer's intention is not to develop a methodology of the *Geisteswissenschaften*, nor an aesthetic theory, but a fundamentally new approach in philosophy, indeed even a new ontology. He is concerned with the universality of hermeneutics and the ontology of language.[17]

If, as I have argued, we are justified in characterizing pre-Hegelian philosophy by its close ties to the natural sciences, it may be illuminating to see how Gadamer marks the contrast between natural sciences and *Geisteswissenschaften*. The core of his view can be condensed into two theses. (1) The typical, and also the highest, form of cognition in the human or social realm is not discovery or explanation of facts but understanding. (2) Understanding is not an activity performed according to certain methodological rules, but rather consists in moving to one's place in the continuing tradition. An italicized sentence in Gadamer's *Wahrheit und Methode* reads: 'Understanding is itself to be conceived not so much as an act of subjectivity but rather as a move into a place within the occurring tradition.'[18] In order to see in what sense these principles break radically with the traditional epistemological model it is useful to observe that, according to Gadamer, a mere change of sides, i.e., from the natural to the socio-historical sciences, would not have been sufficient to transform philosophy into its new shape. In a careful discussion of Dilthey's ideas, Gadamer shows that extensive historical studies and a historicist self-assessment do not in themselves suffice to reveal a truly historical dimension of knowledge. According to his analysis, the main reason for this shortcoming is to be sought in Dilthey's having invoked the paradigm of the natural sciences. Dilthey believes that the scientific and cognitive character of history can only be secured by attaining objectivity. He wants to complete the enterprise that began under the aegis of the *natural* sciences by an *historical Enlightenment*. What this means in practice is simply that Dilthey pursues the ideal of grasping past documents completely and in full congruence with the facts they express. A quotation will shed light on what Gadamer has in mind: 'The interpreter is absolutely simultaneous with his author. That is the triumph of philological method, . . . Dilthey is completely possessed by the idea of this triumph. On it he founds the equivalence of the *Geisteswissenschaften* [with the natural sciences]' (Gadamer 1960: 227). This interpretation of Dilthey by Gadamer accords with the fact, emphasized by problem historians, that critical historical method emerged simultaneously with the New Science. (The critical treatments of the Bible by Hobbes and Spinoza are instances.) Moreover, it fits in with the idea that a realistic problem history depends essentially on the possibility of objective philology (Bréhier 1975: esp. 170). Like

---

[17] Gadamer 1960: Vortwort; see also 'Die Universalität des hermeneutischen Problems', in Gadamer 1967a:101–12.

[18] Gadamer 1960:275. The German original of this singly important sentence should be quoted: 'Das Verstehen ist selber nicht so sehr als eine Handlung der Subjektivität zu denken, sondern als Einrücken in ein Überlieferungsgeschehen, . . .'

problem history, Dilthey's historicism does not transgress the limits of an extended spurious present. Even the intensified perception of history as objective change does not show why we *have to* study history. Gadamer thinks that such a reason only emerges from his radically different epistemological model, that of understanding (*Verstehen*).

Understanding, understood as moving to one's place in the tradition, breaks with the idea of an unaffected observer. The experience gained by this move is construed on the model of the personal relationship which every one of us can develop to another person – the relationship of being a you for an I, one which is different from any relationship you or I may have to a third person (Gadamer 1960: 340 ff). Only by simultaneously finding and actively determining my place with respect to someone else do I come into the position of acquiring knowledge of myself and the other person. Only by finding and simultaneously determining our place with respect to the past do we achieve genuine historical knowledge. The uniqueness of this hermeneutical experience is opposed to the repeatability of experiences in the experimental sciences.[19]

So a further feature of the approach, entailed by theses (1) and (2) above, is: (3) the traditional epistemological opposition between the subjective and the objective is overcome. There is no longer a question as to whether some view is accepted because it accords with the so-called facts or because it accords with previous theories. The model for achieving this perplexing merger is something which is not mysterious at all but a familiar instance of

[19] Gadamer 1960: part 2, II.3.b, esp. pp. 330, 340. This is a decisive feature of Gadamer's view; he takes it from Heidegger. Neither philosopher is looking for universalizable anthropological truths. More accurately: anthropology for them has an ineradicably historical character. David Hoy in his fine analysis of Heidegger's account of history (Hoy 1978) goes wrong when he expects to find a trans-historical anthropology in *Being and Time*, i.e., 'an ontological analysis [that] produces a category characteristic of human existence in general and is not applicable only to a specific culture or historical tradition, such as that of Western Europe' (p. 344). Hoy goes on to say: '[Heidegger] is not suggesting that history is concerned with the *uniqueness* of past events. For Heidegger, the historian should retrieve the existential possibilities of the past age for his own age' (p. 347). Retrieving past possibilities is indeed the whole point of doing history; but which possibilities is a matter of the unique 'faktische existentielle Wahl' that originates out of the future: 'Die Historie . . . zeitigt sich aus der Zukunft' (Heidegger 1926:395). I take this strange phrase to mean something like the simple truth that to write history is inevitably also to continue history actively in view of an anticipated future. It is in this sense that historiography falls short of 'universal validity' (Heidegger 1926:395) – a claim Hoy rightly feels puzzling (p. 348). It is not, therefore, 'subjective'; for each individual belongs to an integrated social culture. It is, however, specific and unique for a given historical (as opposed to individual) situation. How else could Heidegger have believed to add to philosophy by digging into the depths of a unique historical tradition and call it the 'history of being'? Rorty has expressed a decisive insight when he wrote: 'The whole force of Heidegger's thought lies in his account of history of philosophy' (Rorty 1978:257, cf. also 243). All this is deliberately accepted by Gadamer as well. To what extent it implies European intellectual imperialism in our *present* historical situation seems to me an important question. This question should make us feel uneasy enough to search for alternative concepts of essential historicity even though we may not hope to return to something like universal anthropology.

historical occurrence: theological and legal interpretation. The sources, holy books or given laws, are applied to novel situations, and thus new dogmas or new legal precedents are created. Gadamer's philosophical achievement is to promote these occurrences to ontological dignity, i.e., to teach us how they can be viewed as representing the general structure of everything historical.

One final feature needs to be mentioned here: (4) since understanding can only be achieved by an ever renewed attempt to redefine the relationship between the person who understands and that which is understood, Gadamer says, 'in the end, all understanding is an understanding of oneself'.[20]

Let us now ask if the reorientation of philosophy, away from the natural sciences and toward the historical sciences, was successful? In view of (4) it seems clear that full success will require that *all* of history can be accommodated within the model of self-understanding. What does conscious human history consist of? Or better: what is the subject-matter of understanding? (So far I have only talked about the formal structure of historical knowledge.) Gadamer's brief reply presumably would be: the entire cultural heritage as embodied in language, a heritage which comprises nature as well, yet nature as we know it or nature as we have become able to talk about it. Thus Gadamer says: 'Being that can be understood is language' (Gadamer 1960: 450).

This dictum provokes doubts: does it suffice just to understand language? Do we really understand nothing but language? Would we understand language if we understood *only* language? Language is about something after all, something which only occasionally is again language or an intelligible activity of a speaker. Language is also about those conditions of actions and speech which are beyond the reach of human action, i.e., about nature. Do we not understand nature, limited as our understanding may be?[21] My rhetorical questions are meant to convey my uneasiness with the self-sufficiency of a *cosmos intelligibilis* with an idealistic outlook. It seems to me that this idealistic tendency, though separable from the activity of

[20] Gadamer 1960:246. It is illuminating to compare this statement with Gadamer's account of two kinds of experience (1960: part 2, II.3.b). There he claims that, while the repeatable experience of the natural sciences necessarily quenches all historicity, the hermeneutic experience remains as the 'proper' one, because it alone transforms our consciousness and thereby creates the irreducibly historical character of all knowledge.

[21] I am aware of the context in which Gadamer puts forward his claim that everything that can be understood is language. Extending the experience with texts and conversations he comes to talk about the action of things themselves ('das Tun der Sache selbst') which gets hold of us who can speak, so that in this sense the things about which there can be a language have themselves the structure of language. Still more accurately: 'Language is a middle in which the Ego and the world . . . reveal themselves as primordially belonging together' (Gadamer 1960:449f). My criticism is directed precisely against this kind of post-Kantian speculation concerning the unity of world, language and reflexive consciousness.

hermeneutics, is inseparable from the thesis of the universality of hermeneutics.[22] But then the structurally attractive construal of historicity is acquired at a high price: the confinement of the historical to the sphere of language and meaning or, put somewhat differently, the view that history exhausts itself in the self-continuation of conscious culture like a leaven which apparently grows out of itself.

Is that a harmful view? Rorty, a new advocate of hermeneutics, thinks that 'events which make us able to say new and interesting things about ourselves are . . . more "essential" to us (. . .) than the events which change our shapes or our standards of living' (Rorty 1979: 359). This would be an incredibly strong and implausible statement, were it not for the qualification in parentheses left out above which reads: 'at least to us relatively leisured intellectuals, inhabiting a stable and prosperous part of the world'. If we drop the qualification, or if we only doubt the stability (for which there are more reasons than anyone can possibly wish to have), at least two dangers of the hermeneutic view suggest themselves: (1) the underestimation of material novelty, and (2) the lack of adaptation to historical or cultural pluralism.

As to (1), we may agree that the most dramatic and irrevocable changes in history depend, among other things, upon conditions of understanding and self-understanding characterizing a given culture; but they cannot be understood solely with respect to these conditions, let alone be produced from them. The present technological and scientific world is not just the outcome of a transformation of our consciousness, though such transformations are certainly part of it. A major task for our understanding is non-reflexive: it concerns the *material* interaction of man and nature and the *natural* conditions that govern human behaviour in this interaction.

As to (2), the hermeneutic program (Gadamer's, not Rorty's) by its own internal logic (though, perhaps, against its own spirit) always refers to a particular tradition, viz. that tradition with respect to which occupying one's place constitutes the event of understanding. In Gadamer's approach it remains an unsolved problem to analyse the structure of those events of communication that bring together two independent traditions, except in terms of the subordination of one to the other. It might well be that

---

[22] That the idea of a comprehensive and closed world of understanding carries idealistic connotations is made explicit e.g. by Geldsetzer 1968a (see pp. 10–11). Karl-Otto Apel has pointed out the idealistic roots of the *Geisteswissenschaften* (Apel 1967: esp. 35,53). Richard Rorty has cited these passages and argued that the association of idealism with hermeneutics is misplaced (Rorty 1979: VII.4); but he could do so only because he wanted to defend the indispensability of hermeneutics, not its universality. Moreover, he takes hermeneutics as a vehicle of edification rather than truth, whereas Gadamer is far more ambitious when he states: 'Understanding . . . is genuine experience, i.e., an encounter with something that affirms itself as truth' (1960:463).

understanding nature and man's relation to nature trans-culturally will
turn out an essential feature of the analysis of these events.

As a result of the preceding considerations I wish to note the following:
it is possible that the formal structure of historicity described by Gadamer
can be retained while abjuring the exclusive orientation toward the
historical *Geisteswissenschaften*. The contrast between the natural sciences
and the *Geisteswissenschaften* in respect of historicity may well be misleading. Hence, I conclude that it is worth considering possibility (b), mentioned at the end of section II, i.e., the inherent historicity of the natural
sciences.

IV

In the heyday of transcendental philosophy and the autonomy of the
sciences it would have been outrageous to question the trans-historical
character of natural science. The victory of developmental or evolutionary
thinking in the nineteenth century did not alter this situation in principle.
But the growing impact of science upon social life and institutions directed
attention to the conditions of the social production of science and technology. Only then did it become appealing to think in terms of essentially
historical, i.e., non-cumulative and non-convergent, models of scientific
development. After Thomas Kuhn's *The Structure of Scientific Revolutions*
(1962) the new historicist view, though not uncontroversial, became the
common intellectual property of philosophers of science. Yet, as long as we
continue to assume that there is a reality out there called 'nature' that is
invariant, or that changes only unnoticeably slowly throughout the history
of science and technology, it would still seem natural to view science and
technology as the gradual discovery and use of so far unknown territory.
Given this picture, it would seem possible in principle, at least for certain
delimited parts of the territory, to draw something like a final map and to
envisage something like an exhaustive list of uses of its products.

There is nothing in our present scientific knowledge that speaks against
the ontological view underlying this metaphor. Nevertheless, our actual
experience of science does not accord with it. For the successful and
progressive disciplines are *theoretical* in a significant sense, i.e., they have
as objects things and phenomena that we will never perceive directly or
perceive in any sense comparable to that in which a discoverer is said to
perceive a new country. We identify objects solely through the medium of
theories, plus the perception of ordinary things and events. Moreover, the
advanced technical use of nature is inseparable from this kind of identifi-
ability of the invisible. A ready illustration of what I have in mind is not far
to seek in an era we have come to call the atomic age.

One consequence of the theoretical character of science that has recently been well established in the philosophy of science is what we may call the 'local historicity' of research: a new theory can never be judged solely in view of the experimental phenomena for whose explanation it was formulated; in addition, a comparison with previously accepted theories will be required.[23] Furthermore, the successor theories are generally used to interpret their predecessors and to evaluate the limits of their applicability. Einstein's theory of gravitation versus Newton's is a standard example.

This example gives me an occasion to go on to a further observation concerning the historicity of science, an observation that is less commonly made and much more controversial. I want to claim that the natural sciences not only have the property of local but also of 'global historicity'. By this I mean that the discovery as well as the justification of an advanced theory requires the predecessor theory, or rather the chain or net of predecessor theories. At first sight this claim, though perhaps acceptable for discovery, will seem to be clearly false for justification. If the justification of an empirical theory consists in nothing but its empirical adequacy, predecessor theories are irrelevant. Now, in this form, the rejoinder is not even compatible with local historicity. More importantly, the range of conceivable theories that are empirically adequate is much too wide. Its limits are always elusive. It is likely that this range is not even finite. How, then, do we narrow it down to manageable proportions in actual research? In all successfully progressing disciplines this is done with the help of already available and (partly) successful theories. (Of course, not all such theories serve this purpose; the point is that some do. Only in disciplines whose progress is doubtful may global historicity be missing, and their historicity may be of a different kind: not inherent but external.) As an example we may again refer to Newton and Einstein: were it not for Newtonian mechanics and gravitational theory, it would be hard to see how anybody could have discovered general relativity or found its conceptual structure appealing.[24]

Only global historicity permits us to consider a new theory not as a competing alternative but as a corrected continuation of former theories. Without it one could hardly make plausible a thesis which is certainly compatible with present scientific knowledge, though not proved by it: namely that predecessor and successor theories deal with the same reality,

---

[23] On this conclusion leading philosophers as different as Karl Popper and Thomas Kuhn completely agree.

[24] A lot more should be said here: e.g., that specific theoretical features of Newton's theory like the equality of inertial and gravitational mass find an explanation through Einstein's – or that the empirical adequacy of Einstein's theory cannot be ascertained except by using Newton's, (thus assuming the conceptual and numerical compatibility of the two theories), as in the calculation of the observed value of the movement of Mercury's perihelion.

e.g. gravitation. (It is, of course, granted that they deal, at least in part, with the same observable phenomena.) Only global historicity, then, provides the possibility of theoretical progress, since to assume progress excludes conceiving of theoretical change as simple replacement of one theory by another.

When we consider technological progress as well, i.e., the increasing scope and intensity of the interaction between man and nature ('progress' is not here intended as a value term), we will have to allow for the combination of two things: (1) an invariable (or unnoticeably slowly varying) nature beyond human power, *and* (2) a unique history of research into, and use of, nature. Science is only available as something historical, including its claims that are about something trans-historical.

This simple state of affairs is intimately connected with the nature of scientific truth. Only propositions that are, in principle, directly decidable can be true or false in the ordinary and unproblematic sense of the term; in the case of scientific theories, indeed already of single theoretical statements that acquire meaning and testability only within theories, this is not so. Neither Newton's nor (presumably) Einstein's theories of gravitation are simply true or false, although some property that has something to do with the difference between 'true' and 'false' is common to both and separates them both from, say, Descartes' theory of gravitation (the refutation of which Newton deemed worthy of an entire book of his *Principia*).

It is, therefore, impossible to construe scientific theories as entities which might, at the end of research or in a counter-factual ideal case, be construed as a picture of reality which is true in the ordinary sense of the term. Not only was the philosophical dream of a science *a priori* an illusion, the teleological view of scientific knowledge, as advocated by Charles Sanders Peirce or Karl Raimund Popper, is no less impossible.[25] I want to argue the opposite view: the object of science and our knowledge of it are to be assessed not with respect to an imaginary point of convergence in the future, but with respect to the cognitive path of experience and theorizing that has been covered in the past.

It lies beyond the scope of this paper to elaborate and defend this thesis any further.[26] It may, however, be useful to wind up this part of my essay

[25] It is worth noting in the present context that this view helps Gadamer to construct the contrast between science and hermeneutical disciplines which I am trying to demolish. He writes: 'The object of the natural sciences can be determined *idealiter* as that which would be known after the completion of research' (Gadamer 1960:269).

[26] A major point of this elaboration and defence would be to explain why the historical character of science, which I claim to be essential, nevertheless does not entail a historical research practice in science. Here it seems necessary to invoke the non-reflexive character of science: a scientific discipline never includes an investigation of its own activity and development. If, as I shall claim, in the division of research labour philosophy has become

by adding a brief list of points that seem to me to deserve further consideration and may recommend the thesis to the reader. (1) The thesis fits the reality of research, in the sense that scientific achievements always have a beginning but never an end. (2) It is a commonplace to assign a (self-) critical role to science, i.e., to discredit any suggestion that any scientific achievement might be final. (3) Our practical relationship to the world, as far as it is determined by science, is one of facing an open future rather than of aiming at a preconceived goal; this is true for intellectual orientation as well as technological application. In this respect science resembles natural language. This latter serves to cope ever again with novel situations and, for this reason alone, can never become a completed or ideal language, or even admit approximation to such a language as a measure of its adequacy. Similarly, science does not admit the approximation to an ideal type of knowledge as measure of its progress. Finally (4), science is only possible as experience. The experience of an individual does not grow in a short interval of time but only in the course of life. Science, being a kind of social or collective experience, is not even in principle a product of the present (of a lucky moment, as it were) but only of a long history. Only when seen as such can it be understood, and also, one may hope, controlled.

V

It is time now to revert to philosophy and to apply the lesson I tried to extract from science. We have already discussed the intimate connection of science and philosophy, especially during the modern era. We may now draw a conclusion from it: philosophy should be expected to display a relationship to history that closely resembles the relationship of the sciences to history. As long as the sciences aimed at discovering the timeless and eternal order of things, philosophy was led to conceive its task in much the same terms, and conversely. (No hard and fast distinction of philosophy and science is assumed here, let alone a causal direction.) Philosophy investigated the time-transcendent structure of human reason or human nature. When the sciences transgressed preconceived ontological schemes, yet appeared gradually to approach the Truth, philosophy too might hope to find the law of its development in assumptions or anticipations of a final and perfect stage. This pattern can be observed from Hegel until today; names as different as Charles Sanders Peirce, Karl Popper and Jürgen Habermas come to mind in this context.

(or is to become) the consciousness of the scientific world, it would have to carry the entire burden of historicity. Depending on historical conditions the practice of philosophy will then show this feature to a lesser or greater extent (cf. section V below for hints as to what I have in mind).

Furthermore, to the extent to which particular problems can be isolated in the sciences and be investigated apart from their context, and in particular apart from their historical development, philosophy will be, and has been, encouraged to make the same attempt. Frequently, in the past as well as today, this strategy has made sense, and has been as successful as philosophy can be. But some problems will be distorted in an ahistorical or a problem-historical perspective; others will not even be posed. Distortion threatens those problems of high generality I mentioned earlier such as 'What is knowledge?', or 'What are the foundations of morals?'. How can we talk meaningfully about knowledge without taking into account the paradigm case of knowledge, i.e., scientific knowledge with its historical dynamics? How could we do ethics successfully today without giving a central place to the cultural plurality on our planet or to the novel fact that the consequences of our actions affect many future generations? The problems which are not even posed in problem-historical perspectives include all those which themselves have historical content – first and foremost the question of the sources and the goals of science and technology.

The last remark leads me to the point with which I want to wind up this essay. It seems to me that the radical historical turn of philosophy, which I have sketched with special reference to Gadamer, originates from a source that does not become sufficiently visible in Gadamer himself, because he fixes his attention chiefly on the *Geisteswissenschaften*. This source is the experience of science and technology as historical forces, indeed as our historical fate. Only if this experience is recognized can we hope to give an adequate account of the uncompromising historicity of some of the most recent philosophical tendencies. Prominent examples are offered by Heidegger and the late Husserl.

Husserl's treatise on the crisis of European science (Husserl 1934–6) testifies as clearly as one could wish how his uneasiness with modern (natural) science brought him to investigate the history of modern thinking. He, the proponent of an *a priori* analysis of human consciousness, towards the end of his career came to write sentences like the following: 'Since we not only have a cultural-spiritual heritage but also are nothing other than what we have become through our spiritual-cultural history, we have a task that is truly our own. We can approach it properly . . . only through a critical understanding of the totality of history – *our* history' (Husserl 1934–6: 72; ed. Ströker, p. 77). This passage is found in the middle of an analysis of modern natural science and philosophy from Galileo to Kant.[27]

---

[27] Jonathan Rée (Rée, Ayers, Westoby 1978:18) groups Husserl with Wittgenstein, the Vienna Circle and other anti-history revolutionaries. This is correct for the early Husserl; it shows how drastic the reversal of his later years was.

Martin Heidegger's obscure and often repulsive mysticism grows out of a similar concern: the desperate search for a new kind of language or thought ('Denken' as opposed to 'philosophy', which he sees inextricably linked to the scientific tradition) that could account for science and technology as our historical destiny. This is a reason why Heidegger does not turn to extra-scientific wisdom of *any* kind, say Buddhism, but to the Pre-Socratics, and why he thinks that a 'destruction' of the history of European metaphysics is needed in order to grasp the historical contingency of modern European, and thus of planetary, civilization.[28]

These two examples illustrate why we find it difficult, if not impossible, to model philosophy on the traditional (i.e., ahistorical) paradigm of scientific research: science itself as a historical phenomenon has become a major subject-matter for philosophy.[29] Because of the inseparability of science and technology this event affects practical philosophy no less than theoretical philosophy.

Should we then perhaps follow Heidegger and become post-metaphysicians of science?

If I do not want to imply any such recommendation by my emphasis on Heidegger's importance for our theme, it is not so much for the obvious reasons connected with the difficulties of identifying with a particular cultural tradition of inter-war Germany or with Heidegger's forbidding idiosyncrasies. Rather, I am concerned with what I take to be residual misconceptions of science and philosophy in the various so-called 'transcendental' approaches adopted in the German tradition, especially by Husserl, Heidegger and Gadamer. Those authors seem to think that viewing science and technology as something like our historical fate or our historical task requires, first of all, some distance from science – some science-free space, as it were, for intellectual manoeuvering. Husserl, Heidegger and Gadamer, while differing widely in other respects, nevertheless agree in their basic approach to this problem: they seek the

---

28 The germ of Heidegger's approach is already contained in his 1926 publication; there he contrasts everyday life and scientific experience. A further step is a diagnosis of modern thought (1950a). Prominent statements concerning the central outcome of the history of being, technology, are found in 1949, 1953a, and 1953b. There is a lot more scattered material on science and technology in Heidegger; for a survey see Franzen 1975:4.2.1. Loscerbo 1981 is an extended study that shows the pervasiveness of the theme through much of Heidegger's thought.

29 Had Windelband not still worked under the overwhelming influence of Kant and also of Hegel, or had he lived in a time in which the ambivalent dynamics of science were as clear as they are now, he might already have drawn the same conclusion. At least he already viewed science as the main concern of philosophy, as is born out by quotations like the following: 'Die Geschichte des Namens Philosophie ist die Geschichte der Kulturbedeutung der Wissenschaft' (Windelband 1882:20). For him the study of ancient philosophy had its chief purpose in providing 'insight into the origin of Western science in general' (Windelband 1893:1). This is already a Heideggerian theme.

manoeuvering space in the experiences of pre- or extra-scientific life, in the 'Lebenswelt' which includes art and culture.[30] Furthermore, they try to capture these experiences in an autonomous philosophical discipline: a 'transcendental' theory, which aims at demonstrating the conditions that make all methodological investigations of nature and man possible to begin with.[31] (It is to be noted that the later Heidegger replaced the distinction between transcendental philosophy and particular disciplines by the opposition between all traditional disciplines including philosophy and a new way of thinking about being; but I shall not discuss this move here. As far as I can see, it does not affect the following argument.)

Now, it is certainly true that all methodological disciplines originate in common life and that no scientific language could possibly be introduced except with the help of everyday speech. But it is wrong to take this truism as a starting point for an independent philosophical critique of science, and wrong on two counts. (1) The pre-scientific, extra-scientific or science-free *Lebenswelt* is an artefact. Our life has become, as it were, soaked with science and technology. Not only are today's dangers and promises, our fears and hopes, very different from what they used to be in earlier centuries, also beliefs, actions and life plans have changed fundamentally. It is therefore scarcely possible, nowadays, to separate the *Lebenswelt* from the world as viewed and formed by science. The starting point of philosophical analysis can only be a '*scientific Lebenswelt*'. (2) The separation between particular disciplines or sciences and a transcendental philosophical theory is highly questionable. We have good reasons for admitting transcendental *questions* and transcendental *arguments*; but after two centuries of allegedly *a priori* yet actually shifting transcendental *theories*, we should conclude that the attempt at installing an independent philosophical authority has failed. In case of a conflict between the scientist and the philosopher, the latter will normally lose the battle, provided the

---

[30] Husserl (already under the influence of his student Heidegger) takes the 'Lebenswelt' as the starting point of his transcendental critique of science (Husserl 1934–6: part III); his purpose is to retrieve the 'Lebensbedeutsamkeit' of science whose loss is the fundamental problem of his investigation (*ibid.*: §3). Heidegger's famous analysis of everyday experience in his 1926 work marks the starting point for his later critique of technology in which he draws on the contrast between simple life, poetic experience, etc. on the one hand and scientific representation, technological domination, etc. on the other. (For a particularly expressive example among many see Heidegger 1950b.) Gadamer considerably extends the realm of relevant experiences; he wants to include art and culture as formed by historical tradition. This extension is the deeper reason and justification for the orientation towards the *Geisteswissenschaften*; it is not his primary concern to develop a methodology or philosophy of these disciplines (Gadamer 1960: Einleitung, pp. xxv–xxvi; 1967b: esp. 119.

[31] Husserl 1934–6: §§34a, 38–42; Heidegger 1926. Also Gadamer aims at 'something which ... precedes modern science and makes it possible' (1960:xv; cf. also 1967b:119). He accordingly seeks to establish the universality of hermeneutics with the help of an 'ontology' of language (1960: part III).

former does not extrapolate *his* specialty into the single all-embracing theory of the world, in which case he simply turns himself into a philosopher of the *a priori*.

Furthermore, the transcendental approach, especially in its hermeneutic version (*Verstehen as Existenzial* (Heidegger), or an ontology of language (Gadamer)) appears conceptually unsuited to deal adequately with historical novelty. Material interaction and discovery require a coordinate conceptual status alongside reflexive structures of self-experience. This point has already been made against Gadamer in my account of the idealistic implications of universalistic hermeneutics. It seems to apply quite generally to all transcendental approaches, where 'transcendental' refers to an *a priori* theory of subjectivity.

It is, therefore, one thing to grant that Heidegger and Gadamer offer a deep insight into the historicity of philosophy and another thing to accept their specific arguments. They concentrate on the extra-scientific experience of life, or on the *Geisteswissenschaften*, in ways that bypass the unsolved philosophical problem of properly understanding the relationship between these domains and that of scientific experience and scientifically based action. Such understanding, I would suggest, will involve the recognition of the historicity of scientific knowledge.

Briefly summarized, I have tried to argue that philosophy in our tradition is inseparably intertwined with the sciences (in a broad sense of the term), and so the history of philosophy is equally inseparable from the history of the sciences. The sciences, especially the natural sciences in their connection with technology, cannot be adequately understood, let alone managed, except on the basis of our historical experience (if they can be understood or managed at all). This statement will then be true also of philosophy. We need to study the history of philosophy not only to profit from the virtual presence of great past colleagues, nor only to improve our understanding of the genesis of spirit (and, in this sense, our self-knowledge). The history of philosophy is necessary if philosophy is to function as something like a professionalized consciousness of the scientific-technological world – and, we may hope, as its conscience.[32]

[32] Nancy Cartwright, Ian Hacking and Lorraine Daston kindly read a draft of the manuscript and help me to clarify my thoughts; I am aware, however, that I was unable adequately to cope with their criticisms and questions. I learned much from discussions at Johns Hopkins University and the University of Tübingen, in particular from Jerome Schneewind, Richard Rorty and Rüdiger Bubner, as well as from conversations with Hans-Georg Gadamer and Hans-Friedrich Fulda. Norton Wise assisted me in translating quotations from German authors. Last but not least, I am indebted to Richard Rorty for his careful language editing without which the text would hardly have been readable.

REFERENCES

Apel, K.-O. 1967. *Analytic Philosophy of Language and the Geisteswissenschaften*. Dordrecht: Reidel

Bennett, J. 1968. 'Strawson on Kant', *Philosophical Review* 77:340–9

Bréhier, E. 1975. 'The foundations of our history of philosophy', in *Philosophy and History – Essays presented to Ernst Cassirer*, ed. R. Klibansky and H. J. Paton. Gloucester, Mass.: Smith, pp. 159–72

Bubner, R. 1982. 'On Hegel's significance for the social sciences', *Graduate Faculty Philosophy Journal* 8:1–25

Dilthey, W. 1910. 'Aufbau der geschichtlichen Welt in den Geisteswissenschaften', in *Gesammelte Schriften*, vol. VII. Leipzig/Berlin: Teubner, 1927

Franzen, W. 1975. *Von der Existentialontologie zur Seinsgeschichte*. Meisenheim am Glan: A. Hain

Gadamer, H.-G. 1960. *Wahrheit und Methode*. Tübingen: Mohr. All quotations are from the 2nd edition, published in 1965

Gadamer, H.-G. 1967a. *Kleine Schriften I: Philosophie, Hermeneutik*. Tübingen: Mohr

Gadamer H.-G. 1967b. 'Rhetorik, Hermeneutik, und Ideologiekritik', in Gadamer 1967a: 113–30

Geldsetzer, L. 1968a. *Was heisst Philosophiegeschichte?* Düsseldorf: Philosophia-Verlag

Geldsetzer, L. 1968b. *Die Philosophie der Philosophiegeschichte im 19. Jahrhundert – Zur Wissenschaftstheorie der Philosophiegeschichtsschreibung und -betrachtung*. Meisenheim am Glan: A. Hain

Hegel, G. W. F. 1820. *Grundlinien der Philosophie des Rechts*, ed. E. Gans. Quotation is from Hegel, *Sämtliche Werke*, ed. H. Glockner, vol. VII. Stuttgart: Fromann, 1928

Heidegger, M. 1926. *Sein und Zeit*. Quoted from the 11th edition. Tübingen: Mohr, 1967

Heidegger, M. 1949. 'Die Kehre', in *Die Technik und die Kehre*, pp.37–47. Pfullingen: Neske, 1962

Heidegger, M. 1950a. 'Die Zeit des Weltbildes', in *Holzwege*. Frankfurt: Klostermann, pp. 69–104

Heidegger, M. 1950b. 'Das Ding', first published 1951. Quotations are from the later reprint in *Vorträge und Aufsätze*. Pfullingen: Neske, 1954, 4th edition 1978, pp. 157–79

Heidegger, M. 1953a. 'Die Frage nach der Technik', in *Vorträge und Aufsätze*. Pfullingen: Neske, 1954, 4th edition 1978, pp 9–40

Heidegger, M. 1953b. 'Wissenschaft und Besinnung', in *Vorträge und Aufsätze*. Pullingen: Neske, 1954, 4th edition 1978, pp. 41–66

Hoy, D. 1978. 'History, historicity, and historiography in "Being and Time"', in *Heidegger and Modern Philosophy*, ed. M. Murray. New Haven: Yale University Press, pp. 329–53

Husserl, E. 1934–6. 'Die Krisis der europäischen Wissenschaften und die transzendentale Phänomenologie', in *Husserliana*, ed. W. Biemel, vol. VI. Den Haag: Nijhoff, 1962. A selection from this work was edited by E. Ströker, Hamburg: Meiner, 1977

Kant, I. 1781 and 1787. *Kritik der reinen Vernunft.* 1st and 2nd editions. Engl. transl. by N. Kemp Smith, *Critique of Pure Reason.* London/New York: Macmillan, 1929

Loscerbo, J. 1981. *Being and Technology – A Study in the Philosophy of Martin Heidegger.* The Hague: Nijhoff

Mandelbaum, M. 1965. 'History of ideas, intellectual history, and the history of philosophy', *History and Theory, Beiheft 5: The Historiography of Philosophy:* 33–66

Mittelstrass, J. 1977. 'Das Interesse der Philosophie an ihrer Geschichte', *Studia Philosophica* 36:3–15

Oehler, K. 1957. 'Die Geschichtlichkeit der Philosophie', *Zeitschrift für Philosophische Forschung* 11:504–26

Passmore, J. 1965. 'The idea of a history of philosophy', *History and Theory, Beiheft 5: The Historiography of Philosophy:* 1–32

Passmore, J. 1967. 'Philosophy, historiography of', in *Encyclopedia of Philosophy,* ed. P. Edwards, vol. VI: 226–30. New York/London: Macmillan

Rée, J., Ayers, M. & Westoby, A. 1978. *Philosophy and its Past.* Brighton: Harvester Press

Renouvier, Ch. 1885–6. *Esquisse d'une classification systématique des doctrines philosophiques.* Paris

Rorty, R. 1978. 'Overcoming the tradition: Heidegger and Dewey', in *Heidegger and Modern Philosophy,* ed. M. Murray. New Haven: Yale University Press, pp. 239–58

Rorty, R. 1979. *Philosophy and the Mirror of Nature.* Princeton University Press

Windelband, W. 1882. 'Was ist Philosophy?', in *Präludien,* vol. I, 9th edition. Tübingen: Mohr, 1924

Windelband, W. 1889. *Lehrbuch der Geschichte der Philosophie.* All quotations are from the 9th edition by E. Rothacker. Tübingen: Mohr, 1921

Windelband, W. 1893. *Geschichte der abendländischen Philosophie im Altertum,* 2nd edition. Quoted from the 4th edition by A. Goedeckemeyer. Munich: Beck, 1923

Windelband, W. 1914. *Einleitung in die Philosophie.* Tübingen: Mohr

5

Five parables

IAN HACKING

This book presents no monolithic doctrine, but it does have a subversive tone. It will promote a few iconoclastic attitudes, broaden some horizons, and try to make philosophers more aware of the present ferment in approaches to writing history. My own ideas are outlandish enough to get me included in the book, but in such company I should first confess some respect for more hidebound and anachronistic readings of the canon of great philosophers. The pen-friend approach to the history of philosophy can irritate me as much as anyone. A few heroes are singled out as pen-pals across the seas of time, whose words are to be read like the work of brilliant but underprivileged children in a refugee camp, deeply instructive but in need of firm correction. I loathe that, but my first parable, called 'The Green Family', expresses just such an anti-historical message. Descartes (for example) lives, or so I say. My second parable is an instant antidote. It is called 'Brecht's paradox' and is constructed around the fact that Brecht, on reading Descartes, could not help exclaiming that Descartes lived in a world *completely* different from ours (or at any rate Brecht's).

My third parable, called 'Too many words', is self-flagellating. It is about a fairly radical conception about how the history of knowledge determines the nature of philosophical problems. It was once mine. I repeat it now to repudiate the idealist and verbalistic vision of philosophy from which it arose.

The last two parables, called 'Remaking the world' and 'Making up people', are once again complementary and antithetical. In brief, despite all that I have learned from T. S. Kuhn, I think that there is an important way in which history does not matter to the philosophy of the natural sciences, while it does matter to the philosophy of at least some of the human sciences. This will be the hardest of my ideas to explain, but at least for those who prefer theses over parables, there is a thesis there. In some ways it is an old chestnut, but it is roasted, I hope, over new coals.

Parables can be elusive, but all five of mine at least concern different

relations between philosophy and its past. (I) is a reminder that anachronistic reading of some canonical old texts can be a fundamental value in its
own right. (II) recalls that those same texts can speak for a complete
dislocation of ourselves from our past. (III) concerns an exaggerated use of
history for the analysis of philosophical concepts and problems. (IV) is
about history and the philosophy of natural science, while (V) is about
history and the philosophy of some of the social and human sciences. (IV)
draws more on T. S. Kuhn, (V) on Michel Foucault.

I The green family

A short time ago I visited the phoenix city of Dresden which, in addition to
its collections of European art, is home to a remarkable display of Chinese
porcelain. We owe both to the man whom everyone in Saxony calls August
der Stark, although technically he is Augustus II (1670–1733), sometime
king of Poland, and Friedrich Augustus I, elector of Saxony. He is less
admired for his skill as politician and warrior than for his lavish art
collections, his prodigious strength and (in some quarters) for having
fathered the largest number of children on historical record. August
bought any good porcelain he could lay his hands on. His objects are
limited in scope, coming mostly from the period of K'ang Hsi, 1662–1722.
In 1717 he built a small palace for his china, and in the same year he traded
Friedrich Wilhelm I of Prussia a crack regiment of dragoons for 151 vases,
still known as the *Dragonenvasen*. Although he did indeed wield his
sword, not all that effectually, he was no Prussian. August der Stark chiefly
made love, not war. He put his research and development money not into
cannon but chemistry, funding the rediscovery of the ancient Chinese
secret of porcelain manufacture, so that Meissen in Saxony became the first
European porcelain factory. (This was of commercial as well as aesthetic
interest, for in those days porcelain was the main manufactured com-
modity imported into Europe.)

I know little about porcelain. I report without any claim to discernment
that in Dresden my eye was especially caught by work in the style called
'the green family'. New techniques of glazing were developed in one of the
great exporting regions. The results were stunningly beautiful. I do not
single out August der Stark's pieces as the highpoint of Chinese art.
Slightly later work is often more esteemed in the West, and I know well
that very much earlier work has a grace and simplicity that moves the spirit
more deeply. I use the green family rather as a parable of changing tastes
and enduring values.

August der Stark may have loved his china to the point of building a
palace for it, but it was dismissed by later cognoscenti as of no more value

than a collection of dolls. For a century it languished in a crowded cellar, where on dull days you could only barely make out the looming shapes of some of the larger pieces. One man in particular guarded these obscure treasures, Dr Gustav Klemm, and he traded duplicate pieces with other dusty curators to expand what would become the noblest collection of this kind of work in Europe. Only towards the end of the nineteenth century was it returned to light. Then it came out to amaze and delight not only scholars but transients such as me. During the last European war the china went into the cellars again, and survived the Dresden massacre. Then all the Dresden collections went to Moscow for care and custody. They returned in 1958 to be housed in the noble rebuilt rooms of the Zwinger palace.

One could use this adventure to tell two opposite stories. One says: here is a typical human tale of wealth, lust, changes in taste, destruction, survival. Only a sequence of accidents created the Chinese export trade of objects suited to a certain European fashion for chinoiserie around 1700, and then brought some characteristic examples under one lavish roof, saw them lapse from public taste, witnessed a revival, a firestorm and a return. It is a mere historical fact that Leibniz (for example) doted on Chinese work, for such was the fashion of his time. Likewise I, more ignorantly, gape at it too, conditioned by present trends. It was not, however, for Wolff, Kant or Hegel to admire. In short there were periods of admiration and times when these pieces were despised, unlit, unloved. It will be like that again, not only in Europe but also in the land of their manufacture. In some years they will be condemned as an example of early subservience to the bourgeoisie of Europe and its colonies (the green family was a big hit with the planter families in Indonesia). In other years it will come out of Chinese cellars and be invested with an entirely different aura. *Evidently there is no intrinsic value in this stuff, it goes up and down in the scale of human admiration as the wind blows.*

Relativists seldom state their position so crassly, but that is roughly what they think. No one pretends that the conclusion, 'there is no intrinsic value in this stuff' follows from the events described in my example, but I wish to urge, against that conclusion, a slightly more empirical claim which is, I think, supported by the historical facts. I hold that no matter what dark ages we endure, so long as cellars save for us an adequate body of work by the green family, there will be generations that rediscover it. It will time and again *show itself.* I do not need to be reminded that porcelain will show itself only under certain conditions of wealth, pride, and human eccentricities (such as the bizarre practice of crossing disagreeable borders to wander around a strange institution that we call a museum).

I claim no intrinsic value for the green family to be found in heaven, but only an essentially human value, one tiny instance of an inherently human bundle of values, some of which manifest themselves more strongly at one time, some more strongly at another. Achievements created by humans have a strange persistence that contrasts with fashion. Most of the junk that we create has no such value. A sufficiently broad experience of the older private European collections – where objects are kept more for reasons of historical piety than of taste – assures us that being museumized is almost irrelevant to worth. August's collection is special, as its systematic survival and revival bear witness.

What has this to do with philosophy? The resurgence of historicism in philosophy brings its own relativism. Richard Rorty has captured it, or is thought to have captured it, in his powerful book, *Philosophy and the Mirror of Nature*. I was happily innoculated against that message. Just before *Mirror* appeared, I had been giving a course introducing undergraduates to the philosophers who were contemporaries of the green family and August der Stark. My hero had been Leibniz, and as usual my audience gave me pained looks. But after the last meeting some students gathered around and began with the conventional, 'Gee, what a great course.' The subsequent remarks were more instructive: 'But you could not help it . . . what with all those great books, I mean like Descartes. . .' They loved Descartes and his *Meditations*.

I happen to give terrible lectures on Descartes, for I mumble along saying that I do not understand him much. It does not matter. Descartes speaks directly to these young people, who know as little about Descartes and his times as I know about the green family and its time. But just as the green family showed itself to me, directly, so Descartes shows himself to them. My reading list served the function of the Zwinger gallery: it is the porcelain or the reading itself, not the gallery or lecture room, that does the showing. The value of Descartes to these students is completely anachronistic, out of time. Half will have begun with the idea Descartes and Sartre were contemporaries, both being French. Descartes, even more than Sartre, can speak directly to them across the seas of time. Historicism, even Rorty's, forgets that.

A novice needs food, then space, then time, then books, and then an incentive to read, and often that is hardly enough, for just as with the green family, Descartes will have his ups and downs. In London 150 years ago, Spinoza was the rage and Descartes ignored. Neither goes down well in Dresden or Canton today. Both will be much read there in the future, if physical and human conditions permit, or so I say.

As for our more immediate surroundings, any of ten thousand lecture courses would serve as the gallery for Descartes to show himself. It may be my bumbling attempt to locate Descartes in the problematic of his day; it may be Rorty's de-struction; or it may be any one of the standard pen-friend-across-the-seas-of-times courses. I give no argument for my conviction, but invite only experience. I mimic G. E. Moore holding up his hand before an audience of jaded sceptics. Most of us are too jaded even to remember the initial way in which Descartes spoke to us. That is the point of my parable. I gave, from my own recent past, a parallel to just that first speaking. I invite readers to invent or recall their own personal parallel. But if you resist, let me point once more: Hegel dominated the formation of Dewey, and perhaps that of Peirce, and also that of the upstarts Moore and Russell who laid waste to him within a few years. Hegel has, however, long lain fallow among those who read and work in English. Yet I need only point to the author of our opening chapter, Charles Taylor (whose expositions have much to do with the new anglophone practice of reading Hegel) to remind you that Hegel is back. The francophone was, a little earlier, even more hindered when attempting to read Hegel, until Jean Hypolyte provided the gallery within which Hegel would once again show himself. But now we even find Michel Foucault, although he may be seen in print as the denier of the substantiality of 'the text', willing in conversation to admit with glee, when asked for his reaction to the *Phenomenology of Spirit*, that it is *un beau livre*. As indeed it is. That is what it is for a writer such as Hegel to speak directly, once again, first to the French, and later to us, after decades of oblivion.

II Brecht's paradox

Having stated some conventional wisdom, I must at least record the opposing wisdom. I do find it very hard to make sense of Descartes, even after reading commentaries, predecessors and more arcane texts of the same period. The more I make consistent sense of him, the more he seems to me to inhabit an alien universe. That is odd, for he formed French philosophical writing and continues to provide one of its dominant models. I shall not here argue my problems using pedantic scruples. Instead I shall take a few notes written down by Bertolt Brecht early in 1932, when he, too, had been reading Descartes with consternation.

Brecht is useful because his reaction is so direct. 'This man must live in another time, another world from mine!' He is not troubled with niceties. His complaint is a robust astonishment at Descartes' central proposition. How could thinking possibly be my guarantee of my existence? What I *do* is what assures me of existence: but not just any doing. It is doing with purpose, especially those acts that are part of the work that I do. Brecht is a writer. His labour is writing. He is well aware of the paper in front of him. But it is not *that* awareness which (in the manner of Moore) makes him certain of its existence. He wants to write on the paper, and does so. He possesses the paper with his inscriptions, he changes it. Of that he can have no doubt. He adds, a trifle ironically, that to know anything about the existence of the paper, without manipulating it, would be very difficult.

Brecht notoriously writes from an ideology. His next comment is headed, 'Presentation of capitalism as a form of existence, that necessitates too much thinking and too many virtues.' It is in praxis and not in theory that he and his being are constituted. Implicitly turning to Berkeley, he remarks that one can perfectly well doubt whether a tree over there exists or not. But it would be a bit troublesome if no trees or the like existed, for then we would be dead for lack of oxygen. *That* truth may be known by theory, but it is the practical interaction with trees that is at the core of that certainty.

Some will feel that Brecht lives in another world, a world less familiar than that of Descartes. You may dissent from Brecht's seemingly simple-minded ideology and still feel his cry of astonishment at that Cartesian utterance. I am not saying that Pyrrhonism is unthinkable. People go through intellectual operations that lead them to sceptical utterances, and then go through other operations that have the form of relieving them from scepticism. I have no quarrel with that. I am not urging those linguistic 'paradigm case' arguments of a couple of generations ago, in which it was claimed that one could not coherently use English to express sceptical problems. Brecht directs me to a more central worry. How could someone with the deepest seriousness make existence depend upon thought? How relieve real doubt by a chain of reflections which culminates in 'even when doubting, I think, and when thinking, I am'? The step to *res cogitans* seems transparent compared to that first thought. Curiously Hintikka makes a quasi-Brechtian hermeneutic move, when he claims that the *cogito* is to be heard as a performative utterance in the sense of J. L. Austin. I can see that: a modern orator, whose labour is talking, may talk to prove he exists. We have all heard people whom we sarcastically describe in just those terms. But that is not what Descartes is up to, nor are readers of Hintikka usually persuaded by the 'performative' interpretation of the *cogito*.

I am not drawing attention to concepts in Descartes that have been transmuted ('substance') or which have died ('realitatis objectivae', a term well translated by Anscombe and Geach as 'representative reality'). We can, with pain, reconstruct those. Brecht is protesting something at the very core of Descartes. No being of my time, asserts Brecht, can seriously intend the basic Cartesian sentence.

I agree. I have also said in my first parable that generation after generation loves the *Meditations* and feels at home with the text. I think that is a paradox about history and philosophy without resolution. 'You can do the history better' – 'the students are taken in by Cartesian prose style, they only think they understand it and empathize with it' – those are mere comforting kinds of talk, that fail to grasp the seriousness of the Brechtian reaction, or fail to grasp the seriousness of the students to whom Descartes speaks directly. Naturally you do not need to use Brecht to make this point. I thought it useful to remind ourselves that while we philosophers beat around the bush, an alert and inquisitive outsider can at once go to the heart of what is unintelligible about Descartes.

III Too many words

Brecht connects the rise of capitalism with twin vices: too many virtues, too much thinking. Those are not our vices. Our problem is too many words: too much confidence in words as the be-all, the substance of philosophy. Perhaps Richard Rorty's *Philosophy and the Mirror of Nature*, with its central doctrine of 'conversation', will some day seem as linguistic a philosophy as the analysis emanating from Oxford a generation or two ago. To recall what that was like, it is best to think of routines rather than the occasional inspiration of a master such as Austin. We read in a book on Kant's ethics, for example, that: 'A discussion which remains strictly within the bounds of ethics would have no purpose beyond that of analysing and clarifying our moral thinking and the terms we use to express that thinking.' The author, A. R. C. Duncan, also quotes Sidgwick's definition from page 1 of *Ethics*: 'the study of what is right or of what ought to be, so far as this depends upon the voluntary acts of individuals'. Duncan says that he and Sidgwick have the same conception of ethics. Alas poor Sidgwick, poor Kant, who thought they were studying what is right or what ought to be! We might speak of the linguistic blindfold here, a blindfold that allows one to copy a sentence from page 1 of Sidgwick without being able to read it. Gustav Bergmann wrote of 'the linguistic turn' in philosophy, an evocative phrase that Rorty used as the title of an anthology of the period. As Rorty's remarkable collection shows, the linguistic turn was compelling, and in retrospect seems to have been too compelling. There are, however, subtler linguistic blindfolds than ones that make us read Kant as a philosopher of language. To avoid discourtesy I shall tug at my own. It issued in a book such as *The Emergence of Probability* and a solemn lecture to the British Academy about Leibniz, Descartes, and the philosophy of mathematics. The latter ended by saying that 'the "flybottle" is shaped by prehistory, and only archaeology can display its shape'. Such grandiloquent stuff evidently showed I had been reading Foucault, but significantly I had chiefly been reading *Les Mots et les choses*, a work that does not so much emphasize *mots* at the expense of *choses*, as have a strong thesis about how words impose an order on things.

It is easy to state a series of premises leading up to my historico-linguistic point of view. Most of them will seem commonplace until they are totted up. They once stood for my methodology. I stated them as such at a meeting of the Cambridge University Moral Sciences Club in the spring of 1974. Several contributors to the present volume were in the audience, including one of the editors, Quentin Skinner, whom I may hold as witness.

1. *Philosophy is about problems.* This is not an eternal truth. It became fixed in English with titles such as *Some Main Problems of Philosophy* (Moore, Lectures at Morley College, London, winter, 1910–11), *Some Problems of Philosophy* (James 1911), *The Problems of Philosophy* (Russell 1911).
2. *Philosophical problems are conceptual.* They arise from facts about concepts, and from conceptual confusion.
3. *A verbal account of concepts.* A concept is not an abstract non-linguistic entity grasped by our minds. It is to be understood in terms of the words that we use to express the concept, and the contexts in which we use those words.
4. *Words in their sites.* A concept is no more than a word or words in the sites in which it is used. Once we have considered the sentences in which the word is used, and the acts performed by uttering the sentences, and the conditions of felicity or authority for uttering those sentences, etc., we have exhausted what there is to be said about the concept. A strict version would say we have exhausted the concept when we have considered (*per impossibile*) all the actual specific utterances of the corresponding words. A less strict version would allow us to contemplate circumstances in which the word could be used, but in fact is not. Rigour inclines me towards the strict version, but the loose version is more popular.
5. *Concepts and words are not identical.* This is because, in addition to synchronic ambiguity, the same words may, through various kinds of change, come to express different concepts. But concepts are not to be multiplied beyond necessity. Evidence for difference in concept is provided by difference in site: the word is used by different classes of people to do different things. I still admire one theory of how to do this, which is not often thought of in this connection: that of Paul Ziff's *Semantic Analysis*. In parity, we must admit that at different times the same concept may be expressed by different words within the same community. A Ziffian inclination makes me more cautious about this than most people; I take seriously Fowler's *Modern English Usage* and its claim that British English knows only one type of exact synonym, e.g. 'furze' and 'gorse'. Even

today, when I find that the word 'determinism' begins in German around 1788, and that its usage in terms of efficient causes rather than predetermining motives begins in all European language around 1860, I am surprisingly inclined to say that a new concept comes in with this use of the word.

6. *Revolutions.* Ruptures, mutations, epistemological breaks, cuts – whatever metaphor you wish – occur in bodies of knowledge. Typically a concept, category or mode of classification may not survive a revolution intact. Even if we preserve the same word, it may express a new concept superseding an old one. We need not succumb to the excesses of incommensurability here. We need not suppose that post-revolutionary speakers have trouble understanding pre-revolutionary ones who stick to the old ways. But it does follow from this, plus the preceding premise, that concepts may have beginnings and endings.

7. *Problematic concepts.* At least one important class of conceptual confusions arises with concepts that came into being with a relatively sharp break. There is a trivial way that can happen, simply because people have not had time to work things out.

8. *Persistent problems.* There is also the less trivial cliché that some philosophical problems persist throughout the life of a concept. Some problems are as old as the hills, but others are specific and dated, and we may even have the view that some died so effectively so long ago that not all the artificial hermeneutic resuscitation in the world will bring them back to life again. We also know the flybottle phenomenon of the same bundle of arguments being proffered again and again, from generation to generation. Now we are near the end of our journey, and pass to sheer speculation, that the problem arises because of whatever it was that made that concept possible. It is as if a problematic concept had an unhappy consciousness.

9. 'This *uphappy, inwardly disrupted* consciousness, since its essentially contradicted nature is for it a single consciousness, must forever have present in the one consciousness the other also; and thus it is driven out of each in turn in the very moment when it imagines it has successfully attained to a peaceful unity with the other. . .'

Item (9) is not a premise but a project whose influence has been ample. Marx and Freud are the giants spawned by Hegel, but philosophers know the model too. In analytic philosophy it is as strongly connected with therapy as it is in Freud. The most sustained therapists were the linguistic analysts who thought that once linguistic confusions had been removed, philosophical problems would disappear. Then there were the non-linguistic analysts, of whom John Wisdom is the most notable, and who made explicit comparisons with psychotherapy. Wittgenstein had some influence on the formation of Wisdom's ideas, but I find less 'therapy' mentioned in Wittgenstein's own work than many other readers do. The

Hegelian project, whatever its provenance, leads on to my final premise. It is the most improbable one.

10. *Concepts have memories*, or at any rate, we in our very word patterns unconsciously mimic the phylogeny of our concepts. Some of our philosophical problems about concepts are the result of their history. Our perplexities arise not from that deliberate part of our history which we remember, but from that which we forget. A concept becomes possible at a moment. It is made possible by a different arrangement of earlier ideas that have collapsed or exploded. A philosophical problem is created by the incoherencies between the earlier state and the later one. Concepts remember this, but we do not: we gnaw at problems eternally (or for the lifetime of the concept) because we do not understand that the source of the problem is the lack of coherence between the concept and that prior arrangement of ideas that made the concept possible.

The therapy model would teach that we should solve or resolve our problems by undertaking their prehistory. I strongly dissociate myself from that model. It is extraneous to the unhappy consciousness story. About ten years ago an eclectic Norwegian psychiatrist remarked to me in conversation that Freud was wonderful for *explaining* mental phenomena, from slips through dreams to neuroses. The explanations were often splendid, the best in the market, although so far as curing people goes Freud is neither particularly good nor bad. The remark about cure has its tedious partisans pro and con. The remark about explanation was, for me exhilarating. Partly because of positivist training, I was not supposed to believe in explanations that did not have corresponding predictions. Now I could at once admit that Freud's and Freudian explanations of dreamwork and of much odd behaviour were simply wonderful. But don't count on cure.

This negative premise (don't expect therapy) concludes the basis for my model of the *explanation* of (some) philosophical problems. One had to understand the prehistory of problematic concepts, and what made them possible in order to grasp the nature of the philosophical problems. One would explain the problems. This need have no effect on whether the problems remained troubling to you. Those who look for solutions of philosophical problems will get no help from their explanation.

On the other hand, an explanation of the concept 'philosophical problem' (according to premise (1), a dated concept in the sense of premise (5)) would, I hope, make one more uncomfortable about the very idea of solving philosophical problems.

I can caricature these premises as a pinch of this and a pinch of that, but until we get up to the very end, *they were the commonplaces of a perfectly conventional training in analytic philosophy*. Even at the end, where there was more historicizing than philosophical analysis wanted, the extra ideas were scarcely novel.

Why do I no longer like these premises? At first, not for their emphasis on language or the past. Instead because, as many could have forewarned me, of the opening premise. One was in the business of 'solving' philosophical problems. Despite a gallant attempt to do that in connection with probable reasoning, and a briefer flirtation with that approach in the philosophy of mathematics, I was not doing that. But had I not succeeded in the task of explaining the existence and persistence of the problems? Well, no one else likes the explanations as much as I do: a good warning!

I now think I was doing something else. I was embarking on a study of the development of different styles of reasoning, an historical task that I believe to be of great importance. I have been able to formulate this only much more recently, thanks to hints from a book by A. C. Crombie, *Styles of Scientific Thinking in the European Tradition*. I should have learned earlier from a book that is still more often mentioned than read: Ludwig Fleck's *Genesis and Development of a Scientific Fact*, which has many interesting things to say about a *Denkstil*, even though, about that time (1935) the very word was about to be abused by terms such as 'Jewish style of thought'. Fleck outlived those terms. (His profession was public health. He was a gifted medical experimenter who in 1942 managed to publish a paper on the diagnosis of Typhus. That was in *Gazeta Żydowska*, the Lvov Jewish underground unperiodical. After 1945, when he was turning 50, and had got out of the camps, he published more than 100 medical papers about experimental research, until his death in 1961.)

Once you give up the first 1911 premise, that philosophy is about problems, none of the rest are very stable. In one way they are terrifyingly stable, for they are part of the idealist gambit that so permeates Western philosophy. Philosophy is about problems, problems arise from words, solutions must be about words, and 'conversation' ensues. Even when conversation says it rejects the premises, it ensues. Occasionally someone yelps. An example is C. S. Peirce, the only able experimenter in our canon, who when he saw what verbalists had done to his word 'pragmatism' yelped 'ic' and invented the word, if not the deed, of pragmaticism. Pragmatism is nominalist and idealist, both, but Peirce's pragmaticism, as he cantankerously averred, is realist all the way. Although it has views about how words have meanings, it does not reduce philosophy to words. Nor does Fleck, so utterly sensitive to styles of reasoning, for the experimenter cannot afford idealism nor its present form of verbalism. An instructive task for a more critical author than myself would be to check out if every post-Copernican revolution honoured by Kuhn had not been triggered by work in the laboratory, deeds, not thoughts; manipulation, not thinking.

I have laid bare one sequence of premises leading up to one way of doing philosophy historically. It fits the theme of this series of essays. Internally, within this sequence of parables, it has at least one other role. It suggests to me that a well-articulated methodology may lead one to interesting work to which the methodology is in fact entirely irrelevant. If the present volume succeeds, it will propound methodologies that matter only in that they produce interesting work to which the methodologies are irrelevant.

IV Remaking the world

No one from his generation has had a more dramatic impact on the philosophy of science than T. S. Kuhn. Any discussion of the relation between history and philosophy of science will begin with *The Structure of Scientific Revolutions*. This is odd, because he wrote entirely about natural science, indeed about the physical sciences. There is a time-honoured opinion that history matters to the very content of the human sciences, while it does not matter much to the natural sciences. If Kuhn had succeeded in historicizing our understanding of natural science, his achievement would have been revolutionary. I want to show why he did not succeed, and to give another twist to the old idea about a difference between natural and social science. This is in no sense a criticism of Kuhn. I believe that the totality of the work of this historian places him among the major philosophers of this century. Philosophers usually respond only to *Structure*. His work on experiments, measurement, and the second scientific revolution (all published in *The Essential Tension*) are of comparable importance. His latest historical book, *Black Body Theory and the Quantum Discontinuity, 1894–1912*, is what *Structure* is all about, and it is a notable achievement. Yet it is possible to learn from Kuhn in the most thorough way possible, and still to hold that there is a sense in which he did not succeed, and could not have succeeded, in historicizing natural science.

My distinction comes out at the level of one of the older philosophical disputes. It concerns nominalism. The most extreme version of nominalism says that we make up the categories that we use to describe the world. That is a most mysterious doctrine, which is perhaps why, like solipsism, it is almost never maintained. The problem is that we cannot understand why the world is so tractable to our systems of naming. Must there not be some natural kinds in the world for our invented categories to latch on to? Does not that refute strict nominalism?

I hold that Kuhn has importantly advanced the nominalist cause by giving some account of how at least an important group of 'our' categories come into being in the course of scientific revolutions. There is a construction of new systems of classification going hand in hand with certain interests in describing the world, interests closely connected with the 'anomalies' on which a community focuses in times of 'crisis'. At the same time this cannot lead us to a *very* strict nominalism, for the anomalies 'really' do have to appear to be resolved in order for a revolutionary achievement to be recognized. Removal of anomaly is never enough, Kuhn has taught, because all sorts of social conditions are needed for a revolution to 'take'. But reality has to go some part of the way – more than a wilder, stricter, nominalism would allow.

My contrast with the social sciences is as follows. In natural science our invention of categories does not 'really' change the way the world works. Even though we create new phenomena which did not exist before our scientific endeavours, we do so only with a licence from the world (or so we think). But in social phenomena we may generate kinds of people and kinds of action as we devise new classifications and categories. My claim is that we 'make up people' in a stronger sense than we 'make up' the world. The difference is, as I say, connected with the ancient question of nominalism. It is also connected with history, because the objects of the social sciences – people and groups of people – are constituted by an historical process, while the objects of the natural sciences, particular experimental apparatus, are created in time, but, in some sense, they are not constituted historically.

It must be clear that I am groping for a complex distinction between social and natural science. Perhaps I should warn against the most superficial distinction of all. It is curious, even comical, that physical scientists have paid little attention to Kuhn. Science journalists may now fill their articles with the word 'paradigm', but it is not a word that plays any role in reflection about serious research. It is quite the opposite in the social and psychological sciences. Kuhn's *Structure* had hardly appeared in print when presidential addresses to annual meetings of the American Psychological Association and the American Sociological Association avowed their need for paradigms. It has always seemed to me that Kuhn was a good deal clearer about his use of his famous word than most of his readers, including presidents of learned societies. When I claim that there is a sense in which Kuhn has not succeeded in historicizing physical science, it is not because his terminology has had more of a fad in the social sciences. Quite the contrary: it may be that the impact of Kuhn on social sciences is a sign of their lack of self-understanding.

Let us first recall philosophical reaction to Kuhn's book. He was accused of a scandalous undermining of rationality. 'Normal science' did not seem to have any of the virtues that a previous generation of positivists ascribed to science. Even worse, revolutionary change was not cumulative, nor did it occur because there was good reason for making the change, sound evidence for the new post-revolutionary science. Part of the philosophical guild defended its entrenched rights, and protested that history could never teach us anything about scientific rationality. The historian might exhibit some events in the history of science, but the philosopher would always be required to say whether those events were rational or not.

Thus the first wave of philosophical reaction was on the score of rationality, and people still do debate Kuhn's contribution, if any, to the methodology of science. He himself was a bit bemused by this reception, as is shown by his 1973 lecture, 'Objectivity, value judgment, and theory choice'. He subscribed to the traditional values after all – theories should be accurate, consistent, broad in scope, simple, and fruitful in new research findings. He insisted that these desiderata were not in general decisive. Moreover, the relative weights given to these considerations vary from research group to research group, from discipline to discipline, and from one era of science to another. Finally, the sheer rough and tumble of research is too messy for there to be any systematic algorithm. Kuhn was, however, no irrationalist demeaning these common-sense values, and I think the rumour of a 'rationality crisis' provoked by Kuhn was exaggerated.

Another theme of Kuhn's was less discussed, at first, than rationality: an anti-realism, a strong temptation, it appears, towards idealism. Not only are revolutions 'changes in world view' – not a very daring statement, but Kuhn is 'tempted' to say that after a revolution one 'lives in a different world'. Today, some twenty years after the book was published (a period during which Kuhn completed his monumental study of the onset of quantization), he has returned to that theme. People do see the world differently: what better evidence than that they draw it differently! He illustrates this with the first drawings of Volta's electric batteries. When we examine them closely we want to say that the cells cannot have been made like that, for they simply would not work. The voltaic cell, I may add, is no minor invention, but one of the fundamental tools of all science. It came into being in 1800, coinciding with the revival of the wave theory of light, of infra-red radiation and much else that had no immediate place in Newtonian Physics. Volta's invention was fundamental because it provided a steady current of electricity, and hence deflected the magnetic compass. Therefore it created a new epoch, that of electromagnetism.

Kuhn's 'temptation to speak of living in a different world' suggests that he is an idealist, one who holds, in some way, that the mind and its ideas determine the structure of our world. I think he is no idealist, and urge that we should think not of the post-Kantian realist/idealist dichotomy, but of the older, scholastic, realism/nominalism distinction. Kuhn is not among those who challenge the absolute existence of scientific entities or phenomena, nor among those who query the truth conditions for theoretical propositions. Instead he believes that the classifications, categories and possible descriptions that we deploy are very much of our own devising. But rather than leaving this as a mystery about how human categories come into being, he now makes the creation and adjustment of schemes of classification part of his definition of a revolution:

What characterizes revolutions is, thus, change in several of the taxonomic categories prerequisite to scientific description and generalization. That change, furthermore, is an adjustment not only of criteria relevant to categorization, but also of the way in which objects and situations are distributed among pre-existing categories.

I read that as a species of nominalism, and name it revolutionary nominalism, because the transitions in systems of categories occur during those revolutionary breaks with the past whose structures Kuhn proposes to describe. It is also, of course, an historicized nominalism, because it gives an historical account (or is it only an historical metaphor?) of the genesis and transformation of systems of naming. It also has the great value of being local rather than global, for although Kuhn includes big events among his revolutions (Lavoisier, Copernicus) he insists that most revolutions apply only within a small community of, say, one hundred main researchers.

Kuhn's revolutionary nominalism invites histories of category change, but it may seem that the objects of the sciences, although described by changing systems of categories, are not themselves historically constituted. Yet what are the objects? Do they include voltaic cells, for example? Do they include such phenomena as the deflection of a magnetic needle by a steady electric current, or Faraday's more ingenious devices, the electric generator and the electric dynamo? These are not eternal items in the inventory of the universe, but came into existence at very specific times. Nor am I content to say that the inventions are dated, while the phenomena and laws of nature that they employ are eternal. I have been urging for some time that one of the chief activities of the experimenter in the physical sciences is quite literally to create phenomena that did not exist before. Moreover most of physical science (as opposed to astronomy) is about phenomena that did not exist until people brought them into being. What physicists have from the 1870s been calling 'effects' (the photo-electric effect, the Zeeman effect, the Compton effect, the Josephson effect) are mostly phenomena which do not exist, at least in a pure state, anywhere in unpolluted nature, yet they are arguably what physics is, or has come to be, *about*. A more detailed and more guarded statement of this idea is given in my recent book *Representing and Intervening*. I put it in a more blatant way here to suggest that there is a case (of sorts) for saying that the very objects of physical science are not merely recategorized and rearranged, as Kuhn says, but brought into being by human ingenuity.

If I go to this extreme, is not my proposed distinction between human and natural science in ruins? Is it not the case that the objects of natural science become 'historically constituted'? I do not think so. Indeed I have developed a return to serious consideration of experimental science precisely to urge a good many realist, anti-idealist, anti-nominalist conclusions. I claim in the 'representing' half of *Representing and Intervening* that in principle no debates at the level of theorizing will settle any of those realism/anti-realism debates in the philosophy of natural science. I urge, in the 'intervening' half, that recognition of the facts of experimental life and of changing the world leads powerfully to scientific realism. You will detect one source of my admiration for Brecht's direct materialism that puts 'manipulation' rather than 'thinking' as the source of realism. My 'experimental realism' no more invites nominalism than Brecht's materialism. I think that the physical phenomena that are created by human beings are rather resilient to theoretical change. Kuhn's own example of the voltaic cell serves me well.

Kuhn writes that Volta saw his invention on analogy with the Leyden jar. Volta's description of it is strange, and we cannot credit his drawings, for they build in the wrong analogies. But the thing worked. Current did flow. Once that had been done physics never looked back. Likewise, the photo-electric effect was perhaps first produced in 1829 by Becquerel. Various photo-electric manifestations were induced throughout the nineteenth century. One can construct a Kuhnian argument that the effect was not properly 'discovered' until the time of Lenard (1902) or even Einstein and the theory of photons (1905). Certainly once we had the theory we were able to use the phenomena we had begun to create. Automatic doors at supermarkets, and television, were not too far behind. But if (as some have urged) the photon approach needs drastic revision or revolutionary rejection, the supermarket doors will still go on working. Phenomena are resilient to theory. Elementary physics may teach a completely different story about how they work, but work they will. Even if, to re-quote Kuhn, 'there is an adjustment not only of criteria relevant to categorization, but also of the way in which objects and situations are distributed among pre-existing categories', the phenomena which we have created will still exist and the inventions will work. We may lose interest in them. We may replace them by more useful or interesting phenomena. We might lose the skills needed to produce a phenomenon (no one can work brass today the way that a nineteenth-century laboratory assistant could work brass, and I am sure most of the old skills for polishing lenses are now obsolete). I am the last philosopher to forget the radical changes in experimental technology. I still hold that the objects of the physical sciences are largely created by people, *and* that once created, there is no reason except human backsliding why they should not continue to persist.

Thus I claim that Kuhn leads us into a 'revolutionary nominalism' which makes nominalism less mysterious by describing the historical processes whereby new categories and distributions of objects come in to being. But I assert that a seemingly more radical step, literal belief in the creation of phenomena, shows why the objects of the sciences, although brought into being at moments of time, are not historically constituted. They are phenomena thereafter, regardless of what happens. I call this 'experimental realism'.

Never shy to add a few more 'isms' to our ismically troubled world. I would say that my position is strikingly similar to that evolved by Gaston Bachelard's 'applied rationalism and technical materialism'. No other philosopher or historian so assiduously studied the realities of experimental life, nor was anyone less inclined than he to suppose that the mind is unimportant (his applied rationalism). Fifty years ago he was teaching that epistemological breaks occur in science (e.g., 'the photo-electric effect represents an absolute discontinuity in the history of the sciences'). At the same time he believed in scientific accumulation and *connaissance approchée*. What we accumulate are *experimental techniques* and *styles of reasoning*. Anglophone philosophy of science has too much debated the question of whether theoretical *knowledge* accumulates. Maybe it does not. So what? Phenomena and reasons accumulate.

Having thus made a slight obeisance towards Bachelard I pass to one of his spiritual descendants, namely, Michel Foucault. I shall try to be aware of one of Addison's warnings in *The Spectator*. 'A few general rules, extracted out of the French authors, with a certain cant of words, has sometimes set up an illiterate and heavy writer for a most judicious and formidable critic.'[1]

V Making up people

At the end of a recent review of Rorty's *Consequences of Pragmatism*, Bernard Williams first quotes Rorty quoting Foucault, 'the being of language continues to shine ever brighter on the horizon'. He then goes on to say that unless we keep sense

[1] *Spectator* 291 (Saturday, 2 Feb.):1711–12.

that science finds ways out of the cell of words, and if we do not recover the sense that pursuing science is one of our essential experiences of being constrained by the truth, we shall find that the brightness of language on the horizon turns out to be that of the fire in which the supremely bookish hero of Canetti's *Auto Da Fé* immolated himself in his library.

Such games of meta-meta-quoting invite a little burning, but I have two reasons for quoting Williams. The minor one, something of an aside, is that Williams himself may be trapped within the cell of words. The way out of Williams' cell is not to be constrained by the truth but to create phenomena. Only within a theory-dominated verbalistic philosophy of science is 'pursuing science one of our essential experiences of being constrained by the truth'. Let us take a recent example of an important discovery. The event in question happened three months ago. It bore out some guesses made by Fermi many years before. He thought that there must be a particle, a weak elementary particle or boson W, which was in some sense the 'carrier' of weak neutral currents (just as the electron carries ordinary charged currents). Around 1970 people were trying to find W, but then the high energy physics community switched to studying weak neutral currents themselves. They regarded W as a mere hypothetical entity, a figment of our imagination. Only in this decade was the search resumed, at very much higher energy levels than Fermi had thought necessary. Finally, in January 1983, CERN announced it had located W in proton-antiproton decay at 540 GeV. There is a complex history of science story to tell about the shift away from a search for W and then back. There certainly were constraints, but not 'constraints of truth'. I do not suppose there is a true theory of truth, but there is an instructive one, namely the redundancy theory, which says that 'p is true' says no more than p. If something verbal constrained the earlier experimenters, it was a p, not the truth of p. What really constrained research workers was a need for greater energy sources; one had to wait for the next generation in order to create the sought for phenomena involving proton-antiproton decay. There were constraints all over the place, but none of them were constraints of truth, unless by vicious semantic ascent we express the constraints using the redundant word 'true'.

The redundancy theory of truth is instructive but defective. I refer not to its formal defects, but to its philosophical ones. It makes it seem as if 'is true' is merely redundant, but harmless. I think that it does invite semantic ascent, and takes us up the ladder to that cell of words in which philosophers, not excluding Williams, confine themselves. If there is an interesting theory of truth to discuss at the moment, it will lie in Foucault's own 'suggestions to be further tested and evaluated':

'Truth' is to be understood as a system of ordered procedures for the production, regulation, distribution, circulation and operation of statements.

'Truth' is linked in a circular relation with systems of power which produce and sustain it, and to effects of power which it induces and which extend it.

We should, if we have a philosophical interest in truth, care about how statements come into being as candidates for being true or false, and as possible objects of knowledge. But even here 'truth' is redundant, for we are concerned simply with how statements come into being.

So much by way of aside. What of Williams' critique of Foucault? My second thoughts on *The Order of Things* not withstanding, Williams' remarks seem curiously misplaced. Foucault's books are mostly about practices and how they affect and are affected by the talk in which we embed them. The upshot is less a fascination with words, than with people and institutions, with what we do for people and to people. He does have a noble obsession with what he takes to be oppression: the asylum, the prison, the hospital, public hygiene and forensic medicine. His view of these practices may be entirely wrong. Some say that he has already done untold harm to wretched disturbed people who are released on the streets of the American metropolis because Foucault has convinced doctors that the disturbed ought not to be constrained. But one thing is clear. Without wishing in any way to undervalue the important political activities of Charles Taylor, Foucault, vastly more than anyone else invited to contribute to this volume, has not been locked in a cell of words. Moreover, it is precisely his intellectual work, his philosophical work, that directs our attention away from our talk and on to our practices.

I am not denying that Foucault is verbal. Few people have read his first book, about the surrealist Raymond Roussell. Roussell seems to be the very epitome of the man in the cell of words. One of his books is 'How I have written some of my books'. He says he would try to find a sentence such that, by changing one letter in one of the words, you change the meaning of each of the words in the sentence, as well as the grammar. (I hope no one at MIT hears of this.) Then you write down the first sentence at the front of your novel, and carry on until you end your book with the second sentence. He wrote a book, 'Impressions of Egypt', and then toured Egypt to make sure nothing in the book was true. He came of good stock. His mad rich mother chartered a yacht to make a voyage to India. When she got near the coastline she screwed up her telescope, said, 'Now I have seen India' and sailed home. Roussell killed himself. This can all be read at one level as the hyperparisian linguistic obsession. But a caricature, even if lived seriously, may also be read as directing us to the exact opposite.

Whatever be the point of the Roussell phase, let us consider the main sequence of Foucault's work, the madhouse, the clinic, the prison, sexuality, and in general the intermeshing of 'knowledge' and 'power'. I have remarked that Kuhn says nothing about the social sciences or knowledge of human beings. Likewise Foucault says nothing about the physical sciences. His remarks about what we charmingly call the life sciences are chiefly, although not entirely, directed at how we interfere with human lives. I have heard Foucault criticized for being scared of physical science. Let us instead consider the hypothesis that there is something fundamentally correct about the division of labour, Kuhn to the physical sciences, and Foucault to human affairs.

I shall focus on only one thing, making a specific contrast with Kuhn's revolutionary nominalism. The problem with scholastic nominalism, I said, is that it leaves our interaction with, and description of, the world a complete mystery. We can well understand why the word 'pencil' nicely sorts out some objects. We manufacture pencils; that is why they exist. Nominalism about human artefacts is no problem. It is nominalism about grass, trees and stars that is the problem. How can our words fit the earth and heavens, if there are not, prior to us, grass, trees and stars? A strict and universal nominalism is a preposterous mystery. What, however, about categories applying to people?

People are alive or dead, tall or short, strong or weak, creative or plodding, foolish or intelligent. These categories arise from the nature of people themselves, although we are by now well aware how 'intelligence' can be warped by quotients. But consider the categories so much worked over by Foucault, involving madness, criminality and other kinds of deviancy. Consider even his assertion (which I do not quite believe) about what a soldier was in medieval times, and what he became with the new institutions of discipline and uniform: soldiers themselves became different kinds of people. We may begin to grasp at a different kind of nominalism, which I call *dynamic nominalism*. Categories of people come into existence at the same time as kinds of people come into being to fit those categories, and there is a two-way interaction between these processes.

That is not very sensational, as most of the interesting things about us are what we choose to do, or try not to do, how we behave or misbehave. I subscribe to G.E.M. Anscombe's view in *Intention*, that by and large intentional action is action under a description. So there have to be descriptions. If we can show that descriptions change, some dropping in, some dropping out, then there simply is a change in what we can (as a matter of logic) do or not do. One can reread many of Foucault's books as in part stories about the connection between certain kinds of description coming into being or going out of existence, and certain kinds of people coming into being or going out of existence. More important, one can do this kind of work explicitly oneself. I study the dullest of subjects, nineteenth-century statistics. It turns out to be one aspect of what Foucault calls a 'biopolitics of the population', that 'gave rise to comprehensive measures, statistical assessments, and interventions aimed at the entire social body or at groups taken as a whole'. What do I find at the beginning of the great avalanche of numbers, around 1820? Nothing other than the statistics of deviancy, of madness, suicide, prostitution, vagrancy, crime against the person, crime against property, drunkenness, *les miserables*. These vast arrays of data are called *analyse morale*. We find constant subdivisions and rearrangements of, for example, the mad, as the counting progresses. We find classifications of over 4000 different criss-crossing motives for murder. I do not believe that mad people of these sorts, or these motives for murder, in general existed until there came into being the practice of counting them.

Constantly new ways of counting people were devised. New slots were created into which people could fall and be counted. Even the decennial censuses in the different states amazingly show that the categories into which people fall change every ten years. This is partly because social change generates new categories of people, but I think the countings were not mere reportings. They were part of an elaborate, well-meaning, indeed innocent creating of new kinds of ways for people to be, and people innocently 'chose' to fall into these new categories.

Foucault writes of 'two poles of development', one being the biopolitics, the other, an 'anatomopolitics of the human body' concerned with the individual, the body and its actions. That is not something I know enough about to make informed judgment. I did follow up one lead, however, and contend that at least one kind of insanity was invented, and then disturbed people to a certain extent chose to be mad in that way. The case is multiple personality. No more than one or two multiples are recorded, per generation, up to 1875. Then there is a host, and this kind of insanity had a quite explicit political role. Pierre Janet, the distinguished psychiatrist, recounts how one Félida X, who attracted much attention in 1875, was of supreme importance. 'Her history was the great argument of which the positivist psychologists made use at the time of the heroic struggles against the spiritualist dogmatism of Cousin's school. But for Félida, it is not certain that there would be a professorship of psychology at the Collège de France.' Janet held precisely that professorship. After Félida there was a torrent of multiple personalities, which has not quite dried up. Do I mean that there were virtually no multiples before Félida? Is it not just that doctors merely failed to record them? I may be in error, but what I mean is that only after the doctors had done their work was there this syndrome for a disturbed person to adopt. The syndrome bloomed in France, and then moved to America, which is now its home.

I have no idea what such a dynamic nominalism will amount to. Let us however consider its implications for history and philosophy of the human sciences. Like Kuhn's revolutionary nominalism, Foucault's dynamic nominalism is an historicized nominalism. But there is something fundamentally different. History plays an essential role in the constitution of the objects, where the objects are the people and ways in which they behave. Despite my radical doctrine about the experimental creation of phenomena, I hold the common-sense view that the photo-electric effect is timeless at least to this extent: if one does do certain things, certain phenomena will appear. They never did appear until our century. We made them. But what happens is constrained by 'the world'. The categories created by what Foucault calls anatomopolitics and biopolitics, and the 'intermediary cluster of relations' between the two politics, are constituted in an essentially historical setting. Yet it is these very categories in terms of which the human sciences venture to describe us. Moreover, they bring into being new categories which, in part, bring into being new kinds of people. We remake the world, but we make up people. Just before the warning about heavy writing and of French cant, with which I closed Parable IV, Addison wrote, 'it is very certain that an author, who has not learned the art of distinguishing words and things and of ranging his thoughts and setting them in proper lights, whatever notions he may have, will lose himself in confusion and obscurity'. I think that we shall lose ourselves in confusion and obscurity for some time yet, in the so-called social and human sciences, because in those domains the distinction between word and thing is constantly blurred. It is precisely experimental methods that I take to be essential to the physical sciences and which, I claim, make Kuhn's historicized revolutionary nominalism fall short of a strict nominalism. The experimental methods of the human sciences are something else. The lack of a sharp distinction between word and thing is at the root of Wittgenstein's famous concluding remark, that in psychology (and the like) 'there are experimental methods and *conceptual confusion*'. Here Foucault's 'archaeology' may yet prove useful, not in order to 'display the shape of the flybottle' but at least to grasp the interrelations of 'power' and 'knowledge' that literally constitute us as human beings. That would be the strongest impact of history upon philosophy. But until we can do that job better, it will have to remain one more parable, deliberately open, like all parables, to far too many interpretations.

6

Seven thinkers and how they grew: Descartes, Spinoza, Leibniz; Locke, Berkeley, Hume; Kant

BRUCE KUKLICK

Literary, philosophical, and historical studies often rely on a notion of what is *canonical*. In American philosophy scholars go from Jonathan Edwards to John Dewey; in American literature from James Fenimore Cooper to F. Scott Fitzgerald; in political theory from Plato to Hobbes and Locke; in literary criticism from Aristotle to T. S. Eliot (or perhaps Harold Bloom); in economic thought from Adam Smith to John Maynard Keynes. The texts or authors who fill in the blanks from A to Z in these, and other intellectual traditions, constitute the canon, and there is an accompanying narrative that links text to text or author to author, a 'history of' American literature, economic thought, and so on. The most conventional of such histories are embodied in university courses and the textbooks that accompany them. This essay examines one such course, the History of Modern Philosophy, and the texts that helped to create it.

If a philosopher in the United States were asked why the seven people in my title comprise Modern Philosophy, the initial response would be: they were the best, and there are historical and philosophical connections among them. This is a quick answer because reflection usually makes the philosopher slightly uncomfortable. In England Modern Philosophy is: Descartes; Locke, Berkeley, Hume; and only recently Kant. In France it is heavily weighted the other way – toward Cartesian rationalism: Descartes, Geulincz, Malebranche – and then a quick trip through the eighteenth century to Kant. In Germany we have what might be called a *Drang nach the Critique* – Liebniz, Wolff, Kant.[1] Analyzing how the American group

---

[1] My knowledge of English ideas comes from the examination schools of Oxford and Cambridge. But Scruton 1981 indicates that the American version may be now at least Anglo-American. A good example of French treatments is Brehier, 1930 and 1938. Descartes and Cartesianism get eighty pages; Malebranche, twenty-eight; John Locke and English Philosophy, twenty-five; Hume, seventeen; Condillac, eighteen; Rousseau, fifteen. Some classic German treatments are cited later in the text.

was established contributes, at least, to refining my philosopher's answer
to the question, 'Why them?'; but also says something about the business
of writing the history of philosophy.[2]

I begin with the history of ideas in the sixteenth and seventeenth century.
An important strand in the thought of the Renaissance humanists was their
criticism of what they saw as the Aristotelian logic-chopping of the
scholastics. The humanists argued that philosophy had to be the guide to
life and that the scholastics, in concentrating on certain aspects of
Aristotle's logic, had removed philosophy from the affairs of men. On the
contrary, some of the humanists urged that rhetoric had to be elevated to an
equal place with logic; one would then have the ability not only to grasp the
truth but to convince others of it. This notion received its most extreme
statement in the work of Peter Ramus, whose *Dialecticae* was critical to
European intellectual controversy in the century after its initial publication
in 1543. Ramus invented a new way of understanding the world – his
dialectic – which synthesized logic and rhetoric. The novel method was a
mode of analysis that enabled the learned to grasp the structure of certain
propositions and, therefore, if the propositions were true, the structure of
the world *and*, finally, the compelling manner of expressing these truths.
Ramist humanism was the philosophic backbone of much Calvinist
theology, and in England was important to the writing of the late-
sixteenth-century Puritans in Cambridge, Alexander Richardson and
William Ames. Ames in particular was a figure of eminence in the early
seventeenth century. He never set foot in the New World, although he was
planning such an expedition on his death in the second quarter of the
century. Amesean ideas and texts, however, were central to the American
Puritans and formed the core of their thought in the seventy-five-year
period after the founding of Harvard in 1636. In 1714 the American Samuel
Johnson, soon to be a tutor at Yale and known to be a teacher of Jonathan
Edwards, wrote his *Encyclopedia of Philosophy*. This book does not
embody abiding knowledge about the universe, but it does embody the
received philosophical erudition in early-eighteenth-century America.
And Johnson himself was regarded before his apostasy – he converted to
Episcopalianism – as a leading New England thinker. In the *Encyclopedia*
he gave a brief sketch of philosophy since Adam. The summary of
developments since the apostolic age bears quotation at length:

From Greece philosophy was introduced into Italy and thence into Germany,

---

[2] Studies of our understanding of the history of philosophy are rare, but a recent excellent
book is Loeb 1981. Readers ought also to consult: the special issue of *The Monist* 1969;
Mandelbaum 1976; and Walton 1977. One study reflecting on the formation of the
American literary tradition which has also been useful is Baym 1981. Skinner 1978 also
takes up the concerns of the canonical.

Holland, Spain, France, and England. In these countries not a few of the greatest men were found; for their doctrine was Christian. Among these innumerable men the principal sects were Platonists, Peripatetics, and Eclectics. The leader of the eclectic sect was that great man, Ramus, at whose feet, as it were, there followed Richardson and then Ames, the greatest of them, followed him; and we follow Ames.

Voilà! Here is the tradition that was the first focus of speculation in America: Plato, Aristotle, Peter Ramus, Alexander Richardson, William Ames, and Samuel Johnson of Yale.[3]

This is a mildly inaccurate view of the tradition in the early eighteenth century. Toward the end of the seventeenth century Cartesian thought, usually interpreted as an extension of Ramist ideas, was read and esteemed in America. And after 1690 a highly rationalistic version of Locke became known. By the middle of the eighteenth century it is fair to say that the group of thinkers I have just mentioned was no longer taken to encapsulate all wisdom. The new philosophical learning of Locke (and Newton) had become popular, although it was still a Locke comprehended in a Cartesian context – a Locke seen through the lens of the English rationalist Newtonian Samuel Clarke. This Locke was mainly used in 'modernizing' Calvinist theology – this is the burden of the work of Jonathan Edwards.[4] By the end of the eighteenth century in America, philosophy had begun to emerge as an independent enterprise, but there was no longer an agreed and coherent set of doctrines to which a few men had contributed. On the one hand, the tradition crucial to the Ramist world view had ceased to be important for the high religious thinkers working with the new framework that Edwards had established. On the other hand, philosophers in the American colleges had begun to view Descartes and Locke as 'great men', whose works had to be read; but the two were not conceived as forming or being part of a developing dialogue.

The turn of the century marks the beginning of a recognizably 'modern' tradition. The thought of the British and French enlightenment attractive to the likes of Franklin and Jefferson was viewed with hostility by more theologically and philosophically informed thinkers. Hume in particular was regarded with both fear and contempt. But in an adulterated Scottish Enlightenment theologians and philosophers found an antidote to Hume that began a half-century-long love affair between American thinkers and the 'natural' realism of the Scots. Theologians in divinity schools who used philosophy as a backdrop for their studies, and philosophers in the American colleges who worked on recognizably philosophical problems

[3] This account draws on Flower and Murphey 1977 (the quote from Johnson in *ibid.*: 1, 20); and Murphey 1979.
[4] The basis for my summary is from Flower and Murphey (1977:1 365–73).

on their own, both swore allegiance to Thomas Reid and found in his work a series of persuasive answers to Hume's skepticism. As the nineteenth century wore on a clear tradition of thought emerged. Read in the light of subsequent developments in Scotland, Locke was interpreted in a manner allied to the one that textbooks present today – that of a common-sense realism and empiricism; the rationalist Locke became less important and so too did his predecessor Descartes. And the extraordinary triumph of Reid and his followers made Hume a minor figure. There was a natural transition from the empiricist Locke to the empiricist Reid, but this Locke was still not our Locke. He was someone who, whatever his virtues, exemplified the major defect of seventeenth-century thought – adherence to a representative theory of knowledge. The passage from Locke to Reid consisted in the latter's correcting the mistake of the former by a theory of direct perception. Reid's thought was seen to have been strengthened in its details by his student, Dugald Stewart. Moreover, well into the second half of the nineteenth century Americans believed that in the work of Sir William Hamilton the Scottish position had overcome Kant's criticism of Reid in the *Critique of Pure Reason*. Hamilton was a man of immense erudition; he brought German thought to Britain in the 1830s and held the Chair of logic and metaphysics at Edinburgh. In the United States he was recognized as having refined Scottish ideas to take account of whatever was valuable in Kant. So here we have a second tradition in America, one that was dominant until 1870 or thereabouts: Locke, Reid, Stewart, and Sir William Hamilton.

In 1865 John Stuart Mill published his *Examination of the Philosophy of Sir William Hamilton*; Mill was at the zenith of his career and Hamilton, who had been dead ten years, could not respond. Mill was also able to play on the fragmentary and unsystematic character of Hamilton's corpus – much of his work had been posthumously published by his students – and to convict Hamilton of what seemed to many to be obvious contradictions. Writing in a masterly polemical style, Mill demolished Hamilton's reputation – not only in Britain but also in the United States.

The success of Mill's *Examination* is the crucial event in understanding the development of the contemporary view of Modern Philosophy in America, but it was not a personal success for Mill. On the negative side he not only ruined Hamilton but also destroyed the credibility of the entire Scottish reply to Hume. Mill left only Locke standing. On the positive side Mill made what I would roughly call the position of skeptical empiricism again something to be conjured with. But it was not Mill, either in *The Examination*, or his *Logic*, who became required reading; rather, Hume was given the empiricist place of prominence.

Mill's *Examination* was well known in American philosophic circles by

1870 and within ten years the outlines of the twentieth-century tradition were established. For in casting about for an 'answer' to Hume, the theologically oriented philosophers in America began to confront *The Critique of Pure Reason* directly rather than through the vehicle of its Scottish interpretations. In England, Kant was also important, but the deep religious skepticism. Philosophers were pleased to learn and come to United States long after he had gone out of fashion in England. In America the respectable Kant replaced the tarnished Hamilton as the conqueror of religious skepticism. Philosophers were pleased to learn and come to believe that, in awakening Kant from his dogmatic slumbers, Hume led directly to his successor and to his refutation. Thus, the beginning of Modern Philosophy: Locke, Hume, Kant.

I want to sketch how this outline was filled in, but it is first necessary to say something about the intrusion into American philosophical discourse of the textbook in the history of philosophy. The American college library had for a long time been the repository of textbooks used to inculcate philosophy. These texts were of two sorts – rewritten extracts of the thoughts of favored thinkers or synoptic original surveys of the field of moral philosophy with a few pat solutions to problems in what we might call the philosophy of mind. In 1871 and 1873 the two volumes of Friedrich Überweg's *History of Philosophy from Thales to the Present Time*[5] was translated from German – it had originally been published from 1862 to 1866. Überweg's work was popular in the United States but actually only exemplified the growing interest in speculative quarters of 'the history of philosophy' as conceived of in Germany. What this meant for the Americans was that philosophy consciously came to be seen, first, as a collective endeavour in which humanity had *'embodied in scientific conceptions its views of the world and its judgements of life'* – to quote the 1893 American translation of Windelband's *History*.[6] Second, it came to be seen as a dialectic in which there was an intrinsic drive in the very nature of thought – to paraphrase the still sophisticated American *History of Philosophy* of Frank Thilly.[7] Finally, it came to be seen as leading inevitably through the Germans to the superior ideas of the present. As Arthur Kenyon Rogers said in his extraordinary *Student's History of Philosophy*, he achieved the purposes of his book 'through the medium of a somewhat mild reproduction of the Hegelian philosophy of history'.[8] Rogers' book was first published in 1901 but went through many editions and reprintings. It is a proof text of an American 'History of Modern Philosophy'. The German

[5] Überweg 1871, 1873.   [6] Windelband 1893: 9 (italics in original).
[7] Thilly 1914: 1–2. The preface of the third edition, revised (Thilly and Wood 1956:v–viii), should also be read.
[8] Rogers 1907: vi. This 'New Edition, Revised' is the earliest one I have been able to obtain.

works are not, but in the last two decades of the nineteenth century they stood as models for the Americans of what a genuine history of modern thought should be like and the way thinkers ought to be linked.

These models in conjunction with the three philosophers still viable after Mill's attack – Locke, Hume, and Kant – were all that was essential to produce something more than a series of 'great thinkers' or even a dominant tradition of discourse – the *canon* of Modern Philosophy. To show how it was filled in I first call attention to an indigenous renewal of interest in Descartes, and a concern for Berkeley inspired by the American respect for the British neo-Hegelians.

Kant raised for the Americans the whole issue of the intelligibility of representational realism, and they found in Descartes a realist on whom could be blamed a whole series of errors that Kantian thought could correct. Locke too was a representational realist, but in the United States he was not merely and solely an epistemologist; he was also the intellectual father of the Constitution. He was 'America's philosopher', 'the great and celebrated Mr Locke', whose claim on American affections dated from the Revolution. Descartes' place in the canon is in part a testimony to the culture's veneration for Locke, and in part testimony to the desire of the nineteenth-century American thinkers to engage in philosophical scapegoating. Descartes emerged as the leading *rationalist*. Uninterested in scientific observation, he could be contrasted to the empiricist Locke. This development was intellectually coordinate with the rise of German idealism, which in its most extravagant form could be seen as the unfortunate fruition of an unbridled rationalism. But this fruition would only be revealed after World War I. In the late nineteenth century, Cartesian rationalism was singled out to highlight what was sensible about Lockean empiricism.

Berkeley emerged as a major figure for different reasons. Here the Americans were influenced by British idealists who resurrected Berkeley as a precursor of their own Hegelian doctrines. The Americans drew on the work of Alexander Campbell Fraser and Thomas Hill Green: the first rediscovered Berkeley for English readers; the second led the fight in Britain for acknowledging the reality of the self as conscious entity.

Charles Peirce's influential articles of the 1870s and Josiah Royce's enormously significant 1885 *Religious Aspects of Philosophy* typify what happened to Descartes and Berkeley in the United States. Neither American was a defender of Cartesian representational realism, but each of them – Royce on the strength of Peirce's example – took Descartes as the prime example of what had gone wrong with modern philosophy and of the crucial arguments for a series of erroneous views: dualism, *a priori* theorizing about science, and the causal theory of perception. Their responses to Berkeley were more complex: Peirce wanted to maintain Berkeley's pluralistic idealism while damning his nominalism; Royce thought of Berkeley as someone halfway along the road to the correct position of absolute idealism. For both Americans, nonetheless, their treatment of Berkeley functioned similarly to their treatment of Descartes – Descartes underwent a revival that placed him at the beginning of the canon; Berkeley entered the canon from nowhere. Certainly, in the case of Berkeley, one can see that his interpolation into the group of thinkers as someone chronologically between Locke and Hume led subsequently to the *post hoc ergo propter hoc* conclusions that Berkeley followed Locke's assumptions and that Hume, getting Berkeley's message, followed them completely. So Descartes was elevated in part because no one was willing to attack Locke; and Berkeley's elevation reflected in part the impact of the metropolis on the province.

It is more difficult to see how Descartes' successors were joined to the other five. Spinoza and Leibniz were both late-comers to the canon and even today, I suspect, are most likely to be dropped from 'Modern Philosophy' if one gets bogged down in the *Meditations* or if one wants to spend a great deal of time on *Human Understanding*. I have an educated guess about them.

In 1892 Royce wrote a widely read study called *The Spirit of Modern Philosophy*. As George Herbert Mead recalled, there should be 'a special edition of *The Spirit of Modern Philosophy* bound in tooled morocco with illuminated borders and initialed paragraphs and illustrated with Raphaelite art – to symbolize what it meant to young men when Royce first taught in Cambridge'.[9] The second half of this book tried to show how Royce's idealism was compatible with Darwin, but the first half was a history of philosophy. Although Royce's work was admittedly idiosyncratic, he was a leading authority. What he meant by Modern Philosophy was a survey of the (for him) more or less contemporary post-Kantians – Fichte, Hegel, and Schopenhauer. But his conception of what to us is the period of Modern Philosophy is intriguing. Its culmination was Kant; and before that Royce conceived the period as containing two eras. First, 'the deepest speculator' of the seventeenth century, Spinoza; second, the period 'from Spinoza to Kant'.[10] Why such veneration for Spinoza? Simply put: Royce saw Spinoza as the philosopher before Kant most clearly embodying the truth Royce had reached in 1892 – the truth of absolute idealism.

Some fifteen years later another tract for the times was written that is important for understanding the history of philosophy as it was then conceived. In the first chapter of *Pragmatism* William James distinguished between tough- and tenderminded philosophers, between what he called

[9] Mead 1916–17:169.   [10] Royce 1892: 41, 9.

empiricists and rationalists. James' understanding of the history of philosophy *per se* is not at issue, but among other things James called attention to Spinoza and Leibniz as monist and pluralist minds, and to Leibniz as someone who was a pluralist despite being a rationalist – according to James' typology rationalists were monists, empiricists were pluralists. For the purposes of this discussion it needs to be pointed out that James' work is most concerned to validate his own pluralism in a climate of contemporary discussion that he perceived as entirely if wrong-headedly monistic. Royce was a crucial antagonist, and the dispute between him and James defined the limits of philosophical debate in the United States for a generation. James surely was aware of the great prominence that Royce had given to Spinoza. While even a casual acquaintance with James' view of Leibniz makes apparent that he was no defender of Leibniz's optimism, it is also apparent that James was eager to find in the speculative past a set of issues similar to the ones that impelled his own thinking. My hunch is that Spinoza and Leibniz occupy the places they do as tokens of the importance of the monist–pluralist debate of the early twentieth century. Only some such view of the flowering of the canon – that is, of a team of Spinoza and Leibniz – explains why Leibniz is more usually depicted as the successor (or alternative) to Spinoza, rather than (with equal plausibility) the critic of Lockean empiricism. So we have: Descartes, Spinoza, Leibniz. I have already intimated that in America the rationalism of modern philosophy was an outgrowth of the impact of absolute idealism in the late nineteenth century. Here is more evidence to the same effect. In the United States James did much to credit the existence of the tradition of rationalism; he also did much to discredit its worth in contrast with empiricism, pluralism, and a respect for science.

Descartes, Spinoza, Leibniz; Locke, Berkeley, Hume; Kant. But that is not the end of the story. The question that ought to occur is: but what happened to Hegel? And the straight answer to that question is: although he may have been knocked about previously, he was killed in World War I.

In late-nineteenth-century American philosophical circles there were more Hegelians of various sorts than one could shake a stick at. Although Royce was not a Hegelian, his conception of the history of thought led to and through Hegel. Even William James, as I have pointed out, tended to define himself in opposition to Hegel's followers. George Sylvester Morris, who for a time presided over the not inconsequential Hopkins–Minnesota–Michigan axis of burgeoning professional philosophy, better exemplified the sort of powerful figure who encouraged the study of Hegel. Morris was additionally the translator of Überweg's *History of Philosophy*. Nonetheless, the best example is the work of Morris' Hegelian student John Dewey.

In 1884 Dewey wrote an article entitled 'Kant and philosophic method'. What one finds in the essay is a full conception of the twentieth-century history of philosophy evidently deriving from mid-nineteenth-century German ideas about speculative history. Dewey argued that there was an inner logic in the history of thought that led through the empiricists and rationalists to Kant and his heir, inheritor, and completer, Hegel. Four years later in 1888 Dewey published a significant book on *Leibniz's New Essays Concerning the Human Understanding*, part of a series edited by Morris analyzing great treatises of German philosophy. But the intent of *Leibniz's New Essays* was not simply to interpret Leibniz. Dewey also wanted to reconstruct the canon he had so recently sanctioned. The treatment of Leibniz was Hegelian: Dewey found in him answers to the questions of moment to late-nineteenth-century American students of German idealism. He wrote that Leibniz anticipated the treatment of perception of the natural world that came to fruition with idealism; Leibniz's concern was how the physical contained within it the seeds of the spiritual. More than that, Dewey was concerned to show that most of the empiricist tradition was irrelevant to understanding the course of modern philosophy. The canon was Locke (with the *Essay*), Leibniz (in his rebuttal of Locke), Kant, and Hegel. Dewey argued that although the common understanding was that Hume had awakened Kant from his dogmatic slumbers, it was more vital to recognize that prior to the awakening, Leibniz had already programmed Kant to write what he wrote after his sleep.[11] Suffice it to say that Hegel was very much part of the canon at the end of the nineteenth century.

During the first decade of the twentieth century his standing diminished with the rise of various forms of domestic realism. Yet the anti-idealist movement might have been a dubious challenge to Hegel's place in Modern Philosophy were it not for the war. The hysterical academic outcry against all things German from 1914 to 1918 is a well documented part of American social history, and there is no need to rehearse it here. In philosophy, however, it is worthwhile to note that the hysteria led to a vendetta against absolute idealism especially in so far as it had a social dimension – this monstrous form of Teutonic egoism in political life was a root cause of the war. After the war Hegel became, for Americans, a silly, pompous, and *defeated* figure, unworthy of the great tradition. Indeed, the wonder is not that Hegel vanished, but that Kant remained. And in line with this development the Kant who remained was not the Kant pregnant with elements of transcendent metaphysics. It was rather the Kant whom C. I. Lewis expounded, the austere transcendental epistemologist, not the transcendent metaphysician. To make the point in terms of the canon: the

[11] See Dewey 1969:428–35.

Kant of the canon synthesizes rationalism and empiricism; he is much less the father of Hegel.

Nothing I have said should be taken to imply that the seven men were not in some sense the best philosophers from 1605 (Bacon's *Advancement of Learning*) to 1788 (Reid's *Essay on the Active Powers*). Nor do I wish to dispute that there may be prominent philosophical or historical connections, or both, to be made among these thinkers. What I do want to say is that neither the intrinsic merits of the seven nor the connections among them are themselves sufficient to account for the place they hold as exemplars of Modern Philosophy.

In a complex fashion the canon reflects victors' history, 'complex' in two ways. First, the canonical seven were not just living disputants for the late nineteenth century to argue with; they were also emblems of the *problems* that gripped the important American philosophers and, accordingly, the whole philosophic community of that era. In terms of its impact in the period, Mill's *Examination* is far and away the book of most consequence that I have written about. Yet Mill did not make himself either in the *Examination* or the *Logic* a member of the canon; what he did was to point towards crucial problems – skepticism and its refutation – that Hume and Kant symbolized. Similarly, one cannot find a defender of Descartes' position in America; what one does find is that Descartes was believed to have set a cardinal problem. The relation of consciousness to its object in knowing was a puzzle that had to be resolved. For American philosophers Descartes had gotten things all wrong – Peirce and Royce at times almost depict him as a fool – but his work outlined a key epistemological issue. As I have argued, Spinoza was central to Royce's conscious canon, but it was Descartes, with whom Royce is more involved, who was first canonized. So it is victors' history *not* in the sense that the Golden Age merely contributed its personal heroes, but victors' history in the sense that the Golden Age bequeathed to us the men who were its deepest concerns *incarnate*.

Part of my purpose in presenting my earlier brief retrospect of traditions and great thinkers in the seventeenth, eighteenth and the first part of the nineteenth centuries was to indicate that things have changed.

The second way in which Modern Philosophy complexly represents victors' history is that the canon has been frozen in conjunction with the relegation to the university of the learning of all philosophic material. The historical profession has rigidly defined 'natural' historical periods – Renaissance, Reformation, and Modern history – and the philosophical profession has donated the entrenched course that is the subject of this essay. It is arguable that the institutionalization and bureaucratization of philosophy in the university may preserve the present canon, whatever historians might find to be the connections in the seventeenth- and eighteenth-century traditions and whatever they might find to be the intentions of the thinkers in these traditions. And the canon might be preserved whatever its relevance to living philosophical problems, although of course its existence also shapes philosophy's sense of what constitutes a problem worthy of study. Modern Philosophy may be 'there' in the curriculum almost like a museum piece. For those who established it the seven were fellow disputants as well as a repertoire of problems; today, if anything is significant, it is the problems. The reason for this development is that the course unit system may have constrained philosophers to pay homage to ancestors whom they no longer truly worship. So the history is victors' history in a second way: the system of higher education might have extended the length of the victory that was won well beyond what might have happened had the university not come to monopolize the study of philosophy and sealed the victory in ways that may have little to do with ideas at all. Surely, as this essay makes clear, traditions alter. But one reason why I have limited my use of the word 'canon' to the seven is to trade on its sacred connotations. We no longer dispute which books of the Bible are canonical, but we also no longer use them as the guide to life.

I want to conclude by elaborating on an issue that has in part propelled me to make this historical excursus. The excursus calls into question the enterprise of writing what is called the history of philosophy.

The enterprise obviously has an intrinsic evaluative dimension. Scholars write narratives about people somehow *worthy* of study. A history that dwelt equally on all persons who considered themselves to have had philosophic thoughts, or that allocated space to every such person on the basis of the size of the corpus of writings, would be rejected out of hand.

It is legitimate to write a history of philosophy governed by what was influential in a given era; that is, a study of thinkers whom others at the time regarded as significant. But such studies have a limited value and do not encapsulate the critical aspects of what we take to be 'the history of philosophy'. For example, we would acknowledge the usefulness, but also the constricted views, of a history of continental rationalism from, say, 1630 to 1730 that barely mentioned Spinoza and gave great attention to Christian Wolff as the fruition of the tradition. On the other side the notion of 'the history of philosophy' is not captured by the idea of a narrative about thinkers merely important to a contemporary writer; we want to rule out the approach of Bertrand Russell in *A History of Western Philosophy*. To return yet again to Kant's slumber, we don't want to say that Kant was awakened only to fall asleep again; we recognize that it is of little value to attribute importance or lack of importance to Kant on the basis of what some particular authority like Russell happens to believe.

The explication that best gets at what I think is the common understanding of the history of philosophy is something like the Charles Peircean conception of the continuing commitments of a temporally extended community. Somehow, we think, the community of philosophers – those who are living, those who are dead, and those who are yet to come – weeds out what is transient and holds on to what is enduring in the thought of the past: at any given time the accepted canon is likely to be flawed, containing unworthy philosophers or thoughts; but the best guide to have to what is worthwhile is the contemporary consensus of the competent; and it is likely that the philosophic wisdom captured by the group of worthies immortalized at any given time is more likely to reveal genuine wisdom than the group immortalized at some substantially earlier time; and the ultimate criterion for significant inclusion in the tradition is the imprimatur of some hypothetical future community that the present one fallibly and imperfectly tries to achieve. That is, what I have called the common conception bears a strong resemblance to that enunciated in Rogers' *Student's History* of 1901, depending on 'a somewhat mild reproduction of the Hegelian philosophy of history'. The developments that successive histories recount somehow reflect a growing order and intelligence.

It seems to me that my story of the evolution of the twentieth-century canon must cast some doubt on this last assertion. It may be that my history displays the cunning of reason. But I am more persuaded that if anyone thinks the cunning of reason is around, it is because this cunning is presumed. What the history *displays* is that various individuals possessed a modicum of varying kinds of philosophic talents. That canonical wisdom is attributed to someone may hang in part on something like 'intrinsic ability' validated by, attested to, or equated with the work of the community. But certainly histories of philosophy that rely on this sort of criterion for determining who to include, or that propound some theory of speculative advance or underlying structure, miss a great deal.

Consider intellectual elements that appear to be non-rational. Ideology was a factor – for example, the commitment to absolute idealism or to Locke. So too were what, for want of a better word, I would call certain tropes – for example, rationalism *versus* empiricism, monism *versus* pluralism. The struggle between philosophic fathers and their sons was also important: for example, Peirce's dislike of Descartes, or Dewey's veneration of Hegel. Finally, there are speculative fashions and fears: how else explain Berkeley and Hume?

Consider the non-intellectual social influences. The religious tone of nineteenth-century America helped to make Kant; the position of the

United States as a cultural province of England helped to make Berkeley; the reverence for Locke as the intellectual hero of the Constitutional period helped to make Descartes; World War I helped to break Hegel; and the academic clout of the most important American thinkers of the late nineteenth and early twentieth centuries enabled a certain vision of the seventeenth and eighteenth centuries to prevail.

Elevation to the canon also depends on disorder, on luck, on cultural transitions that if not random certainly do not reflect overriding purpose, on scholarly power-plays, and on the sheer glacial inertia of the institutions of higher education.[12] If history shows us this rag-tag result, then the common conception of the history of philosophy is no different from any other I have surveyed. The 'history of philosophy' is just a history of philosophers thought worthwhile by some other philosophers during a certain time.

We do not write the (or 'a') history of philosophy; what we write are histories of philosophers whom we think, or others think, are great.[13] R. G. Collingwood taught us long ago that historical narratives are answers to questions. My analysis of the history of modern philosophy then suggests that initially the questions historians of philosophy asked were: what past philosophers are great; and how are they connected to what interests us now? More recent historians of philosophy have even further reduced interrogative complexity. They ask only: how are the conventionally great

---

[12] A quantitative example may be of interest here. Frederick Copleston's justly praised multi-volume *History of Philosophy* contains several volumes on Modern Philosophy very much in the American vein. There are eighty pages on Hume and then a chapter less than half that length on 'Hume, For and Against', discussing responses to Hume; here Reid is allocated five pages (Copleston 1964). Does anyone really believe that Hume is fifteen times the philosopher Reid is? Or that those 'for' Hume, who wrote both before and after him, were so much less distinguished representatives of his kind of position that they should be regarded as just footnotes to him? And how does one justify a short omnibus chapter on these responses to Hume and a short book – the next in the series – on Kant when the latter is conceived, in the American style, as a further response? My questions are not meant to be *merely* rhetorical.

[13] Murphey (1979) takes this position, calling it historicism as opposed to presentism. But it seems to me he conflates two questions: The first is: (1) Can we recover the intentions of past thinkers or must we interpret them in such a way as to learn only what is significant to us? Those who say we can recover intentions would, I think, be called historicists; those who say we cannot, or write so that we learn only what is significant to us, are presentists. The second question is the one this essay is implicitly concerned to answer: (2) Can we write a certain kind of history of thought without evaluative presumptions about what a certain limited group takes to be worthwhile? The answer to this question, I am constrained to say, is no, and Murphey agrees. But how one answers (2) does not imply any answer to (1). Murphey seems to think that a *no* to (2) implies historicism. Not so. Indeed, it seems to me that if we are skeptical about the value of conventional history of philosophy, historicism will be more difficult to maintain. The recovery of intentions depends on our ability to isolate the community the author meant to communicate with and, so, to rule out meanings not available to him. A *no* to (2), I think, calls into question our ability to isolate this community; but this is not a topic to be explored in this essay.

philosophers related to what interests us now? I would suggest, in conclusion, that these are not particularly subtle queries. They avoid all variety of exploration of past ideas in exchange for learning what a sub-group of philosophic practitioners thinks is worthy in past thinking. The enterprise of the conventional history of philosophy does not rest on a mistake; but it does rest on a feeble inquisitiveness about the past.[14]

REFERENCES

Baym, Nina. 1981. 'Melodramas of beset manhood: how theories of American fiction exclude women writers', *American Quarterly* 33:123–39

Brehier, Emile. 1930. *The History of Philosophy*, vol. v, *The Eighteenth Century*, trans. Wade Baskin. Chicago: University of Chicago Press, 1967

Brehier, Emile. 1938. *The History of Philosophy*, vol. iv, *The Seventeenth Century*, trans. Wade Baskin. Chicago: University of Chicago Press, 1966

Copleston, Frederick. 1964. *History of Philosophy*, vol. v, *Modern Philosophy*, part ii, *British Philosophy*. New York: Doubleday

Dewey, John. 1969. *The Early Works of John Dewey, Volume 1, 1882–1888*. London and Amsterdam: Southern Illinois University Press

Flower, Elizabeth, and Murphey, Murray G. 1977. *A History of Philosophy in America*. 2 vols. New York: Putnams

Kuklick, Bruce. 1977. *The Rise of American Philosophy*. New Haven: Yale University Press

Kuklick, Bruce. 1985. *Churchmen and Philosophers: From Jonathan Edwards to John Dewey*. New Haven: Yale University Press (forthcoming)

Loeb, Louis E. 1981. *From Descartes to Hume*. Ithaca, New York: Cornell University Press

Mandelbaum, Maurice. 1976. 'On the historiography of philosophy', *Philosophy Research Archives*. Bowling Green, Ohio: Philosophy Documentation Center, Bowling Green State University Press

Mead, George Herbert. 1916–17. 'Josiah Royce – a personal impression', *International Journal of Ethics* 27:168–70

Monist. 1969 (59 (4), October). *Philosophy of the History of Philosophy*

---

[14] There are two omissions in this essay that are worth noting. First, anyone well-read in the primary philosophical literature of the period will know that there are historical gaps in the narrative. I believe a more detailed account would not change the narrative's basic outlines. But such an assertion would not convince anyone who is not already convinced. I would rather emphasize that the purpose of the essay is not to give a close account of the developments but to talk about a novel sort of problem in the history of ideas.

The second omission involves my decision not to elaborate the philosophical arguments that led to the shifts I have written about. The reason for this omission is not that the arguments were unimportant or that I am unable to construe them. A number of the arguments are considered *ad nauseam* in Kuklick 1977, and attention should particularly be called to Mill's critique of Hamilton and the response to it which are discussed in Chapters 1–7. On Dewey the reader might consult Kuklick 1985 (forthcoming). These arguments are absent from this paper, not just because it is short and because I do not want to repeat myself; again, the purpose of the essay is to raise a different sort of issue in the history of ideas.

Murphey, Murray G. 1979. 'Toward an historicist history of American philosophy', *Transactions of the Charles S. Peirce Society* 15:3–18

Rogers, Arthur Kenyon. 1907. *A Student's History of Philosophy*, new edn rev. New York: Macmillan

Royce, Josiah. 1892. *The Spirit of Modern Philosophy*. Boston and New York: Houghton Mifflin

Scruton, Roger. 1981. *From Descartes to Wittgenstein: A Short History of Modern Philosophy*. London: Routledge and Kegan Paul

Skinner, Quentin. 1978. *The Foundations of Modern Political Theory*. Cambridge and New York: Cambridge University Press

Thilly, Frank. 1914. *History of Philosophy*. New York: Henry Holt

Thilly, Frank, and Wood, Ledger. 1956. *History of Philosophy*, 3rd edn rev. New York: Holt, Rinehart, and Winston

Überweg, Friedrich. 1871, 1873. *History of Philosophy from Thales to the Present Time*. New York: Charles Scribner's Sons

Walton, Craig. 1977. 'Bibliography of the historiography and philosophy of the history of philosophy', *International Studies in Philosophy* 9:3–34

Windelband, Wilhelm. 1893. *A History of Philosophy with Especial Reference to the Formation and Development of its Problems and Conceptions*, trans. James H. Tufts. New York: Macmillan

◁ ═══════════════════════════ ▷

7

'Interesting questions' in the history of philosophy and elsewhere

WOLF LEPENIES

Die Einzelwissenschaften wissen oft
gar nicht, durch welche Faeden sie
von den Gedanken der grossen Philosophen
abhaengen.

Jacob Burckhardt

I Introduction: a glance at the history of science

It was a philosophical system that provoked one of the most powerful attacks on historical thinking to date, or at least the overemphasis on it. Friedrich Nietzsche's early essay on *The Use and Abuse of History* (1873–4) scorned the predominance of history in nineteenth-century German culture, as an unmistakable sign of decadence for which above all one man was responsible – Hegel, who identified reason in everything historical and for whom eventually the highest and final stage of the world process came together in his own Berlin existence. Nietzsche's attack continues to be illuminating even if we remove it from its original context. While dealing with modern science and scholarship, large parts of his essay can also be read as addressing the use and abuse of the history of science, a field in which the illusion of scientific progress and the aberration of historical thinking merge:

The progress of science has been amazingly rapid in the last decade; but consider the savants, those exhausted hens. They are certainly not 'harmonious' natures; they can merely cackle more than before, because they lay eggs oftener; but the eggs are always smaller though the books are bigger.   (Nietzsche 1957:46)

The history of science, with its more than occasional output of very big books, has not enjoyed a particularly good reputation among scientists. Whether written by professional or amateur historians, by practising or by retired scientists, it was always regarded – to paraphrase Nietzsche once more – as entertainment for a race of eunuchs, 'noisy little fellows measuring themselves with the Romans as though they were like them', a compensation for those who could never do science themselves, had stopped doing it or did not do it well enough.

The three kinds of history that Nietzsche proposed to distinguish – the monumental, the antiquarian and the critical – can be found in the history of science as well. No other discipline has taken Nietzsche's advice that the past should only be explained by what is most powerful in the present as seriously as the history of science. The historian of science therefore made it a habit to arrive long after harvest-time, not a welcome, just a tolerated, guest at the thanksgiving dinner of the scientific community, often sinking 'so low as to be satisfied with any food, and greedily [devouring] all the scraps that fall from the bibliographical table'. Irrelevant for the scientist when arousing the interest of the historian, and boring the latter while flattering the former – that was the dilemma the historian of science faced.

His was a textbook history, as Joseph Agassi called it:

In the first edition of his history of physics of 1899 Cajori gave a big minus to all those who believed in electrons. In the second edition, dated 1929, he gave a big plus to the same people. A cryptic explanation for this change of attitudes is to be found in the unbelievably naive preface to his second edition, where he expresses his loyalty to the up-to-date textbook of physics. Thus, whenever the textbook alters, the history of science changes accordingly.   (Agassi 1963:3)

Historians of science, however, did not write just preface or textbook histories because they wanted to please the scientists. In doing this they fulfilled, as a rule, the expectations of the historical profession as well. In a memorandum presented to the Royal Academy of the Sciences in Munich in September 1858, Leopold von Ranke, one of the few historians to be interested in the topic at all, suggested launching a comprehensive series of books on the history of science ('Geschichte der Wissenschaften'). It was obvious to Ranke that these books could only be written in a specific mode: they would have to represent a 'history of scientific *results*'. It was self-evident that the historian of science, always closely associated with the practitioner of his field, must concentrate on the most recent epochs of scientific development, whereas the political historian was allowed to escape into the more remote eras of the history of mankind.

Neither Ranke's engagement and his genuine interest in the development of the history of science, nor the numerous histories of various disciplines and specialities that were indeed written after his proposal had been accepted, helped to integrate the newly established field into the historical profession. Historians were probably convinced that the development of science should be presented in the form of textbook histories, but they could not be persuaded to be pleased with them. That practising scientists and historians of science alike shared Edward Gibbon's view, expressed at the beginning of his *Essay on the Study of Literature* (1764), of the history of the sciences as a story of splendour and happiness did not convince the traditional political historian who, immersed in the masochism characteristic of his discipline, preferred to write the history of empires and thereby, according to Gibbon, that of the miseries of humankind.

Although he shared the belief in a cumulative growth of knowledge and in a continuous progress of scientific thought with the practitioner of science, the traditional historian of science did not just tell a story of heroes and hero worship but pronounced a verdict on the villains at the same time. Not only ingenious forerunners and brilliant yet misapprehended precursors appeared on the stage, there were heretics and swindlers as well, crooks and plagiarists, and in presenting them the history of science was, paradoxically enough, a constant attempt to remind the scientist of those whom he should better forget. Looking like a pantheon to some, like a penitentiary to others, the history of science was, as Gaston Bachelard once described it, a normative discipline with an insatiable interest in errors.

Though I do not want to apologize for drawing this rough sketch of a much more subtle and interesting picture, I would like to point out that there have been rather diverse orientations in the history of science and that some of them could be described as belonging to distinct national traditions of teaching and research. Distinguishing between a mono- and a multi-disciplinary approach and separating idiographic modesty from nomothetic aspirations, one could claim that it has been the Anglo-Saxon attitude in the *history of science* to concentrate on one group of disciplines, i.e., the natural sciences, whereas the broad connotation of *Wissenschaft* has led the German historians of science to deal with diverse fields of inquiry and pay special attention to the inherent differences between them, i.e. between *Naturwissenschaften* and *Geisteswissenschaften*. It is my impression that, presumably due to the influence of neo-Kantian epistemology, the German tradition in the history of science is intrinsically idiographic in a way the Anglo-Saxon tradition, which was also interested in more general patterns of scientific development, has never been. On the other hand, there is a specific French tradition of a more pluralistic orientation, as the designation *histoire des sciences* reveals at once, and not at all afraid of theory building. We must distinguish an important group of French historians of science, for that matter not *historiens historisants* at all, from both their Anglo-Saxon and German colleagues about whom they could have said, like Cournot: 'Ces savants du Nord ne ressemblent pas à nos têtes françaises.' It should be an interesting problem for the history of science itself why this French tradition has remained rather parochial, given the international context wherein the Anglo-Saxon *history of science* has always dominated. It would be equally interesting to ask, I believe, why this epistemologically orientated *histoire des sciences*, ignited and fired up by the bold visions of Gaston Bachelard and solidified by the meticulous empirical research of Georges Canguilhem, has led Michel Foucault and his followers on a path that nowadays turns out to be a blind alley, even though the impressive building on which the sign 'No Exit' has been attached is nothing less than the Collège de France.

II Four philosophers on the history of philosophy

There are not only many histories of philosophy, but also philosophies of the history of philosophy, histories of the philosophy of history and histories of the history of philosophy. Most of them confirm the belief that too much reflection leads but backwards and that the brooding scholar always runs the risk of becoming what Diderot once called 'un système agissant à rebours'. The profusion of books on the history of philosophy does not point to the legitimacy of the genre but rather to the difficulty of achieving it. Condorcet must have been in an ironic mood when he claimed that there is no better indicator for the advancement of a field than the facility with which mediocre books can be written about it.

Heroes and villains make their appearance again in the history of philosophy. For some – like Brucker – it is an index of errors and of infinite examples of misled and misleading thought. It is often a story of dilemmas (Renouvier) yet at the same time – at least in Hegel's retrospective view – 'a succession of noble minds'. It is hardly surprising that textbook histories of philosophy read very much like textbook histories of science, since they are written from a distinct philosophical point of view. The influence of protestant orthodoxy and of Leibniz is manifest in Brucker (*Historia critica philosophiae*, 1742–4) as well as in Tiedemann (*Geist der speculativen Philosophie*, 1791–7) and Tennemann's history of philosophy (*Geschichte der Philosophie*, 1798–1819) reveals its Kantian origin no less than that of H. Ritter (*Geschichte der Philosophie*, 1829–53) its Hegelian spirit (Delbos 1917).

I shall not continue to discuss histories of philosophy. This would be a task for which I am neither prepared nor sufficiently competent. Despite what I have said so far, valuable studies like the *Histoire de l'histoire de la philosophie* of Lucien Braun – incidentally a student of Georges Canguilhem – have been written about the subject. We must remember, however, that it is always philosophical *research* which is analysed there. But it is not at all obvious that the history of philosophy should have played the same role in philosophical research and publications, as it did in the *teaching* of philosophy and, to use Robert Merton's term, in the oral transmission of philosophical knowledge.

There is a deep anti-historical mood in all philosophy, a continuous and continuously astonishing confidence of the philosophizing *ego* in its abilities to procure and to enjoy the peculiar charm that only a definite and complete knowledge can provide, knowledge brought, as Kant said in the *Prolegomena*, 'to such completion and fixity as to be in need of no further change or be subject to any argumentation by new discoveries' (Kant 1950:115). In this respect, philosophy is a nostalgic discipline, yet one which can only be fulfilled in the present, never in the past. The history of philosophy seems as superficial to dogmatic philosophers as it seems futile to sceptic ones. It becomes a disease of the mind (Nietzsche) and finally the death certificate that philosophy fills out for itself when at the end it is reduced to the point where it can write only its own history (Troeltsch).

Philosophy's past is, of course, not of the same sort as, for example, the past of chemistry. A chemist might have heard of, or even read, Lavoisier, but it would simply be a waste of time, and not make much sense, for him to replicate the experiments from the *Traité élémentaire* in his laboratory. Philosophers, however, though allowed to mistrust Descartes' radical doubt, to dislike the monadology of Leibniz, or to detest Hegel's view of the State, can hardly dismiss Descartes, Leibniz and Hegel as being simply out-of-date. The past of philosophy is alive because it possesses an inexhaustible ability to generate polemic (Gueroult). This quality can only be preserved, most philosophers claim, as long as the philosophical past is stripped of its historical context. 'Presentism' never sounds like a reproach to philosophers, certainly not to those like Hegel who declared that there is no past at all in philosophy, only a present. Therefore, most histories of philosophy are either mere classifications and chronologies or a critique of dogmas and doctrines. Only rarely do they attempt to interpret a past philosophy in its cultural context.

Let me now turn to four philosophers and say something about their views on the history of philosophy. Among them, Descartes exemplifies the anti-historical mood characteristic not only of philosophy but of many histories of philosophy as well. Hegel substitutes teleology for history. Dilthey interprets philosophy as a specific cultural system. Husserl attempts to overcome the dangers of historical relativism by trying to (re-) establish philosophy as a rigorous science. By talking, if only briefly, about these four philosophers, I want to indicate how the history of philosophy is intricately interwoven with a philosophy of history and in principle is reduced to it.

Cartesian travels

Having been to France and Bavaria, to Poland and Prussia, to Switzerland, Italy, Holland and Sweden, René Descartes was a widely travelled philosopher probably ranging, in terms of mileage, at the upper end of a scale, whose lower end must certainly be occupied by Immanuel Kant. Except for a very short sea-trip that resulted in a lengthy footnote on sea-sickness in his *Anthropology from a Pragmatic Point of View*, Kant never left his native Koenigsberg in East Prussia. Descartes, and a new epoch in philosophy with him, begins with a piece of travel literature. This is, I suggest, how we should look for a moment at the *Discours de la Méthode* (1637).

It is a narrative as well as a treatise and from its beginning strikes a rather intimate tone:

> I was then in Germany, where the occasion of the wars which are not yet ended had called me; and as I was returning to the army from the coronation of the Emperor, the onslaught of winter stopped me in a district where, finding no conversation to divert me, and furthermore, by good fortune, having no cares or passions to trouble me, I remained all day alone in a heated room, where I had complete leisure to review my own ideas.   (Descartes 1965:11)

Descartes' search for truth in the sciences is a story of disappointment with book learning and disillusionment about worldly experience. The fallacies of those who in their behaviour follow the examples of books are obvious:

> But I believed I had already given sufficient time to languages, and even to reading the books of the ancients, both their histories and their myths. For conversing with men of past ages is somewhat like traveling. It is good to know something of the mores of different peoples, in order to judge our own more soundly, . . . But when one spends too much time traveling, one must eventually become a stranger to one's own country; and when one is too much interested in the practices of times past, one usually stays ignorant of the practices of the present.   (Descartes 1965:7)

By now,· at the latest, it can seem hardly original to call Descartes' *Discourse* a piece of travel literature: this is the author's, not the reader's, metaphor. By using it, Descartes displays what one might call the philosopher's dilemma. I am not sure about the influence of Descartes in this respect but it strikes me that the ethnographer's dilemma, a *leitmotiv* from Rousseau to Lévi-Strauss, sounds like a variation on the Cartesian theme, expressing as it were the problems of travel abroad where Descartes had addressed the problems of travelling back into the past.

Of course, Descartes did not only travel back into the past, but to other countries as well. Eventually, the experiences of the ethnographer enhance the scepticism of the historian: other mores are no more satisfying than ancient books, and the philosopher's belief 'in anything that had been taught to me only by example and custom' completely disappears.

Thus, a disenchantment and a break with its own past mark the beginning of modern philosophy. The history of philosophy can at best satisfy an exotic desire, for we can imagine nothing so strange and unbelievable that it has not been said by some philosopher. Yet this anti-historical attitude is very carefully set in a precise historical context. Descartes did follow Guez de Balzac's advice to provide a history of his mind and of its heroic fight against the *géants de l'école* (Letter of 30 March, 1628). By doing this, a rather common desire for biographical continuity and coherence was fulfilled. The arguments of those who tried to show where and how often Descartes made a chronological mistake in his account are quite beside the point. It is hardly essential here whether he got his dates right or wrong, but it is important to realize that Descartes wanted us, his readers, to know that there was a moment of illumination that led him in his meditations to the conclusion that he, instead of letting himself be guided by past philosophers, would from now on only be guided by himself: according to the *Cogitationes privatae*, it was 10 November 1619.

Descartes' travels in time and space led him back to the philosophizing *ego*. Neither imaginary travels in the world of books nor real travels in the book of the world can provide the sound and firm knowledge necessary for the foundation of philosophy. This knowledge the philosopher can only find in himself, alone but secure in a heated room on a cold winter's day.

Hegel's rehearsal

In his *Lectures on the History of Philosophy* (2nd edition 1840) Hegel declared that Descartes' influence rested above all in 'his setting aside all former pre-suppositions and beginning [philosophical thinking] in a free, simple and likewise popular way' (Hegel 1974:III,221). Descartes had said that thought must necessarily commence from itself so the philosophies which came before were for ever after set aside. It was Descartes' rejection of past philosophies that secured him his place in the history of philosophy. Yet Descartes could not just be praised. With him a new epoch in the history of philosophy began, but he set to work in 'a quite simple and childlike manner, with a narration of his reflections [just] as they came to him'. Reproachful as they may sound, these remarks were nevertheless made by Hegel in a rather detached mood: Descartes had to be criticized, but he could not be blamed. There was, according to Hegel, a necessity for the appearance of his own as well as any other philosophy.

For Hegel, the history of philosophy could easily be distinguished from the history of science by its manifest disadvantage: there was no clear conception of the subject of philosophy and subsequently no consensus whatsoever about its past and its possible future accomplishments. Voluminous and even learned histories of philosophy had been written but they were only devoted to what Hegel called the 'external existence and external history of philosophy' from which any true philosophical insight was notoriously absent. The authors of all preceding histories of philosophy were like animals which listened to the notes but to whose senses the harmony of a musical piece could not penetrate.

After having dismissed in his maestro-like manner as common and superficial all previous ideas regarding the history of philosophy, this 'battlefield covered with the bones of the dead', Hegel expressed his conviction that there is nothing arbitrary in the activity of the thinking mind and that whatever takes place there must be rational. The study of the history of philosophy is thus an introduction to philosophy itself. Philosophy, a system in development, is nothing but its own history. The usual price had to be paid for such a structuring of history: teleology. This history of philosophy, called a theodicy by Hegel himself, becomes a revelation 'of what has been the aim of the spirit throughout its history', a long and complicated rehearsal, sounding at first ragged and insecure, then constantly improving and climaxing in grandiose harmony, not just a potpourri, as the untrained ear surmised, but one long and coherent piece that Hegel, as it turned out in the end, not only conducted but also arranged, corrected and, who knows, perhaps even composed.

In order to develop his ideal of a truly philosophical history of philosophy, Hegel often compared it with the history of science. Yet a comparison with the history of art is equally if not even more appropriate. There is perhaps no other work as close to Hegel's *History of Philosophy* as the *History of Ancient Art* by Johann Joachim Winckelmann, whom Hegel could not but praise as one who suggested a new view and opened up fresh perspectives in the world of art. For Winckelmann, perfect beauty was to be found in the remote past, in the origin of Greek art; for Hegel, ultimate truth was eventually revealed in the actual present of his own philosophy. For Winckelmann, aesthetics prevailed upon the history of art, as a particular philosophy of history prevailed upon Hegel's history of philosophy.

Dilthey's archives

A history of Hegel's youth was among the last works that Wilhelm Dilthey was able to complete, one of his many attempts, as he himself described it, to recall the life of a philosopher and to reconstruct a philosophical system from manuscripts ('aus den Papieren zu schreiben'). Trying to understand the evolution of philosophical thought, Dilthey's own contributions to the history of philosophy are unmistakably written against Hegel in Hegelian spirit. In deliberate contrast to Hegel, for instance, the development of philosophy is explained by Dilthey not as a progressive change in abstract thinking but as an integral part of a broader cultural history. For a long time the history of philosophy had been confined either to the biographies of famous philosophers or to the history of important philosophical disciplines and specialities. A truly 'scientific' history of philosophy would require the acquisition of the philological method as well as the break-through of historical thought, i.e., evolutionary thinking (*Entwick-lungsdenken*). These two presuppositions were available above all in German philosophical thought, and Hegel had profited enormously from them when he gave unity to the history of philosophy by revealing the structure of its development.

Yet Hegel was not able to write the history of philosophy in a broader cultural context. The first glimpses of such a cultural history of philosophy could be seen in Sainte-Beuve's *Port-Royal*, in Buckle's *History of Civilization in England* and in Hippolyte Taine's *Histoire de la littérature anglaise*.

The culture of a nation and of a time is represented in its theology and literature, in its sciences and in its philosophy. Dilthey thought that the history of one of these layers of culture could not be written without taking into consideration all the others. Yet among them philosophy was privileged in a crucial way. Poetry and religion provided guidance for humankind but lacked the solid basis of the positive sciences. These, by contrast, could help man to explain nature but could no longer tell him how to lead his life or help him to understand the world. Only philosophy could do both. It was a combination of a science and a *Weltanschauung*, and the history of philosophy always had to reconstruct and display this double picture.

Philosophical biographies had been described by Dilthey as the first and immature attempts to write the history of philosophy. There is nothing surprising in the fact that he himself wrote the 'lives' of Schleiermacher and of Hegel and strongly advocated biographical research. For Dilthey, the historical nature of man was his higher nature and biographies were the best way to demonstrate this anthropological insight. The history of philosophy was not a system, as Hegel had conceived it, it was an instrument: anthropologically rooted changes in world-views could be detected, located and measured with its help. Listening to Dilthey as he talks about the necessity to reconstruct the context and to retrace the development of philosophical systems not just from published books but from the philosophers' original manuscripts, he resembles a field-worker more than an armchair-philologist. Dilthey's history of philosophy is an anthropology carried out in the archive.

Husserl's beginnings

Hegel's conception of the history of philosophy led not only to the weakening of scientific approaches in philosophy, but also to historicist and sceptical misunderstandings of it and finally to a decadent form of philosophy – a totally non-committal taxonomy of *Weltanschauungen*. Edmund Husserl drew this picture in his persistent attempt to turn philosophy into a rigorous science. His critique was by no means idiosyncratic. At the beginning of the twentieth century a widespread feeling of malaise prevailed in philosophy. Neither the extremely systematic approach to its history by Hegel nor its 'anthropological' underpinning by Dilthey had left any valuable orientation. Eventually, Jaspers seemed to substitute psychology for philosophy, talking about the different world-views that he encountered in the history of philosophy like a psychiatrist who, unable to offer a cure to his patients, is glad at least to be able to classify their maladies (Rickert 1920–1).

Husserl, however, deplored the decadence of philosophical thought and the fragmentation of philosophical systems since the middle of the nineteenth century. There were simply too many schools, branches and specialities. Philosophers still met from time to time but never their philosophies. This crisis, though not the first in the history of philosophy, led to an unprecedented state of anarchy, since the positive sciences, too, no longer showed self-assurance about their procedures and results. This contributed to the widespread feeling that Europe's traditional values had become obsolete. Responsible for this deplorable situation was not least the fact that modern philosophy's premature attempt to become more scientific had merely brought about the autonomy, and separation from philosophy, of both the natural and human sciences, without thereby improving its own disciplinary status. It not only failed to become more 'scientific', but also faced the difficult problem of determining its relationship to these new and promising fields of knowledge. Husserl's attempt to develop philosophy as a science in the strict sense of the term had nothing to do with the imitation of 'pure mathematics and the exact natural sciences, which we can never cease to admire as models of rigorous and highly successful scientific disciplines' (Husserl 1970: 3–4). The idea of a naturalist philosophy, advocated by 'experimental fanatics', had to be rejected along with the introspection of the historicist. Husserl tried to philosophize without assumptions; his was the ideal of a presuppositionless philosophy. Philosophy could only become reputable again by establishing itself as a 'science of true beginnings, of origins'.

Philosophy as a rigorous science could only be developed as transcendental phenomenology, in a brisk move that turned away from the opinion of past and present philosophers and toward the things themselves. But although the opposition of transcendental phenomenology to historical considerations (Ricoeur) became clear from its very beginning, the history of philosophy was not at all neglected by Husserl. The historical reflections of the *Crisis*, for example, were not chosen simply 'for the sake of an impressive presentation' (Husserl 1970:xxix (Translator's Introduction)); they were not an accidental aspect of his method. On the other hand it is obvious that Husserl in many places – in the historical passages of the early and programmatic paper on 'Philosophy as a rigorous science' (1910–11), in the long introductory 'Critical history of ideas' that opened his lectures on first philosophy (1923–4), in the *Crisis* (1938) itself and also in the historical accounts in many of his lectures – tried above all to show 'that earlier philosophers were unable to solve the problems he would proceed to solve by means of phenomenology' (1970:xxviii). Husserl casts a retrospective glance at past philosophies only to reassure himself of these deficiencies; he turns over the pages of the vast *errorum index* that the history of philosophy forms in preparation for a better book, looking back at the history of philosophy as a mental preparation, a spiritual motivation to found the one and only true philosophy: phenomenology.

When Edmund Husserl was invited, by the Institut d'études germaniques and by the Société française de Philosophie, to give four lectures as an 'Introduction to transcendental phenomenology' in February 1929, he spoke in the Amphithéâtre Descartes of the Sorbonne. Hardly a more appropriate place could have been found for the first presentation of what Husserl, in the published version, later called his *Cartesian Meditations*. When, at their end, Husserl had fully developed his key idea of the phenomenological *epoché*, it had become clear how extensively he had repeated and varied a Cartesian theme, and had equally tried, like Descartes in his *Meditationes*, to get rid of all prior opinions and to make a new beginning, 'de . . . commencer tout de nouveau dans les fondements'.

Husserl saw both Descartes and himself as 'beginning philosophers' (*anfangende Philosophen*). In writing on Descartes he showed an elective affinity for the latter's work, perhaps the only such affinity to be found in his reflections. Philosophy was always, Husserl said, a rather personal affair, and yet the *Meditationes* were not only a document of Descartes' philosophizing, they were still a model for all new beginnings in philosophy. It was to their own detriment that the positive sciences did not take much notice of the *Meditationes*, and Husserl even attempted a sort of counterfactual reconstruction of the history of European philosophy, asking himself what might have happened if the germ of Descartes' philosophy had not been inhibited in its growth and development.

Of course, Husserl could not merely continue where Descartes had let off. Descartes belonged to those who make a discovery – that of the *ego cogito* in his case – but do not know what they have discovered. Husserl's *Cartesian Meditations* point to the deficiencies of Descartes as well as to the failures of the positive sciences. Phenomenology is the grandiose, maybe too grandiose, attempt to filfil a promise and to correct a mistake.

The phenomenological *epoché* is also an historical one, although Husserl even goes so far as to evoke the historical circumstances under which Descartes wrote in order to justify his own attempt to create a renaissance of the *Meditationes*, asking himself whether the unfortunate present in which he lives does not correspond to the miserable past that provoked Descartes' philosophy. In referring to Descartes, however, Husserl does not want to return to a philosophical system of the past. He is interested in the reconstitution of the very *idea* of philosophy, not in the reconstruction of the cultural context or the historical development of a specific philosophy. Ideas and propositions are stored in the history of philosophy and we may use them for our purposes, not caring too much whether they came from Kant or Thomas, Darwin or Aristotle, Helmholtz or Paracelsus. We should be less interested in Descartes than in the philosophical motives of his *Meditationes* that are eternally valid (*Ewigkeitsbedeutung*). When, at the end of his beginnings, Husserl quotes Augustine – 'Noli foras ire, in te redi, in interiore homine habitat veritas' – the reader cannot help remembering Descartes who, three hundred years earlier, had already asked the philosopher to stay home, to look into himself and not to travel back into the history of philosophy any more.

III A history of the middle range

I now wish to develop an alternative to the notion of the history of philosophy presented so far. Fortunately, this alternative can be found in the writings of the same philosophers I have mentioned already. I shall concentrate on Hegel's contribution.

Before speaking of the history of philosophy as a system of development in idea, a revelation of what has been the aim of spirit throughout its history and, finally, as a true theodicy, Hegel dismisses 'the common ideas' regarding the history of philosophy. Diligently reading the *Annales* and ridiculing the naive historiographies of yesteryear, we can only nod in assent when Hegel declares that a mere collection of facts constitutes no science and that 'the narration of a number of philosophical opinions as they have arisen and manifested themselves in time is dry and destitute of interest'.

Reviewing different *genres* of the history of philosophy, however, rejection and appraisal are not the only modes of Hegel's assessment. There is indifference as well. So what I suggest is simply to alter the Hegelian triad: to take for granted what he rejected, to reject what he praised, to praise what left him cold:

Philosophy has a history of its origin, diffusion, maturity, decay, revival; a history of its teachers, promoters, and of its opponents – often, too, of an outward relation to religion and occasionally to the State. This side of its history likewise gives occasion to interesting questions.   (Hegel 1974:1,9)

Distinguished from the history of its 'inner content' these aspects belonged to the 'external history' of philosophy. Although Hegel said much more about this kind of history, and gave the impression that he might come back to it later once the internal history of philosophy had been written, there is no doubt that the 'interesting questions' were of only secondary importance to him.

If we keep in mind that Hegel granted to the external history of philosophy some, if minor, importance, it becomes possible to read his programmatic statements on two different levels. That a philosophy belongs to its own time and is restricted by its own limitations can be interpreted, as Hegel usually did, in the perspective of his philosophy of history: each philosophy was then regarded as the manifestation of a particular stage in history, as a link in the whole chain of spiritual development. But when Hegel warned, for example, that 'we ought not . . . to make an ancient philosophy into something quite different from what it originally was', and cautioned 'not to introduce foreign matter' in the presentation of philosophical ideas, he tried above all to preserve the context of a specific philosophy:

The particular form of a philosophy is thus contemporaneous with a particular constitution of the people amongst whom it makes its appearance, with their institutions and forms of government, their morality, their social life and the capabilities, customs and enjoyments of the same; it is so with their attempts and achievements in art and science, with their religions, warfares and external relationships, likewise with the decadence of the States in which this particular principle and form had maintained its supremacy, and with the origination and progress of new States in which a higher principle finds its manifestation and development.   (Hegel 1974:1,53)

Once our attention has been directed to these 'interesting questions' we encounter them at times and in places when and where we would hardly ever have expected them. Thus, to give but one example, Edmund Husserl, embarking upon the history of the very idea of philosophy and claiming its coherence by virtue of a 'concealed unity of intentional interiority' ('verborgene Einheit intentionaler Innerlichkeit'), suddenly stops and begins to wonder whether the view – utterly wrong in his eyes – that experimental psychology must become the basis of philosophy may not have a lot to do with the deplorable fact that the natural sciences in his time are housed in the philosophy departments and that the majority of the scientists there regularly appoint psychologists to chairs in philosophy (Husserl 1910–11:321).

I do not know what contributions to a history of philosophy that concentrates on Hegel's 'interesting questions' exist already. What I do know, however, is that important fragments of it can be found in the philosophies of the past, rarely in prominent places, mostly hidden somewhere, in footnotes and afterwords, in minor works and occasional pieces, seemingly illegitimate but disturbingly present. The contours of a new history of philosophy begin to emerge, where – to mention but two of the 'old' metaphors – roots and birthdays are less important than branches and baptisms. Not yet in possession of plain answers, still searching for 'interesting questions', this will be a history of the middle range, to borrow Robert Merton's notion. It will be located somewhere between Dilthey's anthropological systems and his philological procedures. It will be neither as sacred as Hegel's theodicy nor as superficial as his 'common ideas', but rather as down-to-earth and secular as his external history.

IV The history of philosophy in disciplinary context

Not all philosophers travel, but almost all of them are architects, like Descartes who compared the evolution of philosophy to the development of an ancient town. A small hamlet in the beginning, it became a great city in the end, though badly planned, with 'here a large building, there a small', and with streets that were crooked and uneven. Casting an aesthetic eye upon this city, Descartes decided to build a better one, 'designed and completed by a single architect', laid out by himself, a philosophical engineer, 'on a plain according to his own imagination'. A wish for architectural purity and the joy of planning prevail in the history of philosophy. Thus Descartes suggests – since the whole city cannot be completely rebuilt – 'considering each of [its] buildings by itself'. Kant, in almost the same words, defines a science as a system in its own right that 'architecturally' must be treated as a 'self-subsisting whole, . . . a separate and independent building, . . . and not as a wing or section of another [one]' (*Critique of Judgment*, §68). Finally, Hegel, in order not to confuse the treatment of the history of philosophy, speaks out in favour of its separation from other allied departments of knowledge.

Purity of this sort may be – although even here I am not sure – useful for epistemology, but it certainly has its dangers for historical research in general and especially for what I shall call from now on the history of disciplines.

In order to demonstrate what I understand by this genre, I must go back to the writings of my philosophers – and be, alas, once more disobedient to their precepts. Indeed I tend to think that for a historian the old, matured cities that Descartes dislikes are a much better place to live in than the 'regular districts' he promises to design, and that a look at '[the] history of the other Sciences, of culture and above all the history of art and religion' might – *pace* Hegel – enrich the history of philosophy. In his 'Analytic of teleological judgment', Kant distinguished between *principia domestica* – principles of a science inherent in that science itself – and foreign principles, *principia peregrina* – resting on 'conceptions that can only be vouched for outside that science'. Kant said that these sciences rely on *lemmata*, auxiliary propositions that they acquire 'on credit from another science'. Once again this might be a useful distinction for epistemological or, for that matter, metaphysical purposes, but such distinctions are useless for historical purposes, unless we put them in motion. Looking at their beginnings and their development, we will find that there are not just sciences of foreign and of domestic principles, not just *principia domestica* or *peregrina*, but always processes of domestication and peregrination, constantly changing their direction and their pace. The history of disciplines is an attempt to describe and to understand this movement – not in a search for the architectonic of pure reason, 'the doctrine of what is really scientific in our knowledge' (*Critique of Pure Reason*, B 861), but for examples of an historical architecture, telling us how something came to be regarded as scientific.

To use Quentin Skinner's formulations, the history of disciplines tries to recover intentions, to reconstruct conventions and to restore contexts. It starts with the rather trivial observation that the cognitive, the historical and the institutional environments of disciplines consist first of all of other disciplines, and that an 'economy of resources' (Abrams) requires that each discipline that tries to articulate, to systematize and to institutionalize or professionalize a set of ideas and practices, also try to distinguish itself from other existing disciplines. It will usually imitate few and criticize many. This is one elementary presupposition for gaining the recognition of academic peers and the support of the broader public.

Disciplinary identities cannot simply be ascribed once and for all by recourse to the 'ultimate meaning' of a science. They are acquired, challenged, maintained and changed under specific historical and cultural circumstances. A discipline claims a *cognitive identity*, the uniqueness and coherence of 'its intellectual orientations, conceptual schemes, paradigms, problematics, and tools for inquiry'. At the same time it has to find a *social identity* 'in the form of its major institutional arrangements' (Merton 1979). Finally, an *historical identity* must be acquired, the reconstitution of a disciplinary past to which in principle all members of a scientific community would agree to belong. The proof of cognitive identity serves a theory programme primarily by distinguishing it from established or competing disciplines. Its social identity is achieved through organizational stability which makes it more fit to survive the permanent academic struggle. Claims on an historical identity distinguish it from competitors, yet at the same time prevent premature differentiation in the discipline. I should emphasize strongly that processes of institutionalization imply acts of refusal: disciplines acquire their identities not only through affirmations but through negations as well. They must not only declare whom they want to follow but also whom to abandon. For these strategies of intrusion and avoidance the reputation of disciplines is of utmost importance: cognitive, social and historical identities are usually formed after the model of some discipline of higher reputation, whereas claims to uniqueness or the imitation of the lower ranks remains the exception to the rule. On all three levels of identity formation processes of selecting, rejecting, storing and retrieving alternative orientations can be observed.

This perspective has become important in recent years, not only in the history of the human and of social sciences, but in the history of the natural sciences as well (Graham, Lepenies and Weingart 1983). There the insight is growing that there may be less rationality in the laboratory and much more reasoning in the research report than had hitherto been assumed. Elsewhere, I have used this perspective for the analysis of historical as well as present-day relations between academic disciplines and have tried to give an explanation of why this perspective, in my view, has begun to challenge some of the more traditional views of the history of science mentioned at the beginning of my paper. In a somewhat bulky reader on the history of sociology (Lepenies 1981) I tried to assemble contributions that (1) discussed the relationship between theory building in sociology and the historiography of the field, (2) assessed the importance of narratives, biographies and autobiographies for the acquisition of sociology's historical identity, (3) related theory groups, schools and processes of institutionalization, (4) addressed the distinction between the history of sociology proper and the history of empirical social research as the difference between a history of discontinuities and a history of continuity, (5) retraced interdisciplinary relations and conflicts, (6) identified national sociological traditions, and (7) followed the changing contacts between some of them.

If asked to give one example for this history of the sciences, I would mention the work of Georges Canguilhem, whose study of the complicated relationship between the disciplines and the life sciences in the nineteenth century will remain a model of precision and insight (Canguilhem 1950).

Husserl suggested arranging the social world with its *alter egos* 'into associates (*Umwelt*), contemporaries (*Mitwelt*), predecessors (*Vorwelt*) and successors (*Folgewelt*)'. Looking at the social world of disciplines one could distinguish the traditional history of science as a history of predecessors and successors from the proposed history of disciplines as a history of associates and of contemporaries. Sequences of influence are now less important than a web of interdisciplinary relations, and the prehistory of the present does not attract as much attention as the emerging genres and disciplinary ethnographies of the past (Geertz 1983).

V A first example: Wundt and his journals

I wonder whether this perspective of a history of disciplines could not play a somewhat more important role in the history of philosophy than it has done so far. The succession of philosophical ideas, opinions, systems and doctrines would still be of major interest, but it would neither be told naively as a simple narrative nor judged once and for all from a higher philosophical point of view. Instead, it would be reflected in the branching of philosophical specialities, in the shifting and exchanges of philosophical centres and peripheries, in the formation of distinct national attitudes in and toward philosophy and, last but not least, in the migration of philosophical thought into other fields of knowledge and into other academic disciplines, and its storage and transformation there.

The cause for Hegel's complaint – that there are 'no bounds . . . left to Philosophy' – should become a strong reason for a renewed interest in its history. The history of any discipline must perforce be written in relation to others, for example, to those disciplines it idolizes, imitates as models, joins as allies, tolerates as neighbours, rejects as competitors or denigrates as inferiors. This is equally true of philosophy. After all, is not the history of Western philosophy the story of its weakening domination of disciplines, first of the natural sciences, and then, shortly thereafter, over the human and social sciences? Is it not a story of faltering and successful segregations and failing rapprochements, of late attempts to restore a unity between philosophy and its unfaithful offspring, for which Husserl's *Crisis*, his plea for philosophy as a rigorous science, is perhaps the most grandiose example? Rather than advocating the painting of such vast panoramas, however, I should like to see sketches that depict philosophy in smaller disciplinary context, a series of stills which, shown one after the other, acquire a film-like quality and reveal not just objects, but their changing relation, their appearance and disappearance in a relatively stable frame of reference.

I can only offer a few examples, of a rather parochial nature, of the history of philosophy in a disciplinary context. These are mostly examples of what should or might be done, not of what has been done already. Almost all of them are confined to the human and the social sciences.

A history of philosophy in disciplinary context would certainly have to concentrate on two processes: on the differentiation of approaches, branches, and specialities *in* philosophy, as well as on the separation of fields of knowledge *from* philosophy. It is my impression that both processes have indeed been minutely described and even interpreted, though often controversially. Lacking, however, are attempts to relate these processes to one another. The separation of psychology from philosophy – if this ever took place – is perhaps the best documented case so far (Woodward and Ash 1982). This separation climaxed in Husserl's attack on psychologism as the most impertinent attempt to 'regard reason as dependent . . . upon something non-rational in character' (Wild 1940:20), an attack which at the same time nourished the phenomenologists' hope that psychology eventually might become the foundation of all other disciplines, once it had been radicalized enough to reach the philosophical dimension (Gurwitsch 1966:68).

In order to illustrate how complicated and surprising in detail these processes of separation and reconciliation have been, I should like to give but one example. It concerns the 'origin' of experimental psychology, normally associated with the 'founding' of Wilhelm Wundt's laboratory in Leipzig in 1875. In 1883, Wundt launched a new journal to promote his psychological views. Its first number contained articles on induction and apperception, on colour charts, on the logic of chemistry, on the free will, on the notion of substance in Locke and Hume and on the measurement of odour and sound. It was a journal that promoted experimental psychology and it could only bear one title: *Philosophische Studien*. A year later, at the end of the first volume, Wundt declared that he had very deliberately not included any programmatic statement in the journal's first issue. The articles themselves had to demonstrate what the reader could expect to find in the new journal. Nevertheless, stated Wundt with a grin, objections had been raised against the title of the journal by those philosophers who, longing to read papers on 'Immanent and transcendent problems', on the 'Notion of being' and on the most recently found 'Typographical error in

Kant's works' – all titles of imaginary articles are Wundt's, not mine – had been disappointed and dismayed. Speculative philosophers and philosopher-writers were appalled to realize who was about to join their high society ('Seit wann hat man gehört, dass diese und ähnliche Dinge es wagen, die gute Gesellschaft der Philosophie ungemütlich zu machen?') and declared that they had no competence to understand what was going on in psychology but that they disliked it anyway. Had he known these complaints in advance, Wundt rather stubbornly concluded, he would have switched to the title *Philosophische Studien*, even if, originally, he had another in mind.

Only in retrospect, it seems, did the title of Wundt's new journal sound polemical, somehow like a *nom de guerre*, by which the newly established experimental psychology claimed to be a legitimate part of philosophy, capable of influencing other philosophical fields like epistemology and demonstrating in a conspicuous way that the question of what was to be regarded as a truly philosophical problem was far from being settled. Experimental psychology resembled a philosophical eclecticism *in vivo*.

Twenty years later, the last issue of the *Philosophische Studien* appeared. Counting the two volumes of the *Festschrift* for Wundt, twenty volumes in all had been published. Wundt contributed an afterword (Schlusswort), nostalgically looking back at the heroic beginnings of experimental psychology when the Leipzig Institute was nothing but a modest private enterprise. Addressing the problem of the journal's title again, Wundt now openly declared that it had been deliberately polemical, 'ein Kampfestitel'. However, and this he had *not* said before, the title was directed not only against the philosophers who refused to take the necessary introductory courses in psychology, but against natural scientists as well, especially those physiologists who scorned as unscientific anything that was even remotely related to philosophy.

At the beginning of the twentieth century Wundt saw himself and his psychology in a rather uncomfortable position. In the natural sciences, speculative *Naturphilosophie*, the natural philosophy of the nineteenth century that seemed completely out-of-date twenty years earlier, was on the rise again and made the cautious and rather restrained epistemological view of Wundt and his followers look like a reactionary philosophy. On the other side, so-called 'pure philosophers', rejecting any scientific method, and especially that of experimental psychology, had arrived at the conclusion that it was about time to expel psychology altogether from philosophy. Wundt, however, reaffirmed his conviction that the sciences finally would give up all speculative dreams and that philosophers would realize the futility of their attempt to promote a psychology that was as unscientific as possible. Terminating the *Philosophische Studien* at this moment should not be regarded, Wundt hastened to add, as expressing any resignation. Despite its title the journal had been too parochial in many respects, being mainly an organ of Wundt's own institute in Leipzig and its psychology. Now, a new journal of a more universal orientation had been founded, the *Archiv für die gesammte Psychologie* – whose editor was E. Meumann in Zurich – which would carry on what Wundt and his journal had begun twenty years before.

In these last words, written in February 1903, Wundt says that he had already wondered whether it was finally time to give up the old name of the journal and to choose one which would more clearly avoid the scientific Scylla of physiological reductionism as well as the philosophical Charybdis of speculative *Naturphilosophie*: namely, *Psychologische Studien*. It seemed, however, that this reflection, after the founding of the *Archiv*, was now only a *cura posterior*.

Three years later, a new psychological journal appeared. The editor was Wilhelm Wundt. Its title was *Psychologische Studien*. In his foreword, written in December 1904, Wundt could not help referring to the farewell address that he had written when the *Philosophische Studien* was discontinued. The change of names did not have to be justified again, since the reasons he had given for it two years before remained the same and were still valid. What had to be justified was that the journal appeared at all. The reasons were suddenly obvious, even though Wundt had not been able to anticipate them a short time before. The *Archiv* had been founded to enhance the diversity of psychological approaches and to provide a 'neutral' place of publication for them. By now, however, so many different and diverse psychologies were mushrooming that it became increasingly difficult to identify Wundt's peculiar approach among them. The *Philosophische Studien* had primarily consisted of papers from the Leipzig Institute. The *Psychologische Studien* would be strictly reserved for them. Another and perhaps more important reason for the publication of the old journal under a new title was that in the *Archiv* problems of applied psychology had become equally as important as problems of theoretical psychology.

Wundt tried to protect a place where the 'pure theoretical interest' of psychology could be pursued. Whereas the title *Philosophische Studien* once claimed that psychology was a legitimate part of philosophy, the title *Psychologische Studien* was now expressing the hope that philosophical orientations would not disappear altogether from psychology.

I have sketched this story – Wundt's own – in order to indicate how complicated the story of the so-called separation of psychology from philosophy has been. There are many facets of it that I cannot discuss here. Two aspects, however, I should at least like to mention. First, processes of specialization do not necessarily imply the narrowing of approaches and perspectives. Seen in a broader, interdisciplinary context, they can, as is the case with Wundt and his journals, express the contrary desire. They may preserve the universality of an early theory programme. Second, we realize again how important the question 'What's in a name?' remains for the history of disciplines (Stocking 1971). There is not much meaning in the names of dogmas and specialities – or in the names of journals, for that matter – and, as Lamennais already knew, whenever doctrines become endangered, there are always words at hand that can swiftly replace them.

VI Other examples: sociologists at home and abroad

It might be worthwhile to re-interpret the role of philosophy in the context of emerging new disciplines, particularly in the nineteenth century, as that of a *reference discipline*, influencing the selection of theory programmes, methods, institutional arrangements and historical orientations for other fields of knowledge and specialities. (My own point of reference here is Robert K. Merton's formulation of reference group theory.)

Nowhere, it seems to me, did philosophy, or at least a substantial part of it, fulfil this reference function with greater facility than in nineteenth-century German intellectual life. In a time of growing contempt for philosophy in general, neo-Kantianism became the accepted referee in a fierce competition of academic disciplines. Not only were these classified and their mutual relations defined on an *inter*disciplinary level, but on the *intra*disciplinary level epistemological frames of research activities were interpreted, and theoretical as well as methodological alternatives were evaluated. For a long time the public images of the natural sciences and of the *Geisteswissenschaften* were shaped less by experiences of laboratory life or involvement in the understanding of a text than by statements of philosophers who claimed to have figured out what the idiographers or the nomothetics ought to do. When, at the turn of the century, Karl Lamprecht and Kurt Breysig challenged the traditional orientation of German historiography by propagating their allegedly scientific method of cultural history, they failed for many and complicated reasons, but above all because they underestimated how secure their discipline now felt with its idiographic paradigm, and how unwilling it was to risk an epistemological comfort that had been provided from the outside. The debate on the two cultures shows how alive the distinctions that the neo-Kantians propagated still are. One cannot help thinking, in this respect, of philosophy not only as referee and as an interpeter, but at the same time as a *tertius gaudens*, able to prolong and even to intensify and to profit from a conflict by claiming to settle it once and for all.

Philosophical anthropology and the sociology of knowledge

The static view of specialities as simply pieces of established disciplines is somewhat altered if one uses the frame of reference I have presented so far. Rather than regarding them as parts, one could look at them as particles that move back and forth from one discipline to another and are constantly changing while they move. Consider philosophical anthropology and the sociology of knowledge, for example. Both originated in a philosophical context; confining the analysis to the German case one could even say that they were both 'created' by one philosopher, Max Scheler. Both can be regarded as results of a certain exhaustion philosophy suffered at the end of the century: when its traditional ways of thinking reached an impasse it moved certain ideas to its own periphery, and finally tried them out on foreign territory.

As their names suggest, we normally regard philosophical anthropology as a more philosophically oriented field than the sociology of knowledge. Scheler wanted to develop a speciality in preparation for his future metaphysics – but that was the sociology of knowledge, not philosophical anthropology. The crucial distinction between them is not a static one in terms of intrinsic properties of a single field, but a dynamic one in terms of changing relations between several areas of knowledge. Philosophical anthropology always got the best of two worlds, defining itself as the empirical part of a philosophy that grew increasingly ashamed of its speculative past, and as the philosophical part of a social science that was still in search of its transcendental foundations. The sociology of knowledge, on the other hand, was scorned as sociologism by one side, and as philosophical speculation by the other. The reason for this unequal treatment is once again a distinction in context rather than in content. Philosophical anthropology was regarded as a home-made speciality, originating and remaining in German philosophy and German social thought alone, whereas the sociology of knowledge was a much more international enterprise. After 1945 the philosophers Helmuth Plessner and Arnold Gehlen, both prolific scholars who had further developed Max Scheler's philosophical anthropology, became heads of sociology departments, thus demonstrating the flexibility of their speciality. It was in the German context alone that the *Wissenssoziologie* of Karl Mannheim, the most advanced version of the sociology of knowledge, was propagated as an attack on philosophy and rejected as such. In the Anglo-Saxon context, however, it was dismissed as mere philosophy, being called by Karl Popper, the Anglo-Saxon from Vienna, not sociology at all, but merely 'a Hegelian version of Kantian epistemology'.

Sociology as positive philosophy

Having – after many and sometimes dangerous excursions in unfamiliar regions – finally arrived in the somewhat safer territory of my own discipline, I shall not leave it again in this paper. What I want to do in concluding is to indicate how the intricate relationship between philosophy and sociology could be retraced in the context of a history of disciplines. I can mention the French case only briefly, but I shall discuss the history of German sociology in more detail.

In launching the new discipline of sociology, Auguste Comte tried to emancipate it from philosophy while borrowing the latter's well-established academic reputation. He attacked two preceding philosophies, the theological and the metaphysical, only to create a third and better one: positive philosophy. The foundation of sociology was interpreted by himself not as an act of upheaval, but as a loyal attempt to create a better philosophy, one that would no longer depend on revelation or speculative thought but be firmly grounded in observation and experiment. When the first volume of *La Philosophie positive*, the journal of the Comtian school, appeared in 1867, it opened with Littré's programmatic article on the three philosophies. There was, as Littré claimed, a logical classification as well as a teleological evolution of all disciplines and both of them culminated in the new field of sociology. Once and for all, the discovery of the natural and didactic hierarchy of the disciplines remained Auguste Comte's achievement. The legitimacy of sociology was assured since a decisive point of no return had been reached in this development: never again would theology and metaphysics be able to gain a foothold where positive philosophy had succeeded. Given its quasi-religious character and the positivists' attempt to create something like a non-theological form of worship, this was a little bit too much for many of Comte's readers, among whom the brothers Goncourt, after having read his book *La Philosophie positive*, made the sarcastic remark: 'Très bon livre, s'il y avait un peu plus de positivisme!'

Durkheim, Comte's follower and critic, reversed his strategy. While Comte – probably the founder of sociology and certainly its most unsuccessful institution-builder – tried above all to win the necessary academic recognition for the sociologist by borrowing his intellectual legitimacy from the philosopher, Durkheim concentrated on assuring a specific cognitive identity – 'independent from all philosophy', as he said in the *Rules of Sociological Method*. However, he shrewdly endorsed the hegemony of philosophy and history in the universities, and even accepted for quite a while the auxiliary role of sociology as part of the philosophy curriculum (Karady 1979). The history of French sociology in the twentieth century is not least a story of its philosophical heritage, which was continually denied and attacked, yet always remained influential. Lévi-Strauss's prophecy that the philosophical ancestry of French sociology, which had played some tricks on it in the past, might 'well prove, in the end, to be its best asset' (Lévi-Strauss 1945:536) was confirmed only twenty years later: due to its philosophical orientation, French sociology by and large had not only resisted the empirical rigour of American sociology, it had finally even become – at least in the eyes of French sociologists – its bad philosophical conscience (Bourdieu and Passeron 1967).

The hidden unity of German sociology

In Germany, sociology for a long time gained only a weak institutional identity. That Germany was a country with sociologists but no sociology was not only deplored in the Weimar republic, but had already been said in the nineteenth century and was to be repeated after World War II as well. The conventional wisdom of the quasi-natural disparity of German social science loses ground, however, when philosophy and sociology are regarded in a common context.

In the introduction to his *Lectures on the History of Philosophy* Hegel had already tried to distinguish a peculiarly German pattern of the development of philosophy and the sciences from that in the other European countries. Whereas outside Germany 'the sciences and the cultivation of understanding had been prosecuted with zeal and with respect', philosophy there was no longer even remembered. Only in Germany did it remain important. 'We have received', Hegel solemnly declared, 'the higher call of Nature to be the conservers of this holy flame . . .'

No one in Germany obeyed Hegel's call more faithfully than the historian Heinrich von Treitschke, who believed that each German was born with a metaphysical instinct: lying in the woods blood dictated to him that he lie, aesthetically and philosophically, on his back while the others, and especially the Latins, lay crassly on their stomachs (Trilling 1963:235). When Treitschke attacked the new social science in his influential PhD dissertation (*Die Gesellschaftswissenschaft*) in 1859, he disclaimed its right to be established as a new field of inquiry at all. There were sociological viewpoints in other disciplines which should certainly be preserved, but there was no need for sociology as an autonomous science. As such it was even dangerous, since it accepted – in order to achieve its cognitive independence from history and the traditional political sciences (*Staatswissenschaften*) – the separation of society from the state. Yet Treitschke's attack on sociology was a polemic of bad conscience, as it seems. In many letters written before and after its publication, he expressed disgust with his own essay and with the unfortunate topic he had chosen for it, having been too young to deal with it anyway (Letters of 11 November 1858; 26 December 1858; 19 January 1859; 25 January 1859). The reader gets the impression that the author attacks only half-heartedly, that he is engaged in a battle that he is not too eager to win and that he would rather not have plotted in the first place. One reason for this attitude is certainly the fact that Robert von Mohl, against whom Treitschke wrote his small book, had been and would continue to be one of his most influential patrons and protectors. An implicit agreement, at least an attempt to achieve one, prevails in Treitschke's polemic. I found a minor yet revealing hint of such an understanding when I was writing this paper. The copy of Treitschke's book *Die Gesellschaftswissenschaft* that I needed had to be ordered through interlibrary loan. It finally arrived, a first edition from Yale's old 'College Library', obviously Treitschke's opponent's personal copy. The handwritten dedication on the front page read: 'Hern Geh. Rath Robert von Mohl in besonderer Verehrung der Verfasser.'

In 1935, Hans Freyer, author of the influential pamphlet *Revolution from the Right* (1932) and certainly one of the conservative outriders of Nazism, although he was never to join the party or any of its organizations, published an article on the present tasks of German sociology ('Gegenwartsaufgaben der deutschen Soziologie'). The title was somewhat dubious since it could be interpreted as a piece of 'German' sociology – that is, sociology based on a racist ideology and on eugenics. The article was an attempt to convince the Nazi leaders not to abolish the social sciences, since they could serve ideological purposes so well. Freyer, whatever his political motivations were, tried to retrace a specific origin and a peculiar cognitive identity of sociology that distinguished it from British as well as from French social science. The most important characteristic of German sociology was its close alliance to philosophy.

There was something paradoxical in Treitschke's attack after all, Freyer said. The opposition of civil society and the State as two different spheres had its origin with Hegel himself, and the new discipline of sociology could claim him as one of its founders, in addition to Herder, Kant, Fichte and Schleiermacher. German sociology was distinguished from both its Anglo-Saxon and its French counterparts by the fact that it did not express any belief in evolutionary social progress. The development of the West towards an industrial class society was described in cold blood, neither rejected nor accepted, seen as a transitory stage, a state of chaos that had to be endured before a new societal order could be born. Civil society was not at all an expression of the natural law of society, as shortsighted English economic theorists believed; it was an historical phenomenon and sociology was the attempt to understand it as such. In this sense, German sociology was, much more than French and British social science, historical and empirical at the same time, yet always able, due to its philosophical orientation, to reflect the meaning and structure of society and State in general. That it was safe from confounding civil society with the natural system of society explained the realism of German sociology. This realism was neither provided by a positive methodology nor by a value-free orientation but by its philosophical legacy, a sociological transformation of Hegel's philosophy of right that was carried out in truly Hegelian spirit.

In this regard, Freyer continued, Treitschke and his opponents were not at all on different sides; since they all agreed in detesting the historical situation that had created sociology, this consensus was much more important than the dissension about the concrete shape and orientation of the new discipline. The late and therefore precipitate industrialization of Germany found the German sociologists on the alert. Since they knew the English model, they regarded this process with open eyes and without inner reservation as the French did. A longing to overcome modern civil society had first found its expression in German philosophy; it was continued and preserved in German sociology. Sociology was both the expression and the verdict of industrial society.

In this paper I cannot attempt to discuss Freyer's article in its historical context. It is important because it represents a tradition in German sociology that tries to establish and to conserve its coherence as a philosophical discipline. There is no paradox in the statement that a certain anti-sociological attitude that characterizes German philosophy has its origin in the same historical context as a specific 'German' tradition of sociology. For Nietzsche, who was the first and the most convincing anti-sociologist, the decadence of sociology was not least expressed in its weakening of philosophical interest. Of course, this was not a revival of Hegelianism, but rather a reaction against it. It is important in this context that both a certain conservative tradition of German sociology as well as a specifically German version of anti-sociological thought in philosophy can only be understood as attempts to revive the close relation between sociology and philosophy or to deplore its loss.

The diversity and incoherence of German sociology has always been regretted by its practitioners and maliciously exposed by its foes. Once we put sociology and philosophy in a common context, however, an astonishing picture begins to emerge. It becomes obvious that there is a specific epistemological perspective that gives German sociological thought a hidden unity and coherence. At the turn of the century this unity expressed itself above all in a common interest in Kantian philosophy which would, many suggested, provide a sound basis for the social sciences. In this respect, Kant and not Hegel appears as the 'founding father' of German sociology. (Yet another question is whether Kant, influencing Durkheim through Renouvier and Brunschwicg, for example, has not been the founding father of European sociology in general. His profound and enduring influence may distinguish the European from the American tradition in the social sciences.)

I cannot go into all the details here. I shall just point to one minor detail in order to explain what I have in mind. In the English edition of *Wirtschaft und Gesellschaft* prepared by Günther Roth and Claus Wittich – which has been highly praised and rightly so – the title of Weber's first chapter is translated as 'Basic sociological terms' and thus misses an important, if not the most important, aspect of the chapter. For in the German original, the title 'Soziologische Kategorienlehre' has a Kantian connotation that can be found in the most diverse systems of German sociology. It reflects the conviction that sociology, for all its legitimate attempt to distinguish itself from philosophy, has not lost a transcendental orientation in the exact Kantian sense of the term. 'Transcendental' does not mean something that passes beyond all experience, 'but something that indeed precedes it *a priori*, but that is intended simply to make knowledge of experience possible', as Kant said in the *Prolegomena* (Kant 1950:122–3).

In this sense a transcendental approach characterizes the emerging German sociology. Weber's categories are an expression of it, as are Simmel's quest for the social *a priori* and his attempt to begin sociology with a Kantian question: How is society possible?

German sociology has not only always been deplored for its diversity. Its development has also been characterized by discontinuity. After World War II it seemed as if the German sociologists, diligently re-educating themselves, succumbed to an empiricism that was even duller than that of the American colleagues they imitated. This picture is not completely false, given the differentiation of sociological specialities and their place and reputation in the sociological field. It is, however, completely misleading if one looks at sociology as a whole and puts it, once again, in a common context with philosophy. All of a sudden one realizes that the most important German sociologists had, in different ways, preserved their philosophical interests and orientations. Both the emigrant Plessner and the non-emigrant Gehlen developed their sociological views on the basis of a philosophical anthropology. Both the emigrant René Koenig and the non-emigrant Helmut Schelsky, favourably inclined towards Kantianism, agreed that sociology had to have a transcendental orientation, that it needed a conceptual system which was prior to all empirical work. Theodor W. Adorno and Karl R. Popper, both emigrants, who sparked a long and bitter confrontation in the history of postwar German sociology

('Positivismusstreit'), at least agreed in jointly opposing any strict separation of philosophy and sociology.

So it turns out, in the end, that German sociology, seen in a broader
environmental and historical context, was much less disperse and discontinuous than has often been claimed. It was always difficult to detect a sense
of belonging and of solidarity among German sociologists. This sense,
however, immediately becomes apparent once these sociologists transcend
the boundaries of their profession and enter the philosophical arena.
Certainly, they still disagree. But they seem to have left the minor (though
really disturbing) quarrels behind in order to agree on major (though more
remote) issues – like citizens who daily find new reasons to ignore and even
detest each other yet gleefully join as compatriots when they happen to
meet abroad.

VII Conclusion: the lady vanishes

I wonder whether this curious relationship between sociology and philosophy – exemplified by but certainly not restricted to the German case –
does not tell us something about the history of philosophy in general. I do
not want to join a somewhat scholastic discussion, musing when and why
and with what right philosophy was or should have been theology's or
someone else's *ancilla* or *domina*. Rather, since I am more interested in
degrees and patterns of visibility than in status problems, I shall confess my
high esteem for that trained Jesuit Alfred Hitchcock and suggest that the
history of philosophy be retraced in disciplinary context as a story called
The Lady Vanishes.

Someone rather old with whom we lately have been acquainted –
conspicuously old-fashioned in look and manners, yet very witty
sometimes, all too often whistling an awkward tune – is threatened,
attacked and finally disappears. While we regret her fate (though not too
much, for she was very old-fashioned indeed) we can suddenly hear her
tune again, familiar by now because we could not help whistling it
ourselves from time to time. There she is, in a place where we would never
have expected to meet her and, twinkling, she is telling us what really
happened while we thought that she was gone forever.*

* This essay was written while I was a member of the School of Social Science at the Institute
for Advanced Study, Princeton, New Jersey, during the academic year 1982–3.

REFERENCES

Agassi, Joseph. 1963. *Towards an Historiography of Science (History and Theory Supplement 2)*. The Hague: Mouton

Ash, Mitchell G. 1981. 'Academic politics in the history of science: experimental psychology in Germany, 1879–1941', *Central European History* 14:255–86

Bouglé, Célestin. 1926. 'Die philosophischen Tendenzen der Soziologie Emile Durkheims', in *Jahrbuch für Soziologie. Eine internationale Sammlung*, ed. G. Salomon, 1:47–52. Karlsruhe: G. Braun

Bourdieu, Pierre and Jean-Claude Passeron. 1967. 'Sociology and philosophy in France since 1945: death and resurrection of a philosophy without subject', *Social Research* 34(1):162–212

Boutroux, Emile. 1910–11. 'Wissenschaft und Philosophie', *Logos* 1:35–56

Braun, Lucien. 1973. *Histoire de l'Histoire de la Philosophie*. Paris: Edition Ophrys

Canguilhem, Georges. 1950. *Essai sur quelques problèmes concernant le normal et le pathologique*, 2nd edn. Paris: Les Belles Lettres

Castelli, Enrico. 1956. 'La Philosophie de l'histoire de la philosophie', *Philosophie* 1956:9–17

Delbos, Victor. 1917. 'Les Conceptions de l'histoire de la philosophie' (1), *Revue de Métaphysique et de Morale* 24:135–47

Descartes, René. 1965. *Discourse on Method, Optics, Geometry, and Meteorology*. Translated, with an Introduction, by Paul J. Olscamp. Indianapolis, Indiana: Library of Liberal Arts

Descartes, René. 1967. *Discours de la méthode* [1637]. Texte et commentaire par Etienne Gilson. 4th edition. Paris: Librairie Philosophique J. Vrin

Dilthey, Wilhelm. 1921a. *Weltanschauung und Analyse des Menschen seit Renaissance und Reformation* (Gesammelte Schriften II). Leipzig/Berlin: Teubner

Dilthey, Wilhelm. 1921b. 'Archive der Literatur in ihrer Bedeutung für das Studium der Geschichte der Philosophie' (1889), in *Gesammelte Schriften* 4:555–75. Leipzig/Berlin: Teubner

Erdmann, Benno. 1878. 'Die Gliederung der Wissenschaften', *Vierteljahresschrift für wissenschaftliche Philosophie* 2: 72–105

Farber, Marvin (ed.). 1940a. *Philosophical Essays in Memory of Edmund Husserl*. Cambridge, Mass.: Harvard University Press

Farber, Marvin. 1940b. 'The ideal of a presuppositionless philosophy,' in Farber 1940a:44–64

Freyer, Hans. 1935. 'Gegenwartsaufgaben der deutschen Soziologie', *Zeitschrift für die gesamte Staatswissenschaft* 95:116–44

Geertz, Clifford. 1983. *Local Knowledge. Further Essays in Interpretive Anthropology*. New York: Basic Books

Gerlach, Otto. 1899. 'Kant's Einfluss auf die Sozialwissenschaft in ihrer neuesten Entwicklung', *Zeitschrift für die gesamte Staatswissenschaft* 55:644–63

Graham, Loren, Wolf Lepenies and Peter Weingart (eds.). 1983. *Functions and Uses of Disciplinary Histories*. Dordrecht: Reidel

Gueroult, Martial. 1956. 'Le Problème de la légitimité de l'histoire de la philosophie', *Philosophie* 1956:45–68

Gurwitsch, Aron. 1966. *Studies in Phenomenology and Psychology*. Evanston, Ill.: Northwestern University Press

Hartmann, Nicolai. 1921. 'Max Scheler', *Kant–Studien* 33:IX–XVI.

Hegel, G. W. Fr. 1974. *Lectures on the History of Philosophy* (2nd edition 1840), translated from the German by E. S. Haldane and Frances H. Simson. 3 vols. London: Routledge, Kegan Paul, and New York: The Humanities Press

Heinemann, Fritz. 1926. 'Die Geschichte der Philosophie als Geschichte des Menschen', *Kant–Studien* 31:212–49

Husserl, Edmund. 1910–11. 'Philosophie als strenge Wissenschaft', *Logos* 1:289–341

Husserl, Edmund. 1950. *Cartesianische Meditationen und Pariser Vorträge* [1929] (Husserliana I) ed. S. Strasser. The Hague: Martinus Nijhoff

Husserl, Edmund. 1956. *Erste Philosophie [1923/24]. Erster Teil: Kritische Ideengeschichte* (Husserliana VII), ed. R. Boehm. The Hague: Martinus Nijhoff

Husserl, Edmund. 1970. *The Crisis of European Sciences and Transcendental Phenomenology. An Introduction To Phenomenological Philosophy.* Translated, with an Introduction, by David Carr. Evanston, Ill.: Northwestern University Press

Kant, Immanuel. 1907. *Critique of Pure Reason* [1781], translated into English by F. Max Mueller, 2nd edition, revised. New York: Macmillan

Kant, Immanuel. 1950. *Prolegomena to Any Future Metaphysics [Which Will Be Able to Come Forth as Science* (1783)], with an Introduction by Lewis White Beck. Indianapolis, Ind.: Library of Liberal Arts

Kant, Immanuel. 1973. *The Critique of Judgment* [1790], translated with Analytical Indexes by James Creed Meredith. Oxford: Clarendon Press

Karady, Victor. 1979. 'Stratégies de reússite et modes de faire-valoir de la sociologie chez les durkheimiens', *Revue française de sociologie* 20: 49–82

Klein, Jacob. 1940. 'Phenomenology and the history of science', in *Farber* 1940a:143–63

Kuhn, Thomas S. 1971. 'The relations between history and history of science', *Daedalus* 100(2):271–304

Lepenies, Wolf. 1978. 'Wissenschaftsgeschichte und Disziplingeschichte', *Geschichte und Gesellschaft*, 4:437–51

Lepenies, Wolf. 1980. 'Transformation and storage of scientific traditions in literature', unpublished manuscript. Princeton, NJ: Institute for Advanced Study

Lepenies, Wolf (ed.). 1981. *Geschichte der Soziologie*, 4 vols. Frankfurt am Main: Suhrkamp

Lévi-Strauss, Claude. 1945. 'French sociology', in *Twentieth-Century Sociology*, ed. G. Gurvitch and W. E. Moore, pp. 503–37. New York: Philosophical Library

Littré, Emile. 1867. 'Les trois philosophies', in *La Philosophie Positive*, ed. E. Littré and G. Wyrouboff, 1:5–30. Paris: Librairie Germer Baillière

Merton, Robert K. 1979. *The Sociology of Science. An Episodic Memoir.* Carbondale, Ill.: Southern Illinois University Press

Merton, Robert K. 1980. 'On the oral transmission of knowledge', in: Merton and Riley, *Sociological Traditions from Generation to Generations.* Norwood, NJ: Ablex Publication Corporation, pp. 1–35

Nietzsche, Friedrich. 1957. *The Use and Abuse of History* [1873–4]. Translated by Adrian Collins with an Introduction by Julius Kraft. Indianapolis, Ind.: Liberal Arts Press

La Philosophie de l'Histoire de la Philosophie. 1956. Rome: Istituto di Studi Filosofici, Università di Roma, and Paris: Librairie Philosophique J. Vrin (Bibliothèque d'Histoire de la Philosophie)

Ranke, Leopold von. 1888. *Abhandlungen und Versuche. Neue Sammlung.* Leipzig: Duncker

Rickert, Heinrich. 1920–1. 'Psychologie der Weltanschauungen und Philosophie der Werte', *Logos* 9:1–42

Rueschemeyer, Dietrich. 1981. 'Die Nichtrezeption von Karl Mannheims Wissenssoziologie in der amerikanischen Soziologie', in *Soziologie in Deutschland und Oesterreich 1918–1945*, ed. M. Rainer Lepsius, pp. 414–26, Sonderheft 23/1981. Kölner Zeitschrift für Soziologie und Sozialpsychologie

Schütz, Alfred. 1940. 'Phenomenology and the social sciences', in Farber 1940a:164–86

Simon, W. M. 1965. 'The "Two Cultures" in nineteenth-century France: Victor Cousin and Auguste Comte', *Journal of the History of Ideas* 26:45–58

Stocking, George W., Jr. 1971. 'What's in a name? The origins of the Royal Anthropological Institute: 1837–1871', *Man* 6:369–90

Treitschke, Heinrich von. 1859. *Die Gesellschaftswissenschaft. Ein kritischer Versuch.* Leipzig: S. Hirzel

Treitschke, Heinrich von. 1929. *Briefe und Gedichte* (Aufsätze, Reden und Briefe, vol. 5), ed. Karl Martin Schiller. Meersburg: Hendel

Trilling, Lionel. 1963. *Matthew Arnold*, 2nd edition [1939]. London: Unwin

Weber, Max. 1968. *Economy and Society. An Outline of Interpretive Sociology*, ed. Günther Roth and Claus Wittich, 3 vols. New York: Bedminster Press

Wild, John. 1940. 'Husserl's critique of psychologism: its historic roots and contemporary relevance', in Farber 1940a:19–43

Woodward, William R. and Mitchell G. Ash (eds.). 1982. *The Problematic Science. Psychology in Nineteenth-Century Thought.* New York: Praeger

Wundt, Wilhelm. 1883. 'Schlusswort zum ersten Bande', *Philosophische Studien* 1:615–17

8

The Divine Corporation
and the history of ethics

J. B. SCHNEEWIND

I

In studying the history of philosophy we are often tempted to project our current concerns with problems and methods backwards. One reason we may do this is that we cannot read any text intelligently without having some interpretative approach of our own, however inchoate it may be. In contemporary Anglo-American philosophy, both learning and teaching have been largely ahistorical. In looking at earlier texts, consequently, the framework we use to try to understand them naturally tends to be the one we use in our daily philosophical work. It is likely to seem obviously appropriate, and perhaps we do not have another one available.

There are particular drawbacks to this approach in studying the history of ethics. It is widely held that modern philosophy begins with Descartes and is essentially defined by its epistemological concerns. These in turn are seen as motivated by the new science and the cognitive challenge it contained for religious doctrine. Of course it is recognized that morality was involved in religion. But Bacon and Descartes and Locke did not make ethical issues central to their philosophy, and it seems to be Christianity as a theory of the world, rather than as a way of life, that is ultimately at issue in their writings. So when we teach a course called 'the history of modern philosophy', we usually teach the history of epistemology and metaphysics, and we do not ordinarily offer a comparable course, held to be of equal importance, on the history of modern ethics. The history of ethics is seen, if it is seen at all, as a dependent variable. This accords well with that strain of contemporary ethics which sees moral philosophy as centering on those close relatives of epistemology, the topics of meta-ethics. In this connection it is interesting to note that there is a widely accepted pattern for teaching the history of modern epistemology and metaphysics from Descartes to Kant (one whose own history is explored in this volume by Professor Kuklick), but no similar widely accepted pattern for teaching the history of modern ethics. Of course it is possible that there is no really independent life to the history of thought about morality, that modern ethics simply arose out of changes in the best views available about knowledge and the ultimate constitution of the universe. I believe, however, that this is not so. And if it is not, then an interesting question arises as to why it has so long been assumed that it is. Rather than speculate on that issue here, I shall concentrate on sketching an alternative way of looking at the history of modern ethics.

The period with which we will be concerned begins at the end of the sixteenth century, with the work of Montaigne, who opens up the modern era in moral thought, and Hooker, who gave the older view its last great articulation in English. It extends through the time of Kant, Bentham, and Reid two centuries later. I will indicate how we can see the course of philosophical thought about morality during this period as centering on certain specifically ethical issues – issues of cooperation, justice, and responsibility. I do not want to deny that changes in metaphysics and epistemology, as well as in religious belief, were vitally important to thought about morality. But morality sets its own requirements for an adequate theory, and changes in those other areas of thought have their importance for morality through the medium of a dynamic arising out of those requirements. That dynamic is what gives the history of modern ethics its central problem and therewith its independence.

Before moving to my main theme, I want to make a remark about the kind of help I hope this paper can give. To use the terms now current, I seek predominantly an internal rather than an external explanation of the history of ethics between approximately the time of Montaigne and that of Kant. An internal explanation of a succession of philosophical positions sees the succession as developing from argumentative or rational considerations, using for the most part, common terms, and resting – consciously or not – on shared assumptions. An account which involves holding that some common assumption was dropped by a later thinker will still be largely an internal account if it stresses ways in which the later view is best understood as working out the consequences of dropping one, but not others, of the beliefs earlier thinkers held. In giving priority to a search for an internal explanation, I do not mean to suggest that external considerations are unimportant or unavailable – far from it. But I think we must have the best internal explanation we can get of an historical development in philosophy before we are in a good position to look for external explanations.

One reason for this is that we would like to understand the work of earlier thinkers as philosophers. On our own understanding of what philosophy is, it involves argument and the working out of the full logical implications of a principle or a position. So we want the historian of philosophy to explain earlier thinkers, and their conversations, in ways that bring out their philosophical aspects. We are not content if we are told simply that they came to hold certain views – never mind why – and that these views influenced later writers – never mind how. An important intellectual historian tells us, for example, that the Enlightenment was 'always moving from a system of the universe in which all the important decisions were made outside of man to a system where it became the responsibility of man to care for them himself'.[1] This may be true. Indeed I think it is. But I do not understand it philosophically until I can see what rational steps led various thinkers from the earlier 'system' to the later one. And to see this is to have an internal explanation of the change.

More generally I think that the most satisfying account possible of why someone believes something is one which shows that what is believed either is true or is the proper outcome of a compelling argument from premises the person accepts, and that the person was in a good position to notice this. We may need to appeal to external factors to explain why the thinker was in a position to notice a truth or to see previously unnoticed implications of some of his beliefs. But we feel – surely correctly – that the fact that someone noticed the truth of some proposition or saw the soundness of an argument from his own beliefs to a new conclusion must be a strong explanation of why the person came to believe what he did. If such an explanation is available and correct, it seems to make unnecessary any search for further, non-rational, accounts of why the person held the belief. It seems then that it is only where internal explanations of the history of thought cannot be found that we must turn to external explanations; and if this is so, then it is evident why we should begin our work by seeking internal accounts.

Now this view leads, as one historian of political thought rightly complains, to 'a kind of history which always tends essentially to trace things back to their origins, to the first beginnings of the ideas which it sees at work . . . Philosophers are tempted to push upstream until they arrive at the source. Historians must tell us how the river made its way, among what obstacles and difficulties.'[2] The danger of supposing that philosophical views must be shown to be simply developments of one absolute originating point is real. So is the danger that the contexts in which philosophical positions develop will be ignored. If we really want to be historians, even when our subject is philosophy, we must be aware of these dangers. We must be ready to look for and acknowledge points at which there are radical discontinuities within the history of philosophy. But one way to locate such points is to push the search for internal explanations until we

[1] See Wade 1971:21, where the view is attributed to Cassirer.   [2] Venturi 1971:2–3.

fail to find them. Then we will be in a situation where we must look for
external explanations. Certainly many of the considerations which help us
understand how a thinker came to be in a position to grasp a new truth or
new argument are external. Questions about why certain issues become
salient at a given time, about why some once common assumptions are
generally abandoned but others are not, about why a line of thought took
one turn but ignored another that was equally available, may often require
externally based answers. But there is no *a priori* way to tell what sort of
explanation will be available. Only detailed study of particular developments can tell.

II

It is uncontroversial that a long-standing Christian view of morality
dominated thought at the beginning of the period I shall be considering.
But an inadequate grasp of the logic of that position has hampered our
ability to see its role in future developments. It is often supposed that the
one essential issue about a religious morality is whether or not it is
voluntarist or intellectualist: whether morally right acts are right simply
because God commands us to do them, or whether, by contrast, God
commands us to do them because they are, in themselves, right. This
problem, of significant concern to theologians, is of considerably less
moment to morality as such. Interest in it, sometimes rekindled by concern
with the so-called naturalistic fallacy, simply serves to distract attention
from what is a far more important aspect of morality when that is viewed as
under the aegis of a Divinity of the sort Christianity teaches. My effort to
present a heuristic for the history of ethics must begin, therefore, with a
sketch of a model of the religious position which brings out the features I
think more important. I say 'model' because, while I think my outline
captures the important features of a wide variety of actual positions, it
deliberately leaves open a number of options about how the details are to
be filled in. My sketch ends by portraying what I label 'the Divine
Corporation', but it begins simply with some remarks about the division of
labor and about cooperation. What I say should be obvious – perhaps
painfully so – but none the less true for all that.

Consider, then, the idea of a cooperative endeavor, in which agents join
to produce a good that no one of them could produce alone. Each
participant has a task or set of tasks. The tasks for each can be set out in
rules laying down the duties of a station. It is the joint or successive
performance by each of the duties of his or her station that brings about the
good. There may or there may not be a separate, higher order, station, or
set of stations, for the function of supervision or management. But neither

a supervisor nor a first-order worker is personally responsible for the production of the good. Still, it would be unreasonable, in many instances, for participants to limit themselves strictly to their formally stated responsibilities and to refuse to go beyond them. We usually suppose that each agent has a general responsibility – over and above those listed as the duties of his or her station – to keep an eye on the way things are working out, and to step in to make up for the defective performance by others, or for unforeseen contingencies. So even though no single worker has an assigned responsibility described as 'bringing about the good which the group aims at producing', each has some vague responsibility for keeping that good in view and adjusting his or her activities accordingly. And each participant would be liable to censure or perhaps penalty should this general responsibility be ignored.

That each agent should have this vague general responsibility for the outcome is not a necessary feature of cooperative ventures. On the contrary, it can only reasonably be attributed under certain conditions. These conditions may be present or absent in varying degrees. It seems plain, for instance, that as the participants understand less and less about the good to be produced, their liability to be criticized if they simply do their specific duties decreases. The less each understands about the contributions the others are to make, the less each is liable to criticism for minding his own business. To the extent that there is, and is known to be, a strong back-up system, so that misfortunes or failures by others will be remedied, one's vague general responsibility for adjusting one's actions by keeping an eye on the results will be decreased. If one's supervisor has made it very clear that one is paid for carrying out one's own duties strictly, looking neither to left nor to right, then, again, one's liability to criticism for doing this is minimized.

Imagine, then, that you have a job with clearly defined responsibilities within a huge cooperative venture. Your supervisor must coordinate the efforts of large numbers of other workers, who are unknown to you. The supervisor in turn reports to a still higher director, one of many, all ultimately controlled by a brilliant administrator, who is known to keep the vast international ramifications of the complex, multi-faceted, covert operation under review. You would, I think, be quite wrong in interfering with the tasks of others. It would be inexcusable for you to suppose that you could see well enough what was meant to result from another's work to intervene, to think that the chief administrator had failed to foresee all the contingencies, or to arrogate managerial responsibilities to yourself. In such a case one's responsibilities set strict limits to one's liability to criticism or penalty. Or at least this is true within the sphere of operation of the corporation. A sergeant who carries out direct orders from his company commander and assigns all-night garbage pail washing to a rambunctious platoon in sub-zero weather may not be liable to military criticism if two of the men catch pneumonia and die. But it is arguable that he has incurred other liabilities. A secret service agent may carry out his duties impeccably, winning nothing but praise from the Firm, and yet be open to serious reproach from other points of view. If we want an organization within which our responsibilities set a *complete* limit to our liabilities – where we should do our own duty, regardless of the consequences – we must take some further steps. The good we are helping to produce must be supremely important, yet far too complex for us to understand. The supervisor must be supremely efficient. He must never make mistakes about how to divide the labor. He must foresee every contingency and must be powerful enough to cope with any emergency. He must be so fair that there can be no doubts about his employment practices. Thus he must give all the agents adequate instructions about their tasks; he must assign them jobs within their powers; and he must reward them on the basis of their merits. Last, but not least, he must be too good ever to assign any duties that would be improper from any point of view. This just cooperative endeavor is the Divine Corporation, and its administrator is obviously unusual. In the Western world, indeed, he is generally thought to be unique.

III

The vision of the universe as a Divine Corporation carries with it a certain understanding of moral laws which in turn has important implications for the task of the moral philosopher.

The laws by which God structured the inanimate and subhuman parts of the cosmos and those through which the human and higher parts were ordered are not basically different in kind. They are God's bidding to his creatures, and all must obey. But there is a difference between the ways in which they do so. The inanimate and non-rational parts of the universe conform to their laws (to the extent they do: one cannot expect perfect conformity in less than perfect beings) automatically, without requiring any sort of conscious awareness of those laws. Rational creatures – humans, and presumably angels – conform through conscious choices, guided by some degree or kind of awareness of their laws. The difference in the role consciousness plays in keeping natural and moral agents acting in appropriate ways leads to one significant difference between the laws of the two realms. Both sorts of law must be universal. They must determine how every entity of the kind they govern is to behave. Thus laws governing humans, like those governing other natural kinds, must apply to all humans as humans, whatever special laws there may be for subgroups within the species. (The Divine Corporation does not as such require a hierarchical or class structure within human societies.) Moreover both sorts of law must be the supreme determinants of behavior for the beings they govern. God's designs cannot, after all, be thwarted. But in addition to being universal and supreme, the laws governing humans must have a feature which laws for non-rational creatures need not. They must be such that humans can knowingly and deliberately do what the laws require. For if people could not act in accordance with moral laws, those laws could not structure the human contribution to the cosmic good at all; and if we could not act in full awareness that we are doing as they direct, the difference between rational and non-rational creatures would disappear. This third feature I shall label with the barbarous term 'performability'.

These three features of the laws of the moral world can also be seen as natural consequences of a Divine Corporation view of morality. It is a requirement of such a view, as I said, that the head of the firm be completely just. To guarantee our motivation, the tasks he sets for us are of supreme importance to each of us. It is therefore only just that we should be able to know what they are and be able to do them. If performance is the condition of our obtaining our wages, it would be unfair if some had harder and some easier tasks, or if some were better equipped to do their jobs and therefore found them less onerous. For the reward is essentially the same for each worker. So the work we must do to qualify for it must in some fundamental respect be the same for everyone, and everyone must be equally able to do it. On this view, therefore, the moral world is a just world, and as members of it we are involved in a just cooperative venture.

The natural philosopher then has the task of explaining the non-rational world. Perceptible disorder and irregularity exist in it, but they must be understandable somehow in the light of underlying order and purpose. Moral philosophy has an analogous task with respect to the moral world – the world of agents governed through their awareness of universal, supreme, and performable laws. There, too, apparent disorder and irregularity must be shown to be explicable in terms of order and of subservience to God's designs. There is no sharp discontinuity between natural and moral philosophy, but there are some differences. The moral philosopher tells us the substance of the laws of the moral world, as the natural philosopher does those of the natural world. In addition the moral philosopher must offer an account of the universality, supremacy, and performability of the moral laws – must, that is, explain how there can be a distinctive moral world. But in an important way moral philosophy, unlike natural, does not tell us anything new. The natural philosopher will discover hitherto unknown aspects of the workings of the natural world, and his instruction about them may teach us new ways of using the part of creation God made to serve us. Moral philosophy, by contrast, is corrective rather than instructive. Its usefulness lies not in discovering novelties but in removing the errors into which we are persistently tempted to fall. It thereby clears the way for us to live by the untheoretical guidance which must be available to all of us.

Not everyone, either before our period or during it, would have agreed that there is a moral world. But the Christian view of morality leads naturally, as I have indicated, to the conviction that there is, and offers a powerful account both of its inner structure and of its apparent disorder. As Christian beliefs came under attack and were weakened or wholly abandoned, the accounts that could be given of the structure and possibility of the moral world were forced to shift also. My main suggestion is that we will best explain the development of modern ethics by seeing it as resulting from attempts to defend belief in the reality of the moral world, viewed as a just cooperative venture, while accommodating changes in, or departures from, the religious underpinnings of that belief.

IV

I have tried to show that an important principle is involved in the dynamics of any venture in which people are at work to produce a good which no one of them alone could produce. The principle is that individual responsibility for the successful outcome of a joint endeavor varies inversely as the complexity of the enterprise and the perfection of the director. The Divine Corporation embodies this principle no less than other such ventures. But the idea of the Divine Corporation as I have so far sketched it is ambiguous or loose in a number of important ways. The Corporation requires a number of elements, each of which can be interpreted in various ways. Differing views about one element will require different ways of understanding other elements, or the relations among the elements, if the structure of the Corporation is to be preserved. This ambiguity or openness to multiple interpretations is what makes it possible to use the model in understanding a wide range of positions. I will give some examples.

Let me begin with the good to be produced by the agents working in the Corporation. So far I have talked as if their work must result in a product which is different from the work itself. This is the view of it held by the many Divine Corporation theorists who took the product to be the happiness of humanity. But other positions are possible. The Corporation might be considered on the analogy of a ballet company or an orchestra, where the product is not in the same way separable from the activities of the performers. It might then be held that our contribution to the cosmic order, or to displaying the full glory of God, is simply our behaving in the ways God has shown us to be fitting. This view of the purpose of the cooperative endeavor shades over into another one, which, like it, plays down the importance of consequences. God, it may be noted, can bring about any conceivable state of affairs, except one, regardless of our cooperation. The one thing he cannot produce by himself is our free decision to cooperate, our voluntary choice of doing as God directs. Perhaps the unique contribution humans make to the cosmic display of God's glory is the proper ordering of their own soul or wills.

Next there is, of course, the question of the nature and status of the laws governing the moral world – surely one, if not the sole, element of significance. It may be held, perhaps on theological grounds, that moral principles are laws made necessary by God's decree and transmitted to us as marking out our roles in declaring his glory. Then we would have neither a rational grasp of the laws themselves nor much understanding of how our assignment contributes to the cosmic good. Alternatively, it might be argued that each principle taken by itself must be inherently reasonable, and that God enforces the principles because they are so. Then their rationality might be self-evident to us, even though we still might not understand fully how the role they define for us makes its cosmic contribution. If on the other hand we suppose that the purpose of the cooperative venture is to make everyone happy, then it is natural to think that moral laws are, at least from God's point of view, general rules about utility. From the human perspective such rules always have exceptions. So to preserve universality we might argue that God always requires his creation to work by general laws. Or we could hold that the laws are absolute for us simply because of our subordinate position within the Corporation.

These options about the nature or status of the laws of the moral world are of course closely linked to the options about how agents can come to be aware of what they are to do. Here major constraints are imposed by the need to account for performability. If, for instance, moral laws are taken to be discoverable by reason, the philosopher must explain how it is that all people have essentially equal abilities to know moral truths. The cognitive theorist will probably move to an intuitionist position, at least as regards morality, since it seems plain that people do not have equal ability to reason about complex issues; and it was commonly held that people do have equal ability to grasp intuitive truths. To avoid intuitionism, with its connection to theories involving innate ideas, or else as one way of accommodating theological voluntarism, the theorist might offer a non-cognitivist account of moral awareness. This may give an easy account of performability, since it can help with the motivational issue as well as the availability of guidance. But then the requirement of universality demands an account of why moral emotions or the moral sense should be the same in everyone. In any case a Divine Corporation theorist will tend to hold that there is a *consensus gentium* about morals, and will need to explain any serious exceptions there seem to be to this.

Perhaps the most interesting feature of epistemology in Divine Corporation theories is that its main task is to help in explanation. Justification of moral principles as such is not the issue. The assumption is made that all or most of us are aware of what we ought to do, and are in agreement on the main points. Epistemology is called in to show why this is so. There is no call to generate, or to remove, deep skeptical doubts about morality as a whole. Arguments, epistemological and otherwise, are given about which specific principles best reveal the substance of the moral world. And a philosopher may well produce an argument to show that moral principles are rational or are purely emotional. But the point in either case is to support some particular explanatory account of the just cooperative venture of which we are all a part.

Finally there is the interpretation of the motives of the agents in carrying out their assignments – the old question of human nature. To indicate the full range of ambiguity involved here I must point out that the Corporation as so far sketched might involve only the *coordination* of the work of various agents, and need not involve their full cooperation. If someone were employing workers to produce a good which only joint effort could bring about, but the employees did not know that they were working with others on such a project, we could not say they were *cooperating* with one another. Allowing the employees to know there are other agents beside themselves, even allowing them some knowledge of the aim or point of the joint enterprise, still would not entitle us to call their work cooperative. It is at best coordinated. The agents are cooperating only if in addition to the conditions so far given, it is also true that at least one of the reasons each agent has for doing his or her work is a desire to help bring about the good which the venture is meant to produce.

Consider first workers in a merely coordinated venture. They are presumably working solely for their own ends: each has taken the job for its wages, and so far none has a basis for questioning his or her assignment. If each knows there are other employees and knows something of the point of the joint venture, but is still working solely for the wages, it turns out that there is an analog of the principle I have said is at work within a truly cooperative venture. We can see this by imagining a worker in a coordinated venture who wants to increase his wages. He knows there are others involved and knows the point of the venture. If the employer is fair, he can reasonably suppose that he will be rewarded in proportion to his contribution to the good which, for whatever reasons, the director wants brought about. The worker might then reasonably think he could increase his contribution by making up for slackness in the performance of others, or by doing things that are important but are being left undone. But the more complex the venture is and the more perfect the director, the less reasonable it is for the employee to think that he can really increase his contribution to the good and thus come to merit higher wages by going beyond his responsibilities. In the limiting case of the Divine Corporation he would have no reason to think he could increase his wages in this way. The employee's duties would be absolute for him, despite the fact that God sees his work as being for a purpose. The Divine Corporation can thus model some features of morality whether we take the corporation to involve coordination or full cooperation.

Consider, then, the questions that arise if cooperation is involved. Here at least part of the motivation for participating is a desire to help bring about the good. This need not be the same as a desire for that good itself, though it may be. If the good to be jointly produced is truly a common good – one which is a good for each and all of the agents, in addition to being the good for which God created the whole enterprise – then any of several accounts may be offered of how we each find our own happiness in that good. If it is not a common good in this way, then a different account will have to be offered of why we participate. We may also see this as the question of whether the persons who are the agents in the Divine Corporation have within them a source of order, essential to their nature, which leads them to act as members of a just cooperative venture, or whether, as in a coordinated enterprise, they must be induced or compelled to act appropriately by external sanctions and rewards. On any account of motivation, the need to explain the supremacy of moral laws is as important as the need to account for their performability; and the philosopher must also leave room for an account of why we do not always act in accordance with the laws of the moral world.

V

So far I have kept my discussion of the Divine Corporation away from historical realities. I have only tried to show how the idea might be embodied in a wide variety of positions having the common essential feature of relying on the logic of coordination or cooperation under a perfect supervisor. I do not mean to suggest that every possible variant was actually exemplified. Nor do I want to say that Divine Corporation ethics was dominant at the beginning of our period in the unqualified and bare form I have given it. On the contrary, religious doctrines about the necessity of Divine grace, in stronger, anti-Pelagian, or in weaker, semi-Pelagian, forms always raised difficulties about performability, while skepticisms of various kinds led to doubts about universality, and Stoicism and Machiavellianism raised questions about supremacy. But I do want to claim that the Divine Corporation represents what became increasingly central to the moral teaching of Christianity. As a result, the model can serve some useful purposes for the historian.

First, it helps us understand the structural and dynamic features of an important succession of actual, influential positions. St Thomas Aquinas and his numerous followers in the natural law tradition, both on the Catholic and on the Protestant sides, through Suarez and Hooker, hold views which are modelled by the Divine Corporation. So too do the 'modern' natural law thinkers descending from Grotius. We do not find thinkers like Pufendorf, Burlamaqui, and Vattel of great philosophical interest today, because the philosophical part of their work, as distinct from their concerns with politics and international law, so often merely repeats what had been worked out earlier. But they represent what I believe to have been the common framework of thought of the educated part of the world during the seventeenth and eighteenth centuries. The philosophers we study from that period draw our attention in part because they modify, depart from and eventually abandon that framework. It is crucial to our understanding of them to know what they were departing from, to see why they departed, and to note how far they went. Thus the Divine Corporation is useful not only as a starting point but also as a benchmark. To the extent a philosopher stays close to it we may view him as conservative; to the extent he breaks away, as innovative. This gives us some rough measure of change in moral philosophy in terms that could have been used by the thinkers of the period we are trying to understand, and not just in our own terms.

Second, the idea of the Divine Corporation helps us to see the history of ethics as controlled by a concern for the moral world as a just cooperative enterprise. By bringing before us the complex whole into which the elements of the moral life must fit, whatever philosophical interpretation of them is given, it reminds us not to attach undue explanatory importance to philosophical debates about any one of the elements alone. A change in interpretation of one element will require other changes in a philosophical explanation of the moral world. A grasp of the dynamic that links these changes is perhaps the most important tool that the idea of the Divine Corporation gives us for understanding the history of ethics during our period.

In what follows I shall try to illustrate this by tracing very hastily the changes that led to the positions of Reid, Bentham, and Kant. With their work we come, I believe, to the culmination of the classical period of modern ethics and to the transition to a new period. If the idea of the Divine Corporation can help to explain how their positions emerge reasonably from earlier views, it has served its purpose.

VI

The basic change in religious thought during the period that concerns us was the rejection, to as great an extent as possible, of appeals to mystery and incomprehensibility as central to adequate accounts of the Christian faith. This change leads to dramatic results for the explanation of morality within the Divine Corporation. When we can understand neither the corporate good to which we are contributing nor our own role in producing it, and when we believe in constant providential supervision of life, it is only rational – so I have argued – to treat our duties as absolute. This holds whether we are each motivated solely by self-interest or not. Consequently the philosopher explaining the moral world needs an account of those duties which yields such a view of them. As God's purpose comes to be thought more comprehensible, and as our part in helping it becomes plainer, there is less and less reason to treat duties in this way. This is particularly true as one moves away from seeing God primarily as a just judge, and toward thinking of him rather as the Benevolent Author of Nature. Then his end will be our happiness, not an incomprehensible display of infinite glory; and if happiness is the goal, our part in bringing it about is more easily grasped. This tendency is reinforced when, like the theists and deists, one insists that after the Creation God intended the world to operate without unpredictable special providences – that he set the world-machine going, and then let it alone. For then we must cease to think that an intelligent power rectifies our errors and omissions and makes up for accidents. More of the responsibility for doing so must rationally be thought to be our own. There is thus more and more good reason to understand morality in terms of our responsibility for looking to the *point* of our duties – to the good our cooperative efforts are to produce – for direct guidance in action.

At the same time there are good reasons to resist this utilitarian tendency. As we would expect, it can be challenged on the ground that utilitarianism finds it hard to explain how each of us can know what to do. We also find another kind of reasoning. Our moral experience, and not appeal to religious doctrine, is used as a source of argument against utilitarian views. Our moral experience carries rational weight because, in a Divine Corporation theory, God must have given us ways of being aware of what is required of us. Hence the experience through which each of us learns how to act must reflect the realities of the moral world. And as that experience is equally available to all of us, it gives us common data from which to argue reasonably. Butler is the *locus classicus*. Admitting that the only positive moral character we can attribute to God is goodness, he agrees that God looks at the world as a utilitarian. But we are not in God's position. We do not know enough to be utilitarians, and our moral experience shows us that we have particular duties of other kinds:

> as we are not competent judges, what is upon the whole for the good of the world, there may be other immediate ends appointed us to pursue, besides that one of doing good, or producing happiness. Though the good of the creation be the only end of the Author of it, yet He may have laid us under particular obligations, which we may discern and feel ourselves under, quite distinct from a perception that the observance or violation of them is for the happiness or misery of our fellow-creatures. And this is in fact the case.   (*The Works of Bishop Butler* 1, 166n)

Butler elsewhere gives ample detail in support of this last contention. His target is in part Hutcheson, who argues that while we have a moral sense to guide us – thus avoiding worries about performability – its dictates are best mapped by a utilitarian law. If Butler makes the latter conclusion implausible, others criticize the non-cognitivism as unable to account for universality. The predictable result of these moves is a reassertion of intuitional views in Price and ultimately in Reid.

Reid gives us the last and most minimal of Divine Corporation theories in the eighteenth century. Indeed it is doubtful whether he should be thought of as a Divine Corporation theorist at all. He holds that moral principles are self-evident, and that everyone has sufficient intuitive grasp of them to guide action by them. Intuition is construed in a way that gives it the same role in explaining our knowledge of nature as it has in explaining our knowledge of morality. Since Reid thus has quite general grounds for allowing that ordinary moral beliefs carry rational weight, it looks as if he need not rely on the Butlerian belief that our moral faculty is God-given. And it also looks as if Reid does not think that action in accordance with the self-evident principles of morality is meant to serve any end whatsoever beyond conformity itself. He thus seems to advocate the kind of deontological view later made familiar by Prichard and Ross. But if in this respect he is out of the realm of Divine Corporation theory, there is another side to his position that is not. He holds that our ordinary moral beliefs are the test we are to use when we try to construct theories about the general laws of morality. And with this test in mind he concludes, against Hume, that no simple basic law is adequate. There are some seventeen intuitively evident axioms of morality. No reduction of them to any one principle is possible. At this point Reid's independence of reliance on the deity ends. Reid must have God available to guarantee that our intuitions reveal a moral world, not a chaos. God is needed to assure us that the apparently arbitrary list of moral axioms is complete and that the axioms do not conflict. In particular, Reid appeals to God to show that prudence, which is self-evidently required, does not conflict with the demands of benevolence, justice, and the other equally self-evident principles of morality. Against the monistic utilitarianism of someone like Bentham, who will not allow of any appeal to God as an explanatory entity, Reid could have only two lines of argument. One is to claim that the best explanation of the fact that we all share the same moral beliefs is that they result from accurate perception of underlying moral reality. The other is the appeal to self-evidence. But Bentham claims that the best explanation of such common moral beliefs is that they arise simply from social and psychological conditioning. Reid is thus left with only the epistemology of general intuitionism as the basic line of defense of a pluralism of moral principles against utilitarian monism. At this point we begin to face the issues that became central in the next phase of the history of ethics.

VII

The task for secular moral theories during the period from Montaigne to Kant is set by the ability of Divine Corporation theories to account for morality as it is present in the society of the times; and that morality had largely been shaped by teachings which were informed by the presuppositions of the Divine Corporation. Thus secular moralists were forced to duplicate in their theories many of the features of Divine Corporation views. This is strikingly evident in the work of Hobbes, and is a feature of Hume's view as well. A brief comment about them will help to bring out the originality of Bentham and Kant, and show why I take these later thinkers to mark the end of one understanding of the problems of moral philosophy and the beginning of another. I think it obvious that both Hobbes and Hume find ways to replicate that relation between absolute moral laws and a good which is produced by coordination or cooperation, which is essential to Divine Corporation views. It is also clear that each finds a surrogate to take on at least some of the functions of God in such views. The point I want to stress here has rather to do with their view of the task of moral philosophy. Amid many differences between them, this is a point of agreement.

Their agreement is that the moral world does not hold together only because each individual within it understands the whole explanation of morality, far less because each deliberately uses the philosophical account of morality in making moral decisions. Indeed, Hobbes and Hume would agree that there would be considerable danger to the moral world if such a thing should occur. The citizens, for Hobbes, are to understand morality as a matter of the Golden Rule, supplemented by carefully regulated preaching of the laws from the pulpit. His own books are addressed to the ruler – not to the masses for further debate. Hume, without thinking so much central control is needed, sees the moral world as held together by our sentiments. He explains how they are naturally coordinated to do the job, but he does not suggest that each of us should transform his explanation into a principle which we would then use in making our decisions. There may possibly be some room for 'correcting our sentiments' at the margins of the moral world, but deliberate use of theory is not what gives the moral world its basic order.

The rejection of this view of the limits of moral philosophy, and its replacement by the belief that each agent can deliberately contribute to a proper moral order by consciously using a principle of action discovered by a philosopher, is the work of Bentham and Kant.

With Bentham the change does not result so much from internal philosophical motivation as from a deep conviction that the social world needs to be reformed. Accepting no cosmic principle of order, Bentham abandons the Divine Corporation stance entirely, since he sees no reason to suppose that our moral beliefs up to this time have any value as guides in this endeavour. Before we can know their value, we must have a rational criterion which we can deliberately use to assess them. He thinks, of course, that he has such a criterion. Not only can it be used by rulers to lead the reshaping of their societies, it can be used by individuals making their own decisions. Bentham thus does not offer the utilitarian principle as the explanation of a moral world which we can be confident we already, somehow, inhabit. It is rather to guide us in making by ourselves and for ourselves a community which will be moral. There is no one else who can take the responsibility for doing so.

Bentham shows us how radically the task of the moral philosopher changes if we do not suppose that there is anything like the supervisor for a Divine Corporation, not even Nature. The philosopher must now also give rational grounds for this principle, strong enough to convince people who may very well hold convictions opposed to it. Questions of how each agent can figure out or come to know what to do in particular cases acquire an importance they did not have in Divine Corporation theory and its secular analogs. And questions about how, and whether, a moral first principle of this description can be proven come to have a new and far greater significance. Once again we are at the beginning of a new period of moral philosophy.

VIII

My story must end with Kant; and in the light of that story, his position is extraordinarily complex and, I believe, profoundly ambivalent. Only necessity drives me into the folly of trying to present an analysis of his place in the history of ethics at the end of a paper.

If Kant were the deontologist pure and simple that he has often been taken to be, he would have gone even further than Reid in abandoning Divine Corporation views of morality. He would have extracted the element within such views that stresses the absoluteness of one's duties and made it into the whole of what is distinctively moral. He would thus have denied the teleological significance of absolute duties which is central to Divine Corporation views. He would have shown that one can account for the universality of moral demands by noting their transparent rationality. He would have avoided Reid's need to use God to guarantee the coherence of morality by showing that there is only one moral principle. He would have shown that performability can be assured because it is easy to apply the one principle, and because we are free always to do as morality demands. And he would have guaranteed the supremacy of morality by his insistence on its uniquely categorical character. It is of course this last claim that leads readers to think Kant sees morality as entirely cut off from any concern with the teleological point of performance of duty. But this reading of Kant is not adequate. Numerous commentators have shown why, and the matter is perhaps no longer in doubt. I want here only to note a way of bringing it out that shows simultaneously an important respect in which Kant is still deeply inside the Divine Corporation tradition.

We can see this by noting Kant's frequently repeated view that virtue or moral goodness is to be understood as worthiness to be happy. It is important to see that this is a seriously question-begging account for Kant to use. One of his avowed aims is to show that morality is binding on us regardless of whether (we believe that) God exists and rewards and punishes us. But the notion of deserving something – good or bad, reward or punishment – only makes sense in a context in which some system of distributing goods and evils according to pre-established rules or criteria is in force. Given such a practice, then it is indeed obvious that those who abide by the rules or meet the criteria (or do so 'best', if that is pertinent) deserve the established rewards, and that those who break the rules deserve the punishments. Lacking such a context, no sense can be given to the notion of desert. The assertion that someone deserves a better break than life has given him really comes to no more than the use of a metaphor to express the feeling that it would be nice if the person had had a better life. Thus in simply taking it for granted that virtue can be defined in terms of deserving happiness, Kant reveals how thoroughly he assumes a point of view which makes perfect sense in a just world of which a Divine Corporation view is true, but makes none if we live in a neutral universe.

Of course there is an important way in which Kant does not simply take it for granted that we live in a just world. Rather, he argues that morality requires us to believe that we do. Our moral actions, he holds, are not to be done for the sake of their consequences. They are to be done simply because they are required by the moral law. None the less, all rational acts have purposes, and so must the acts required by morality. Kant thinks he can show that the world required by morality as its outcome is one in which happiness is distributed according to merit. Now if it is not reasonable to act purposelessly, and if we cannot take as our purpose something we know or believe to be impossible, then we must believe that such a world is possible. And to believe that a just world is possible, we must – so Kant notoriously concludes – also believe that there is a God who can make it so, for humans alone cannot control those aspects of Nature which must fall into line if a just moral world is to be brought about. In short Kant cannot conceive of morality except in a world structured as the Divine Corporation structures it. Instead of seeing the absolute character of the demands of duty as resulting from prior knowledge that we live in such a world, he sees those demands as giving us our sole justification for believing that we do.

It is well known that this part of Kant's general position created enormous difficulties for him. I do not refer to his moral arguments for the existence of God and the immortality of the soul, which bother us more than they worried him. I refer rather to his difficulty in explaining convincingly how morality can be perfectly independent of religious belief and its assurances of rewards for virtue, while at the same time holding that morality requires us to project a religious view of the world in which we act. If Kant's refusal to give up the latter part of this complex belief testifies to the tenacity of his commitment to a Divine Corporation view of morality, there is another side of his thinking that shows plainly his reluctance to remain within those confines. Kant always believed that the ability of the parts of God's world to direct themselves as parts of an ordered whole gave more sublime proof of God's glory than would a need for his constant intervention and direction. The upshot of this in Kant's mature thought is not only the Rousseauvian conviction that moral insight is equally available to every normal human. It is the belief that conscious use of articulated knowledge of the moral law would not disrupt, would instead strengthen, moral order. He sees his principle, therefore, both as explanatory of our deepest moral convictions – as in Divine Corporation theory – and as directive of our choices – as in Bentham's view. But in his historical and political writings, the directive function comes to have more and more of a role. We are to think of ourselves as being like God in one respect. We are required to make the world into a just moral community. The moral law shows us the conditions to which it must comply if it is to be one in which we as rational agents can willingly participate. Kant thus seems increasingly to treat the moral world as an historical task rather than as a metaphysical or religious assurance. That his view is indeed a descendant of the Divine Corporation is borne out by this turn in his thought. As I have pointed out, it is a result of the dynamic of the Divine Corporation that as God's supervision and activity lessen, man's responsibility increases. Like Bentham, though in a much more complex fashion, Kant did not really think we could leave it up to God.[3]

REFERENCES

Venturi, Franco. 1971. *Utopia and Reform in the Enlightenment*. Cambridge: Cambridge University Press

Wade, Ira O. 1971. *The Intellectual Origins of the French Revolution*. Princeton: Princeton University Press

The Works of Bishop Butler, ed. J. H. Bernard. London: Macmillan, 1900

[3] I am most grateful to J. J. Katz, Thomas Nagel, Quentin Skinner, David Sachs, Richard Rorty, and John Rawls for their comments on earlier versions of this paper.

◁ ═══════════════════════════════════ ▷

9

The idea of negative liberty:
philosophical and historical perspectives

QUENTIN SKINNER

I

My aim is to explore a possible means of enlarging our present understanding of the concepts we employ in social and political argument.[1] The prevailing orthodoxy bids us proceed by consulting our intuitions about what can and cannot be coherently said and done with the terms we generally use to express the concepts involved. But this approach might with profit be supplemented, I shall argue, if we were to confront these intuitions with a more systematic examination of the unfamiliar theories within which even our most familiar concepts have sometimes been put to work at different historical periods.[2]

One way of proceeding with this line of thought would be to offer a general defence of this view about the 'relevance' of the history of philosophy for the understanding of contemporary philosophical debates. But I shall instead attempt to make a more direct, if more modest, contribution to the theme of the present volume by focusing on one particular concept which is at once central to current disputes in social and political theory and is at the same time overdue, it seems to me, for this type of historical treatment.

[1] I am very grateful to Thomas Baldwin, John Dunn, Richard Flathman, Raymond Geuss, Susan James, J. G. A. Pocock, Russell Price, James Tully and my co-editors for reading and commenting on earlier drafts of this article. To Thomas Baldwin and Susan James I am especially indebted for many discussions and much essential help. An earlier version of the present essay formed the basis of the Messenger Lectures I delivered at Cornell University in October 1983. I made further revisions in the light of the many helpful criticisms I received at that time, especially from Terry Irwin, John Lyons and John Najemy.

[2] I am thus developing a line of thought originally outlined at the end of Skinner 1969:52–3. That argument in turn owed an obvious debt to the formulations contained in the Introduction to MacIntyre 1966 and in Dunn 1968, two studies by which I have been much influenced. I should add that, if I am reminded at the outset that the thesis of incommensurability, as defended in particular by Feyerabend 1981, serves to question the very idea of pursuing the line of thought I have in mind, I can only reply that one of the subsidiary though far from modest hopes I entertain for my present argument is that it may do something (at least in relation to theories about the social world) to question the thesis of incommensurability itself.

The concept I have in mind is that of political liberty, the extent of the freedom or liberty of action available to individual agents within the confines imposed on them by their membership of political society.[3] The first point to be observed is that, among English-speaking philosophers of the present time, the discussion of this topic has given rise to one conclusion which commands a remarkably wide measure of assent. It is that – to cite the formula originally owed to Jeremy Bentham, and more recently made famous by Isaiah Berlin – the concept of liberty is essentially a 'negative' one. Its presence is said to be marked, that is, by the absence of something else; specifically, by the absence of some element of constraint that inhibits the agent concerned from being able to act independently in pursuit of his[4] chosen ends. As Gerald MacCallum expresses the point, in a form of words that has become standard in the current literature, 'whenever the freedom of some agent or agents is in question, it is always freedom from some constraint or restriction on, interference with, or barrier to doing, not doing, becoming or not becoming something' (MacCallum 1972:176).[5]

It would be no exaggeration to say that this assumption – that the only coherent idea of liberty is the negative one of being unconstrained – has underpinned the entire development of modern contractarian political thought. We already find Thomas Hobbes expressing it at the outset of his chapter 'Of the liberty of subjects' in *Leviathan*, in which he presents an extremely influential statement of the claim that 'liberty or freedom signifieth (properly) the absence of opposition' and signifies nothing more

---

[3] Discussing this concept, some philosophers (for example Oppenheim 1981) prefer to speak of social freedom, while others (for example Rawls 1971) always speak of liberty. As far as I can see, nothing hangs on this difference of terminology. Throughout the following argument I have accordingly felt free (or at liberty) to treat these two terms as exact synonyms and to use them interchangeably.

[4] Or her, of course. But in the course of this article I shall often allow myself the convenience of treating 'his', 'he', etc., as abbreviations, where appropriate, for 'his or her', 'he or she', etc.

[5] Note the implication that if a negative analysis of liberty always takes a triadic form (as MacCallum here suggests) it will always include at least an implicit reference to the agent's possession of an independent, unconstrained will, in consequence of which he is able to act freely in pursuit of his chosen ends. It is true that this has sometimes been questioned. John Gray, for instance (1980:511), argues that 'freedom must be regarded as basically a dyadic rather than as a triadic concept', a claim he defends by appealing to Isaiah Berlin's criticism of MacCallum for the latter's supposed failure to appreciate that 'a man struggling against his chains or a people against enslavement need not consciously aim at any definite further state' (Berlin 1969:xliii note). But it is surely evident that the struggling man of Berlin's example is someone who wishes at once to be free from an element of interference, and at the same time to be able (freely, independently) to do or be or become something – at the very least, to become a man free from the constraints imposed by his chains and in consequence (and *eo ipso*) free to act should he choose to do so. It seems clear, in short, that the purported counter-example misses MacCallum's point, which is that, when we say of an agent that he or she is unconstrained, this *is* to say that he is capable of acting at will – or of choosing to remain inactive, of course.

(Hobbes 1968:261). The same assumption, often couched specifically in terms of MacCallum's triadic analysis, continues to run throughout the current literature. Benn and Weinstein, for example, implicitly adopt MacCallum's framework in their important essay on freedom as the non-restriction of options, as does Oppenheim in his recent discussion of social freedom as the capacity to pursue alternatives.[6] And the same analysis is explicitly invoked – with direct reference to MacCallum's classic article – in Rawls' *Theory of Justice*, Feinberg's *Social Philosophy*, and many other contemporary accounts.[7]

It is of course true that, in spite of this basic and long-standing agreement, there have always been disputes among proponents of the 'negative' thesis about the nature of the circumstances in which it is proper to say that the freedom of some particular agent has or has not been infringed. For there have always been divergent beliefs as to what counts as opposition, and thus as the sort of constraint that limits the freedom as opposed to merely limiting the ability of agents to perform actions. Far more important, however, for the purposes of my present argument is the widespread endorsement of the conclusion that – as Charles Taylor puts it in his attack on the consensus – the idea of liberty is to be construed as a pure 'opportunity concept', as nothing but the absence of constraint, and hence as unconnected with the pursuit of any determinate ends or purposes (Taylor 1979:177).

It is typical of negative theorists – Hobbes is again a classic example – to spell out the implications of this central commitment in polemical terms. The aim of doing so has generally been to repudiate two contentions about social freedom – both occasionally defended in the history of modern political theory – on the grounds that they are incompatible with the basic idea that the enjoyment of social freedom is simply a matter of being unobstructed. One of these has been the suggestion that individual liberty can only be assured within a particular form of self-governing community. Put most starkly, the claim is that (as Rousseau expresses it in *Du Contrat Social*) the maintenance of personal freedom depends on the performance of public services. The other and connected suggestion often attacked by negative theorists is that the qualities needed on the part of each individual citizen in order to ensure the effective performance of these civic duties must be the civic virtues. Again, to put it starkly (as Spinoza does in the *Tractatus Politicus*), the claim is that liberty presupposes virtue; that only the virtuous are truly or fully capable of assuring their own individual freedom.

By way of responding to these paradoxes, some contemporary theorists

---

[6] See Benn and Weinstein 1971:201; Oppenheim 1981:65.
[7] See Rawls 1971:202; Feinberg 1973:11, 16.

of negative liberty have simply followed Hobbes in insisting that, since the liberty of subjects must involve 'immunity from the service of the commonwealth', any suggestion that freedom involves the performance of such services, and the cultivation of the virtues necessary to perform them, must be totally confused (Hobbes 1968:266). Isaiah Berlin remarks, for example, at the end of his celebrated essay, 'Two concepts of liberty', that to speak of rendering myself free by virtuously performing my social duties, thereby equating duty with interest, is simply 'to throw a metaphysical blanket over either self-deceit or deliberate hypocrisy' (Berlin 1969:171). The more moderate and usual riposte, however, has been to suggest that, whatever may be the merits of the two heterodox claims I have singled out, they are certainly not consistent with a negative analysis of freedom, and must point instead to a different conception – perhaps even a different concept – of political liberty. This appears to be Berlin's own view in an earlier section of his essay, where he concedes that we might entertain a secularized version of the belief that God's service is perfect freedom 'without thereby rendering the word "freedom" wholly meaningless', but adds that the meaning we should then be assigning to the term cannot possibly be the one required by a negative account of liberty (Berlin 1969:160–2).

Despite these strictures, the more fairminded defenders of negative liberty have sometimes conceded the possibility of constructing a coherent – even if an unfamiliar – theory of social freedom in which the liberty of individuals might be connected with the ideals of virtue and public service.[8] As Berlin in particular has emphasized, all that needs to be added to begin to make sense of such claims is the ultimately Aristotelian suggestion that we are moral beings with certain true ends and rational purposes, and that we are only in the fullest sense in possession of our liberty when we live in such a community and act in such a way that those ends and purposes are realized as completely as possible (Berlin 1969:145–54).

Some contemporary writers have added, moreover, that we *ought* to insert this further premise, and to recognize that (in Charles Taylor's words) freedom is not merely an 'opportunity' but an 'exercise' concept, that we are only free 'in the exercise of certain capacities', and thus that we 'are not free, or less free, when these capacities are in some way unfulfilled or blocked' (Taylor 1979:179). Having made this move, such theorists characteristically go on to observe that this at least commits us to

---

[8] But by no means all have been so fairminded. Strict followers of Hobbes (such as Steiner 1974–5, Day 1983 and Flew 1983) insist that the only coherent account that can possibly be given of the concept of liberty is the negative one. And, insofar as MacCallum's analysis suggests a negative understanding of freedom as the absence of constraints upon an agent's options (which it does), this is also the implication of his account and of those that depend on it.

considering the reinstatement of both the claims about social freedom so firmly repudiated by Hobbes and his modern disciples. First of all, as Taylor suggests, if human nature does indeed have an essence, it is certainly not implausible to suppose – as many ancient philosophers in fact supposed – that its full realization may only be possible 'within a certain form of society' which we need to serve and uphold if our true natures, and hence our own individual liberty, are both to reach their fullest development (Taylor 1979:193). And secondly, as Benjamin Gibbs, for example, puts it in his book on *Freedom and Liberation*, we can hardly resist the further conclusion, once we acknowledge that our liberty depends upon 'attaining and enjoying those cardinal goods appropriate to our natures', that the practice of the virtues may be indispensable to the performance of just those morally worthwhile actions that serve to mark us out as 'consummately free' (Gibbs 1976:22,129–31).

Much of the debate between those who think of social freedom as a negative opportunity concept and those who think of it as a positive exercise concept may thus be said to stem from a deeper dispute about human nature. The argument is *au fond* about whether we can hope to distinguish an objective notion of *eudaimonia* or human flourishing.[9] Those who dismiss this hope as illusory – such as Berlin and his many sympathizers – conclude that this makes it a dangerous error to connect individual liberty with the ideals of virtue and public service. Those who believe in real or identifiably human interests – Taylor, Gibbs and others – respond by insisting that this at least makes it arguable that only the virtuous and public-spirited citizen who serves the State is in full possession of his or her liberty.

This in turn means, however, that there is one fundamental assumption shared by virtually all the contributors to the current debate about social freedom. Even Charles Taylor and Isaiah Berlin are able to agree on it: that it is only if we can give a content to the idea of objective human flourishing that we can hope to make sense of any theory purporting to connect the concept of individual liberty with virtuous acts of public service.

The thesis I propose to defend is that this shared and central assumption is a mistake. And in order to defend it, I shall turn to what I take to be the lessons of history. I shall try to show that, in an earlier and now discarded tradition of thought about social freedom, the negative idea of liberty as the mere non-obstruction of individual agents in the pursuit of their chosen ends was combined with the ideas of virtue and public service in just the manner nowadays assumed on all sides to be impossible without incoherence. I shall thus try to supplement and correct our prevailing and

---

[9] For emphasizing and tracing the implications of the fact that some such conception lies at the heart of most 'positive' views of liberty, I am greatly indebted to Baldwin 1984.

misleadingly restricted sense of what can and cannot be said and done with the concept of negative liberty by examining the record of the very different things that have been said and done with it at earlier phases in the history of our own culture.

II

Before embarking on this task, however, one obvious query about this way of proceeding must first be answered. It might well be asked why I propose to examine the historical record at this juncture instead of attempting directly to develop a more inclusive philosophical analysis of negative liberty. My answer is not that I suppose such purely conceptual exercises to be out of the question; on the contrary, they are the hallmark of the most probing and original contributions to the contemporary debate.[10] It is rather that, in consequence of certain widespread assumptions about the best methods of studying social and political concepts, it is apt to seem much less convincing to suggest that a concept *might* be coherently used in an unfamiliar way than to show that it *has* been put to unfamiliar but coherent uses.

The nature of the assumptions I have in mind can readily be illustrated from the current literature on the concept of liberty. The basic postulate of all the writers I have so far mentioned is that to explicate a concept such as that of social freedom is to give an account of the meanings of the terms habitually used to express it. And to understand the meanings of such terms, it is further agreed, is a matter of understanding their correct usage, of grasping what can and cannot be said and done with them.[11]

So far so good; or rather, so far so Wittgensteinian, which I am prepared to suppose amounts in these matters to the same thing. These procedures next tend to be equated, however, with giving an account of how *we* generally employ the terms involved. What we are thus enjoined to study is 'what we normally would say' about liberty, and what we find 'we do not want to say' when we reflect about the uses of the term in an adequately self-conscious way.[12] We are told to stay 'as close to ordinary language as possible', the reason being that the highroad to understanding a concept

[10] I have in mind especially MacCallum 1972 and Baldwin 1984.
[11] For explicit presentations of these postulates, applied to the case of 'explicating' the concept of freedom, see for example Parent 1974a:149–51 and Oppenheim 1981:148–50,179–82.
[12] Parent 1974b:432–3. Cf. also Benn and Weinstein 1971:194 on the need to study 'what in general one can appropriately say' about the term 'freedom' in order to understand the concept, and their attack on Parent's account in 1974:435 on the grounds that it is 'so evidently contrary to standard usage' that 'one is bound to mistrust the characterization of freedom which makes it even possible'.

such as that of liberty is to grasp 'what we normally mean' by the term 'liberty'.[13]

This is not to say that 'ordinary language' is to have the last word, and most of the writers I have been discussing are at pains to distance themselves from so widely discredited a belief. On the contrary, it is assumed that, once we begin to move towards a position of equilibrium between our intuitions about concepts and the demands of current usage, it may well prove necessary to adjust what we are disposed to say about a concept such as that of liberty in the light of what we find ourselves saying about other and closely connected concepts such as rights, responsibility, coercion and so forth. The true goal of conceptual analysis – as Feinberg for example formulates it – is thus to arrive, by way of reflecting on 'what we normally mean when we employ certain words', at a more finished delineation of 'what we had better mean if we are to communicate effectively, avoid paradox and achieve general coherence'.[14]

As the above quotations reveal, however, the question is still about what *we* are capable of saying and meaning without incoherence. Given this approach, it is easy to see how it comes about that any purely analytical attempt to connect the idea of negative liberty with the ideals of virtue and service will be liable to appear unconvincing, and vulnerable to being dismissed out of hand. For it is obvious that *we* cannot hope to connect the idea of liberty with the obligation to perform virtuous acts of public service except at the unthinkable cost of giving up, or making nonsense of, our intuitions about individual rights. But this in turn means that, in the case of all the writers I have been considering, only one of two responses can be offered to someone who insists on trying to explicate the concept in such a counter-intuitive way. The kinder is to suggest that – as Berlin for example tends to put it – they must really be talking about something else; they must 'have a different concept' of liberty.[15] But the more usual is to contend – as for example Parent does – that they must simply be confused. To connect the idea of freedom with such principles as virtue or rational self-mastery, as Parent patiently reminds us, fails to convey or even connect with 'what we ordinarily mean' by the term 'liberty'. From which he concludes that any attempt to forge such links can only result in a confused misunderstanding of the concept involved.[16]

It is in the hope of preventing myself from being ruled out of order in this

[13] For this injunction see Oppenheim 1981:179.
[14] See Feinberg 1973:2. For similar commitments, see Parent 1974a:166, Raz 1970:303–4, and Oppenheim 1981:179–80, who cites both Feinberg and Raz with approval.
[15] See Berlin 1969, esp.154–62; cf. Ryan 1980:497.
[16] Parent 1974a:152, 166, and 1974b:434. Cf. also Gray 1980:511, who insists that, by reflecting on 'intelligible locutions having to do with freedom', we can dismiss MacCallum's contention that the term always denotes a triadic relationship.

fashion before the argument gets under way that I propose to eschew conceptual analysis and turn instead to history. Before doing so, however, one further preliminary note of warning must be sounded. If there is to be any prospect of invoking the past in the manner I have sketched – as a means of questioning rather than underpinning our current beliefs – we shall have to reconsider, and indeed repudiate, the reasons usually given for studying the history of philosophy by the leading practitioners of the subject at the present time.

For a representative discussion of these reasons, furnished by an eminent practitioner, consider the Introduction to J. L. Mackie's revealingly titled book, *Problems from Locke*. This opens by articulating the basic presupposition of much contemporary work in the history of philosophy: that there is a certain determinate range of problems that go to make up the discipline of philosophy, and that we can therefore expect to find a corresponding range of historical treatments of these problems, some of which may prove to be 'of continuing philosophical interest'.[17] It follows that, if we want a usable history, there are two guidelines to be observed. The first is to concentrate on just those historical texts, and just those sections of just those texts, in which it is immediately apparent that familiar concepts are indeed being deployed to construct familiar arguments with which we can then take direct issue. Mackie gives clear expression to this rule when he remarks in his Introduction that he 'makes no attempt to expound or study Locke's philosophy as a whole, or even that part of it which is to be found in the *Essay*', since his aim is exclusively to discuss 'a limited number of problems of continuing philosophical interest' which happen to be raised and considered at various points in Locke's work (Mackie 1976:1).

The second guideline is that, since the reason for exhuming the great philosophers of the past is to help us arrive at better answers to our own questions, we must be prepared as much as necessary to recast their thought in our own idiom, seeking to produce a rational reconstruction of their beliefs rather than a picture of full historical authenticity where these two projects begin to collide. Again Mackie offers a particularly clear statement of this commitment, observing that the main purpose of his work 'is not to expound Locke's views or to study their relations with those of his contemporaries and near contemporaries, but to work towards solutions of the problems themselves' (Mackie 1976:2).

The value of following these rules, we are finally assured, lies in their capacity to provide us with a ready and easy way of dividing up our intellectual heritage. If we come upon a philosophical text, or even a bit of

---

[17] Mackie 1976:1. According to the most optimistic formulations, such historical treatments may sometimes be of *permanent* philosophical interest. See for example O'Connor 1964:ix.

an otherwise interesting text, in which the author begins to discuss a topic which (as Mackie puts it) 'is not a live issue for us', the proper course of action is to reallocate it for study under the separate heading of 'the history of ideas' (Mackie 1976:4). This is held to be the name of a distinct discipline that concerns itself with issues 'of purely historical' as opposed to 'intrinsically philosophical' significance.[18] Sometimes it is rather strongly implied that it is hard to see how these issues (not being 'live') can have much significance at all. But it is usually allowed that they may well be of interest to those who are interested in such things. It is just that such people will be historians of ideas; they will not be engaged in an enquiry of any relevance to philosophy.

I have no wish, of course, to question the obvious truth that there are large continuities in the history of modern philosophy, such that it may sometimes be possible to sharpen our wits by arguing directly with our elders and betters. I do wish to suggest, however, that there are at least two reasons for questioning the assumption that the history of philosophy should be written as though it is not really history. One is that, even where we feel confident in saying of some earlier philosopher that he is in effect inhabiting a timeless continuum, and is arguing about an issue of contemporary relevance in a wholly contemporary style, we can hardly claim to have understood the philosopher in question, to have arrived at an interpretation of his thought, as long as we remain content simply to explicate and comment on the structure of his arguments. I shall not pursue this objection here, but I take it that to mount an argument is always to argue *with* someone, is always to reason for or against a certain conclusion or course of action. This being so, the business of interpreting any text that contains such forms of reasoning will always require us (to speak over-schematically) to follow two connected lines of approach which seem to me ultimately inseparable, though they are often separated in such a way that the second is overlooked. The initial task is obviously to recapture the substance of the argument itself. If we wish, however, to arrive at an interpretation of the text, an understanding of why its contents are as they are and not otherwise, we are still left with the further task of recovering what the writer may have meant by arguing in the precise way he argued. We need, that is, to be able to give an account of what he was *doing* in presenting his argument: what set of conclusions, what course of action, he was supporting or defending, attacking or repudiating, ridiculing with irony, scorning with polemical silence, and so on and on through the entire gamut of speech-acts embodied in the vastly complex act of intended communication that any work of discursive reasoning may be said to comprise.

[18] For a representative recent statement of the issue in these exact terms, see for example Scruton 1981:10–11.

One of my doubts about the prevailing approach to the history of philosophy is that it systematically ignores this latter aspect of the interpretative task. I now turn to my other criticism, which I propose to treat at much greater length. It is that the notion of 'relevance' contained in the orthodox approach is a needlessly constricting and indeed a philistine one. According to the view I have been outlining, the history of philosophy is only 'relevant' if we can use it as a mirror to reflect our own beliefs and assumptions back to us. If we can do this, it takes on 'intrinsic philosophical significance'; if we cannot, it remains 'of purely historical interest'. The only way to learn from the past, in short, is to appropriate it. I wish to suggest instead that it may be precisely those aspects of the past which appear at first glance to be without contemporary relevance that may prove upon closer acquaintance to be of the most immediate philosophical significance. For their relevance may lie in the fact that, instead of supplying us with our usual and carefully contrived pleasures of recognition, they enable us to stand back from our own beliefs and the concepts we use to express them, perhaps forcing us to reconsider, to recast or even (I shall next seek to suggest) to abandon some of our current beliefs in the light of these wider perspectives.

To open the pathway towards this broader notion of 'relevance', I am thus pleading for a history of philosophy which, instead of purveying rational reconstructions in the light of current prejudices, tries to avoid these as much as possible. Doubtless they cannot be avoided altogether. It is deservedly a commonplace of hermeneutic theories that, as Gadamer in particular has emphasized, we are likely to be constrained in our imaginative grasp of historical texts in ways that we cannot even be confident of bringing to consciousness. All I am proposing is that, instead of bowing to this limitation and erecting it into a principle, we should fight against it with all the weapons that historians have already begun to fashion in their efforts to reconstruct without anachronism the alien *mentalités* of earlier periods.

III

The above remarks are excessively programmatic and in danger of sounding shrill. I shall now attempt to give them substance by relating them to the specific case I have raised, the case of what can and cannot be coherently said and done with our concept of negative liberty. As I have already intimated, my thesis is this: that we need to look beyond the confines of the present disputes about positive *versus* negative liberty in order to investigate the full range of arguments about social freedom developed in the course of modern European political philosophy; and that this quest will bring us to a line of argument about negative liberty which has largely been lost to view in the course of the present debate, but which serves to cast some doubt on the terms of that debate itself.

The missing line of argument I should like to reinstate is the one embedded in the classical and especially Roman republican theory of citizenship, a theory that enjoyed a brilliant though short-lived revival in Renaissance Europe before being challenged and eventually eclipsed by the more individualistic (and especially contractarian) styles of political reasoning that triumphed in the course of the seventeenth century. The success of that challenge, especially as presented by such avowed enemies of classical republicanism as Thomas Hobbes, was so complete that it soon came to seem truistic to assert that – as Hobbes had argued – any theory of negative liberty must in effect be a theory of individual rights.[19] By the time we reach the controversies of the present day, we find this assumption so deeply rooted that, in a work such as Robert Nozick's *Anarchy, State and Utopia*, it is made to stand at the outset as the one unquestionable axiom upon which the whole conceptual framework is then raised.[20] But the issue had not always appeared in this light. As Hobbes' republican critics vainly tried to point out at the time, there was never any reason to accept Hobbes' disingenuous contention that, in construing liberty as a right, he was merely proffering neutral definitions of terms. On the contrary, as James Harrington in particular sought to argue in his *Oceana* of 1656, such an account of liberty deserved to be viewed not merely as a contentious but a gravely impoverished one.[21] To espouse it involved turning one's back on the political traditions of 'the ancients', especially the Roman stoic ideal of liberty under the law. It also involved – an even more impoverishing effect – ignoring the lessons more recently taught by that most learned disciple of the Roman moralists, Niccolò Machiavelli, whom Harrington praised as 'the only politician of later ages', and whose *Discourses* on Livy he described as the most important attempt to retrieve and apply an essentially classical understanding of political liberty to the conditions of post-medieval Europe (Harrington 1977:161–2).

[19] For the background to this development, and for an important discussion of Hobbes' views about individual rights, see Tuck 1979. For the same assumptions as a background to Locke's thought, see Tully 1980.

[20] Thus the opening sentence of Nozick 1974 reads: 'Individuals have rights, and there are things no person or group may do to them (without violating their rights).' See Nozick 1974:ix.

[21] For the background to this contention, see Pocock 1981. Pocock has done more than anyone to revive this Harringtonian perspective and elucidate its Machiavellian sources. See Pocock 1975, to which I am greatly indebted. For the general suggestion I am making here to the effect that, as a means of gaining a more critical perspective on our current assumptions and beliefs, we should revert to those historical moments at which our present orthodoxies were still unorthodox, see also Charles Taylor's contribution to the present volume.

With these judgments of Harrington's – soon to be echoed by Spinoza –
I find myself in complete agreement, and my principal aim in what follows
will simply be to enlarge on them.[22] I shall attempt to show, that is, that the
Roman stoic way of thinking about political liberty is indeed the tradition
we need above all to recapture if we wish to provide a corrective to the
dogmatism about the topic of social freedom that marks both Hobbes'
Leviathan and the writings of more recent theorists of natural or human
rights. And I shall concentrate on Machiavelli's *Discourses* on Livy as – to
cite Spinoza's estimate – the most acute and helpful reworking of the
classical theory in the annals of modern political thought (Spinoza
1958:313). I shall thus be concerned to develop an historical thesis about
Machiavelli's intentions in the *Discourses* as well as a more general
argument about the value of trying to recover what I take to have been
Machiavelli's line of thought. My historical thesis – which I can only hope
for the moment to present in a regrettably bald and promissory style[23] – is
that, while there are of course many things that Machiavelli may be said to
be doing in the *Discourses*, perhaps his most central concern is to address –
partly to question, but chiefly to reiterate – that view of *libertas* which had
lain at the heart of Roman republican political thought, but had subsequently been obliterated by the very different understanding of the
concept characteristic of the middle ages.[24] My more general thesis I have
already stated: that to recapture the structure of this theory as far as
possible in its own terms may in turn help us to enlarge our own
understanding of negative liberty.

IV

Machiavelli defines what it means to be a free man in the course of the
opening two chapters of Book I of his *Discourses*. But his main discussion
of social freedom is launched in the ensuing sequence of chapters, in which
he considers what ends and purposes men commonly seek within political
society, and in consequence what grounds they have for valuing their
liberty. As a preliminary to this discussion, however, he first of all notes

[22] I also try to enlarge on them, for another aspect of Machiavelli's views about social
freedom, in Skinner 1983, an article which can be read as a sequel to this present one.

[23] I hope shortly to publish a monograph on the republican idea of liberty, presenting and
documenting more fully the various claims made here in an unavoidably abbreviated form.
Note that, in what follows, all references are to Machiavelli 1960, and all translations are my
own, although I must express my thanks to Russell Price for very helpful correspondence
about some of the problems of translation posed by Machiavelli's text. Note too that, since
I make it contextually clear whenever I am citing from the *Discourses*, I have felt free merely
to put page references to this source in my own text, without in each case adding
'Machiavelli 1960'.

[24] For this view of political liberty, see especially Harding 1980 and references there.

that, in all polities of which history makes any mention, there have always been two roughly distinguishable groups of citizens, who have always had contrasting dispositions (*umori*), and have accordingly had different reasons for prizing their freedom to pursue their chosen ends (137). On the one hand there are the *grandi*, the rich and the powerful, whom Machiavelli sometimes equates with the nobility (139). Characteristically their chief desires are to obtain power and glory for themselves and avoid ignominy at all costs (150,203). They often desire these ends so passionately, moreover, that they pursue them intemperately,[25] their intemperance taking the form of what Machiavelli calls *ambizione*, a tendency to strive for pre-eminence at the expense of everyone else (139,414).[26] These attitudes serve to explain why the *grandi* place such a high value on their personal liberty. For their principal aim is obviously to remain as free as possible from any obstruction (*sanza ostaculo*) in order to act in such a way as to acquire glory for themselves by way of dominating others (176,236). As Machiavelli concludes, such an elite 'desidera di essere libera per comandare' (176).

As well as the *grandi*, there will always be the rank-and-file of ordinary citizens, the *plebe* or *popolo* (130). Their main concern will usually be no more than to live a life of security, 'without anxieties about the free enjoyment of their property, without any doubts about the honour of their womenfolk and children, without any fears for themselves' (174). But they too are prone to feel these desires passionately, and in consequence to pursue them in an intemperate style. In their case the tendency to intemperance takes the form of what Machiavelli calls *licenza*, 'an excessive desire for freedom', a wish to avoid any intervention in their affairs on the part even of a legitimate government (134,139,227). As a result, the *popolo* also exhibit a very high – indeed, an even higher – regard for their personal liberty (139). For their basic aim is obviously to remain free so far as possible from all forms of interference in order to lead their own undisturbed lives. As Machiavelli again summarizes, 'desiderano la libertà per vivere sicuri' (176).

By now it will be evident that this account of why all citizens value their freedom is at the same time an account of what Machiavelli means by speaking of the freedom of individual agents within political society. What he clearly has in mind is that they are free in the sense of being unobstructed in the pursuit of whatever ends they may choose to set themselves. As he

---

[25] That is, by what Machiavelli calls *straordinari* methods. Note that these are methods which, as Cicero or Livy would put it, are *extra ordine*. But to act *recte et ordine* (another favourite phrase of Livy's) is to fulfil one of the two criteria for behaving *temperantia*, with temperance. (Cf. note 32 below.) Hence we may say that *straordinari* methods are, for Machiavelli as for his classical sources, instances of intemperance.

[26] For the best account of the role of *ambizione* in the whole of Machiavelli's political thought, see Price 1982.

puts it in the opening chapter of Book I, to be a free man is to be in a position to act 'without depending on others'. It is to be free, that is, in the ordinary 'negative' sense of being independent of any constraints imposed by other social agents, and in consequence free – as Machiavelli adds in the same passage with reference to collective agents – to act according to one's own will and judgment (126).

It is important to underline this point, if only because it contradicts two claims often advanced by commentators on the *Discourses*. One is that Machiavelli introduces the key term *libertà* into his discussion 'without taking the trouble to define it', so that the sense of the word only emerges gradually in the course of the argument.[27] The other is that, as soon as Machiavelli begins to make his meaning clear, it transpires that the term 'liberty' as he uses it 'does not bear the sense' we should nowadays attribute to it; on the contrary, 'it must be taken in a wholly different sense'.[28]

Neither of these contentions seems warranted. As we have just observed, Machiavelli begins by stating exactly what he means by speaking of individual liberty: he means absence of constraint, especially absence of any limitations imposed by other social agents on one's capacity to act independently in pursuit of one's chosen goals. But as we saw at the outset, there is nothing in the least unfamiliar about assigning the term 'liberty' this particular sense. To speak of liberty as a matter of being independent of other social agents, and in consequence able to pursue one's own ends, is to echo one of the most familiar of the formulae employed by contemporary theorists of negative liberty, with whose basic framework of analysis Machiavelli appears to have no quarrel at all.

Given that we all have various goals we are minded to pursue, it will obviously be in our interests to live in whatever form of community best assures us the freedom to pursue them, whether the goals we have in mind are those of power and glory for ourselves, or merely the secure enjoyment of our property and family life. The next question that arises, then, is clearly this: in what form of polity can we most reliably hope to maximize our liberty to pursue our chosen ends?

By way of answering this question, Machiavelli introduces – at the start of Book II – an unfamiliar but pivotal claim into his discussion of social freedom. The only form of polity, he maintains, in which the citizens can hope to retain any freedom to follow their own pursuits will be one in which it makes sense to say that the community itself is 'living a free way of life'. Only in such communities can ambitious citizens hope to acquire

[27] Renaudet 1956:186. For similar judgments see Pocock 1975:196; Cadoni 1962:462n; Colish 1971:323–4.
[28] Guillemain 1977:321; Cadoni 1962:482. For similar judgments see Hexter 1979:293–4; Prezzolini 1968:63.

power and glory, 'rising by means of their ability to positions of prominence' (284). Only in such communities can ordinary members of the *popolo* hope to live in security, 'without having any anxiety that their property will be taken away from them' (284). Only in a free community, a *vivere libero*, are such benefits capable of being freely enjoyed (174).

But what does Machiavelli mean by predicating liberty of entire communities? As he makes clear at the start of Book I, what he means by the term 'liberty' when he uses it in this way is exactly what he means when he speaks of the freedom of natural as opposed to corporate bodies. A free city is one that is 'not subject to the control of anyone else', and is thus able, in virtue of being unconstrained, 'to govern itself according to its own will' and act in pursuit of its own chosen ends (129).

Putting these two claims together, we thus arrive at the following thesis: the continued enjoyment of our personal liberty is only a possibility, according to Machiavelli, for members of self-governing communities in which the will of the body politic determines its own actions, the actions of the community as a whole.

It remains to ask what form of government is best suited to the maintenance of such a *vivere libero* or free polity. Machiavelli thinks it possible, at least in theory, for a community to enjoy a free way of life under a monarchical form of government. For there is no reason in principle why a king should not organize the laws of his kingdom in such a way that they reflect the general will – and thus serve to promote the common good – of the community as a whole.[29] Generally, however, he insists that 'without doubt this ideal of the common good is properly served only in republics, where everything tending to promote it is alone followed' (280). Accordingly, the most precise statement of Machiavelli's thesis is as follows: it is only those who live under republican forms of government who can hope to retain any element of personal liberty to pursue their chosen ends, whether those ends involve the acquisition of power and glory or merely the preservation of security and wealth. As he puts it in a crucial summarizing passage at the start of Book II, this makes it 'easy to understand why an affection for a *vivere libero* springs up in all peoples'. For experience tells us that, whether we are interested in power and glory, or merely in the secure accumulation of wealth, it will always be best for us to live in such a polity, the reason being that 'no cities have ever been able to expand in either of these ways – either in power or in wealth – except when they have been *state in libertà*' (280).

This conclusion – that personal liberty can only be fully assured within a self-governing form of republican community – represents the heart and

---

[29] For this possibility see Machiavelli 1960:154, 193–4, 388–90, and for an excellent discussion of this point see Colish 1971:345.

nerve of all classical republican theories of citizenship. Among more recent proponents of negative liberty, however, it has usually been dismissed as an obvious absurdity. Hobbes, for example, seeks to dispose of it by the typical device of sheer assertion, declaring in *Leviathan* that 'whether a commonwealth be monarchical or popular, the freedom is still the same' (Hobbes 1968:266). And this contention has in turn been reiterated by most defenders of negative liberty in the course of the contemporary debate. Our next task must therefore be to enquire into the reasons Machiavelli offers for insisting, on the contrary, that the preservation of negative liberty actually requires the maintenance of one particular type of regime.

V

The key to Machiavelli's reasoning at this stage is to be found in his account of the place of *ambizione* in political life. As we have already seen, he believes that the exercise of ambition is invariably fatal to the liberty of anyone against whom it is successfully directed, since it takes the form of a *libido dominandi*, a willingness to coerce others and use them as means to one's own ends. We next need to recognize that this disposition to act ambitiously arises, according to Machiavelli, in two distinct forms, neither of which we have the least hope of fighting off unless we are members of a self-governing community.

One of these forms we have already encountered. It arises – to cite Machiavelli's terminology – 'from inside' a community, and reflects the desire of the *grandi* to achieve power at the expense of oppressing their fellow-citizens. This is an ineliminable threat, for the *grandi* we have always with us, and they are invariably disposed to pursue these selfish goals. These they characteristically seek to attain by gathering around themselves groups of *partigiani* or partisans, aiming to use these 'private forces' to wrest control of the government out of the hands of the public and seize power for themselves (e.g. 452, 464). Machiavelli distinguishes three main ways in which ambitious *grandi* can usually manage to acquire such partisans. They can seek to have themselves re-elected to public offices for excessive periods, so becoming sources of increasing patronage as well as objects of increasing personal loyalty (e.g. 452–3, 455–6). They can lay out their exceptional wealth to purchase the support and favour of the *popolo* at the expense of the public interest (463–4). Or they can use their high social standing and reputation to overawe their fellow-citizens and persuade them to adopt measures more conducive to the promotion of sectional ambitions than the good of the community as a whole (e.g. 207, 236). In every case the same chain-reaction is set up: 'from partisans arise factions in cities, from factions their ruin' (148). The moral is that 'unless a city manages to devise various ways and means of beating down the *ambizione* of the *grandi*, they will quickly bring it to ruin' and 'reduce it to servitude' (218).

The other form of *ambizione* Machiavelli describes is said to arise and threaten free communities 'from outside'. At this point the pervasive image of the body politic in effect carries the full weight of the argument. For the parallel between natural and corporate bodies is said to extend to their having the same dispositions. Just as some individuals seek the quiet life while others go in quest of power and glory, so too with bodies politic: some are content 'to live quietly and enjoy their liberty within their own boundaries', but others are ambitious to dominate their neighbours and coerce them into acting as client states (e.g. 334–5). As always, ancient Rome is cited as the best illustration of this general truth. Due to *ambizione*, the Romans waged continuous war on all the peoples surrounding them, attaining their own 'supreme greatness', their own power and glory, by conquering each neighbour in turn, overthrowing their *libertà* and subjecting them to the service of Rome (e.g. 279, 294).

As with individual *grandi*, so with entire communities, this disposition to act ambitiously is altogether natural and ineliminable. Some communities are never 'content to keep themselves to themselves', but are always 'seeking to dominate others', from which it follows that 'neighbouring princes and republics always feel a natural hatred for each other, the product of this *ambizione di dominare*' (129, 426). Moreover, just as the clients of ambitious *grandi* find themselves coerced into serving their patron's ends, so too the citizens of any polity that becomes the client of another will automatically forfeit their personal liberty, since they will find themselves forced to do their conqueror's bidding as soon as their community is reduced to servitude (e.g. 129, 334–5, 426). It follows that any city desirous of preserving its liberty must always be ready to conquer others, for 'unless you are prepared to attack, you are liable to be attacked' (199, 335). The moral in this case is that 'you can never hope to make yourself secure except by the exercise of power' (127).

There are in short two threats to personal as well as civic liberty arising from the omnipresence of *ambizione*. How are they to be fought off? Consider first the danger of 'servitude arising from outside'. To meet this threat, the members of a free community must obviously follow the right methods and cultivate the right qualities for effective defence. These Machiavelli takes to be the same for political as for natural bodies. The right method is to establish military ordinances to ensure that 'your own citizens act as the defenders of their own liberty', thereby preventing them from adopting the lazy and effeminate alternative of hiring or relying on others to fight on their behalf (186–9). To rely on hired soldiers, Machiavelli repeatedly warns, is a sure way to ruin your city and forfeit your own liberty, simply because their only motive for fighting is 'the small amount of pay you give them'. This means that they 'will never be faithful, never so much your friends as to be willing to lay down their lives in your cause'. By contrast, a citizen army will always be striving for its own glory in attack, its own freedom in defence, and will therefore be far more willing to fight to the death (231; cf. 303, 369). Machiavelli is not of course saying that a city which defends its body with its own arms will thereby guarantee its citizens their liberty. Against overwhelming odds, as the Samnites discovered in their struggles against Rome, there is ultimately no hope of avoiding servitude (279, 285). But he is certainly admonishing us that, unless we are willing personally to contribute to the defence of our community against external aggression, we shall 'lay it open as a prey to anyone who chooses to attack it', as a consequence of which, sooner rather than later, we shall find ourselves enslaved (144; cf. 304, 334–6, 369).

As for the personal qualities we need to cultivate in order to defend our liberty most effectively, Machiavelli singles out two above all. First of all we need to be wise. But the wisdom we require is by no means that of the consciously sage and sapient, the *savi*, whom Machiavelli (following Livy) usually treats with irony. To be *savio* is generally to lack precisely those qualities of wisdom which are really essential in military (and indeed in civil) affairs (349, 461). The relevant qualities are those required for the forming of practical judgments, the careful and effective calculation of chances and outcomes. They are, in a word, the qualities of *prudenza*. Prudence tells you when to go to war, how to conduct a campaign, how to bear its changing fortunes (e.g. 302, 314, 362). It is one of the qualities by which the greatest military commanders have always been distinguished, commanders such as Tullius and Camillus, both crucial to Rome's early success, each of whom was *prudentissimo* in his generalship (186, 428).

The other quality indispensable for effective defence is of course *animo*, courage, which Machiavelli sometimes couples with *ostinazione*, sheer determination and persistence. Courage is the other leading attribute of the greatest military commanders, as Machiavelli repeatedly stresses in explaining the military successes of early Rome. When Cincinnatus, for example, was called from his plough to mount the defence of his city, he at once assumed the Dictatorship, raised an army, marched forth and defeated the enemy in a dramatically short space of time. The quality that brought him this victory was *la grandezza dello animo*, his high courage. 'Nothing in the world frightened him, nothing alarmed or confused him at all' (458). Courage is also the quality that must above all be instilled in every individual soldier if victory is to be grasped. Nothing is more lethal, nothing more likely to bring 'clear defeat', than 'the kind of accident that has the effect of taking away the courage of an army' and leaving it terrified (487). As the conduct of the French in battle above all reminds us, 'natural fury' is never enough; what is needed is fury disciplined by persistence or, in a word, courage (484).

Even if 'external' ambition is successfully fought off, there is still the more insidious danger that the same malign disposition will arise 'from within' your city, in the breasts of its leading citizens, and thereby reduce you to servitude. How is this to be forestalled? Machiavelli again argues that, in the first instance, this is a matter of establishing the right laws and ordinances, and again alludes to the metaphor of the body politic in describing what laws are required. They must be such as to prevent any single limb or member of the body from exercising an undue or coercive influence over its will. But this means that, if the laws governing the behaviour of the community are to express its general will, rather than merely the will of its active and most ambitious part, there must above all be laws and institutions capable of serving as a *temperamento* – a means of tempering, a curb – to control the selfish *ambizione* of the rich and the nobility (423). For as Machiavelli repeatedly affirms – citing a metaphor much invoked by Virgil as well as Livy and Cicero – unless the *grandi* are 'bridled' and 'held in check' (*a freno*), their natural intemperance will quickly lead to disorderly and tyrannical results.[30]

Finally, in civic as in military affairs, there are certain qualities that all citizens must cultivate if they are to act as vigilant guardians of their own liberty. Once more Machiavelli singles out two above all. Again the first is said to be wisdom, but again this is not the wisdom of the professional sage. Rather it is the worldly wisdom or prudence of the experienced statesman, the man with practical ability to judge the best course of action and to follow it out. This quality is not merely said to be indispensable for effective political leadership; it is also a central thesis of Machiavelli's political theory that no community can ever hope to be 'well-ordered' unless it is brought to order by such a *prudente ordinatore*, such a worldly wise organizer of its civic life (129–30, 153, 480). In addition it is no less crucial that all citizens who aspire to take a hand in government, to help in upholding the freedom of their community, must be men of prudence. If we ask, for example, how it came about that ancient Rome was able, over so long a period, to institute 'all the laws needed to preserve her freedom', we discover that the city was continually organized and reorganized 'by very

[30] See Machiavelli 1960:136 and cf. also 142, 179–80, 218, 229–31, 243–4, 257, 314. For the classical idea of the *temperamentum* that Machiavelli also cites, see Cicero, *De Legibus*, III.10.24. For the image of the curb or bridle see Virgil, *Aeneid*, 1.541 (a passage to which Machiavelli appears to allude at 173) and 1.523. For the use of the same metaphor by Livy, *Ab Urbe Condita*, see e.g. 26.29.7.

many men who were *prudenti*', and that this constitutes the key to explaining her success (241–4).

The other quality every citizen must cultivate is a willingness to avoid all forms of intemperate and disorderly behaviour, thus ensuring that civic affairs are debated and decided in an orderly, well-tempered style. At this point, taking up the Roman ideal of *temperantia*, Machiavelli closely follows his classical sources – notably Livy and Cicero – in dividing his discussion into two parts. One aspect of *temperantia*, as Cicero had explained in *De Officiis*, consists in that set of qualities a citizen needs to acquire if he is to advise and act in a truly statesmanlike way. And the most important of these, he repeatedly declares, are *modestia* and *moderatio*.[31] Machiavelli completely agrees. 'There is no other way for an adviser to act than to do so *moderatamente*' and 'to defend his opinions dispassionately and with *modestia*' (482). The other requirement of *temperantia*, Cicero had added (1.40.142), is that everyone should behave 'with orderliness' (*ordine*), a sentiment echoed in Livy's insistence on the need to act *recte et ordine*, in a right and orderly way.[32] Again Machiavelli completely agrees. To maintain a *vivere libero*, the citizens must avoid all *disordine* and behave *ordinariamente*, in an orderly way. If intemperate and disorderly methods (*modi straordinari*) are permitted, tyranny will result; but as long as temperate methods (*modi ordinari*) are followed, freedom can be successfully preserved over long periods of time (146–9; cf. 188, 191, 242, 244).

Machiavelli helpfully summarizes his entire argument towards the end of Book I in the course of explaining why he believes that the cities of Tuscany 'could easily have introduced a *vivere civile*' if only a prudent man (*uno uomo prudente*) had arisen to lead them 'with a knowledge of ancient statecraft'. As grounds for this judgment he mentions the fact that the members of the communities in question have always displayed *animo*, courage, and *ordine*, temperance and orderliness. From which it follows that, if only the missing ingredient of *prudente* leadership had been added, 'they would have been able to maintain their liberty' (257).

VI

Hobbes assures us in *Leviathan* that

> the liberty whereof there is so frequent and honourable mention in the histories and philosophy of the ancient Greeks and Romans, and in the writings and discourse of those that from them have received all their learning in the politics, is not the liberty of particular men, but the liberty of the commonwealth. (Hobbes 1968:266)

---

[31] Cicero, *De Officiis*, 1.27.93; cf. also 1.27.96; 1.40.143; 1.45.159.
[32] For example, Livy *Ab Urbe Condita*, 24.31.7; 28.39.18; 30.17.12.

We can now see, however, that Hobbes has either failed to grasp the point of the classical republican argument I have sought to reconstruct, or else (a far more probable hypothesis) is deliberately attempting to distort it. For the point of the argument is of course that the liberty of commonwealth and the liberty of particular men cannot be separately assessed in the way that Hobbes and his epigoni among contemporary theorists of negative liberty have all assumed. The essence of the republican case is that, unless a commonwealth is maintained 'in a state of liberty' (in the ordinary negative sense of being free from constraint to act according to its own will) then the individual members of such a body politic will find themselves stripped of their personal liberty (again in the ordinary negative sense of losing their freedom to seek their own goals). The grounds for this conclusion are that, as soon as a body politic forfeits the capacity to act according to its general will, and becomes subject to the will either of its own ambitious *grandi*, or some ambitious neighbouring community, its citizens will find themselves treated as means to their masters' ends, and will thereby lose their freedom to pursue their own purposes. The enslavement of a community thus brings with it the inevitable loss of individual liberty; conversely, the liberty of particular men, *pace* Hobbes, can only be assured under a free commonwealth.

To grasp this point, moreover, is at the same time to see that there is no difficulty about defending both the claims about social freedom which, as we saw at the outset, contemporary philosophers have been apt to stigmatize as paradoxical, or at least as incompatible with a negative view of individual liberty.

The first was the suggestion that only those who place themselves whole-heartedly in the service of their community are capable of assuring their own liberty. We can now see that, from the perspective of classical republican thought, this is not to state a paradox but a perfectly straight-forward truth. For a writer like Machiavelli, the liberty of individual citizens depends in the first place on their capacity to fight off 'servitude arising from outside'. But this can only be done if they are willing to undertake the defence of their polity themselves. It follows that a readiness to volunteer for active service, to join the armed services, to perform one's military services, constitutes a necessary condition of maintaining one's own individual freedom from servitude. Unless we train ourselves to act 'like those who kept Rome free with their own arms', unless we are 'prepared to act in such a way as to defend our fatherland', we shall find ourselves conquered and enslaved (237, 283).

Personal liberty also depends for Machiavelli on preventing the *grandi* from coercing the *popolo* into serving their ends. But the only way to prevent this from happening is to organize the polity in such a way that each and every citizen is equally able to play a part in determining the actions of the body politic as a whole. This in turn means that a readiness to serve in public office, to pursue a life of public service, to perform voluntary services, constitutes a further necessary condition of maintaining one's own liberty. Only if we are prepared 'to act in favour of the public' (452), 'to do good for the community' (155), to 'help forward' and 'act on behalf of' the common good (153–4), to observe and follow everything required to uphold it (280) can we in turn hope to avoid a state of tyranny and personal dependence.

Cicero had already laid it down in De Officiis (1.10.31) that individual and civic liberty can only be preserved if *communi utilitati serviatur*, if we act 'as slaves to the public interest'. And in Livy there are several echoes of the same astonishing use of the vocabulary of chattel slavery to describe the condition of political liberty.[33] Machiavelli is simply reiterating the same classical oxymoron: the price we have to pay for enjoying any degree of personal freedom with any degree of continuing assurance is voluntary public servitude.

I now turn to the other contention that contemporary writers have generally held to be incompatible with a negative analysis of individual liberty. This is the connected suggestion that the attributes required on the part of each individual citizen in order to perform these public services effectively must be the virtues, and thus that only those who behave virtuously are capable of assuring their own freedom. If we revert to Machiavelli's account of the qualities we need to cultivate in order to serve our polity in war and peace, we can readily see that this too appears, from the perspective of classical republican thought, to be a perfectly straightforward truth.

We are said to need three qualities above all: courage to defend our liberty; temperance and orderliness to maintain free government; and prudence to direct both our civic and military undertakings to the best effect. But in singling out these attributes, Machiavelli is of course invoking three of the four 'cardinal' virtues listed by the Roman historians and moralists, all of whom agreed that – to cite Cicero's formulation in De Inventione – the overarching concept of *virtus generalis* divides into four components, and that these are 'prudence, justice, courage and temperance' (II.53.159). As we have seen, moreover, Machiavelli also endorses both the major claims advanced by the classical republican theorists about the significance of these qualities, claims that are most systematically developed by Cicero in De Officiis. One is that these four qualities are precisely the attributes we need to acquire if we are to perform our highest earthly duties, those of serving our community in war and

---

[33] For example, Livy, *Ab Urbe Condita*, 5.10.5.

peace; the other is that our capacity to secure our own liberty together with that of our *patria* both depend entirely on our willingness to perform these *officia*.

It is of course true that Machiavelli's analysis differs from Cicero's in one immensely important respect. For he silently makes one alteration – small in appearance but overwhelming in significance – to the classical analysis of the virtues needed to serve the *communes utilitates*: he erases the quality of justice, the quality that Cicero in *De Officiis* had described as the crowning splendour of virtue (1.7.20).

This is not to say that Machiavelli fails to discuss the concept of justice in the *Discourses*. In fact he follows the Ciceronian analysis of the concept almost word for word. Cicero had argued in *De Officiis* that the essence of justice consists in the avoidance of *iniuria*, of harm contrary to *ius* or right (1.7.20). Such harm arises in one of two ways: either as the product of fraud or of 'brutal' and 'inhumane' cruelty and violence (1.11.34–5; 1.13.40–1). To observe the dictates of justice is thus to avoid both these vices, and this duty lies equally upon us at all times. For in war, no less than in peace, good faith must always be kept and cruelty eschewed (1.11.34–7). Finally, the observance of these duties is also said to be in our interests. If we behave unjustly, we shall not only cheat ourselves of honour and glory; we shall undermine our ability to promote the common good and thereby to uphold our own liberty (1.14.43; cf. III.10.40–III.25.96).

Machiavelli completely agrees with this account of what constitutes the virtue of justice. But he flatly repudiates the crucial contention that the observance of this virtue is invariably conducive to serving the common good. This he regards as an obvious and disastrous mistake, and this dissenting judgment takes us to the heart of his originality and his subversive quality as a theorist of statecraft. He responds in the first place by making a firm distinction between justice in war and peace, arguing that in warfare both forms of *iniuria* are frequently indispensable. Fraud is often crucial to victory, and to treat it as inglorious is absurd (493–4). The same is no less true of cruelty, a quality that marked the very greatest of Rome's generals, such as Camillus and Manlius, and proved in each case to be vital to their success (448–54). Moreover, the same lessons apply with almost equal force in civic affairs. Although fraud in this case is detestable, it is often essential to the achievement of great things (311–12, 493). And although cruelty may similarly stand as an accusation against anyone who practises it, there is no denying that it will often have to be practised, and will always have to be excused, if the life and liberty of a free community are to be successfully preserved (153–4, 175, 311–12, 468, 494–5).

This represents an epoch-making break with the classical republican analysis of the cardinal virtues; its suddenness and completeness can hardly be overemphasized. But it is scarcely less important to emphasize that this represents Machiavelli's sole quarrel with his classical authorities. The rest of his analysis of *virtù* and its connections with *libertà* is impeccably Ciceronian in character. He not only centres his entire account around the qualities of courage, temperance and prudence; he regularly refers to these attributes as elements of virtue as well as preconditions of liberty. When generals or entire armies are described as exhibiting *animo*, they are also said to be displaying an element of *virtù* (e.g. 231, 310, 484–5). When a community and its members attain the characteristic of *ordine*, of being *bene ordinata*, they are again said to be in possession of an element of *virtù* (e.g. 379–80). When civic and military leaders are commended for *virtuoso* behaviour, this is often because they are said to have exhibited exceptional *prudenza* (e.g. 127–9, 186, 454). In all these cases, the qualities that assure liberty are cardinal virtues.

It is true that this is to offer an unorthodox reading of Machiavelli's views about the meaning and significance of *virtù*. Chabod summarizes the more usual view of the matter when he declares that '*virtù*, in Machiavelli, is not a "moral" quality as it is for us; it refers instead to the possession of energy or capacity to decide and act' (Chabod 1964:248). But I am not denying this; as far as it goes, this is of course correct. The widest use to which Machiavelli consistently puts the term *virtù* is in speaking of the means by which we achieve particular results; the means, as we still say, by virtue of which they are achieved (e.g. 172, 295, 354, 381). As a result, when he comes to speak of those results in which he is principally interested in the *Discourses* – the preservation of liberty and the attainment of civic greatness – he consistently uses the term *virtù* to describe the human qualities needed for these successes to be achieved. Speaking of *virtù* in these connections, he is thus speaking of abilities, talents, capacities. Of generals and armies he frequently remarks that the quality which enables them to defeat their enemies, to win great victories, is their *virtù* (e.g. 184, 279, 452). And in discussing the role of *virtù* in civic affairs, he likewise uses the term to describe the talents needed to establish cities, impose orderly government, prevent faction, avoid corruption, maintain decisive leadership and uphold all the other arts of peace (e.g. 127, 154, 178–9).

My objection to Chabod's type of analysis is merely that it does not go far enough.[34] We still need to ask about the *nature* of the talents or abilities that serve to bring about great results in civic and military affairs. And if we press this further question we find, as we have seen, that Machiavelli's answer comes in two parts. On the one hand we need a certain ruthlessness, a willingness to discount the demands of justice and act with cruelty and

[34] The same seems to me to apply to Price 1973, although this is the best available discussion of the uses of the term *virtù* throughout Machiavelli's political works.

perfidiousness when this is necessary to uphold the common good. But on the other hand, the remaining qualities we need are said to be courage, temperance and prudence. At the heart of Machiavelli's political theory there is thus a purely classical message, framed in the same play on words that the classical republican theorists had all exploited. If we ask in virtue of what qualities, what talents or abilities, we can hope to assure our own liberty and contribute to the common good, the answer is: in virtue of the virtues.

VII

In the light of the above attempt to outline the structure of a classical republican theory of freedom, I now wish to revert to the current disputes about the idea of negative liberty from which I started out. The historical materials I have presented, I shall conclude by suggesting, are relevant to these disputes in two related ways.

They show us, in the first place, that the terms of the contemporary debate have become confused. It is agreed on all sides that a theory of liberty which connects the idea of social freedom with the performance of virtuous acts of public service would have to begin by positing certain ends as rational for everyone to pursue, and then seek to establish that the attainment of those ends would leave us in the fullest or truest sense in possession of our liberty. This is of course a possible way of connecting the concepts of freedom, virtue and service. It is widely (though I think mistakenly)[35] held to be Spinoza's way of doing so in the *Tractatus Politicus*, and it certainly seems to be Rousseau's way of doing so in the *Contrat Social*. It is by no means the only way of doing so, however, as present-day analytical philosophers are apt to suppose. In a theory such as Machiavelli's, the point of departure is not a vision of *eudaimonia* or real human interests, but simply an account of the 'humours' that prompt us to choose and pursue our various ends. So Machiavelli has no quarrel with the Hobbesian assumption that the capacity to pursue such ends without obstruction is what the term 'liberty' properly signifieth. He merely argues that the performance of public services, and the cultivation of the virtues needed to perform them, both prove upon examination to be instrumentally necessary to the avoidance of coercion and servitude, and thus to be necessary conditions of assuring any degree of personal liberty in the ordinary Hobbesian sense of the term.

---

[35] Because such interpretations underestimate the extent to which Spinoza is restating classical republican ideas, especially as developed by Machiavelli in the *Discourses*. But for an excellent corrective, together with full references to rival accounts, see Haitsma Mulier 1980.

This brings me to the other way in which the classical republican theory is of relevance to contemporary arguments. As a consequence of overlooking the possibility that a theory of negative liberty might coherently have the structure I have just sketched, a number of philosophers have proceeded to enunciate further claims about the concept which they take to be statements of general truths, but which are in fact true only of their own particular theories of negative liberty.

One of these has been the Hobbesian claim that any theory of negative liberty must in effect be a theory of individual rights. As we have seen, this has reached the status of an axiom in many contemporary discussions of negative liberty. Liberty of action, we are assured, 'is a right'; there is a 'moral right to liberty'; we are bound to view our liberty both as a natural right and as the means to secure our other rights.[36] As will by now be obvious, these are mere dogmas. A classical theory such as Machiavelli's helps us to see that there is no conceivable obligation to think of our liberty in this particular way. Machiavelli's is a theory of negative liberty, but he develops it without making any use whatever of the concept of individual rights. While he often speaks of that which is *onesto*, or morally right, I know of no passage in his entire political writings where he speaks of individual agents as the bearers of *diritti* or rights.[37] On the contrary, the essence of his theory could be expressed by saying that the attainment of social freedom cannot be a matter of securing our personal rights, since it indispensably requires the performance of our social duties. To those who respond – in the manner of Machiavelli's scholastic contemporaries and their contractarian descendants – that the best way of securing our personal liberty must nevertheless be to conceive of it as a right, as a species of moral property, and to defend it absolutely against all forms of external interference, the classical republican theorists have an obvious retort. To adopt this attitude, they maintain, is not merely the epitome of corrupt citizenship, but is also (like all derelictions of social duty) in the highest degree an instance of imprudence. The prudent citizen recognizes that, whatever extent of negative liberty he may enjoy, it can only be the outcome of – and if you like the reward of – a steady recognition and pursuit of the public good at the expense of all purely individual and private ends.

As we have seen, however, contemporary theorists of negative liberty have not lacked their own retort at this point. They have gone on to denounce the underlying suggestion that it may be in our interests to

---

36 For these claims see respectively Day 1977:270; Day 1983:18; McCloskey 1965:404–5.
37 Colish 1971:345–6 claims that 'Machiavelli often connects *libertà* with certain private rights' and 'clearly identifies freedom with the protection of private rights'. I can find no textual warrant for such assertions in any of Machiavelli's political works. For a good corrective to such anachronistic claims, see Sasso 1958:333–41.

perform our duties as dangerous metaphysical nonsense. But it will now be evident that this too is a mistake. Machiavelli believes of course that as citizens we have a duty (*ufficio*) to perform (482), that duty being to advise and serve our community to the best of our abilities. So there are many things, he repeatedly tells us, that we ought to do and many others that we ought to avoid. But the reason he offers us for cultivating the virtues and serving the common good is never that these are our duties. The reason is always that these represent, as it happens, the best and indeed the only means for us 'to do well' on our own behalf, and in particular the only means of securing any degree of personal liberty to pursue our chosen ends (e.g. 280). There is thus a perfectly clear and unmetaphysical sense in which, although Machiavelli never speaks of interests, it is fair to say that he believes our duty and our interests to be one and the same. He is celebrated, moreover, for the chilling emphasis he places on the idea that all men are evil, and can never be expected to do anything good unless they can see that it will be for their own good to do it. So his final word is not merely that the apparent paradox of duty as interest enunciates, once more, a straightforward truth; like his classical authorities, he also believes that it states the most fortunate of all moral truths. For unless the generality of evil men can be given selfish reasons for behaving virtuously, it is unlikely that any of them will perform any virtuous actions at all.

REFERENCES

Baldwin, T. 1984. 'MacCallum and the two concepts of freedom', *Ratio* (forthcoming)

Benn, S. and Weinstein, W. 1971. 'Being free to act, and being a free man', *Mind* 80:194–211

Benn, S. and Weinstein, W. 1974. 'Freedom as the non-restriction of options: a rejoinder', *Mind* 83:435–8

Berlin, I. 1969. *Four Essays on Liberty*. Oxford: Oxford University Press

Cadoni, G. 1962. 'Libertà, repubblica e governo misto in Machiavelli', *Rivista Internazionale di filosofia del diritto* 39:462–84

Chabod, F. 1964. 'Il segretario fiorentino' in *Scritti su Machiavelli*. Turin: Einaudi

Colish, M. 1971. 'The idea of liberty in Machiavelli', *Journal of the History of Ideas* 32:323–50

Day, J. 1977. 'Threats, offers, law, opinion and liberty', *American Philosophical Quarterly* 14:257–72

Day, J. 1983. 'Individual liberty', in A. Phillips Griffiths (ed.), *Of Liberty*. Cambridge: Cambridge University Press

Dunn, J. 1968. 'The identity of the history of ideas', *Philosophy* 43:85–104

Feinberg, J. 1973. *Social Philosophy*. Englewood Cliffs, NJ: Prentice-Hall

Feyerabend, P. 1981. 'On the "meaning" of scientific terms', in *Realism, Rationalism and Scientific Method: Philosophical Papers, Vol. I*. Cambridge: Cambridge University Press

Flew, A. 1983. '"Freedom is slavery": a slogan for our new philosopher kings', in A. Phillips Griffiths (ed.), *Of Liberty*. Cambridge: Cambridge University Press

Gibbs, B. 1976. *Freedom and Liberation*. Brighton: Sussex University Press

Gray, J. 1980. 'On negative and positive liberty', *Political Studies*. 28:507–26

Guillemain, B. 1977. *Machiavel: L'anthropologie politique*. Geneva: Librarie Droz

Haitsma Mulier, E. 1980. *The Myth of Venice and Dutch Republican Thought in the Seventeenth Century*. Assen: Van Gorcum

Harding, A. 1980. 'Political liberty in the Middle Ages', *Speculum* 55:423–43.

Harrington, J. 1977. 'Oceana' in J. Pocock (ed.), *The Political Works of James Harrington*. Cambridge: Cambridge University Press

Hexter, J. 1979. *On Historians*. London: Collins

Hobbes, T. 1968. *Leviathan*, edited by C. B. Macpherson. Harmondsworth: Penguin Books

MacCallum, G. 1972. 'Negative and positive freedom', in P. Laslett *et al.* (eds.), *Philosophy, Politics and Society*, fourth series. Oxford: Basil Blackwell

McCloskey, H. 1965. 'A critique of the ideals of liberty', *Mind* 74:483–508

Machiavelli, N. 1960. *Il principe e discorsi*, ed. S. Bertelli. Milan: Feltrinelli

MacIntyre, A. 1966. *A Short History of Ethics*. New York: Macmillan

Mackie, J. 1976. *Problems from Locke*. Oxford: The Clarendon Press

Nozick, R. 1974. *Anarchy, State and Utopia*. New York: Basic Books

O'Connor, D. 1964. 'Preface' to *A Critical History of Western Philosophy*. London: Collier Macmillan

Oppenheim, F. 1981. *Political Concepts*. Oxford: Basil Blackwell

Parent, W. 1974a. 'Some recent work on the concept of liberty', *American Philosophical Quarterly* 11:149–67

Parent, W. 1974b. 'Freedom as the non-restriction of options', *Mind* 83:432–4

Pocock, J. 1975. *The Machiavellian Moment*. Princeton, NJ: Princeton University Press

Pocock, J. 1981. 'Virtues, rights and manners', *Political Theory* 9:353–68

Prezzolini, G. 1968. *Machiavelli*. London: Robert Hale

Price, R. 1973. 'The senses of virtù in Machiavelli', *European Studies Review* 3:315–45

Price, R. 1982. '*Ambizione* in Machiavelli's thought', *History of Political Thought* 3:383–445

Rawls, J. 1971. *A Theory of Justice*. Cambridge, Mass.: Harvard University Press

Raz, J. 1970. 'On lawful governments', *Ethics* 80:296–305

Renaudet, A. 1956. *Machiavel*. 6th edition. Paris: Gallimard

Ryan, C. 1980. 'The Normative Concept of Coercion', *Mind* 89:481–98

Sasso, G. 1958. *Niccolò Machiavelli: Storia del suo pensiero politico*. Naples: Istituto Italiano

Scruton, R. 1981. *From Descartes to Wittgenstein: A Short History of Modern Philosophy*. London: Routledge and Kegan Paul

Skinner, Q. 1969. 'Meaning and understanding in the history of ideas', *History and Theory* 8:3–53

Skinner, Q. 1983. 'Machiavelli on the maintenance of liberty', *Politics* 18:3–15

Spinoza. 1958. 'Tractatus Politicus', in A. G. Wernham (ed.), *The Political Works*. Oxford: Oxford University Press

Steiner, H. 1974–5. 'Individual liberty', *Proceedings of the Aristotelian Society* 75:33–50

Taylor, C. 1979. 'What's wrong with negative liberty', in A. Ryan (ed.), *The Idea of Freedom*. Oxford: Oxford University Press

Tuck, R. 1979. *Natural Rights Theories: their Origin and Development*. Cambridge: Cambridge University Press

Tully, J. 1980. *A Discourse on Property*. Cambridge: Cambridge University Press

PART II

◁ ══ ▷

10

The sceptic in his place and time

M. F. BURNYEAT

I

Nowadays, if a philosopher finds he cannot answer the philosophical question 'What is time?' or 'Is time real?', he applies for a research grant to work on the problem during next year's sabbatical. He does not suppose that the arrival of next year is actually in doubt. Alternatively, he may agree that any puzzlement about the nature of time, or any argument for doubting the reality of time, is in fact a puzzlement about, or an argument for doubting, the truth of the proposition that next year's sabbatical will come, but contend that this is of course a strictly theoretical or philosophical worry, not a worry that needs to be reckoned with in the ordinary business of life. Either way he *insulates* his ordinary first order judgements from the effects of his philosophizing.

The practice of insulation, as I shall continue to call it, can be conceived in various ways. There are plenty of philosophers for whom Wittgenstein's well-known remark (1953:§124), that philosophy 'leaves everything as it is', describes not the end-point but the starting-point of their philosophizing. There are many who accept one or another version of the idea that philosophy is the analysis or, more broadly, that it is the meta-study of existing forms of discourse – an idea going naturally with the thought that, while a certain amount of revision may be in order, in general philosophy must respect and be responsive to these forms of discourse in the same way as any theory must, in general, respect and be responsive to the data it is a theory of. Others again have invoked Carnap's (1950) distinction between internal and external questions: ordinary inquiries about when and where things happen are inquiries which go on by recognized procedures within the accepted spatiotemporal framework of science and everyday life, whereas philosophical questions and the doubts that inspire them are external questions, about the framework itself, as to whether it provides the best way of speaking about places and times.[1] But I am not here

[1] Carnap, I should emphasize, is no insulator, but a verificationist who denies that external

concerned with the credentials of these and other accounts of the practice
of insulation. For I believe that, at least in some central areas of philosophical discussion, the sense of a difference between philosophical and ordinary
questions lies deep in most of us: much deeper than any particular
articulation of it that you might meet yesterday or today in Harvard,
Oxford or California.

Admittedly, there are those who, influenced perhaps by Quine, would
be reluctant to accept any of these views or to have anything to do with
insulation. For them, as for Quine, philosophical reflection and ordinary
thought are to be seen as a single fabric, no part of which is immune from
the effects of revisions and puzzlements elsewhere. But it is one thing to say
this, another to make sure that you fully believe it. One test is how you
react to the following argument: It is true that *yesterday* my body was for
some time *nearer to* the mantelpiece than to the bookcase; therefore, it is
false that space and time are unreal. In my experience,[2] nearly everybody
protests that this argument of Moore's (1925) is the wrong *sort* of argument
to settle a philosophical dispute about the reality of space or time. They feel
strongly that philosophical scepticism cannot be straightforwardly refuted
by common sense. But the corollary of this must be that common sense
cannot be refuted by philosophical scepticism. And indeed, when we look
at the paper which has contributed more than any other single factor to
keeping alive an interest in scepticism during these days of exact philosophy, Thompson Clarke's famous essay 'The legacy of skepticism' (1972),[3]
we find that his starting-point, the foundation of the whole thing, is the
thesis that the judgements and knowledge-claims we make in ordinary life
are immune (that is his word) from philosophical doubt. Insulation, it
turns out, is a two-way business. It protects ordinary life from philosophy
and it protects philosophy from ordinary life and G. E. Moore, and you
cannot buy the one protection without the other. Alternatively, if you do
want your philosophizing to connect with first order concerns, you had
better keep it sober.

I hope that I have said enough for you to recognize the phenomenon I
am pointing to: if not in yourselves, then in others and in the philosophy of
our time. My thesis is going to be that it is precisely that, a phenomenon of
our time. This sense of the separateness, sometimes even the strangeness, of

questions have cognitive content. Consequently, he thinks of frameworks as up for
acceptance or rejection on pragmatic grounds: whole frameworks could be swept away, if
they proved inconvenient. But Stroud 1979, rejecting the verificationism and restoring
meaning to philosophical debate, does render the internal–external distinction equivalent
to insulation.

[2] Compare Stroud 1979:279.

[3] Clarke's influence is acknowledged in Stroud 1979: 297 n. 41; 1983:434, n. 11; Cavell 1979:
xii, xx–xxi; Nagel 1979:19, 27.

philosophical issues is not a timeless thing, intrinsic to the very nature of philosophy. It is a product of the history of philosophy.[4] I shall tell of a time when insulation was not yet invented, when philosophical scepticism did straightforwardly clash with common sense, and people took it seriously precisely because they saw it as a genuine alternative to their ordinary views. If my thesis is correct, there will be historical questions to ask about when, and by whom, and why insulation was invented: questions the answers to which might help to explain the atmosphere of 'belatedness' (if I may borrow a term from literary criticism) that so often surrounds twentieth-century philosophical discussions of scepticism. All that thrashing about to discover a way to take the sceptic seriously, and to insist that he is still very much alive, betrays a feeling that the important dealings with scepticism took place long ago. Which I think is true. But I shall come to the historical questions in due course. First, I must establish that once upon a time scepticism was a serious challenge and no one thought to insulate it from affecting, or being affected by, the judgements of ordinary life.

II

The first philosophers to title themselves sceptics, in both the ancient sense (*skeptikos* means 'inquirer') and in the modern sense of 'doubter' (for which their word was *ephektikos*, 'one who suspends judgement'), were the members of the Pyrrhonist movement founded by Aenesidemus in the first century BC.[5] Their use of these words was designed to distinguish their type of philosophy both from that of the Academics and from that of the dogmatic schools. Pyrrhonist inquiry, we are told, has a unique feature: it does not terminate either in the discovery of the truth, as the dogmatic philosophers claim theirs does, or in the denial of its discoverability, which is the conclusion argued for by the Academics.[6] This was more than a theoretical distinction. In the ancient context to appropriate *skeptikos* and *ephektikos* to flag a type or school of philosophy was a dramatic and

---

[4] So also, of course, is the corrective reaction which flies the banner of 'applied philosophy': a volume could be written on the presuppositions of that phrase.

[5] For the Pyrrhonist titles of allegiance, see Sextus Empiricus, *Outlines of Pyrrhonism* 1. 7, Diogenes Laertius, IX. 69–70; on the history of the word *skeptikos*, see Janáček 1979; Striker 1980:54 n. 1; Sedley 1983:20–3.

[6] S.E., *PH* I. 1. 'Argued for' can of course be taken two ways: (a) 'argued for but not necessarily endorsed', (b) 'argued for and endorsed'. The difference between (a) and (b) sums up the difference between the dialectical aims of the Academy under Arcesilaus and Carneades (third to second centuries BC) and the dogmatizing Academy of Philo (second to first century BC). For the complexities of the historical transition from (a) to (b), see Couissin 1929; Sedley 1983; Frede in this volume.

fundamentally new declaration that from now on scepticism, inquiry and doubt, was to be a philosophy to live by.[7]

Not only were the Pyrrhonists the first self-proclaimed sceptics, it was above all their ideas which represented scepticism to the modern world when the writings of Sextus Empiricus (*circa* 200 AD) were rediscovered and published in the sixteenth century.[8] The sixteenth century was in fact the time when Pyrrhonism achieved its greatest impact. As Richard Popkin (1979) has taught us, the rediscovery of Sextus played a major role in shaping modern philosophy's preoccupation, from Descartes onwards, with the task of finding a satisfactory rebuttal of sceptical arguments. For a long time this meant a rebuttal of the arguments in Sextus Empiricus. Thus the notion of scepticism which we find in Sextus Empiricus can claim to be the original one, both for antiquity and for modern times. And it so happens that as far back as Gassendi and, I think, Montaigne we find an interpretation of Pyrrhonian scepticism according to which the sceptic does practise insulation of a kind – of what kind, we shall shortly see.[9]

This interpretation will provide a useful point of departure, first because Montaigne and Gassendi were two of the thinkers most closely involved in the modern revival of Pyrrhonian scepticism; secondly because their brand of insulation is still to be met with in modern accounts of ancient scepticism;[10] and thirdly because in the modern literature on ancient scepticism the Montaigne–Gassendi type of insulation competes with another, different notion of insulation which is itself something I would

[7] Sadly, the Pyrrhonists failed to persuade the world to observe the distinction between themselves and the Academics. The Academics came to be called, retrospectively, *skeptikoi* and *ephektikoi* because the distinction was disputed or ignored (Aulus Gellius, XI. 5; *Anonymi Prolegomena Philosophiae Platonicae* 21–5 Westerink; cf. S.E., *PH* I. 221–2). In the course of time the blanketing nomenclature, combined with insensitivity to the difference adverted to in n. 6, gave modern philosophy, and subsequently modern scholarship (including modern scholarship concerned with the beginnings of modern philosophy), a gravely distorted picture of pre-Pyrrhonist scepticism. I would not deny outright the propriety of referring to Arcesilaus and Carneades as 'the Academic sceptics'; it is too late now to undo tradition. But I believe, and will argue at length elsewhere, that there was a real and fundamental difference, not only between Pyrrhonism and the dogmatic scepticism of Philo, but also – and here perhaps I diverge from Frede, at least in emphasis – between Pyrrhonism and the dialectical arguments for sceptical conclusions put forward by Arcesilaus and Carneades. That is why I start my consideration of the history of scepticism at the point where the sceptic first got his name.

[8] The qualification 'above all' is necessary because a full treatment must reckon with the earlier presence of Cicero's *Academica* as a source for 'Academic scepticism'. But it was Sextus who made scepticism a major issue for the modern world: see Schmitt 1983 for a summary of the results of historical research in this area.

[9] In their separate and quite different ways both Gassendi (most accessible in Brush 1972) and Montaigne 1580 frustrate the attempt to find in them a single, consistent interpretation of Pyrrhonism: see Walker 1983 on the former, Cave 1979: pt. II, ch. 4 on the latter. But the insulation I shall be speaking about stands out more clearly than rival tendencies.

[10] E.g. Hallie 1967, Striker 1983.

like to situate in a historical perspective designed to highlight changes in the role that scepticism has played at different periods.

So now to business.

III

The key text for all insulating interpretations is *Outlines of Pyrrhonism* (abbreviated *PH*) 1.13, which draws a contrast between certain things the sceptic assents to, and certain others he does not assent to. The contrast defines the scope of Sextus' scepticism, and our decision as to where the line is drawn will determine our interpretation of the scepticism:

When we say that the sceptic does not dogmatize, we are not using 'dogma' in the more general sense in which some say it is dogma to accept anything (for the sceptic does assent to the experiences he cannot help having in virtue of this impression or that: for example, he would not say, when warmed or cooled, 'I seem not to be warmed or cooled'). Rather, when we say he does not dogmatize, we mean 'dogma' in the sense in which some say that dogma is assent to any of the non-evident matters investigated by the sciences. For the Pyrrhonian assents to nothing that is non-evident.[11] (*PH* 1.13)

To begin with, we can ask what Sextus means by saying that the sceptic does assent to experiences (*pathè*), like that of being warmed, which are bound up with the use of the senses and, more generally, with the having of impressions (*phantasiai*), whether of sense *or of thought*. (I italicize these words as a quick warning not to take the quoted paragraph as confining the sceptic's assent to sense-impressions. Although the example here is a sense-impression, in Sextus 'impression', 'experience', 'appearance' are not restricted to the sensory,[12] and readers more familiar with British Empiricist ideas and impressions than with Hellenistic epistemology should beware of importing the former into the latter.) But this assent, which is elsewhere and often called assent to appearances, is itself unclear, or at least has been the subject of dispute.[13] The dispute, in a nutshell, is this: if one

---

[11] My translation of this key passage is an attempt to put into tolerable English the results of minute analysis, by several hands, of nearly every word and phrase occurring in it (Frede 1979; Burnyeat 1980; Barnes 1982). Any nuances that may remain doubtful or in dispute will not, I believe, affect the present discussion.

[12] See Burnyeat 1980:33–7.

[13] Frede 1979 *versus* Burnyeat 1980. The present paper began as a further contribution to this debate, and an attempt to outflank my opponent. But he, meanwhile, has moved to a new position (in his contribution to this volume), and some of my earlier arguments relied on a thesis, that 'dogma' just means 'belief', which has been dented by Sedley 1983: nn. 57 and 67 and in correspondence earlier, and smashed by Barnes 1982. My revised position, like that of Barnes, should still be regarded as an alternative to Frede 1979, but it joins with Frede's current concern to see the whole issue in a broader historical framework extending into modern times. As always, I owe much to discussion of these matters with Michael Frede.

gives the sceptic a generous notion of appearance, the area of his assent expands and the scepticism contracts, while conversely scepticism spreads and assent draws back if (as I do) one takes a more restricted view of appearance. Let me explain in a little more detail.

Sextus directs us to understand every statement he makes, however expressed, as a record of his experience (*pathos*) telling us how things appear to him (*PH* 1.4, 15, 135, 197, 198–9, 200; *M* XI.18–19). If he means 'appear' in its non-epistemic sense, *PH* 1.13 implies that the sceptic's assent is restricted to experiential reports like 'It feels warm to me here', 'This argument strikes me as persuasive'. He may say 'It is warm', 'It is a sound argument', but what he means is 'I have the experience of its appearing so'. If, on the other hand, 'appear' carries its epistemic sense, to talk about how things appear is simply to talk in a non-dogmatic way about how things are in the world. We will no doubt want further elucidation of what it is to talk 'in a non-dogmatic way', but *PH* 1.13 now leads us to expect that the sceptic will be content to accept (*eudokein*) a host of propositions like 'It is warm here', 'This is a persuasive argument', just so long as these are understood to make no more strenuous claims than suffice for the purposes of ordinary life.

But we can also ask about the other half of the contrast in *PH* 1.13. What does Sextus mean by saying that the sceptic does not assent to any of the non-evident matters investigated by the sciences? It is this side of the issue I propose to discuss here. Perhaps it will contribute some light on the first area of dispute.[14]

What, then, are the non-evident objects of scientific inquiry? The notion of the non-evident is the notion of that which we can only know about, if we can know it at all, by inference from what is evident. If knowledge of the non-evident is possible, as Sextus' dogmatist opponent believes, it is mediate knowledge as contrasted with the immediate, non-inferential knowledge of what is evident (*PH* II.97–9). The dogmatist's favourite example of something evident is the proposition 'It is day'. If you are a normal healthy human being walking about in the daytime, it is perfectly evident to you that it is day. But we need an example which relates smoothly to the sciences on the one hand and to the sceptic's experience of being warmed on the other. I do not think that Sextus' dogmatist would hesitate to claim, when he is sitting on his stove, that it is quite evident that it is warm. Now, if one takes 'The stove is warm' as an example of something evident, and couples it with the reference to the sciences, it

---

[14] Meanwhile, I have found an ancient ally in *Anonymi Commentarius in Platonis Theaetetum* 61, 1–46 Diels–Schubart. The author distinguishes between the epistemic and the non-epistemic uses of 'appear' and assigns the latter to Pyrrho. This evidence may be significantly closer in time to Aenesidemus than has generally been thought: see Tarrant 1983.

becomes rather natural to suppose – and this is what Montaigne and Gassendi did suppose – that dogma in the sense Sextus wishes to eschew is any scientific pronouncement about, for example, the underlying physical structure which makes warm things warm; any theory about the real nature of heat, perhaps even the assertion or the belief that there is such a thing as the real nature of heat about which a theory could in principle be given.

On this type of interpretation – in honour of Montaigne I should like to call it the country gentleman's interpretation – Pyrrhonian scepticism is scepticism about the realm of theory, which at this period will include both what we would consider philosophical or metaphysical theory and much that we can recognize as science. The non-theoretical judgements of ordinary life are insulated from the scepticism and the scepticism is insulated from them, not because Sextus, like Thompson Clarke, assigns a special status to philosophical doubt, but because he assigns it a special subject matter, different from the subject matters with which the ordinary man is concerned in the ordinary business of life. This is insulation by subject matter or content.

One advantage of the country gentleman's interpretation is that there is no great difficulty in understanding how he can walk about his estate making arrangements for next year's crops while proclaiming himself a sceptic about space and time. There is no difficulty here because what the sceptic suspends judgement about, on this view, is not the spaces and times of ordinary life but the space and time of the natural philosophers. The sceptic is not a man who doubts he is in Cambridge or that he has been talking for at least five minutes. He is a man who is doubtful about the sorts of thing that the natural philosophers say in constructing their theories:

For some define time as the interval of the motion of the whole (by 'whole' I mean the universe), others as that motion itself; Aristotle (or according to some, Plato) defines it as the number of prior and posterior in motion, Strato (or according to some, Aristotle) as the measure of motion and rest, and Epicurus (as reported by Demetrius Lacon) as the concomitant of concomitants, since it accompanies days and nights and seasons, and the presence and absence of feelings, and motions and rests. (*PH* III.136–7)

The sceptic is doubtful about time both because the dogmatic philosophers disagree with each other and there seems to be no way of resolving the dispute (*PH* III.138–40) – hence the recitation of the different accounts of time – and because he is impressed by certain destructive arguments of the kind promulgated later by Augustine and McTaggart against the reality of time (*PH* III.140–50). Not that the sceptic accepts the negative conclusion of the destructive arguments: that would be dogma too, a negative dogmatism. Rather, just as he cannot find a criterion for deciding which among the competing positive views is correct, so equally he cannot decide whether or not the destructive arguments should be preferred to more positive urgings from the other side. The two dogmas, the affirmation and the denial of the reality of time, balance out and the sceptic suspends judgement on the issue and on all theoretical issues connected with time (*PH* III.140). The same goes for space, as will appear below. The sceptic sets aside the heavy pronouncements of the philosophers and the scientists and gets on with the business of daily life in Cambridge.

IV

So far, then, so good. But how well does the country gentleman's interpretation measure up to the texts (besides *PH* 1.13) in which it claims to find evidence of insulation? At first glance it does rather well.

Sextus starts his treatment of *topos* (place) in the *Outlines of Pyrrhonism* with an introductory statement about the scope of his discussion:

Space, or place, then, is used in two senses, the strict and the loose – loosely of place taken broadly (as 'my city'), and strictly of exactly containing place whereby we are exactly enclosed. Our enquiry, then, is concerned with space of the strict kind. This some have affirmed, others denied; and others have suspended judgment about it. (*PH* III.119, tr. Bury 1933–49)

The parallel passage in Sextus' larger work *adversus Mathematicos* (abbreviated *M*), comes not at the beginning but shortly thereafter:

Now it is agreed that, speaking loosely, we say that a man is in Alexandria or in the gymnasium or in the school; but our investigation is not concerned with place in the broad sense but with that in the circumscribed sense, as to whether this exists or is merely imagined; and if it exists, of what sort it is in its nature, whether corporeal or incorporeal, and whether contained in place or not. (*M* x.15, tr. Bury 1933–49)

These announcements focus the inquiry on a conception of place which is familiar from Aristotle: place as the immediate container of a body. Your place, on this idea of it, is the innermost boundary of the body (of air or other material) surrounding you, the boundary which encloses you and nothing else.[15] We may well think such a conception of place a heavily

---

[15] Ar. *Phys.* 212a 5–6; cf. 209b 1. For the bulk of Sextus' discussion, and therefore for ours, this formulation will suffice. But at *Phys.* 212a 20–1 Aristotle refines it to read: 'the innermost *static* boundary of the surrounding body', which is equivalent (boundaries being what they are) to 'the innermost boundary of the surrounding static body'. The point of the refinement is this: the place of X was to be the boundary of Y enclosing X, but if Y is moving, this specifies a carrier or vessel of X rather than X's place (212a 14–18). The solution is to find Z such that Z is static and Z encloses X at the same boundary as Y does. Example: X = a boat, Y = the body of water flowing in the Cayster, Z = the river Cayster as a geographical entity. Thus understood, the refinement does not (*pace* Ross 1936: 57, 575–6) threaten the condition that the place of X is equal to X (211a 28–9) and contains nothing but X (209b 1), and it is wholly unnecessary for Hussey 1983:117–18 to

theoretical one, or at least not an ordinary man's conception of place. Correspondingly, it looks to be a point in favour of the country gentleman's interpretation that Sextus should confine his discussion to the exact or circumscribed sense of 'place'. We could hardly ask for a more explicit statement that his scepticism has no quarrel with ordinary remarks to the effect that someone is in Alexandria.

The country gentleman will be encouraged further by the opening moves in the debate about place. Sextus' usual practice is to set out the arguments in favour of something, match them with the arguments against, and declare a draw: the equal balance of opposing arguments leaves us no choice but to suspend judgement. What the sceptic suspends judgement about is what the dogmatic arguments are for and against. And when we attend to the arguments for affirming that place is real, we find this:

If, then, there exist upwards and downwards, and rightwards and leftwards, and forwards and backwards, some place exists; for these six directions are parts of place, and it is impossible that, if the parts of a thing exist, the thing of which they are parts should not exist. But upwards and downwards, and rightwards and leftwards, and forwards and backwards, do exist *in the nature of things (en tēi phusei tōn pragmatōn)*; therefore place exists.

(M x.7, tr. Bury 1933–49; my emphasis)

It sounds Aristotelian, and it is. To say that there are real directions in the nature of things is to say that physical theory must recognize that directionality is an objective feature of nature, not just relative to ourselves, and this is exactly what Aristotle maintained: 'the kinds or differences of place are up–down, before–behind, right–left; and these distinctions hold not only in relation to us and by arbitrary agreement, but also in the whole itself' (*Physics* 205b 31–4; cf. 208b 12–22).

We get the same message from *M* x.9, which adduces the (Aristotelian) doctrine of natural places:

Further, if where what is light naturally moves there what is heavy naturally does not move, there exists a place proper (*idios topos*) to the light and to the heavy; but in fact the first <is true>; therefore the second <is true>. For certainly fire, which is naturally light, tends to ascend, and water, which is naturally heavy, presses downwards, and neither does fire move downwards nor water shoot upwards. There exists, therefore, a proper place both for the naturally light and for the naturally heavy.

(M x.9, tr. Bury 1933–49 with modifications)

---

contemplate treating 212a 20–1 as an interpolation on the grounds that it identifies the boat's place with the river *banks*. Even the circularity with which the refined definition has been charged (Owen 1970:252, Hussey 1983:117) becomes a benign regress if 'static boundary' = 'boundary of a static body' and Aristotle's cosmology can provide a terminal place for all bodies to be permanently in (209a 32, 211b 28–9, 212a 21–4, 212b 17–22). Sextus in fact exploits the refinement that places must be fixed and unmoving at *M* x. 25, 26, and at *M* x. 30–5 finds it necessary to make a sally against the Aristotelian cosmology.

That each element tends by virtue of its intrinsic nature to its own proper place in the universe is a central tenet of Aristotle's cosmology and a large part of what he means to be arguing for when he opens his own discussion of place in *Physics* IV.1 (cf. 208b 8ff).[16] If this is the positive dogma, the negative dogma set against it will be the denial of these theoretical notions, and the sceptic's suspending judgement will be suspending judgement as to theory. Which leaves him free to indulge in as much use as he likes of the ordinary broad sense of 'place'.

V

But our country gentleman is taking it too easy. To begin with, the arguments just quoted, although Aristotelian in character, do not argue for the existence of place in the narrow as opposed to the broad sense. They argue for the existence of place. Several of the considerations are indeed drawn from natural philosophy, but they make no use of the narrowness of narrow place. Second, we should look more closely at what Sextus says about the broad sense which he is not contesting. And here I must touch briefly on some points of philology.

The key word in *PH* III. 119 is *katachrēstikōs*. To say 'My city is the place where I am' is to use 'place' in the broad sense and thereby to speak *katachrēstikōs*. Bury (1933–49) translates 'loosely' but this does not tell you that the adverb derives from a verb meaning 'to misuse'. To use an expression *katachrēstikōs* is to use it improperly (grammarians still say 'catachrestically') and is contrasted here with using it *kuriōs*, in its proper meaning. So the contrast between broad and narrow place is a contrast between an improper and a proper use of the term. Both uses are current (*legetai dichōs*), but in the proper acceptation of the term, 'place' means that by which we are exactly enclosed. Narrow place is not a technical construct of natural philosophy but what 'place' actually means. In his introductory statement about the scope of his discussion Sextus is saying that it will be concerned only with place properly so called, not with anything and everything that gets called 'place' in the sloppy usage exemplified by such remarks as 'My city is the place where I am'.

In the parallel passage *M* x.15, Bury again translates 'loosely' but the

---

[16] Add *M* x. 10 (cf. *PH* III. 121), which cryptically claims that three of the factors in the (Aristotelian) causal analysis of something's coming to be require the existence of place, viz. the agent, the matter, and the end or *telos*. Although this argument does not appear in Ar. *Phys.* IV. 1, it might have been suggested by 209a 18–22 and the third item confirms that Sextus or his source intended it as an argument using Aristotelian resources (*pace* Bury 1933–49 *ad PH* III. 121). The appeal to Hesiod's Chaos at *PH* III. 121 and *M* x. 11 may be compared with Ar. *Phys.* 208b 29–33, the thought-experiment at *M* x. 12 with 209b 6–13.

On the relation between natural place and containing place, see Machamer 1978.

word now is *aphelōs*. *Aphelōs* occurs a number of times in Sextus Empiricus and elsewhere, and so far as I can see the best gloss on it would be 'without distinctions', with special reference to technical distinctions by which theory or science purports to represent real distinctions in the nature of things.[17] If you say that someone is in Alexandria, you are simply not distinguishing between his place and his city, which we would often describe as the place where he is. You are not picking out his *place*, but the surroundings he shares with his fellow citizens. What Sextus is saying, then, is that the dispute will not be about anything and everything that people call place, but about the attempt to identify for each thing its own unique place in the world, distinct from the places of all other things.

We now have two angles on the scope of Sextus' discussion. He will question the existence or reality of place properly so called, and he will question the idea that each thing has its own unique place in the world. The implication is that these are two ways of specifying the same target.[18] If that is so, Aristotle would be the first to recognize that the target is himself. Not only are the arguments in favour of the reality of place, as Sextus sets them out at *M* x. 7–12, closely modelled on the corresponding arguments in Aristotle's *Physics* IV.1, but it was Aristotle who invented, in all but name, the distinction between broad and narrow place. The distinction ensues rapidly on the decision to identify that which is called place in its own right (*kath' hauto*) with the *idios topos* unique to each thing. Anything else called something's place will be so called derivatively (*kat' allo*): because and in virtue of the fact that it contains the proper place of the thing in question. Thus we are in the heavens as a place because our place properly so called is in the air and the air is in the heavens (*Phys.* 209a 31–209b 1, 211a 23–9).[19]

---

[17] At *PH* I. 17 (cf. *M* VI. 1–2) it is simply the distinction between a narrowly moral and a broader sense of 'correctly'. But at *M* I. 153, 177, 179, 232 the context is the efforts of certain grammarians to regiment language so that gender endings, for example, correspond to gender differences in nature, and *aphelēs* expresses the indifference to such distinctions shown by the common speech of ordinary life. As a term of stylistic analysis, the word signifies a period which is simple, not divided into clauses (*monokōlos*, Ar. *Rhet.* 1409b 16–17), or, more generally, plain unelaborate speech (*M* II. 21, 22, 76, 77). Galen, *Meth. Med.* x. 269, 1–14 Kühn has an extended elucidation, derived from the Methodic school of medicine, the upshot of which is to equate the adverb *aphelōs* with (i) non-dogmatically, (ii) in accordance with the needs of life (*biōtikōs*), (iii) without articulation by distinctions (*mē diērthrōmenōs*) (cf. *M* IX. 218, D.L. VII 84), (iv) not precisely but untechnically and without any special knowledge.

[18] Janáček 1948 assembles evidence that Sextus' regular practice was to write the longer *M* treatment of a given topic with the shorter *PH* version before him. The purpose of *M* is to clarify and expand *PH*, filling in the *Outlines*.

[19] These two passages show Aristotle noticeably happier to use 'in' than to use 'place' of the broad places intermediate between our proper place and the heavens. I guess that this is because the circumference of the heavens not only provides the ultimate derivative place of everything individually, but *eo ipso* constitutes the place proper of everything collectively. That would explain why the 'common' place of *Phys.* 209a 32–3 is defined as that in which all bodies are and is not equivalent (as Ross 1936 *ad loc* would wish it to be) to Sextus'

When Aristotle formulates his definition of place as the immediate container of a body, he too thinks of this definition as positing for each thing a unique place which is that thing's place in the only strict and proper acceptation of the term.

It is of course beside the point to object that this talk of narrow circumscribed place gives a wrong account of English 'place' or Greek *topos*. Nor is it relevant to adduce the scientific superiority of the modern practice of fixing a unique location for something by the method of coordinates. Our concern is with the philosophical presuppositions of an ancient debate, between Sextus and Aristotle, about an older, less abstract method of fixing location by reference to containers and surroundings. My claim has been that both Sextus and Aristotle conceived the debate not as a discussion of a special theoretician's notion of place, but as a discussion of place. They agree that the word 'place' is correctly analysed as requiring a unique place for each thing. It is not just a contextual synonym of 'city' or 'gymnasium' but has its own proper meaning, its own job in the language: assigning to each thing its proper place in the world. Alternatively, and giving the point a more polemical thrust, if the word 'place' has any real work to do in our language and lives, it *presupposes* the possibility of defining, for each thing, a unique place. And since in the context of this ancient debate, the definition has to be through containers and surroundings, we soon reach the result that the only proper place a thing can have is the narrow circumscribed place which Sextus identifies as the target of his questioning. For, as Aristotle saw, this is the only surrounding container which is not shared with something else. If a man's *place*, as distinct from his city or his house, has to be uniquely *his* place, it can only be that boundary of air or whatever which directly surrounds and contains him and nothing else. This is how Sextus can represent his sceptical doubts about narrow circumscribed place as doubts about the reality of place *tout court* (*PH* III.135, quoted below; *M* x.6).

VI

We can check this conclusion, which I have so far defended on philological and historical grounds, against Sextus' argumentative practice. *M* x. 95 introduces a suggestion designed to meet Diodorus Cronus' argument

'broad place'. For all that, 'broad place' is nothing but a convenient label for the derivative uses of 'in' which Aristotle does, inevitably, recognize. I know no evidence to justify Sorabji's (1983: 25–6) assertion that broad place is a Stoic notion. The Stoic contrast is between place (which they define, differently from Aristotle, as the interval occupied by and equal to a body) and room (*PH* III. 124–5, *M* x. 3–4). Sextus refutes the Stoics separately at *PH* III. 124–30 and in the larger work confines himself to the mere mention at *M* x. 3–4; in both discussions of place his main target is Aristotle.

against continuous motion. Diodorus' argument claimed that continuous motion is impossible because a moving object cannot be moving in any place it is not in (obviously), nor in the place where it is (place proper is too narrow to move in), hence it cannot be moving in any place; hence it cannot be moving. The suggested reply is this:

'Being contained in place' has two meanings, they say: (i) in place determined broadly, as when we say that someone is in Alexandria, (ii) in place determined exactly, as the air moulded round the surface of my body would be said to be my place and a jar is called the place of what is contained in it. On this basis, then, that there are in fact two senses of 'place', they assert that the moving object can be moving in the place it is in, viz. place determined broadly, which has extension enough for the processes of motion to occur. (*M* x. 95)

There is the suggestion: in broad place the moving object has plenty of room to get its moving done. Now observe how Sextus rebuts it:

Those who say that 'place' has two senses, place taken broadly and place determined exactly, and that because of this motion can occur in place conceived broadly, are not replying to the point. For place conceived exactly is *presupposed by*[20] place conceived broadly, and it is impossible for something to have moved over broad place without first having moved over exact place. For as the latter contains the moving body, so the broad place contains, along with the moving body, the exact place as well. As, then, no one can move over a distance of a stade without first having moved over a distance of a cubit, so it is impossible to move over broad place without moving over exact place. And when Diodorus propounded the argument against motion which has been set forth, he was keeping to exact place.[21] Accordingly, if in this case motion is done away with, no argument is left in the case of broad place. (*M* x. 108–10, my emphasis; cf. *PH* iii. 75)

The contention is that broad place will not save anything that has foundered on considerations drawn from narrow place. It certainly will not save the Aristotelian account of motion from Diodorus' critique, for we have seen that Aristotle states himself in his own terms the premise that broad place presupposes narrow place.[22]

We need not stop to examine ways in which the Aristotelian description of motion could be reformulated to escape the dilemma, nor the ingenious alternative picture which Diodorus offers whereby a body can be first in

[20] *Proēgeitai*, lit. 'precedes': the context shows that the priority is logical, not temporal.
[21] The rebuttal, like the suggestion it rebuts, presupposes that Diodorus' argument is aimed at ordinary objects moving from one Aristotelian place to another. For remarks of Aristotle's which expose him to Diodorus' attack by implying that a body can move in its place, see *Phys.* 211a 35–6, 212a 9–10. At *M* x. 85–6, 119–20, the same argument treats of 'partless' bodies moving from one 'partless' place to another. On the latter, atomistic application, see Denyer 1981; on the relation between the two applications, Sedley 1977: 84–6; Sorabji 1983: 17–20, 369–71.
[22] Add *Phys.* 241a 8–9: 'It is impossible that any moving object should have moved over a distance greater than itself without first having moved over a distance equal to or less than itself.'

one place and then in another without our ever being entitled to say of it, in the present tense, 'It is moving'.[23] The question we must ask is whether Sextus accepts the presupposition premise.

In the quoted rebuttal he is speaking on behalf of Diodorus, whom he has cast (*M* x. 48) as the dogmatic denier of motion. Sextus' concern is to ensure that the arguments against motion are no less, but also no more, effective than the arguments in favour of it. For this purpose all he needs is that both negative and positive dogmatists accept the premise. However, the reason they accept it is that they regard broad place as derivative from narrow place. In their view, the presupposition is built into the very language of 'place', the proper meaning of which is narrow circumscribed place. In other words, it is in the first instance the dogmatists who would call broad place a catachrestic use of the term.[24] If Sextus does so too (*PH* III. 119, quoted above), this can only be because he does not question the dogmatist's analysis of the language of 'place'. What he questions is whether the project for which this language is designed can be successfully carried through. He questions the entire language game (as he would have chuckled to be able to call it) of locating bodies in their places.

VII

You are asked to fetch a slab and are told that it is in Alexandria. This just says that it is somewhere in Alexandria without indicating exactly where. Locating the slab vaguely in Alexandria presupposes that it can be located precisely at a particular place which is enclosed within the larger whole of Alexandria. The same applies if you are told 'It's in the temple' or 'In the inner shrine'. You can still ask, 'Where in the shrine is it?' So we reach the thought that there is exactly one place which is the slab's place and nothing else's place, and, as Aristotle saw, inevitably this will be narrow place: that envelope of air which directly surrounds and contains the slab and nothing else. If this and this alone is place proper, the fact that we can all agree that the slab is somewhere in Alexandria does not help to show that we can arrive at a clear notion of the place which is the place where it is. It is this precise place that we have to get a clear notion of if we are to vindicate our practice of locating bodies in places.

The pro-arguments in *M* x read quite well as arguments in favour of the

---

[23] See references in the previous note. Comparisons have been made with Russell's view (1914: 144) that 'nothing happens when a body moves except that it is in different places at different times'. But ancient opinion mostly sides with Russell's opponents in taking this to be a denial of motion rather than a theory of it (Ar. *Phys.* 231b 21ff, 240b 8ff, S.E., *M* x. 48).

[24] Note *PH* I. 207: the sceptic uses language 'without distinctions (*adiaphorōs*) [n. 32 below] and, if they wish, catachrestically', i.e. if non-sceptics wish to call it a misuse, he admits the charge.

proposition that we can and do locate things in well-defined places. An important passage not yet quoted is the following:

Moreover, if where Socrates was another man (such as Plato) now is, Socrates being dead, then place exists. For just as, when the liquid in the pitcher has been emptied out and other liquid poured in, we declare that the pitcher, which is the place both of the former liquid and of that poured in later, exists, so likewise, if another man now occupies the place which Socrates occupied when he was alive, some place exists. (*M* x. 8, tr. Bury 1933–49)

What is being argued for is the legitimacy of quite ordinary locating activities, as well as the more theoretical physicists' doctrine of natural places and directions. And here again Sextus is following Aristotelian precedent.[25] Like Sextus' dogmatist, Aristotle mixes considerations drawn from natural philosophy with arguments based on what is said in the common speech of ordinary life. Aristotle and Sextus are not country gentlemen; in both writers the ordinary concern with place and the theoretical concern are seen as continuous with each other.

Sextus' counter-arguments, urging the denial of place, are compatible with this. They fall into two classes: (i) rebuttals of the pro-arguments, chiefly on the score that all talk of right and left, or of Plato being where Socrates was, presupposes the existence of place and cannot without circularity establish it (*M* x. 13–14); (ii) dilemmas of a typical sceptical kind (though partly derived from Aristotle, *Phys.* 211b 5ff) to the effect that absurdities follow whether place is body or void, whether it is form or matter or the limit of a body or the extension bounded by those limits (*M* x. 20–9). What is important for our purposes is the final upshot of the negative arguments:

If the place of a thing is neither its matter, nor the form, nor the extension between the limits, nor again the extremities, of the body, and besides these there is nothing else to conceive it as, we must declare place to be nothing. (*M* x. 29)

It comes to this, that the legitimacy of locating things in places depends on whether or not we can formulate a coherent conception of place in the proper sense of the word. Both in ordinary life and in doing physical theory we take for granted that we can put things in their places. We may do it vaguely, but that presupposes we could be more precise if need be. But could we? Can we defend this practice without circularity? Can we formulate a clear and coherent notion of what a thing's place is? Some say 'Yes', some say 'No', but the sceptic remains in doubt and refrains from judging either way. If that is how the question stands, there is no Gassendi-

---

[25] The replacement argument just quoted from *M* x. 8 (cf. *PH* III. 120) corresponds to Ar. *Phys.* 208b 1–8.

type insulation by subject matter between scepticism and ordinary life.[26]

Finally, it seems to me that only some such interpretation as I have now reached will make adequate sense of the way the topic is concluded in the *PH* version:

> It is possible to adduce many other arguments. But in order to avoid prolonging our exposition, we may conclude by saying that while the Sceptics are put to confusion by the arguments, they are also put to shame by the evidence of experience. Consequently we attach ourselves to neither side, so far as concerns the doctrines of the Dogmatists, but suspend judgement regarding place.
>
> (*PH* III. 13–15, tr. Bury 1933–49)

The arguments are the negative arguments which show that no coherent conception of place can be formulated, so that place is unreal, but here they are set against a positive belief suggested by ordinary experience. What belief? Does ordinary experience directly suggest that one can formulate a philosophically defensible conception of place? I think not. What ordinary experience suggests is that one can locate objects in places. Anyone, claims the *PH* dogmatist, can look and *see* the difference between right and left, up and down, and can see that I am now talking just where my teacher used to talk (*PH* III. 120). Well might a person be ashamed if it turns out he cannot do that. And if he cannot, then of course it will be inappropriate to talk of the 'evidence' of experience: that is the dogmatist's epistemologically loaded description, preparatory to his arguing that ordinary experience *establishes* the reality of place.[27] But what ordinary experience establishes, philosophy must be able to elucidate. Conversely – and this is the sting of the negative critique – what philosophy fails to elucidate, ordinary experience fails to establish (compare *PH* III. 65–6). The abstract question of the nature of place and philosophical questions about defining it come into Sextus' discussion, through the presupposition premise, as attempts to make coherent sense of the mundane activity of putting things in their places (saying where they are).

VIII

I believe that the same conclusion can be drawn from Sextus' discussion of time, but rather than go into further details here I propose to step back to

---

[26] When Gassendi 1658: pt. II, bk. II, chs. 1–6 (selections in Brush 1972: 383–90) criticizes Aristotelian place, his predominant complaint is that it is bad science and wrong-headed metaphysics. I do not deny that insulation by subject matter, between the theoretical and the ordinary, is to be found in antiquity also: the obvious example is the Empirical school of medicine (see Deichgräber 1930). But Sextus firmly repudiates the suggestion that the sceptic could consistently be an Empiric (*PH* I. 236).

[27] There is no parallel to this in the *M* version, because the pro-arguments in *M* have been regimented into *modus ponens* form, without any indication of the epistemological grounding of the categorical premise.

consider the overall strategy within which the debate about time and place is one local scuffle. It is not often that Sextus appears to limit the scope of his scepticism in the way he does with place, which is one reason why I have dwelt on this at length.[28] The overall strategy will show that it would have been very surprising if we had reached any other conclusion than that Pyrrhonian scepticism does not practise insulation by subject matter. Once again, I start with a modern foil.

In his book *Ethics: Inventing Right and Wrong*, J. L. Mackie writes:

> The denial of objective values can carry with it an extreme emotional reaction, a feeling that nothing matters at all, that life has lost its purpose. Of course this does not follow; the lack of objective values is not a good reason for abandoning subjective concern or for ceasing to want anything. (Mackie 1977:34)

Mackie can say this because his whole discussion is based on a very strong version of the modern distinction between first and second order inquiries. He insulates first order moral judgements so securely that he thinks they can survive the second order discovery that all first order value judgements involve error, viz. an erroneous (false) claim to objective truth. The original Pyrrhonists, by contrast, thought that if philosophical argument could cast doubt on the objectivity of values – in their terms, if it could be shown that nothing is good or bad by nature – that would precisely have the effect of making you cease to want anything, or to hope for anything, or to fear anything. Their name for this detached view of one's own life was tranquillity.

The great recommendation of Pyrrhonism is that suspension of judgement on all questions as to what is true and false, good and bad, results in tranquillity – the tranquillity of detachment from striving and ordinary human concerns, of a life lived on after surrendering the hope of finding answers to the questions on which happiness depends. As Sextus explains, it turns out that happiness ensues precisely when that hope is abandoned: tranquillity follows suspension of judgement as a shadow follows its body (*PH* 1. 25–30). In its own way, Pyrrhonian scepticism offers a recipe for happiness to compete with the cheerful simplicity of Epicureanism and the nobler resignation of the Stoic sage.[29]

Now a recipe for happiness must make contact with the sources of unhappiness. It is above all the judgements which underlie the ordinary man's hopes and fears which must be put in doubt and withdrawn if

---

[28] Another case, more commonly cited (e.g. Frede 1979: 114), is Sextus' expression of tolerance towards one kind of sign-inference. On this see Barnes 1982: 12–18, where I would be less hesitant than he to ascribe to Sextus a Humean reduction of the inference to psychological habit.

[29] For more detailed discussions of Pyrrhonian tranquillity, see Hossenfelder 1968, Burnyeat 1980, Annas 1985.

tranquillity is to be achieved. The target of the sceptical arguments is, first, the ordinary man's ordinary belief that it is good and desirable to have money, say, or fame or pleasure (*M* XI. 120–4, 144–6; cf. *PH* I. 27–8); and second, the first order judgements of ordinary life about what is happening in the world around, which bear upon our achievement of these goals (if it is good and desirable to have money, it is important to know where the money is). The method of attack is philosophical argument, but the target is our innermost selves and our whole approach to life. Any attempt to insulate our first order judgements would frustrate the sceptic's philanthropic enterprise of bringing us by argument to tranquillity of soul (cf. *PH* III. 280).

Sextus' discussion of space and time should be seen in this wider perspective. Nowadays, if someone claims that Aenesidemus lived and worked in the first century BC and Sextus Empiricus around 200 AD, we see a big difference between doubting this claim on empirical grounds concerning the historical evidence – it really is frightfully meagre – and doubting the claim on the basis of a philosophical argument to show that the past is unreal. I do not think Sextus has anything like our sense of this difference. For him, anyone who says that Plato now is in the place where Socrates was when he was alive, and intends thereby to make a truth-claim, says something which is open to inquiry in that he can be challenged to give reasons or evidence for his claim and to defend its legitimacy, where this may include (as we have seen) defending a conception of place or the reality of time. If the defence fails, that has much the same effect as failure to produce decent historical evidence. It begins to look as if there is no good reason to believe the statement. And if you can find no good reason to believe a statement, what can you do but suspend judgement about it? All that remains for you is the standard sceptic retreat to a statement which makes no truth-claim, for which, consequently, reasons and legitimacy cannot be demanded, namely, 'It appears to me that Plato now is in the place where Socrates was when he was alive.'[30] That you can say without opening yourself to the sceptical arguments.

But there are other ways this retreat can express itself. Because the sceptic intends no truth-claim, he can say things which, were they intended as truth-claims, would presuppose something he cannot defend. Here is a simple example from another context in Sextus (*M* VIII. 129): in ordinary life one would be happy to say 'I am building a house', but strictly and properly speaking reference to a house presupposes the existence of a house already built. So the phrase is a nonsense, a misuse of language

---

[30] On the importance of the point that statements recording how things appear do not count as true or false, see Burnyeat 1980 and 1982.

(*katachrēsis*).[31] Nonetheless, people use it, just as they use 'man' for 'human being' (*M* VII. 50). And in this detached attitude of the ordinary speaker with respect to the presuppositions of his own language the sceptic finds a model to follow on a larger scale.

It is catachrestic to use 'is' for 'appear' (*PH* I. 135) and to indulge in assertive discourse without intending to affirm or deny anything (*PH* I. 191–2; cf. 207). But the sceptic tells us that, because his sole concern is to indicate how things appear to him (this much, of course, he says in plain language, with the verb 'appear' in its proper meaning), he does not care what expressions he uses (*PH* I. 4, 191). He can afford to be indifferent to the commitments and presuppositions of his vocabulary, because the part of the language he is serious about is the part which enables a speaker to express his non-committal indifference to the question whether what he says is true or false, viz. the vocabulary of appearance. The verb 'appear' (in its non-epistemic sense) is a device available within language for detaching oneself from the presuppositions and commitments of the rest of language. But an equally good alternative is to say what anyone else would say, without worrying whether it is true or false, without being serious about the proper application of the concepts involved.

In this spirit, if the sceptic says that the slab is in Alexandria, it will not be because he doubts that broad place presupposes narrow place. On the contrary, the presupposition is part of the normal workings of the language within which he thinks and speaks his scepticism. He can be unconcerned about the presupposition, if and only if he is unconcerned about whether it is true or false that the slab is in Alexandria. He will happily say that the slab is in Alexandria because, as he means it, this amounts to a statement of (non-epistemic) appearance. He thereby avoids rashly committing himself to distinctions which it takes a great deal of theoretical knowledge (virtually the whole Aristotelian cosmology)[32] to be able to draw.[33]

IX

We are now equipped to re-read Sextus' remark at *PH* I. 13 that dogma in the sense in which the sceptic avoids dogma is assent to any of the non-

---

[31] For the Aristotelian ancestry of this puzzle, and the philosophical depths to which it can reach, see Owen 1978–9.

[32] Cf. nn. 15, 19 above.

[33] It fits this conclusion that in the last chapter of *PH* I, where Sextus discusses common ground between Pyrrhonian scepticism and the Methodic school of medicine and says that the Methodic's use of language is as undogmatic and as unconcerned with distinctions (*adiaphoron*) as the sceptic's, he subsumes this under the sceptic life following appearances (*PH* I. 236–41). *Adiaphoron* is to be compared with *aphelōs* at *M* x. 15, discussed above at n. 17. The adverb *adiaphorōs* is coupled with *katachrēstikōs* at *PH* I. 191, 207; cf. 188, 195, *M* I. 61, IX. 333.

evident matters investigated by the sciences. This looked like support for
the country gentleman's interpretation because it could so easily be taken
to confine the sceptic's judgement-suspending to theoretical statements.
One major problem for this, the country gentleman's, reading is that
Sextus plainly states that the outcome of his critique of the criterion and of
truth is that one is forced to suspend judgement about the things which the
dogmatists take to be evident as well as about the abstruse matters they
describe as non-evident (*PH* II. 95, *M* VIII. 141–2). All statements about
external objects are doubtful, even such simple ones as 'It is day' or 'The
stove is warm'.

Does this mean that the latter statements are non-evident, and hence
dogma too? I used to think so.[34] But now it appears to me that the
distinction between the evident and the non-evident is itself one of those
dogmatists' distinctions which the sceptic makes light of (cf. *PH* II. 97).
The definition of dogma as assent to any of the non-evident matters
investigated by the sciences is explicitly taken from someone else (*PH* I.
13).[35] Sextus will use it, but not for the purpose of insulating the ordinary
from the theoretical. About both sides of the dogmatists' distinction he
speaks with a clear voice: it is impossible not to suspend judgement. All we
need to add is an explanation of why the distinction makes no difference to
the scope of Sextus' scepticism.

The answer, I submit, is the lack of insulation. Every statement making a
truth-claim falls within the scope of scientific investigation because, even if
the statement itself is not at a theoretical level, it will still use concepts
which are the subject of theoretical speculation: concepts such as motion,
time, place, body. If these concepts are problematical, which Sextus argues
they all are, and no line is drawn between philosophical and empirical
doubt, the original statement will be equally problematical. You will have
to suspend judgement about whether next year's sabbatical will come for
you to work on the philosophy of time – and also, of course, about whether
it would matter if it did not.[36]

As I see it, then, the ancient sceptic philosophizes in the same direct
manner as G. E. Moore. Moore is notorious for insisting that a philosophical thesis such as 'Time is unreal' be taken with a certain sort of seriousness,
as entailing, for example, that it is false that I had breakfast earlier today.

---

[34] Cf. n. 13 above.
[35] Cf. Burnyeat 1980:47, n. 48.
[36] This solution to the problem of the status of ordinary life statements in Sextus is a
generalization of that in Barnes 1982:10–12. Barnes works with just one presupposition:
the Pyrrhonist will not judge that the stove is warm because he is unable to satisfy himself
that he has a criterion of truth to ground his judgement. I add: and also because he is unable
to find a satisfactory philosophical elucidation and defence of the concepts involved in or
presupposed by the statement that the stove is warm.

And he thinks it relevant and important to argue the contrapositive: it is true that I had breakfast earlier today, therefore it is false that time is unreal. People always feel that these arguments and attitudes of Moore's miss the point. That is not the way philosophical questions should be treated; it is a naive and wrong sort of seriousness. But I think that Sextus would recognize a kindred spirit. If we look a third time at the texts before us we can see that Sextus' dogmatist argues in a manner exactly like Moore: one thing is to the right, another to the left, therefore there are places; Plato is where Socrates was, so at least one place exists. Compare: here is one hand, here is another, so at least two external things exist.[37] Sextus complains that this is circular; he does not complain that it is the wrong *sort* of argument to establish the thesis that place exists. And he propounds a modal version of the same inference in reverse: it is problematic whether place exists, therefore it is problematic whether Plato *is* where Socrates was or whether one thing *is* to the right of another. Similarly: it is problematic whether anything is good or bad by nature, therefore it is problematic whether it was worthwhile to write this essay. Perhaps it appears to me now that it was not worthwhile. Never mind. If I have achieved the sceptic detachment, this will be a non-epistemic appearance: a thought or feeling which I experience without any concern for whether it is founded in truth or reasons, and so without any diminution of my tranquillity.

X

I have been concerned to show that once upon a time philosophical scepticism had a seriousness which present-day philosophy has long forgotten about. It is now time for a broader canvas and the question when, and by whom, and why insulation was invented. To this end I shall take a brief – very brief, and accordingly less documented – glance backwards and forwards from the period (first century BC to third century AD) in which ancient Pyrrhonism flourished.

First, backwards. The idea that a man's first order judgements are put in doubt if he cannot give a defensible philosophical account of the concepts he is applying is reminiscent of nothing so much as Socrates' well-known habit of insisting that unless Euthyphro, for example, can define piety, he does not know, as he thinks he does, that it is pious to prosecute his father for letting a slave die. The Socratic view that one cannot know any examples falling under a concept unless one can give a definition or account of that concept has been branded 'the Socratic fallacy'.[38] The historical

---

[37] For an ancient parallel to Moore's further claim (1939:148–50; 1953:119–26) that the premise of this argument is much more certain than any philosophical premise that could be used to prove it true (or false), see Cic. *Acad.* II. 17.

[38] Geach 1966.

perspective I have been offering might prepare us to take a more sympathetic, or at least a more complex, view.[39] It is worth pondering the point that when Socrates' interlocutors fail to come up with a satisfactory definition, they are never advised to leave philosophy to those who are good at it, but rather to continue the search for a definition, in order that their life may be rightly directed.

In due course Socrates' insistence on the priority of definitional knowledge became Plato's thesis that you cannot know anything unless you know the Forms which are what definitions specify. And there are other signs that Plato has no inkling of insulation. He quite regularly insists that a philosophical theory must be able to be stated without infringing itself. The thesis of monism, for example, that only one thing exists, is refuted in the *Sophist* on the grounds that it takes more than one word to formulate it (244bd). Again, Protagoras' relativist theory of truth, that a proposition is true only for a person who believes it to be true, is made to refute itself in the *Theaetetus* because it implies that it itself is not true for those who do not believe it to be true. In neither case does it occur to Plato that a philosophical theory might claim a special meta-status exempting it from being counted as one among the propositions with which it deals.

Aristotle might seem a more promising source for insulation. In *Physics* I. 2, for example, he says firmly that the natural philosopher does not have to worry about the arguments of Eleatics like Parmenides and Zeno which purport to show that motion is impossible and that only one thing exists. In natural philosophy one takes for granted that motion and plurality exist: that is a first principle or presupposition of the whole inquiry.

But on closer examination it turns out that what Aristotle is insisting upon is not insulation but the departmentalization of inquiry. He does think that the Eleatic conclusions are directly incompatible with the first principles of natural philosophy. It is just that no science examines the principles which are a presupposition of its having a subject matter to study; e.g. geometry does not consider whether there are points nor arithmetic whether numbers exist. These are questions for another study, which Aristotle calls first philosophy (metaphysics). But he thinks of this higher study as delivering conclusions which the sciences subordinate to it can use as first principles. Whereas twentieth-century philosophy has usually thought of science and metaphysics as quite distinct *kinds* of inquiry (because in our world they usually are), for Aristotle natural philosophy is simply 'second philosophy' (e.g. *Metaphysics* 1037a 14–15). It is a less abstract and less general enterprise than first philosophy, because it deals with one part of the subject matter of first philosophy, and

---

[39] References and discussion in Burnyeat 1977.

secondary to it, because first philosophy has access to the ultimate principles of explanation (*Metaphysics* E. 1). That is all.[40]

The other side of this ancient coin is that it is a mistake to think of Aristotle's *Physics*, in the way twentieth-century philosophical interpreters tend to do, as philosophy *of* science in contrast to science.[41] Aristotle's analysis of the ordinary language meaning of 'place' is as direct a contribution to science as his analysis of the language of pleasure in the *Ethics* is a contribution to practical wisdom. In neither case does Aristotle think of the conceptual analysis as operating independently of first order concerns at a level of its own. It contributes directly to first order knowledge. The reason why conceptual analysis bulks so large in the *Physics* and the *Ethics* is that Aristotle holds a substantive, and in its time revolutionary, thesis to the effect that the ordinary man's ordinary concepts are the best starting point from which to proceed to the understanding of nature, on the one hand, and to the saving of our souls on the other. His very positive dogmatism matches Sextus' scepticism at each uninsulated point.

XI

So when did things change? Who invented insulation?

It was not, I think, Descartes. Descartes had no patience with Gassendi's attempt to limit the scope of the ancient sceptical materials. Indeed it was Descartes' achievement to see that those materials reach much further than the ancient Pyrrhonist had ever dreamed, that they impugn the very existence of the external world in which the Pyrrhonist had looked to enjoy tranquillity.[42] Accordingly, when Gassendi, in keeping with his unwillingness to allow Sextus to doubt ordinary truth-claims as well as theoretical ones, was unwilling to accept that the sceptical doubt of the *First Meditation* was seriously meant to have absolutely general scope, Descartes replied:

My statement *that the entire testimony of the senses must be considered to be uncertain, nay, even false*, is quite serious and so necessary for the comprehension of my meditations, that he who will not or cannot admit that, is unfit to urge any objection to them that merits a reply. (*V Rep.*, HR II. 206)[43]

But then he continues:

But we must note the distinction emphasized by me in various passages, between

---

[40] I do not understand why Kung 1981 thinks that Quine 1951 justifies her finding in Aristotle anticipations of Carnap's distinction between internal and external questions. In any case, the claim depends on ignoring the full range of questions that Aristotle assigns to first philosophy.

[41] So Owen 1961:116, 119, 125–6; Hamlyn 1968: ix; Ackrill 1981: 24; Annas 1981:286.

[42] See Burnyeat 1982.   [43] HR = Haldane and Ross 1931.

the practical activities of our life and an enquiry into truth; for, when it is a case of regulating our life, it would assuredly be stupid not to trust the senses, and those sceptics were quite ridiculous who so neglected human affairs that they had to be preserved by their friends from tumbling down precipices.[44] It was for this reason that somewhere I announced *that no one in his sound mind seriously doubted about such matters* [HR 1. 142–3]; but when we raise an enquiry into what is the surest knowledge which the human mind can obtain, it is clearly unreasonable to refuse to treat them as doubtful, nay even to reject them as false, so as to allow us to become aware that certain other things, which cannot be thus rejected, are for this reason more certain, and in actual truth better known by us.

Thus it is the same range of propositions which Descartes treats as certain for the purposes of practical life and as doubtful for the purpose of an inquiry into truth. There is no insulation of the Gassendi type here. But neither is there any other kind of insulation. Descartes has to insist that his doubt is strictly theoretical and methodological, not practical, precisely because he believes that the judgements of ordinary life really are put in doubt by the sceptical arguments. They are rendered so completely and utterly doubtful that Descartes feels he must construct a provisional code of conduct to keep his practical life going while he is conducting the inquiry into truth. Imagine a modern philosopher launching a seminar on scepticism by drawing up a set of rules for everybody to live by until the sceptical doubts have been laid to rest. That is what Descartes does, at some considerable length, in Part III of the *Discourse on the Method* (HR 1. 95ff). His distinction between the theoretical and the practical is not insulation but a deliberate abstraction of himself from practical concerns, a resolution to remain noncommittal towards everything in the practical sphere until theory has given him the truth about the world and a morality he can believe in.

If not Descartes, then how about Berkeley? Berkeley knew the Pyrrhonist arguments through Bayle[45] and his response was his well-known abolition of the distinction between appearance and reality. If the distinction is made, then Berkeley agrees that the sceptical arguments show we cannot know the truth of any statement about how things really are. The only answer is to say that the way things really are is nothing over and above the appearances. The question is, does Berkeley think this could or should make a difference to the judgements of ordinary life? The answer seems to be that sometimes he does and sometimes he does not.

When in a mood to accommodate the ordinary man, Berkeley will claim or imply that his immaterialist idealism is not an alternative to, but an analysis of, ordinary discourse. It gives the correct account of what we

---

[44] The reference is to a story about Pyrrho retailed at D.L. IX. 62. Other references to ancient sceptics actually living their scepticism are HR 1. 206, II. 335.
[45] See Popkin 1951–2.

ordinarily mean by talking of objects, an account whereby our ordinary statements come out true (1710:§82 *fin.*; cf. §§34–5).

But Berkeley is not always so accommodating to ordinary thought. Consider his well-known injunction to 'think with the learned, and speak with the vulgar' (1710:§51). This is motivated by an admission that on his principles ordinary causal statements like 'Fire heats', 'Water cools', come out false. For in his system only minds have causal efficacy. So if we do continue to say, with the vulgar, 'Fire heats', we will have to do it in much the same spirit as the Copernican continues to speak of the sun rising. Strictly, what the vulgar say is inaccurate, false. This is like Mackie's error theory of moral discourse, but with the crucial difference that Berkeley does not have Mackie's twentieth-century assurance that the distinction between first and second level inquiries smooths over the problem. As Berkeley sees the matter, idealism bears upon at least some ordinary judgements in the way the Copernican theory bears upon the statement that the sun rises.[46]

Thus Berkeley's progress towards insulation is at best qualified and ambiguous. Hume jumps right back to the position we found in Sextus; or at least, that is how it first appears. It is quite essential to Hume's programme that Pyrrhonism should clash directly and drastically with our everyday beliefs. For Hume maintains that if we were the rational creatures we fancy ourselves to be, we would give up, for example, the belief in external objects once we were confronted with the sceptical arguments which show the belief to be unfounded. The fact is, however, that we do not give up the belief. Inevitably, it recaptures our mind when we leave our study for everyday pursuits. It is this resistance of our beliefs to the sceptical arguments which demonstrates for Hume the role in our lives of factors other than reason, namely, custom and imagination. They, not reason, must be responsible for our beliefs if the beliefs do not go away when the reasons for them are invalidated by the sceptic's critique. The whole argument would collapse if our everyday beliefs were insulated by some logical device from that critique, from what Hume calls the impossible rigours of Pyrrhonism.

True, one may see a kind of insulation in the very fact that the beliefs do not go away. But what is important about this is that for Hume it is just a fact, a phenomenon that we may detect in ourselves when we leave the study. If Descartes had been aware of the same phenomenon, he would have had no need of his provisional morality.

---

[46] A nice ancient parallel is Empedocles frag. 9: people speak, incorrectly, of things coming to be and passing away; Empedocles acknowledges that he makes use of this customary mode of speech for the purposes of his own discourse; but he does not retract one iota from his contention that it is mistaken.

The next step is not difficult to predict. It is possible to be more impressed with Hume's account of the impotence of scepticism to budge our everyday beliefs than with his argument from that premise to the impotence of reason. If someone could find a way of preserving the premise while denying the conclusion, scepticism would suffer a dramatic loss of significance.

Which brings us, as many will have foreseen, to Kant. It was Kant who persuaded philosophy that one can be, simultaneously and without contradiction, an empirical realist and a transcendental idealist. That is, it was Kant who gave us the idea that there is a way of saying the same sort of thing as real live sceptics like Aenesidemus used to say, namely, 'The knowing subject contributes to what is known', which nevertheless does not impugn the objectivity of the judgements in which the knowledge is expressed. Where Aenesidemus would cite the empirical factors (jaundice and the like) which obstruct objective knowledge, the Kantian principle that objects have to conform to our understanding is designed to show that our judgements are validated, not impugned, by the contribution of the knowing mind. But Kant can make this claim, famously difficult as it is, only because in his philosophy the presupposition link is well and truly broken. 'The stove is warm', taken empirically, implies no philosophical view at the transcendental level where from now on the philosophical battle will be fought. Empirical realism is invulnerable to scepticism and compatible with transcendental idealism.[47]

In this way, with the aid of his distinction of levels (insulation *de iure*), Kant thought to refute scepticism once and for all. The effect, however, was that scepticism itself moved upstairs to the transcendental level.

I say this because I find it interesting to notice how Thompson Clarke's sceptic repeats some of what Kant said, but in a quite different tone of voice. Clarke's sceptic takes up what is called the absolute point of view and declares that the plain man's knowledge-claims are all very well in the context of ordinary life but they do not embody an absolute knowledge of things as they are in themselves; they are knowledge only in a manner of speaking – the plain man's manner of speaking, which has no foundation outside the practices of ordinary life. So we reach the idea that there are two ways of understanding a statement like 'The stove is warm', the plain way and the philosophical way, and it is only the philosophical claim to an absolute knowledge that the sceptic wants to question. What he questions is precisely that 'The stove is warm' can embody any further or deeper kind

---

[47] These sketchy remarks owe much to Stroud 1983, which may be read in conjunction with Tonelli's (1967) scholarly demonstration that in Kant's day scepticism was still essentially the 'empirical' scepticism of the ancient tradition. For some relevant connections between Kant and Wittgensteinian insulation, see Lear 1982.

of knowledge and truth than the plain man puts into it. Once the Kantian insulation by levels is established, scepticism itself goes transcendental.

The other important thing about Clarke's sceptic, and about most of the references to 'the sceptic' in modern philosophical literature, is that this sceptic has no historical reality. He is a construction of the modern philosophical imagination. The point is that when scepticism goes transcendental, the expression 'the sceptic' has to lose the historical reference it still carries in Hume, its connection with what certain historical figures actually said and thought. It becomes the name of something internal to the philosopher's own thinking, his *alter ego* as it were, with whom he wrestles in a debate which is now a philosophical debate in the modern sense.

XII

Now in recent years it has been argued with much skill and scholarship that something very like a transcendental scepticism is to be found in the texts of the ancient Pyrrhonist tradition, above all at *PH* I. 13.[48] Sextus, on this interpretation, insulates not between subject matters, as Gassendi thought, but between an ordinary and a philosophical way of understanding statements such as 'The stove is warm'. Sextus describes himself as a defender of the plain man and ordinary life. He has no objection to the plain man's manner of speaking, only to the dogmatist's belief that he can achieve a further or deeper kind of knowledge and truth than the plain man requires for the purposes of ordinary life.

It is an attractive interpretation, but the historical perspective I have tried to present suggests, not that it is simply wrong in the way that Gassendi's insulating interpretation is wrong, but that it is anachronistic. Its anachronism is the other side of the anachronism of G. E. Moore. Moore tried to take scepticism seriously. He refused to consider any insulating device of the kind provided by the Kantian distinction between the transcendental and the empirical. But he succeeded only in sounding peculiarly, even outrageously, naive – just because he was tackling scepticism in pre-Kantian terms, as if Kant had not existed. Moore is naive where Sextus is merely innocent, because of course it is true that when Sextus wrote Kant had not existed. The trouble with innocence – the image is very nearly Kant's own (1781: A761) – is that, once lost, it can never be regained.[49]

---

[48] Frede 1979.
[49] This paper owes debts to numerous discussions at different times and places. Two particular sources of inspiration that must be acknowledged are the writings of Barry Stroud, and Burton Dreben's Howison Lectures at Berkeley in 1981.

REFERENCES

Ackrill, J. L. 1981. *Aristotle the Philosopher*. Oxford: Oxford University Press

Annas, Julia. 1981. *An Introduction to Plato's Republic*. Oxford: Clarendon Press

Annas, Julia. 1985. 'Doing without objective values: ancient and modern strategies', in *The Norms of Nature*, ed. M. Schofield and G. Striker. Cambridge: Cambridge University Press

Barnes, Jonathan. 1982. 'The beliefs of a Pyrrhonist', *Proceedings of the Cambridge Philological Society* 208 (N.S. 28):1–29

Berkeley, George. 1710. *A Treatise Concerning the Principles of Human Knowledge*

Brush, Craig B. 1972. *The Selected Works of Pierre Gassendi*. New York and London: Johnson Reprint Corporation

Burnyeat, M. F. 1977. 'Examples in epistemology: Socrates, Theaetetus and G. E. Moore', *Philosophy* 52:381–96

Burnyeat, M. F. 1980. 'Can the sceptic live his scepticism?', in *Doubt and Dogmatism: Studies in Hellenistic Epistemology*, ed. M. Schofield, M. Burnyeat and J. Barnes, pp. 20–53. Oxford: Clarendon Press

Burnyeat, M. F. 1982. 'Idealism and Greek philosophy: what Descartes saw and Berkeley missed', *Philsophical Review* 90: 3–40

Burnyeat, Myles (ed.) 1983. *The Skeptical Tradition*. Berkeley, Los Angeles and London: University of California Press

Bury, R. G. 1933–49. *Sextus Empiricus, with an English Translation*. 4 vols, Loeb Classical Library. London: Heineman and Cambridge, Mass.: Harvard University Press

Carnap, Rudolf. 1950. 'Empiricism, semantics, and ontology', *Revue Internationale de Philosophie* 11: 20–40. Repr. in *Semantics and the Philosophy of Language*, ed. L. Linsky, pp. 208–28. Urbana: University of Illinois Press, 1952

Cave, Terence. 1979. *The Cornucopian Text: Problems of Writing in the French Renaissance*. Oxford: Clarendon Press

Cavell, Stanley. 1979. *The Claim of Reason: Wittgenstein, Skepticism, Morality, and Tragedy*. Oxford and New York: Oxford University Press

Clarke, Thompson. 1972. 'The legacy of skepticism', *Journal of Philosophy* 69:754–69

Couissin, Pierre. 1929. 'Le Stoicisme de la Nouvelle Académie', *Revue d'histoire de la Philosophie*, 3:241–76. English translation in Burnyeat (ed.) 1983:31–63

Deichgräber, K. 1930. *Die griechishe Empirikerschule*. Berlin: Weidmannsche Buchhandlung

Denyer, Nicholas. 1981. 'The atomism of Diodorus Cronus', *Prudentia* 13:33–45

Frede, Michael. 1979. 'Des Skeptikers Meinungen', *Neue Hefte für Philosophie* 15/16:102–29

Gassendi, Pierre. 1658. *Syntagma Philosophicum*

Geach, P. T. 1966. 'Plato's *Euthyphro*: an analysis and commentary', *Monist* 50:369–82

Haldane, Elizabeth S. and Ross, G. R. T. 1931. *The Philosophical Works of Descartes*, 2 vols. Corrected edition. Cambridge: Cambridge University Press

Hallie, Philip P. 1967. Article 'Sextus Empiricus', in *The Encyclopedia of Philosophy*, ed. Paul Edwards. New York and London: Macmillan

Hamlyn, D. W. 1968. *Aristotle's De Anima Books II and III*. Oxford: Clarendon Press

Hossenfelder, M. 1968. *Sextus Empiricus, Grundriss der pyrrhonischen Skepsis*, Einleitung und Übersetzung. Frankfurt am Main: Suhrkamp Verlag

Hussey, Edward. 1983. *Aristotle's Physics Books III and IV*. Oxford and New York: Oxford University Press

Janáček, K. 1948. *Prolegomena to Sextus Empiricus*. Acta Universitatis Palackianae. Olomucensis

Janáček, K. 1979. 'Das Wort *skeptikos* in Philons Schriften', *Listy Filologické* 101:65–8

Kant, Immanuel. 1781. *Critique of Pure Reason*. Translated by Norman Kemp Smith. London: Macmillan and New York: St Martin's Press, corrected edn 1933

Kung, Joan. 1981. 'Aristotle on Thises, Suches and the Third Man argument', *Phronesis* 26:207–47

Lear, Jonathan. 1982. 'Leaving the world alone', *Journal of Philosophy* 79:382–403

Machamer, Peter K. 1978. 'Aristotle on natural place and natural motion', *Isis* 69:377–87

Mackie, J. L. 1977. *Ethics: Inventing Right and Wrong*. Harmondsworth: Penguin

Montaigne, Michel de. 1580. *Apologie de Raymond Sebond*

Moore, G. E. 1925. 'A defence of common sense', in *Contemporary British Philosophy*, second series, ed. J. H. Muirhead, pp. 191–223. London: George Allen & Unwin and New York: Humanities Press. Repr. in G. E. Moore, *Philosophical Papers*. London: George Allen & Unwin and New York: Macmillan, 1959, pp. 32–59

Moore, G. E. 1939. 'Proof of an external world', *Proceedings of the British Academy*, 25:273–300. Repr. in G. E. Moore, *Philosophical Papers*. London: George Allen & Unwin and New York: Macmillan 1959, 127–50

Moore, G. E. 1953. *Some Main Problems of Philosophy*. London: George Allen & Unwin and New York: Macmillan

Nagel, Thomas. 1979. *Mortal Questions*. Cambridge: Cambridge University Press

Owen, G. E. L. 1961. 'Tithenai ta phainomena', in *Aristote et les problèmes de méthode*, ed. S. Mansion, pp. 83–103. Louvain: Publications Universitaires and Paris: Béatrice–Nauwelaerts. Repr. in *Articles on Aristotle*, ed. J. Barnes, M. Schofield and R. Sorabji, vol. 1, pp. 113–26. London: Duckworth, 1975

Owen, G. E. L. 1970. 'Aristotle: method, physics and cosmology', in *A Dictionary of Scientific Biography*, ed. C. C. Gillespie, vol. 1:250–8. New York: Charles Scribners

Owen, G. E. L. 1978–9. 'Particular and general', *Proceedings of the Aristotelian Society* 79:1–21

Popkin, Richard. 1951–2. 'Berkeley and Pyrrhonism', *Review of Metaphysics*, 5:223–46. Repr. in Burnyeat (ed.) 1983: 377–96

Popkin, Richard. H. 1979. *The History of Scepticism: From Erasmus to Spinoza*. Berkeley, Los Angeles and London: University of California Press

Quine, W. V. 1951. 'On Carnap's views on ontology', in W. V. Quine, *The Ways of Paradox and Other Essays*. New York: Random House, 1966, pp. 126–34

Ross, W. D. 1936. *Aristotle's Physics*. A revised text with introduction and commentary. Oxford: Clarendon Press

Russell, Bertrand. 1914. *Our Knowledge of the External World*. London: George Allen & Unwin

Schmitt, C. B. 1983. 'The rediscovery of ancient skepticism in modern times', in Burnyeat (ed.) 1983: 225–52

Sedley, David. 1977. 'Diodorus Cronus and Hellenistic Philosophy', *Proceedings of the Cambridge Philological Society* 203 (N.S. 23):74–120

Sedley, David. 1983. 'The motivation of Greek skepticism', in Burnyeat (ed.) 1983:9–30

Sorabji, Richard. 1983. *Time, Creation and the Continuum*. London: Duckworth

Striker, Gisela. 1980. 'Sceptical strategies', in *Doubt and Dogmatism: Studies in Hellenistic Epistemology*, ed. M. Schofield, M. Burnyeat and J. Barnes, pp. 54–83. Oxford: Clarendon Press

Striker, Gisela. 1983. 'The Ten Tropes of Aenesidemus', in Burnyeat (ed). 1983:95–116

Stroud, Barry. 1979. 'The significance of scepticism', in *Transcendental Arguments and Science*, ed. P. Bieri, R.-P. Horstmann and L. Krüger, Synthèse Library vol. 133, pp. 277–98. Dordrecht, Boston and London: D. Reidel

Stroud, Barry. 1983. 'Kant and skepticism', in Burnyeat (ed.) 1983:413–34

Tarrant, H. 1983. 'The date of Anon. *In Theaetetum*', *Classical Quarterly* 33:161–87

Tonelli, Giorgio. 1967. 'Kant und die antiken Skeptiker', in *Studien zu Kant's philosophischer Entwicklung*, ed. H. Heimsoeth, D. Henrich and G. Tonelli, pp. 93–123. Hildesheim: Georg Olms

Walker, Ralph. 1983. 'Gassendi and skepticism', in Burnyeat (ed.) 1983:319–36

Wittgenstein, Ludwig. 1953. *Philosophical Investigations*, translated by G. E. M. Anscombe. Oxford: Blackwell

◁ ══ ▷

The sceptic's two kinds of assent and the question of the possibility of knowledge

MICHAEL FREDE

Traditionally one associates scepticism with the position that nothing is, or can be, known for certain. Hence it was only natural that for a long time one should have approached the ancient sceptics with the assumption that they were the first to try to establish or to defend the view that nothing is, or can be, known for certain, especially since there is abundant evidence which would have seemed to bear out the correctness of this approach. After all, extensive arguments to the effect that there is no certain knowledge or that things are unknowable play a central role in our ancient sources on scepticism. And thus Hegel, Brandis, Zeller, and their successors were naturally led to take these arguments at face value and to assume that the sceptics were trying to show that nothing can be known. Closer consideration of the matter, though, shows that it cannot have been the position of the major exponents of ancient scepticism, whether Academic or Pyrrhonean, that nothing is, or can be, known. And this for the simple reason that the major ancient sceptics were not concerned to establish or to defend any position, let alone the position that nothing is, or can be, known. In fact, they went out of their way to point out that, though they produced arguments for it, they did not actually take the position that nothing can be known (cf. S.E., *PH* 1. 200–1).[1] And they went on to criticize those who did claim that nothing can be known as being as dogmatic as those philosophers who claimed that something can be known, as being pseudo-sceptics (cf. S.E., *PH* 1. 3,226; Photius, *Bibl.* 212, 169b).[2] Hence, in the following, I will call the position they criticize 'dogmatic scepticism', to distinguish it from the scepticism I want to attribute to the major ancient sceptics and which I will call 'classical scepticism'. I do not by this want to suggest that there are no important differences between Arcesilaus, Carneades, and the Pyrrhoneans. It just

---

[1] Sextus Empiricus, *Outlines of Pyrrhonism* (hereinafter *PH*).
[2] Photius, *Bibliotheke*, ed. R. Henry (Paris, 1959).

seems to me that these differences are minor compared to the difference between classical and dogmatic scepticism.

If there should be a substantial difference between classical scepticism and dogmatic scepticism, the questions arise (1) how it came about that scepticism turned dogmatic, (2) how it came about that scepticism was identified with dogmatic scepticism, so much so that even classical sceptics came to be interpreted as dogmatic sceptics, and (3) whether something philosophically important was lost because one was not aware of classical scepticism as an alternative to dogmatic scepticism. It is these questions I am primarily interested in, but since they only arise if there actually is a substantial difference between classical and dogmatic scepticism, I will first turn to the question whether it can be made out that there is a significant difference.

Traditionally philosophers and historians of philosophy have not seen a substantial difference. For they have treated Arcesilaus, Carneades, and the Pyrrhoneans as if they, just like the dogmatic sceptics, had taken, defended, and argued for the position that nothing can be known. Now this only seems possible if one does not take seriously the classical sceptic's remark that he, unlike the dogmatic sceptic, does not take the position that nothing can be known. And the only reason I can see for not taking this remark seriously is the following: one has reason to believe that the classical sceptic, like the dogmatic sceptic, does have the view that nothing can be known; and thus one thinks that the classical sceptic only says that he does not take this position because he not only cannot consistently claim to know that nothing can be known, but cannot even take the position that nothing can be known, if he wants to preserve consistency with a main tenet of scepticism, namely the principle that one should not commit oneself to any position, that one should suspend judgement, withhold assent on any matter whatsoever. Hence, since I do want to take the classical sceptic's remark seriously, I have to argue either that the classical sceptic in fact does not have the view that nothing can be known or that there is a substantial difference between having a view, on the one hand, and taking a position or making a claim, on the other. Since I believe that there is some sense in which even the classical sceptic might have the view that nothing is, or can be, known, I will try to argue the latter by distinguishing, following the classical sceptic, two kinds of assent such that having a view involves one kind of assent, whereas taking a position, or making a claim, involves a different kind of assent, namely the kind of assent a sceptic will withhold.

But before we turn to this distinction of two kinds of assent, it will be of use to consider the view that one should withhold assent. For it is this view which, supposedly, the classical sceptic tries to preserve consistency with, in denying that he takes the position that nothing can be known.

What, then, is the status of this view that it is wise to withhold assent? To start with, it is the conclusion of an argument the sceptic produces which is supposed to show that the wise man will always withhold assent. But it clearly is not the case that the sceptic, in arguing this way, thinks that he commits himself to the position that it is wise to always withhold assent. For to commit oneself to this position would be to give assent. In this particular case it is easy to see why the sceptic is not committed to the conclusion of his argument. It is an argument drawn from premises which only his opponent, by granting them, is committed to; an argument designed to show his opponent that he is in a dilemma, that he is committed to conflicting claims and hence had better consider the matter further until he is in a position to decide between them. For it is central to the position of his opponent that the wise man often does have the kind of justification for his views which will allow him to give assent. To be shown then that he also is committed to the view that the wise man will never give assent, puts him into a fundamental dilemma.

What is clear in the case of this argument, namely that the sceptic is not committed to its conclusion because he is just trying to show to his opponent that he is committed to a claim which conflicts with his original claim, seems to me to be true of all sceptical arguments. The sceptic never tries to argue for a position, he never argues against a claim in the sense that he tries to establish a conflicting claim and thereby tries to show the falsehood of the original claim. He rather thinks of himself as following Socrates, submitting the claims of others to the kind of test Socrates had subjected them to. Socrates saw himself in the unfortunate position of lacking the knowledge and expertise in ethical matters which others claimed to have. He was more than eager to learn from those who were qualified to speak on these matters. But how, given his own ignorance, would he be able to tell whether somebody really had some special qualification to speak on these matters? The method he used was the following: he would ask the person whose qualification he wanted to test a question to which the person would have to know the answer if he were knowledgeable and expert, qualified to speak on the given subject-matter. He would then try to show by an argument drawn from assumptions accepted by his opponent that his opponent also was committed to a belief which was incompatible with his answer to the original question. In case Socrates succeeded, this would have the effect that the opponent would have to admit that by his own standards of rationality he did not have the required qualification, the expertise or knowledge Socrates was looking for. For if he did have the knowledge he would have sufficient reason to reject one of the two conflicting claims. As it is, he, by his own standards, does not even have any reason to maintain one rather than the other of the two claims. For he must have had some reason for his original claim. But this reason now is balanced by another reason which he is shown to have in support of the conflicting claim. And it is because he is not in a position to adjudicate between the two that he ends in an aporia, that he is in a dilemma, that he does not know what to do about the conflict.

For our purposes one crucial feature of this kind of Socratic argument is that all its premises are supplied by the opponent. Socrates does not have to know their truth, he does not even have to have any view as to their truth, nor does he have to know the truth or have a view as to the truth of the conclusion of his argument, to achieve his aim of finding out whether his opponent can be trusted to know the truth on the matters in question. Another crucial feature is that it not only reveals that the opponent by his own standards lacks the knowledge in question, but that it also shows to the opponent that he would have to give the matter further consideration because, as it is, he does not seem to be even in a position just to make the claim.

What I want to suggest is that Arcesilaus and his followers thought of themselves as just following Socratic practice, and that they understood their arguments in the indicated way. In fact, I believe that they went one step further: they not only did not want to be committed themselves to the truth of the premises and the conclusion of their arguments, they also did not want to be committed to the validity of their arguments. More generally, they thought that their opponents had committed themselves to a certain view as to what counts as knowledge, good reason, sufficient reason, justification, and that their opponents had developed something called 'logic' to formulate canons and standards for argument and justification, canons whose strict application would guarantee the truth of the conclusions arrived at in this way. Since the sceptic wants to see whether his opponent at least by his own standards or canons has knowledge, he in his own arguments adheres to these standards. But this does not mean that he himself is committed to them. He is aware of the fact, e.g., that ordinarily we do not operate by these standards and that it is because his opponents want more than we ordinarily have that they try to subject themselves to these stricter canons; they want 'real' knowledge, certain knowledge.

For these reasons, then, the sceptics also would see no reason why their arguments that it is wise always to withhold assent would commit them to the position that one always should withhold assent. Their arguments just show that this is a conclusion their opponents are committed to. But the sceptics not only produce arguments to the effect that one should withhold assent, they also, as we can see from Sextus Empiricus, are in the habit of saying, at the conclusion of their various arguments against the various claims they address themselves to, that one ought to suspend judgement, to withhold assent on the matter. Since these remarks are not part of the sceptical arguments themselves, one might think that at least now the sceptics are committing themselves to a position in saying that one should withhold assent on this or that matter. And since the sceptics seem to be willing to make this kind of remark on any subject-matter whatsoever, one might even think that this reflects the general position that one should always withhold assent. But, of course, there is another interpetation of these remarks. Their aim might just be to point out to the opponent that by his own standards it would seem that he ought to withhold assent. But since the sceptic has not committed himself to these standards there is also no reason to think, just on the basis of these remarks, that he is committed to the claim that one ought to withhold assent on a particular subject, let alone to the generalization that one always ought to withhold assent.

What reason, then, do we have at all to assume that the sceptic thinks that one ought to withhold assent? I think that what may allow us to assume after all that the sceptic has the view that one ought to withhold assent is the fact that his opponents try to refute the sceptic by challenging this view and that the sceptic accepts that challenge. But one has to keep in mind that the fact that the sceptic accepts the challenge also admits of a different interpretation. The opponent, in challenging the view that it is wise to withhold assent, may be trying to remove one horn of the dilemma into which he has been put by the sceptical argument that the wise man will not give assent, and the sceptic may be taking up the challenge to show that his opponent is not in a position to rule out this possibility and thus to remove the conflict of his beliefs. In fact, I think that in classical scepticism this is one function of, e.g., the accounts of the so-called practical criterion, i.e. I think that it should not be taken for granted that the sceptical accounts of the practical criterion are just straightforward accounts of how a sceptic may proceed in real life. They, first of all, serve the purpose to show that the possibility that the wise man will not give assent cannot be ruled out just because it would be impossible to lead a life, let alone a wise life, without assent. The accounts of the practical criterion are supposed to show that even on the Stoics' own assumptions it might be possible to live without assent. Still, it also seems clear from the way the sceptic's opponents attack the sceptic on this point that they do not regard the sceptic's remarks as just a move in the dialectical game, but think that the sceptic does have the view that one ought to withhold assent. But in what sense could the sceptic have the view that one always ought to withhold assent without involving himself in immediate contradiction? If to have a view is to give assent a sceptic cannot heed his own precept without violating it. Thus we must assume that there is a kind of assent, namely the kind of assent the sceptic will withhold, such that having a view in itself does not involve that kind of assent, if we also want to assume that the sceptic does think that one ought to withhold assent and that he does not thereby involve himself in contradiction.

In what sense, then, could the sceptic have the view that one always ought to withhold assent? The only possibility I see is this: claim after claim it turns out in his experience that given certain standards or canons it seems that one ought to withhold assent. And this might suggest to him, leave him with the impression that, given these standards, one ought to withhold assent. But this does not mean that he is ready to make the claim that one ought to withhold assent. For he knows too well that his claim would invite a sceptical counter-argument. It would be pointed out to him that his experience was quite limited, that it was possibly quite idiosyncratic, that the future might be radically different, etc. Knowing all this he does not feel in a position to make the claim that one ought to withhold assent, but he also still might have the impression that, given certain canons, one ought to withhold assent, just as he might still have the impression that there is motion, and yet not be ready to make that claim because he acknowledges that there are impressive arguments, like Zeno's paradoxes, on both sides of the question and that he is in no position to adjudicate between them. More generally, the reason why he does not feel like making a claim, let alone a claim to knowledge, is that he thinks that there is a philosophical practice of making claims, and in particular a practice of making claims to knowledge, and that to engage in this practice is to subject oneself to certain canons, and that he has the impression that, given these canons, one ought to withhold assent. To be more precise, according to these canons, one has to have some special reason to make a claim, and given what counts as a reason according to these canons, he does not see himself in a position to make a claim, and thus thinks he ought to withhold assent.

I want to emphasize that this view not only has a rather complicated, tenuous status, it also has this further complexity which tends to be overlooked. It is a view relative to the canons and standards of rationality espoused by dogmatic philosophy, which the dogmatic philosopher insists on applying to any claim whatsoever, whether it be in mathematics or in ordinary life. It is only given these standards that it seems that one should withhold assent. But they are not the sceptic's standards, though he does not reject them, either. And thus Sextus often qualifies his remark that we have to withhold assent by saying that we have to withhold assent as far as this is a matter of reason or philosophical reason (*hoson epi tō philosophō logō*; *PH* III. 65; I. 215; II. 26, 104; III. 6, 13, 29, 81, 135, 167). Thus there is room for another kind of assent, though one which will be threatened by the possibility that one ought to conform to the standards postulated by dogmatic philosophy if it should turn out that there is a choice in the matter.

On the basis of this one might try to make a distinction between just having a view and making a claim, taking a position. Just to have a view is to find oneself being left with an impression, to find oneself having an impression after having considered the matter, maybe even for a long time, carefully, diligently, the way one considers matters depending on the importance one attaches to them. But however carefully one has considered a matter it does not follow that the impression one is left with is true, nor that one thinks that it is true, let alone that one thinks that it meets the standards which the dogmatic philosophers claim it has to meet if one is to think of it as true. To make a claim, on the other hand, is to subject oneself to certain canons. It does, e.g., require that one should think that one's impression is true and that one has the appropriate kind of reason for thinking it to be true. To be left with the impression or thought that p, on the other hand, does not involve the further thought that it is true that p, let alone the yet further thought that one has reason to think that p, that it is reasonable that p. Even on the principles of Stoic logic the propositions (i) that p, (ii) that it is true that p, and (iii) that it is reasonable that p, are different propositions, and hence the corresponding thoughts or impressions are different thoughts. And though the propositions that p and that it is true that p may be necessarily equivalent, it does not follow from this that the impression that p involves, or is identical with, the impression that it is true that p.

Now it seems to me that there is such a distinction between having a view and taking a position, but that it is quite difficult to articulate it. And one reason for this seems to be that there is a whole spectrum of distinctions with a very weak notion of having a view at one extreme and a very strong notion of taking a position at the other extreme. The problem is to draw the distinction in such a way that it does correspond to the distinction the sceptics actually made.

One way the sceptics draw the distinction is in terms of two kinds of assent, and since I think that it is a difficulty about the way in which the distinction is to be drawn in terms of two kinds of assent which historically gives rise to dogmatic scepticism, I focus on the distinction thus drawn. But it is important to realize from the outset that this is just one way in which the sceptics draw the distinction, and that they draw the distinction in this way because their opponents speak about assent in such a way that they are in no position to assail the sceptical distinction.

A clue as to how we might distinguish two kinds of assent for the

classical sceptic, we get from Sextus. For Sextus, too, distinguishes two
kinds of assent. Though at times he says that the sceptic invariably
withholds assent, he also says that the sceptic does give assent to those
impressions which are forced upon him (1. 13), or that the sceptic does not
want to overturn those views which lead us, having been impressed by
things in a certain way, towards assent without our will. The addition
'without our will' is crucial. For it guards this kind of assent against the
threat that we might find out that we ought to conform to the canons of
rationality postulated by dogmatism. This kind of assent is not a matter of
choice, unlike the assent of the Stoic wise man. In the first of these passages
Sextus also uses the verb *eudokein* as a variant for the verb normally used in
this context, *synkatatithesthai*. And indeed, the Suida, the Etymologicum
Magnum, and the Lexeis Rhetorikai (*Anecdota Graeca*, 1, p. 260)[3] treat
synkatatithesthai as a synonym of *eudokein*. And if we consider the
ordinary use of this verb it turns out that it might refer to an explicit act of
acknowledgement, approval, consent, acceptance, the kind of thing one
does for a reason. Or it might refer to a passive acquiescence or acceptance
of something, in the way in which a people might accept a ruler, not by
some act of approval or acknowledgement, but by acquiescence in his rule,
by failing to resist, to effectively reject his rule. Correspondingly there are
two ways or senses in which one might accept or approve of an impression.
When the Stoics speak of 'assent', they talk of an act of approval, the kind
of thing one should do for an appropriate reason; they think that to assent
to an impression is to take it to be true, and that one should have good
reason for taking something to be true. But there is also the other sense of
'assent'. One might, having considered matters, just acquiesce in the
impression one is left with, resign oneself to it, accept the fact that this is the
impression one is left with, without though taking the step to accept the
impression positively by thinking the further thought that the impression
is true. One might also not acquiesce in the impression one is left with and
think that the matter needs further consideration. But whether one does or
does not acquiesce in it is not by itself dependent on whether one takes the
impression to be true. Assent may be a purely passive matter. It may be the
case that human beings work in such a way that impressions are more or
less evident to us. Evidence is a purely subjective feature of our
impressions. Now we also attribute different importance to different
questions. We might be constructed in such a way that if we have an
impression on a matter whose degree of evidence does not correspond to
the degree of importance we attach to the matter, we naturally, unless we
are prevented, e.g. by lack of time or energy or have decided to take a risk,
go on to consider the matter further till we get an impression which has a

[3] Ed. I. Bekker (Berlin, 1814).

sufficient degree of evidence. It would not even have to be the case that at a certain point we decide that we now have clear enough an impression and stop to consider the matter further. It may be just the case that as soon as we have clear enough an impression we, without any further thought, act on it. And this may be all acquiescence and assent consist in.

One might object that both cases of assent constitute some kind of acceptance, and that to accept an impression surely is to accept it as true. After all, how could somebody be said to have the view that *p* without thinking that it is the case that *p* or that it is true that *p*?

Here is at least one way in which this might be possible. It might be the case that action does not require that one take the impression one is acting on to be true. It might be the case that action does not, in addition to the impression that *p*, require a positive act of assent or the further thought that it is true that *p*. All that may be needed is one's acquiescence in the impression, and all this may amount to is that in the series of impressions one has reached an impression which produces an action rather than the kind of disquiet which would make one go on to consider the matter further till one reached an impression which one no longer resists and which produces an action. Indeed, one may have the view that *p* without even entertaining the thought that *p*, let alone the further thought that *p* is true. Things may have left us with the impression that *p*, and we may act on that view, without being aware of it. We may leave aside here cases in which something prevents us from realizing that this is the view we have (e.g. cases of suppression or self-deception). For even if we know that we have a certain view and on some occasion act on it, it is not necessary that in order to act on it we on that occasion have to entertain explicitly the corresponding thought and to assent positively to it. An expert craftsman is still acting on his expert beliefs, even though he is not actually thinking of what he is doing when he is acting on them. Indeed thinking of them might interfere with his activity. But having finished his work he might well explain to us which views guided his activity. And for some of these views it might be true that this would be the first time he ever formulated them, either to himself or to somebody else. Nevertheless he could properly claim to have acted on them.

The sceptic might think that his opponents will have to grant that there are these kinds of cases and that they can be characterized in terms of assent to an impression. For even the Stoics assume that the wise man will often act, not on the basis of certain knowledge, but of wise conjecture. He is not omniscient, and his rationality and wisdom are characterized exactly by his ability to be rational or reasonable in his assumptions and actions even when he lacks knowledge, as he inevitably will, in the complex situations of everyday life. Nevertheless he will do what is fitting or appropriate because he will be able, as the Stoics themselves say, to give a reasonable (*eulogon*) account of what he has done. I want to suggest that the past tense of 'what he has done' is to be taken seriously. The view is rather like Aristotle's; the person who has chosen to act in a certain way does not actually have to have gone through some moral reasoning and to have actually decided to act accordingly; what makes the action voluntary rather is that one correctly explain the action after the fact as being done for reasons of a certain kind. Similarly the Stoic wise man, in order to do what is fitting, does not necessarily actually have to go through some reasoning, overtly accept or assent to the conclusion, and act on the basis of this. It rather is that his action in hindsight can be explained in terms of such reasoning. Thus even on the Stoics' theory there will be cases where the wise man, in fact, just acts on an impression of an appropriate kind and where, if we want to talk about assent, the assent consists in nothing but the fact that the wise man does not resist the impression he is acting on, but, in acting on it, implicitly accepts it. This, then, would seem to be a kind of case where acceptance of, or assent to, an impression does not involve taking it to be true. And if this is so, and if withholding assent is counted as an action, one might, e.g., say that the sceptic has the view that one ought to withhold assent in the sense that he might explain his withholding assent in terms of his acquiescence in this impression, pointing out that he is not resisting or fighting against this impression, but implicitly accepts it by acting on it.

Thus the sceptic may have views which account for his behaviour. He behaves exactly in the way in which somebody who believed these views to be true would behave. But he insists that there is no need to assume that action, in addition to the appropriate kind of impression, requires the additional belief that the impression is true.

Now one might also ask the sceptic as to his view on this or that matter. And he might be ready to try to articulate his view. And in this case it might be objected that he now is taking a position as to what he takes to be the truth of the matter. But, as we can see from Sextus, it is open to him to reply that he is merely trying to articulate the views which guide his behaviour, he is merely, as it were, giving an autobiographical report, without taking a stand on the truth of his views.

At this point it is also worth taking note of another crucial fact. It is assumed by Greek philosophers that knowledge and truth are correlatives. For them those things count as truths which on the true account of things would come out as truths. But given that dogmatic philosophy has raised the conditions for what is to count as knowledge, it thereby has raised the requirements for what is to count as true. Now things which we ordinarily would count as true no longer necessarily qualify as such. We might think that it is true that this book is brown. But it might turn out that on the true theory of things this is a mere appearance, that in fact there only is a certain configuration of atoms which may, or may not, produce this appearance. And similarly for all other ordinary truths. It is in this way that dogmatic philosophy creates a global contrast between appearance and truth or reality. For dogmatic philosophy insists on calling into question all the truths we ordinarily go by.

And given this contrast the sceptic, of course, does not take his impressions to be true, i.e. he does not think that his impressions are such that they will come out true on the true theory of things. For what reason would he have to think this? And he can point to the fact that not even the Stoic wise man takes all his impressions to be true in this way. The very point of the doctrine of the reasonable is that it allows the wise man to accept impressions, and thus not to be reduced to inaction, without thereby taking them to be true. It is in this way that the Stoic wise man avoids having false beliefs, even though some of his impressions, however reasonable, may be false. For though he goes by the impression that *p*, he does not accept it as true, but only as reasonable.

Thus one may argue that the Stoics, given their own theory, can hardly reject the suggestion that there is a difference between having a view and taking a position, between just going by an impression and going by an impression because one takes it to be true, between two kinds of assent, merely passive acceptance and active acceptance as true.

There is one important difference between having a view and taking a position which was emphasized by the sceptics and which is still reflected by our ordinary notion of dogmatism. The sceptic has no stake in the truth of the impression he is left with. He is ever ready to consider the matter further, to change his mind. He has no attachment to the impressions he is left with. He is not responsible for having them, he did not seek them out. He is not out to prove anything, and hence feels no need to defend anything. For the dogmatic, on the other hand, something is at stake. It does make a great difference to him whether his impressions really are true and whether he has made a mistake in taking them to be true. For in actively giving assent to them he has become responsible for them, and hence feels a need to defend them and to prove them to be true. The dogmatic, in taking a position, has made a deliberate choice, a *hairesis*, for which he is accountable. But because so much is at stake for him, he no longer is in a position openly to consider alternatives, to realize and accept the weight of objections; he has become dogmatic in his attitude.

If we now apply this distinction of two kinds of assent and corresponding-ly the distinction between having a view and taking a position to the question of knowledge, we might say that the classical sceptic perhaps comes to be left with the impression that nothing is, or even can be, known, whereas the dogmatic sceptic takes the position that nothing can be known. How could the classical sceptic come to have this impression? In his experience it turns out that claim after claim does not pass his scrutiny which, at least given the standards his opponents themselves are committed to, these claims should pass if they were made from knowledge. Thus he naturally is left with the impression that, given these standards, nothing will pass the test and hence that nothing is, or even can be, known. And in the course of time he might even acquiesce in this impression. He might stop to think that this cannot be right and that just some further consideration will change his impression. And yet he might not feel the slightest inclination to claim that nothing can be known. He knows the objections too well: limited experience, experience with the wrong claims, experience with the wrong opponents, one day we will know, etc. And there is, of course, the troublesome tag 'given these standards'. He is not committed to these standards, but he does see their attraction. He himself originally had hoped that by following these standards he would arrive at certain knowledge and thus could adjudicate all the conflicts which were troubling him. But he also knows of powerful arguments against these standards, like the paradox of the liar. He cannot rule out the possibility that other standards would fare better. He is aware of the fact that in ordinary life and in ordinary language we do not subject ourselves to these standards. We do not ordinarily require of somebody who claims to know that he should have the kind of reason and justification for his belief which allows him to rule out all incompatible beliefs, that knowledge has to be firm or certain exactly in the sense that somebody who really knows cannot be argued out of his belief on the basis of assumptions incompatible with it. It seems that ordinarily we only expect satisfaction of these standards to an extent and degree which is proportional to the importance we attribute to the matter in question. And thus, following common usage, a sceptic might well be moved to say, in perfect consistency with his scepticism, that he knows this or that. There is no reason why the sceptic should not follow the common custom to mark the fact that he is saying what he is saying having given the matter appropriate consideration in the way one ordinarily goes about doing this, by using the verb 'to know'. This, in fact, is what we find Sextus doing occasionally (cf. *Adversus Mathematicos* VIII. 157). Aenesidemus obviously was prepared to go so far as to say that a wise man knows that he does not know anything for certain and that if he does know something he is still going to withhold assent (Photius, *Bibl.* 212, 169b 28ff). A sceptic might take the view that all one could sensibly do was to follow this very complicated common practice. But if he would follow this practice it would be with the thought that what one said one knew could be radically otherwise, and that the whole practice of using the verb 'to know' the way we ordinarily do could be radically mistaken. For we cannot, e.g., rule out the possibility that we should subject ourselves to the rigorous standards and canons philosophers have been trying to impose, but which their own claims do not meet. There is the possibility that one day they will be able to formulate a set of canons which will find general acceptance. There is the possibility that one day they will make claims which meet these standards and which will pass the test.

It seems to me that this rather differentiated view is quite different from the dogmatic position that nothing can be known. It is a view the classical sceptic finds himself stranded with, not a position he is out to demonstrate, to establish, to defend, not a position he thinks he has reason to adopt and adopts for that reason. He is not out to show that some particular person, or some group of people, or people in general do not have knowledge, he is not out to show anything. He is willing to find out. But so far, all his search has left him with is the impression that nothing is known. If this is correct then there is a substantial difference between classical scepticism and dogmatic scepticism, and the ancient representatives of classical scepticism were not just deluding themselves when they saw a difference between their own view and that of dogmatic sceptics. But if this is so, then the question does arise how this complex attitude of the classical sceptic collapsed into the dogmatic position that nothing can be known.

It seems that the major step in the direction of a dogmatic scepticism was already taken in antiquity. For, as we saw, already in antiquity some sceptics accused other sceptics of being dogmatic in their assertion that nothing can be known. This is the charge Aenesidemus levels against the late Academics (cf. Photius, *Bibl.* 212, 169b), and a charge, Sextus thinks, which might be levelled against the Academics in general (*PH* 1. 226). Evidence that some late Academics did in fact espouse such a dogmatic scepticism we find at the end of Cicero's *Academica priora* (148). There Catulus is made to say:

I return to the position of my father, which he said to be that of Carneades; I believe that nothing can be known, but I also believe that the wise man will give assent, i.e. will have opinions, but this in such a way that he is aware that he is only opining and that he knows that there is nothing which can be comprehended and known; hence I approve of this kind of withholding assent in all matters, but I vehemently assent to this other view that there is nothing which can be known.

These remarks reveal their dogmatism in the vehemence with which Catulus assents to the impression that nothing can be known, in the strong attachment which he has to this view, an attachment of a kind which is quite alien to the classical sceptic and which is explicitly criticized by Sextus Empiricus (*PH* 1. 230). Moreover it reveals its dogmatism in that it allows the sceptic to have opinions, i.e. beliefs as to how things are. This passage and its context also supply us with some crucial information as to the source of this dogmatism. To start with, it is clear from Cicero's following remarks that he does not think that the view Catulus expresses is the general view of the Academy; Cicero himself thinks that this was not Carneades' view. Secondly, as we can see from Catulus' own remarks, this view is presented as an interpretation of Carneades, but as one which is controversial.

Now we know from the earlier parts of the *Academica* of at least one respect in which this interpretation of Carneades was controversial among Carneades' pupils. We are told that there was disagreement between Clitomachus on the one hand, and Metrodorus and Philo on the other, as to whether, in reality and according to Carneades, the wise man will give assent and hence have opinions. The question is whether we can reconstruct enough of this controversy to see how it might have led to the kind of dogmatic scepticism which we find in the later Academy and which is represented by Catulus' remarks. In this case we also would have some explanation why later authors, like Sextus, entertain the possibility, or even assume as a fact, that Academic sceptics in general were dogmatic. For the view presents itself as an interpretation of Carneades and as the position of the Academy in general.

What, then, could have given rise to the view that according to Carneades the wise man will assent to what is not known, i.e. will have opinions, and how could this lead to the kind of dogmatic scepticism we are considering? The following seems to me to be a possibility. The notion of the probable (*pithanon*) plays a central role in Carneades. Among other things it is a matter of probability for Carneades that nothing can be known (Cic., *Ac. pr.* 110). Now there are two different interpetations of, and attitudes towards, the probable. These seem to correspond to two different interpretations of Carneades' so-called practical criterion. Asked how the sceptic will know what to do if he universally withholds assent, Carneades points out that he will just follow the probable, what seems to be the case, and that depending on the importance of the matter he will go through certain procedures to make sure that his impression is relatively reliable. It is clear that Carneades' account, first of all, is a dialectical move against a dogmatic objection and thus does not commit him to any view at all. But I also think that it does reflect Carneades' view as to how people actually go about gaining an impression they are willing to rely on. And taken this way, it admits of two interpretations. It may be taken just in the sense that this is how human beings in general seem to proceed, or it may be taken in the sense that this is how one ought to proceed if one wants to get a reliable impression, one which, if not true, at least has a good chance to be true. Whereas on the first interpretation it is just noted that human beings, as a matter of fact, go about considering matters in a certain way when in doubt, on the second interpretation proper consideration is regarded as conferring some epistemological status on the impression thus arrived at: it at least has a good chance to be true. And thus, though it is agreed on all sides that the probable is that which seems to be the case, this is interpreted in two different ways. On one interpretation what on due consideration appears to be the case offers us some guidance as to what actually is true. Though we are in no position to say that it is true, we may expect it to have a good chance of being true, to be like the truth (*verisimilis*), or else to be the truth itself (Cic., *Ac. pr.* 7; 32; 66; 99; 107). On the other interpretation the fact that something appears to be the case goes no way to show that it is true; however much it appears to be the case, this does not in itself make it any more likely to be true. The probable is just the plausible, and there is no reason to assume that plausibility and truth, or even evidence and truth, go hand in hand.

Another piece of relevant information seems to be the following: Carneades subscribed to the sceptic tenet that one always should withhold assent. But it also seems to have been agreed that Carneades did say that it sometimes is wise to give assent (*Ac. pr.* 67). Obviously, this needed interpretation, because it had to be made compatible with the general sceptical tenet to withhold assent, but presumably also because Arcesilaus had said nothing of the sort and hence Carneades' remark might be taken to indicate a significant departure from the position of Arcesilaus. Thus we find Clitomachus making a distinction of two kinds of assent, obviously trying to give an interpretation of the distinction which will not commit Carneades to the view that it is wise to have mere opinions (Cic., *Ac. pr.* 104). And it seems clear from Catulus' remarks that the opposing party similarly made a distinction of two kinds of assent, but exactly in such a way that Carneades would be committed to the view that the wise man will have opinions. For Catulus distinguishes between the universal withholding of assent and the vehement assent he gives to the view that nothing can be known and remarks that the wise man will give some kind of assent, i.e. will have opinions.

Now there is an obvious connection between the two interpretations of the probable and the two interpretations of the two kinds of assent already Carneades must have distinguished. To see this we have to notice that the sceptics only sometimes speak of two kinds of assent; at other times they reserve the term 'assent' to the mental act, to something one does for a reason, to the positive acceptance of an impression because one thinks one has reason to take it to be true; and then they refer to the other kind of assent by talking of just following or approving or accepting an impression. At this point they rely on an etymological and conceptual connection between *pithanon* (probable) and *peithestai* (to follow; cf. *PH* I. 230). It is this connection which Cicero tries to preserve when he renders *pithanon* by *probabile* to make it correspond to the verb for 'approve' or 'accept' which he likes to use, namely *probare* (Cic., *Ac. pr.* 99; 139). So the probable quite literally is that which invites approval or assent in the sense in which the sceptic is free to give assent. But now there is a disagreement about this sense, and hence about the way the probable is to be understood, and hence a disagreement as to whether Carneades allows for mere opinion. The dogmatic sceptic seems to take the view that the only kind of assent which is illegitimate is assent of the kind where one takes something to be true, i.e. commits oneself to a belief as to what will come out as true on the true theory of things, as to what would turn out to be true if one really knew what things are like. And since it is one thing to take something to be true and quite another to take it to be probable, he thinks it is quite legitimate to give the kind of assent to an impression which would consist in taking it to be probable. And though we may not be able to ascertain what is to count as true, we can consider the matter with appropriate care and thus arrive at an impression which is probable and then assent to it as probable. But to take something to be probable is, on this interpretation of the probable, to take it to be either true or at least sufficiently like what is true. Thus somebody who does give assent in this sense does have beliefs as to how things are, i.e. mere opinions.

Clitomachus' interpretation of the two kinds of assent, on the other hand, is very much along the lines of the distinction I earlier on attributed to Sextus, as we can see from Cicero (*Ac. pr.* 104), who spells out Clitomachus' view in some detail. On this interpretation, a view one acts on and a view one is willing to communicate do not presuppose either that one takes them to be true or that at least one takes them to be likely to be true, because one has considered the matter carefully. It is rather that, as a matter of fact, we sometimes only act on an impression, if we have considered the matter further, but not because we now think it more likely to be true. It surely is relevant to keep in mind in this connection, though this is not pointed out in our ancient texts, that sometimes we, quite reasonably, act on views which we ourselves find less likely to be true than their alternatives.

Now to take something to be true or at least likely to be true is not the same thing as to take it to be true. And thus even the kind of dogmatic Academic sceptic we are considering can insist that he, too, distinguishes between having a view and taking a position, if to take a position is to take one's impression to be true, and that he does not take a position in saying that nothing can be known. This is what allows him to think that he is still a sceptic and not dogmatic. But since having a view for him might be a matter of actively adopting a view because he thinks that it is true or at least likely to be true, it is only a thin line which distinguishes him from the dogmatic who adopts a view because he takes it to be true. Both have views as to how things are, both may be equally firmly convinced that they are true (remember Catulus' vehement assent), but one believes that the kind of justification or knowledge which would establish the truth of a view is available, whereas the other believes that it is not available. But on the particular question we are concerned with, namely the possibility of knowledge, one cannot be more dogmatic than our dogmatic sceptic already is. For one cannot consistently claim that on the true account of things, i.e. if we really know how things are, it will turn out that nothing can be known. Thus, though there is a fine distinction between the dogmatism of the dogmatists and the dogmatism of late Academic sceptics, this fine distinction entirely collapses when it comes to the view that nothing can be known. To preserve whatever distinction there is, one might distinguish between adopting a view and taking a position and contrast both with having a view. But I will in the following use 'taking a position' in a wide sense to cover both, to emphasize the similarity which – in the eyes of the classical sceptic – dogmatic scepticism has with ordinary dogmatism.

If this should be correct we can see what gives rise to dogmatic scepticism. Having considered a matter carefully one finds oneself with a view which one finds persuasive. But this is now taken to mean that because one has considered the matter carefully the view has some likelihood of being true, though, of course, there is no guarantee or certainty that it is true. Thus Cicero can talk of the probable as the canon of truth and falsehood (*Ac. pr.* 32), and he can talk of the Academic method of arguing pro and con, of considering a matter from all sides, as a method he pursues in the hope of finding what is true or at least very much like the truth (*Ac. pr.* 7). Thus the probability of the impression that nothing can be known, too, is interpreted as the likelihood, though not certainty, that nothing can be known, a likelihood one may be so convinced of that one vehemently assents. By contrast the classical sceptic just finds himself with the view that nothing can be known and may finally acquiesce in it.

Thus a certain interpretation of the Carneadean criterion, and hence the probable, and along with it a certain interpretation of the distinction of two kinds of assent, is the first step on the road to dogmatic scepticism. It allows the sceptic to have opinions as to how things are, as long as he is aware that his opinions are not a matter of certain knowledge. And it allows him to take the position that nothing can be known, if only it, too, is qualified by the proviso that it itself is not a matter of certain knowledge. For given his experience with sceptical arguments it seems at least probable that nothing can be known.

Now the view that, in spite of all the sceptical arguments one has been producing and the effect they have had, one might still be left with an impression as to how things are and that, on the basis of this impression, one may take a position, has an effect on the way sceptical arguments in general and the arguments concerning the possibility of knowledge in particular are viewed. On the old view the sceptical method to argue against any claim, and – by implication – for any claim, since one would argue against the contradictory of a claim as much as against the claim itself, was seen as a purely negative, critical method. It might have been granted that the considerations pro and con might still leave one with an impression, that however much one argued for and against the existence of motion one might still be left with the impression that things move. But it was not assumed that this impression gained any epistemological status in virtue of the fact that one was still left with it after having gone through all the arguments pro and con. Now it comes to be assumed that the sceptical method of arguing pro and con also is a method of truth, a method which allows one to approximate the truth, though it does not guarantee the truth of the resulting impression (cf. Cic., *Ac. pr.* 7). And hence the dogmatic sceptic might well take the view that having carefully considered the Stoic arguments for the possibility of knowledge and the sceptical arguments against it, and finding, on balance, the sceptical arguments to be weightier, he is in a position to claim that nothing can be known.

Moreover, once the sceptic takes the liberty to take positions, his positions, given the eclecticism of the time, tend to become more or less identical with those of the Stoics, except on the question of knowledge itself. Thus he does come to believe in mental items like impressions and mental acts like assents. And he comes to believe in the premises of the arguments the classical sceptics had formulated to show that the Stoics themselves were committed to the view that nothing is, or can be, known. And now these arguments will have a pull on him, which is reflected by the quite unsceptical vehemence with which Catulus assents to the view that nothing can be known. Now sceptical arguments to the effect that nothing can be known can come to be interpreted as arguments which go some way, though not all the way, to establish the truth of the claim that nothing can be known. This, then, is the second major step on the road to dogmatic scepticism. The sceptic now, though qualifiedly, himself espouses the dogmatic framework of concepts and assumptions which seem to make knowledge impossible.

It should be noticed that at this point the classical and the dogmatic sceptic no longer just differ in the kind of assent they might feel free to give, but also in the impressions they give assent to. The difference between classical and dogmatic sceptics does not just consist in the different qualifiers attached to their views. For given his, albeit qualified, trust in the ability of philosophical arguments to get one somewhere, the dogmatic sceptic will have views induced by nothing but such arguments, whereas it would seem that in the case of the classical sceptic such arguments only threaten to undermine even those views which had been induced quite independently of philosophical argument.

Finally, the second step, the acceptance of the dogmatic framework, seems to involve a third step. The classical sceptic had started out being attracted by certain knowledge. He certainly had not committed himself to the view that knowledge is certain knowledge. But the dogmatic sceptic now seems to accept the Stoic view that knowledge has to be certain. In fact, I am inclined to think that Philo provoked such an outcry among dogmatic sceptics because he maintained that though the kind of certain knowledge the Stoics were after was impossible this did not mean that knowledge as such was impossible, that this had never been the position of the Academy, and that hence the supposed break of the New Academy with the Old was an illusion.

In this way, then, we arrive by Cicero's time at the dogmatic sceptical position that since all we ever have are impressions as to how things are and since there is nothing to ever guarantee the truth of an impression, nothing as to how things are can be known for certain.

The next question I raised was how it came about that scepticism came to be identified with dogmatic scepticism, so much so that even classical scepticism was identified as dogmatic scepticism and that to the present day we associate scepticism with the dogmatic sceptical position. To understand this we have to see that scepticism of any form in antiquity soon came to be a dead issue. Dogmatic scepticism did not have a future in later ancient thought. It rather provoked a revival of classical scepticism. For it seems that Pyrrhonism is not so much a revival of Pyrrho's philosophy, but a revival of classical Academic scepticism under the name of 'Pyrrhonism', to distinguish it from the dogmatism which Aenesidemus and Sextus Empiricus associated with the later sceptical Academy. But neither form of scepticism suited the temper of late antiquity; later antiquity found some form of Platonism or other, in Christian or pagan garb, more congenial, and thus scepticism, with some odd exceptions like Uranius in the sixth century (cf. Agathias, *Historiarum libri quinque* II.29, 7),[4] came to be a historical position to be vehemently rejected, rather than to be carefully understood. Thus it was largely a matter of ignorance that in late antiquity scepticism came to be identified with dogmatic scepticism. In the Latin West this was, no doubt, in good part due to Cicero's influence, who

---

[4] Ed. R. Keydell (Berlin, 1967).

himself was a dogmatic sceptic and who, moreover, would be the only substantial source concerning scepticism available to those who did not read Greek. And Cicero's influence was magnified by St Augustine's authority, who for his attack on scepticism in his *Contra Academicos* primarily, if not exclusively, relied on Cicero, but unlike Cicero, gave no indication of the possibility of a non-dogmatic scepticism and treated Carneades as taking the kind of position espoused by Cicero. And given Augustine's standing far into early modern times it is not surprising that the Western view of scepticism should have been determined by him throughout the Middle Ages, especially since for a long time his *Contra Academicos* would have been the only readily available source which discussed scepticism in any detail. And the impression gained from Augustine would be confirmed by the odd remark in the Latin Fathers, Arnobius (*Adv. Nationes* II.9–10)[5] or Lactantius (*Div. Inst.* III. 6),[6] for example. It may also be of relevance in this context that the question of knowledge became a live issue again in the late Middle Ages due in part to Ockham's doctrine of intuitive cognitions. Ockham took the view that cognitions are entities. He also took the view that God, by his absolute power, can destroy any one of two separate entities, while preserving the other. Thus God could preserve a cognition we have while destroying the object of the cognition. And yet Ockham wanted to maintain that there are cognitions, namely intuitive cognitions, which warrant an evident judgement. Naturally his view raised questions. And at least one author, Nicolaus of Autrecourt, in his letters to Bernhard of Arezzo, took the view that, given the doctrine of cognitions or impressions and the doctrine of divine omnipotence, he had to infer 'that every awareness which we have of the existence of objects outside our minds, can be false', and moreover that 'by natural cognitive means we cannot be certain when our awareness of the existence of external objects is true or false' (First Letter, p. 511).[7] Thus the question of the possibility of knowledge came to be a live issue again more or less exactly in those terms in which dogmatic scepticism had formulated it. In fact it may well have been this debate kindled by Ockham which created an interest in Cicero and Sextus Empiricus. An early fourteenth-century manuscript of a Latin translation of Sextus' *Outlines* and a fifteenth-century manuscript of the same translation in any case show a revival of interest in ancient scepticism which must have been generated by developments in medieval philosophy itself.

Thus the West came to think of scepticism as dogmatic scepticism and even thought of classical sceptics as dogmatic sceptics. And the influence of

---

5 Ed. A. Reifferscheid, CSEL IV (Vienna, 1875).
6 Ed. S. Brandt, CSEL XIX (Vienna, 1890).
7 In H. Shapiro, *Medieval Philosophy, Selected Reading* (New York, 1964).

the East during the Renaissance did not change this view. For the Greek East, too, already in antiquity had settled for a dogmatic interpretation of scepticism. This is true for secular authors as much as ecclesiastical authors. To take the latter first, nobody would be able to gather from Clement's discussion (*Stromateis* VIII. v.15.2ff)[8] that not all sceptics asserted it as true that nothing can be known. Similarly Eusebius (*Praeparatio Evangelica* XIV.17.10)[9] talks as if the sceptics took the position that nothing can be known. A particularly striking example of how even classical sceptics are interpreted as dogmatic sceptics is offered by Photius in his report on Aenesidemus' *Pyrrhonean Arguments* (*Bibl.* cod. 212. 169b). Aenesidemus, in reaction to the dogmatism of the later Academy, had tried to revive classical scepticism under the name of Pyrrhonism. But though Photius tells us in the course of his report that Aenesidemus thought that the Academics had become dogmatic in claiming that nothing can be known, he starts out by telling us that Aenesidemus wrote his book to establish the thesis that nothing is known for certain. As for secular Greek writers one may compare the *Anonymous Prolegomena* (p. 21, 1ff)[10] and Olympiodorus' *Prolegomena* (3.32ff).

Thus it was part of the medieval heritage that scepticism should be thought of as dogmatic scepticism and that even classical sceptics should be considered as dogmatic sceptics. But we have to ask why in early modern times, when most of the evidence concerning classical scepticism was available again, and when Cicero and Sextus Empiricus were reread with a new frame of mind, scepticism continued to be regarded as a dogmatical position, either as the extreme scepticism of the Pyrrhoneans or as the mitigated scepticism of the Academics.

I am not in a position to answer this question, but I do have some suggestions as to how it might be answered. There is, first, mere inertia; this notion of scepticism, after all, was the notion inherited from the Middle Ages. Secondly, the early modern debate concerning the possibility of knowledge must have been a continuation of the medieval debate we referred to earlier. It surely is not by accident that the sceptical arguments against causality found, e.g., in Hume are very much like the arguments to be found in Nicolaus of Autrecourt or in Ghazali and Averroes' refutation of Ghazali. But at issue in this debate was a version of dogmatic scepticism. Thirdly, early modern philosophy, in part in following the tradition of late medieval epistemology, in part in reaction to Aristotelianism and Scholasticism, came largely to adopt the framework of dogmatic Hellenistic epistemology and thereby invited dogmatic scepticism. The very term

[8] Ed. O. Stählin, GCS III (Leipzig, 1909).
[9] Ed. K. Mras, GCS VIII. 1 (Berlin, 1954).
[10] Ed. L. G. Westerink (Amsterdam, 1962).

'impressions', for example, may be due to Cicero's influence (*Ac. pr.* 58). Fourthly, dogmatic scepticism satisfied various ideological needs of the time. It could be used to reject Aristotelian science, a curious preoccupation of that period. It could be used to point out the need for faith and revelation. Fifthly, the attitude towards historical philosophical texts was very different from ours. Philosophers of the past were studied as paradigmatic philosophers, as authorities, as exponents of a philosophical position worth considering, i.e. they were approached with a preconception of what one expected from them which was determined by one's own needs. Obviously this attitude is not conducive to an understanding of the history of philosophy. One way in which this may be relevant for our question is this: at least on the face of it, classical sceptics seem to differ from dogmatic sceptics primarily in that the latter allowed the sceptic to have beliefs as to how things are, whereas the former seem to require a life without beliefs. But this seemed so obviously to be such an untenable position that, until very recently, not even historians of philosophy gave it serious consideration. As a result one focussed on the part of classical scepticism which was concerned with the possibility of knowledge, as if that part could be understood in isolation from the classical sceptic's attitude towards belief. But as we have seen the difference between classical and dogmatic scepticism lies exactly in a different attitude towards belief or assent. Thus we only can do justice to the classical sceptic's attitude towards knowledge if we take his remarks concerning belief seriously. Sixthly, when the texts were read again, it must have seemed that there were basically two forms of scepticism in antiquity, Pyrrhonean scepticism, going back to Pyrrho, and Academic scepticism going back to Arcesilaus. Pyrrhonean scepticism seemed hopeless as a philosophical position because one misunderstood the Pyrrhonean attitude towards beliefs and thought that a Pyrrhonean was supposed to live without beliefs. Hence the mitigated scepticism of the late Academy seemed to be the only sceptical position of promise. But remarks in Sextus suggested that the dogmatic scepticism of the late Academy was the position of the Academy in general. For Sextus in part relied on Antiochus for his view of the Academic position, and Antiochus saw Carneades, perhaps Arcesilaus and Carneades, as dogmatic sceptics. Moreover Sextus himself had a vested interest in seeing the Academy in general as dogmatic. After all, the supposed dogmatism of the Academy is the main rationale for Pyrrhonism. Thus, if one concentrates on Academic scepticism as the viable sceptical position, and under the influence of Augustine and Sextus interprets Academic scepticism quite generally as dogmatic, one naturally arrives at a dogmatic conception of scepticism. But a more scholarly reading of Sextus or Cicero would have shown that this had not been the position of the Academy all along.

To turn finally to our last question, it seems to me that early modern philosophy might have profited from a better historical understanding of ancient scepticism and the realization that dogmatic scepticism is only a degenerate form of scepticism. For it was because of this distorted notion of scepticism that the question at issue was understood as the question how we ever could be justified, on the basis of the impressions or ideas which are immediately given to us, to have any views as to how things are, let alone to be certain as to how things are. Descartes answered this question very much along the lines the Stoics had answered it, but Hume, in spite of an obvious tendency to go in this direction, was prevented from answering it in the way in which classical scepticism had answered it, since he to a good extent, too, accepted the dogmatic framework in which the question was posed by ancient dogmatic scepticism. But once we see that this framework in which the question is posed is the framework of dogmatic Hellenistic epistemology and only thus comes to be the framework of ancient dogmatic scepticism, it is easy to realize that the classical sceptic will have no part of it. For all he knows it might be a mistake to distinguish quite generally and globally between how things appear and how they really are. There are some cases where it seems to be useful to make such a distinction, e.g. in the case of illusions, or in the case of deception. But for these cases we have ways to ascertain what really is the case which allow us in the first place to draw, for these cases, a reasonably clear distinction between how things appear and how they really are. But how are we supposed to know what is asked for when we are asked what things are really like in cases where we have not yet already found that out or that things might be quite different from what they appear to be like? In short, I see no reason why a classical sceptic should accept the global contrast between appearance and reality. I also see no reason why a classical sceptic would believe in such mental entities as impressions or ideas. It is not that he is not willing to accept that people have impressions in the sense that one may have the impression that all this is not very clear, or that people have a mind. He explicitly says that he accepts this. But it is one thing to accept this and quite another to believe in mental entities like impressions. There is no reason to think that he believes in mental acts like assents. It is true that he talks as if he accepted impressions and assents. But this is because his opponents believe in these things. And when, for a change, he does use this language to talk about his own attitude, he is careful not to commit himself to the dogmatic assumptions associated with this language. Thus the assent the sceptic is free to give becomes a matter, for example, of his being ready to say 'yes' or 'no' if asked (Cic., *Ac. pr.* II.104). Moreover he has no reason to think that impressions are immediately given and unquestionable. Anybody who has written a paper knows how difficult it is to be clear about one's impressions of the subject which one tries to articulate. Similarly it is by no means easy to tell in detail what the impressions one is acting on actually are like. Again, it is true that the sceptic talks as if there were no question as to what our impressions are when he addresses his opponents. Sextus explicitly says that how something appears to one is not an issue. But by good luck we know from two passages in Galen that a radical Pyrrhonean will also challenge reports of impressions if the question should arise (*De diff puls.* VIII.708ff; cf. XIV.628).[11] Moreover, there is no reason why the sceptic should accept what we do not accept in ordinary life, namely that there is a single answer to the question 'What is to count as knowledge?' What we expect from somebody who knows varies enormously from context to context. What counts as knowledge in an ordinary context may not count as such in the context of a scholarly or scientific discussion where we have higher demands. It also varies with the importance we attach to a matter.

So what in good part has happened is that, because one has failed to understand the classical sceptic's attitude towards belief, one also has failed to understand the peculiar nature and status of the arguments of classical scepticism, one has read and keeps reading them as if they represented the sceptical view of the problem of the possibility of knowledge. In fact, their primary function is to present the dogmatic with the problem he, the dogmatic, is faced with given the dogmatic framework of notions and assumptions within which the dogmatic moves. And we should expect a proper sceptic not only to question the assumptions arrived at within this framework, but the very framework itself. This is what, from the point of view of classical scepticism, the later sceptical tradition failed to do. A better knowledge of the history of philosophy would have made this failure apparent.[12]

---

[11] *Galeni Opera*, ed. C. G. Kühn (Leipzig, 1821–33).

[12] In writing this paper I have been greatly helped by discussions with Myles Burnyeat, John Cooper, Richard Jeffrey, Barry Stroud, and many others, but in particular Charlotte Stough, who took the care to write up her extensive comments on it.

12

The concept of 'trust'
in the politics of John Locke

JOHN DUNN

Because in politics the most fundamental question is always that of what particular human beings have good reason to *do*, and because what they do have good reason to do depends directly and profoundly on how far they can and should trust and rely upon one another, I take the central issue in political philosophy (properly so called) to be that of how to conceive the rationality of trust in relation to the causal field of politics.

In this essay I shall be talking about the thinking of Locke, firstly because I consider that he made a more systematic and determined effort to think about this question than any other and more recent political philosopher, and secondly (and, of course, connectedly) because the attempt to think comprehensively about this conception has essentially disappeared from modern political philosophy, both in its Marxist and in its liberal or conservative variants. (There are, to be sure, important analytical idioms in modern thought – such as game theory – and key moments in the construction of particular political theories – such as Rawls' original position – in which the issue is treated with great assurance.) The explanation of this disappearance is a complicated and somewhat obscure matter, and not one suitable for treatment in this context. But that it is so would be difficult to deny.

I discuss Locke, therefore, not because I wish to argue that we should espouse all – or any – of Locke's own detailed conceptions, but because we do, in my view, have good reason to treat his conception of political philosophy as exemplary – as a model which there is still every ground for our trying to emulate.

To most modern philosophers, the question 'What is the bond of human society? What in the last instance holds it together?' will seem a pretty odd one. There is, to be sure, one entire tradition in modern social theory which is still more or less united in the last instance in the view that what does hold human society together is the indispensability of cooperating in the production of material goods. But this is certainly not intended as a psychological allegation about human dispositions or attitudes. And it remains one of the most pressing difficulties of Marxist theory that its conviction of what *does* secure the reproduction of human social arrangements is not accompanied by any very clear or cogent explanation of just how and why human agents can be confidently expected to be either disposed to, or able to, execute the task which the theory assigns to them (cf. Cohen 1978 and 1982 with Elster 1982). When John Locke in his *Essays on the Law of Nature* described *fides* as the *vinculum societatis* (the bond of society; Locke 1954:212) there is no reason to believe that he drew a clear distinction between what he took to be the central virtues or ethical requirements of a good social life and what he took to be the causal explanation of the existence of such a life. At the time, indeed, he had no particular reason to think especially hard about the latter question. Modern thinkers, by contrast, are inclined to separate out these two questions with some completeness, often electing to confine themselves solely to considering either the internal relations of a set of ethical concepts or the political sociology of the conditions for reproducing a particular regime or mode of production. Those who are interested predominantly in explaining the reproduction of particular social and political patterns would not, on the whole, be inclined to look for answers at the psychological level. (A partial exception would be Barrington Moore's explanation of the historical record of human passivity in the face of injustice (Moore 1978, and cf. Dunn 1982) in terms of imaginative habituation, eked out by rational pessimism.) Even if they were prepared to essay a psychological account of the cement of human society, most modern social thinkers would probably offer a fairly variegated list of contributory factors: greed, fear, lust, conviviality, habit, hope, despair, indolence, an extremely high degree of selective inattention – and so on.

The most famous single criticism of Locke's political philosophy (and in some measure of the entire contractarian tradition) is David Hume's attack in the *Treatise of Human Nature* III.II (esp. sec. 8; Hume 1911:II, 242–3) and more particularly in his essay 'Of the original contract' (Hume 1903:466–7) on the absurdity of any attempt to resolve the obligation of allegiance into the obligation of fidelity, to explain political obligation by invoking the duty to keep promises (see Thompson 1977; Dunn 1983b). There is, in my view, abundant doubt as to how far Locke himself did intend to *explain* political obligation through the duty to keep promises and, more particularly, as to how far it is true to say that he regarded personal consent as a precondition for valid political obligation (Dunn 1980: ch. 3). But what is true is that his moral and political thinking as a whole (and in my view the central burden of his philosophical thinking in its entirety) was directed towards an understanding of the rationality and moral propriety of human trust. What I should like to try to do in this essay is to show how and why this preoccupation dominated his thinking, to show that it was (and is) a coherent preoccupation, and to suggest that modern political philosophy has not gained but lost from its fastidious and scrupulous avoidance of such gross and promiscuously constituted issues. I take it that, to the extent that my purpose is successfully realized, what could reasonably be drawn from the line of argument is, in the first place a fairly robust understanding of the integrity and force of a past piece of philosophical thinking of very high quality and secondly, and much more tentatively, a not necessarily altogether flattering perspective on the tacit framing of much political philosophy in our own day.

The rationality of trust within particular structures of social and political relations is a pressing issue in political understanding in any society of the modern world. It features prominently (and pertinently enough) in the characteristic analyses of the politics of communist states constructed by western scholars, just as it does in those of capitalist states developed by Marxist scholars. It is a salient preoccupation of such ambitious essays on the theoretical assessment of modern society and its travails as that of Jürgen Habermas. But, as far as I know, only one major social theorist has recently chosen to consider it directly. The German functionalist sociologist Niklas Luhmann published ten years ago a lengthy synthetic essay on the problem of trust in modern society. Some of the main lines of thought set out in this work offer an instructive contrast to Locke's approach. Like Locke, Luhmann sees trust as central to sustaining a society in operation. Like Locke again, he sees trust as making possible a massive extension of men's capacity to cooperate, not by means of cognitively rational calculation but through the provision of a measure of buffering between indispensable hopes and expectations which are necessarily partially disappointed. Trust, fundamentally, is a technique for coping with the freedom of other human beings (Luhmann 1979:30), for extending the availability of time and thus rendering possible the choice of delayed gratification (p. 87), for increasing men's tolerance of uncertainty (p. 15), for the contrafactual stabilization of expectations (p. xiv). Without trust, confidence in their own expectations of others, men or women could scarcely nerve themselves to get up in the morning (p. 4). The working of all complex political or economic institutions, government bureaucracies or monetary systems (pp. 50, 69), depends directly upon trust and, at least in part, on trust generated in the more intimate and cognitively accessible contexts of each human being's everyday life (p. 16).

Luhmann's book does not present a particularly bold and clear line of thought. But it does extend this range of judgements, any or all of which Locke might well have shared, in one distinctive direction, a direction dictated by Luhmann's emphatic commitment to a functional conception of society. Modern societies, Luhmann believes, depend less on normative experience and more on purely cognitive assumptions than did their historical predecessors (p. xiv). 'The contrafactual stabilization of experience is the function of normative experience' (p. xiv). This function is less central to modern societies because of the degree to which these require for their working not emotional trust in known and familiar persons but system-trust predicated on the ways in which institutions, practices and the incumbents of distinct roles present themselves to us (p. 22). Individual trust is seldom reflexive in its base, founded upon trust in the viability of trust itself (p. 69); but confidence in economic institutions such as a particular currency is characteristically grounded in this way. Because of this sharp change in the balance between emotional and presentational, between direct and systemic, trust in the operations of earlier societies and in those of today, issues of the rationality of trust today depend for their assessment predominantly on the causal analysis of society, and thus cannot be handled by an ethical theory of the appropriate criteria for the allocation of individual trust (p. 87). This view of the part played by the cognitive apprehension of, and the instrumentally rational response to, social causality in cementing social cooperation is sociologically more plausible in relation to the Federal Republic of Germany of the late 1960s than, for example, to the Great Britain of the early 1980s. But however questionable its sociological judgements, it does indicate one strong contrast between modern social thought and the perspective of Locke: the very limited extent to which the latter's conceptions of rational and moral conduct for individuals or groups in particular contexts depended upon explicit judgements of the causal properties of societies or of particular social institutions. One of the judgements which I shall attempt to press at the end of this essay is that, despite the indispensability of causal analysis of society (Dunn 1980: ch. 10; 1983a), there is considerably more than we normally recognize today to be said for the pre-modern, Lockean, perspective on this question.

Its most important merit is the directness with which it addresses the question of just what particular human beings (ourselves included) have good reason to *do*. A great deal of modern political philosophy, whether utilitarian or Kantian in its moral inspiration (Williams 1981), gives very arbitrary or uncertain accounts of how in a particular historical situation any particular agent has good reason to act. There are, of course, many other types of question which require an answer in political philosophy. But because of the historically given character of political conflict and political power, and the consequent need for the conclusions of political philosophy to intrude themselves into existing fields of force and significance (Dunn 1980: chs. 8, 10), no adequate political philosophy can simply take the form of a theory of what is intrinsically desirable. (It cannot, in the last instance, because the question 'Desirable for whom?' is the prototypically political question.) At the very least any such theory must also offer an account of what sort of claims in the face of what sorts of costs the intrinsically desirable can rationally levy upon individual historical agents or groups of such agents. If these claims constitute at all a heavy burden, it must add at least a sketch of the reasons why such agents would themselves be epistemically well-advised to regard the claims as valid.

Two powerful imaginative tendencies have made it particularly hard to generate such reasons today. One, plainly, is the rather steady pressure of moral scepticism, motivated essentially by the contrast between the presumed epistemic solidity of human understanding of non-human nature and the cognitively relatively whimsical status of judgements of human value. The second is the increasingly alienated vision of the nature of human societies and polities which has developed over the last two and a half centuries. If the entire field of political and social relations surrounding an individual agent is taken as given, and his or her potential contribution to politics is then assessed in purely instrumental terms, virtually all political action will appear as necessarily futile; and the balance between comparatively certain cost and highly uncertain gain will become prohibitively discouraging to political agency (Dunn 1980: ch. 10).

This essay is not the place to try to take the measure of either of these imaginative pressures. But I mention them briefly at this point because they do press so hard on all of us and because, in the realm of politics at least, their conjunction is so obviously culturally malign. John Locke wrestled for forty years with the problems presented by the first: the epistemic status of moral judgements. But, for reasons which I shall try to make clear, he was never compelled to face the menace of the second. The failure of his attempts to rebut moral scepticism[1] mean that we can hardly today employ his philosophy to order, discipline and sustain our own fondest political intuitions – a more important judgement in the United States than in Britain. But the boldness with which he conceived human societies as historical creations for which their members can and should always try to assume an active responsibility can perhaps still be of some real aid. Certainly it seems to me to hold a better and wiser balance between agent responsibility and external social and political causality than any political philosopher or political scientist of the last half century has managed to achieve.

I turn now to the development of Locke's thinking about the place of trust in human life, and consider firstly a justly famous letter, written in his

---

[1] For an illuminating study of Locke's moral thinking see Colman 1983.

late twenties to an unnamed friend, probably Thomas Westrowe (Locke 1976: I, 122). It is the most striking expression of moral scepticism that Locke ever penned. Passion and fancy, not reason, rule human life. Human beings select their beliefs to suit their desires and rational argument has little, if any, power to alter them. 'Men live upon trust and their knowledg is noething but opinion moulded up between custome and Interest, the two great Luminarys of the world, the only lights they walke by.' The diagnosis of this predicament is lengthier, more eloquent and considerably more definite than the remedies which are suggested to meet it. Custom and interest are uncertain and fickle guides and the conclusions which they suggest are surprisingly conventional:

Let the examples of the bravest men direct our opinions and actions; if custome must guide us let us tread in those steps that lead to virtue and honour. Let us make it our Interest to honour our maker, and be usefull to our fellows, and content with our selves. This, if it will not secure us from error, will keepe us from loseing our selves, if we walk not directly straite we shall not be alltogeather in a maze.

Apart from the somewhat erratic pragmatism of the proposed attitude towards the deity, the stalwart conventionality of the recommended response stands in marked contrast with the existential urgency of the predicament identified. As agents, human beings make their own selves; but they do so in circumstances and out of materials emphatically not of their own choosing. Because they have such good reason to distrust the materials with which they must work and the beliefs on the basis of which they must act, and because so much of their lives necessarily depends upon custom and habitual expectation, only the clearest conceptions of virtue, held imaginatively at some distance from the immediate importunities of their own lives, can exercise a benign directive pressure upon these. To continue to act at all, men must be able to trust, to believe with confidence. But they can hope to form beliefs which epistemically deserve their trust only by a subtle and unrelenting suspicion of their own motives and a steady contemplation of ethical models which are wholly independent of their own immediate desires.

In Locke's first extended writings on politics, the *Two Tracts* of the early 1660s dealing with the extent of a magistrate's legitimate authority over indifferent things (actions neither directly commanded nor directly forbidden by God's law), the issue of trust does not explicitly arise. The magistrate's authority derives immediately from the will of God: 'God wished there to be order, society and government among men. And this we call the commonwealth. In every commonwealth there must be some supreme power without which it cannot truly be called a commonwealth; and that supreme power is exactly the same in all governments, namely, legislative' (Locke 1967:231–2). It is not clear that any such power over human life could in principle derive its authority simply from the consent of men (pp. 78, 231). Not only is political power indispensable for human security. It is also compelled by this very indispensability to determine its own scope in practice, since the partiality of individual human judgement and the geographical and cultural variety of men's evaluations precludes their being left to determine its scope in the light of their own individual beliefs. 'Our deformity is others' beauty, our rudeness others' civility, and there is nothing so uncouth and unhandsome to us which doth not somewhere or other find applause and approbation' (p. 146).

None of these considerations simply disappeared from Locke's later thinking; but the practical conclusions which he drew from them notoriously altered sharply. They did so in one sense, as is well known, as a consequence of his involvement in the busy political intrigues of the Shaftesbury entourage. But they did so, perhaps more profoundly, because of the theoretical instability of the position which Locke adopted in his English *Tract*. In this, the magistrate, in the exercise of the authority 'settled on him by God and the people' (p. 150), is uniquely entitled to 'follow the dictates of his own understanding', while all other men, in the matter of indifferent things, must submit their conduct in its entirety to this authority, whether or not they personally believe it to be religiously permissible to do so. In this respect Locke's mature philosophical position, centring on the precept of the *Essay* that 'Men must think and know for themselves' (Locke 1975:19 (Contents Summary, I. IV. 23)), reverts to the perspective set out in his youthful letter to Thomas Westrowe and constitutes a systematic attempt to confront the problems which this raises.

When Locke attempted, not long after writing the *Two Tracts*, to develop a coherent account of the status and binding force of the law of nature, it was the twin threats of the partiality of individual judgement and the cultural heterogeneity of evaluative standards which he took as his major challenges. Each plainly militated against the view that natural law was in any helpful sense innate or that its standing could be established firmly in the general consent of mankind. The former had particularly lethal implications for any attempt to ground men's knowledge of the law of nature upon tradition:

since traditions vary so much the world over and men's opinions are so obviously opposed to one another and mutually destructive, and that, not only among different nations but in one and the same state – for each single opinion which we learn from others becomes a tradition – and finally since everybody contends so fiercely for his own opinion and demands that he be believed, it would plainly be impossible – supposing tradition alone lays down the ground of our duty – to find

out what tradition is, or to pick out truth from among such a variety. (Locke
1954:128–9)

Cultural heterogeneity militates especially severely against any attempt to
ground the law of nature in the general consent of mankind:

there is almost no vice, no infringement of natural law, no moral wrong, which
anyone who consults the history of the world and observes the affairs of men will
not readily perceive to have been not only privately committed somewhere on
earth, but also approved by public authority and custom. Nor has there been
anything so shameful in its nature that it has not been either sanctified somewhere
by religion, or put in the place of virtue and abundantly rewarded with praise.
(1954:166–7)

Individual partiality and cultural heterogeneity do not merely pose practical obstacles to the observance of the law of nature. They also constitute
epistemic obstacles to its reliable identification in the first place.

In practice, in large measure, human beings do learn how to act, what
is virtuous, what is obligatory, what is prohibited or disapproved, from
the responses of other human beings and especially from their speech: *ab
aliis fando* (p. 128). Tradition, therefore, offers a perfectly appropriate
and plausible causal explanation of most of human sentiment and belief
(pp. 126–9). But insofar as this explanation is exhaustive and valid, what it
implies is that the authority behind human moral sentiments and beliefs is
merely the dictates of *men* and not those of reason (p. 128). If the law of
nature were to be learnt from tradition, it would be an example of faith
rather than knowledge, since it would depend upon the authority of a
speaker rather than on the evidence of things themselves (p. 130, and see p.
176). Faith (*fides*) stands in epistemic contrast to knowledge (*cognitio*). But
it also stands in practical contrast to the vice of untrustworthiness. The
virtue of keeping one's promises is the virtue of *fides* (p. 126). If the law of
nature were founded solely in individual worldly advantage and utility, the
duties of human life would be at odds with one another. What reason could
there be, on this presumption, for fulfilling a promise when to do so would
be to one's own personal disadvantage (pp. 212–14)? On the assumption
that individual worldly advantage is the basis of the law of nature, no
coherent account of the content and binding force of human duties can be
constructed. Any real conception of a society is subverted, and with it,
fides (trustworthiness), the bond (*vinculum*) of society (p. 212).

That Locke happens in the *Essays on the Law of Nature* to employ the
same term to mark the epistemic contrast between faith (or belief) and
knowledge and between interpersonal trustworthiness and undependability, in itself tells us only a fact about his Latin vocabulary. But it also
serves handily to draw our attention to three very profound assumptions

behind his thinking: firstly, that any acceptable human society depends upon the recognition of moral duties which cannot be validly derived from the rational assessment of individual worldly advantage; secondly, that the most important and encompassing of these duties is the duty to act towards fellow human beings in a way which deserves their trust; and thirdly, that the most important theoretical question about human duties is the question of how far and in what sense we can *know* the content of these duties, and how far and under what conditions we must rest our assessment of them in the last instance simply on faith. In his letter of 1659 Locke had underlined the compulsiveness and the radical undependability of human moral judgement; but he had also emphasized the extent to which human beings retain the capacity to take responsibility for, to modify and even to dispose of their own beliefs. The *Essays on the Law of Nature* explore the sceptical threat posed by this judgement, without doing much to clarify or to reinforce the optimistic injunction which accompanies it. But they also extend its implications from the existential problems of the individual into the life of civil society at large. Trustworthiness, the capacity to commit oneself to fulfilling the legitimate expectations of others, is both the constitutive virtue of, and the key causal precondition for the existence of, any society. It is what makes human society possible. For Locke (unlike for David Hume) there is a real and potentially systematic antithesis between individual terrestrial interest and individual moral duty; and there is no reason at all to trust in the moral validity of any individual's or even any society's moral socialization. The duty to be trustworthy simply *is* more fundamental than the moral conventions or positive laws of any society, because none of the latter is necessarily morally valid and because, without the former, human society would not be possible at all. It is an individual duty, not a naturally given attribute of human nature – and without its display human society simply cannot exist.

The most dramatic proclamation of this judgement in Locke's works comes in the famous explanation in the *Letter on Toleration* of why it is that, although anyone whose religious beliefs and sentiments do not directly imply the political subversion of a legitimate political authority has a *right* to the toleration of the civil powers, no atheist can possess any such right. His reasons for taking this view go back to a brief section added to the final draft of his 1667 *Essay on Toleration*, in which he had insisted that

the belief of a Deity is not to be reckoned amongst purely speculative opinions, for it [represents] the foundation of all morality, and that which influences the whole life and actions of men, without which a man is to be counted no other than one of the most dangerous sorts of wild beasts, and so incapable of all society.[2]

---

[2] *Bodleian Ms Locke* c 28, ff. 21–32, cited in Locke 1968a:15–16.

One reason given in the *Letter of Toleration* for denying a right of toleration to atheists applies only to those perverse enough to claim such a right in the name of religion. Since Locke's defence of the right to toleration defends this *as* a religious right, he is quite consistent in denying it on these grounds to an atheist. But the first and more striking reason which he gives echoes the judgement of 1667. No one who denies that there is a God is entitled to toleration (1968a:134). For 'neither faith (*fides*), nor agreement, nor oaths, the bonds (*vincula*) of human society can be stable and sacred for an atheist: so that, if God is once taken away, even simply in opinion, all these collapse with him'. (Or, as William Popple's 1689 translation puts it, 'the taking away of God, even only in thought, dissolves all' (p. 134)). Locke's judgement here notoriously clashes directly with that of his Protestant contemporary Pierre Bayle, who denied that there was any reason at all why a society of atheists should not prove perfectly viable in practice (Bayle 1911–12: I, 301–20, 336–50; II, 5–21, 102–51). From the perspective of modern scholars, Bayle's judgement appears self-evidently correct, while Locke's is at best an embarrassingly superstitious anomaly in one of the great advocates of the liberal value of freedom of thought and expression.

In Locke's own thinking, however, there was nothing vaguely anomalous about the judgement. Indeed it lay at the very foundation of his theory of the content and binding force of moral duty. The reason why atheists posed such a threat was not a causal hypothesis about the degree to which on any given occasion they would in practice prove emotionally susceptible to the authority of the law of opinion or reputation (the moral traditions of the community to which they belonged) (*Essay* II. xxviii, 10–12 (Locke 1975:353–7)). Rather, it was a logical presumption about the necessary absence for them of any good reason, in the last instance, for curbing their own selfish and socially destructive desires. It was the rational implications of atheism for human practice, not its external and contingent causal pressure upon human moral dispositions, which expelled it from the protected arena of free intellectual exploration. Almost any set of religious, or moral, or speculative opinions *might* in Locke's view contingently affect men's moral demeanour for the worse. But this consideration alone could not possibly justify the repression of any particular set. What was unique about atheism was that if its premise was once accepted, then it rationally *should* affect men's moral demeanour as a whole dramatically for the worse.

If trustworthiness, fidelity, the keeping of agreements and promises, and respect for oaths were in this way the bonds of human society, what in Locke's eyes *makes* society possible at all, it is obviously important to understand how he conceived the extent of human trustworthiness in practice and what he considered to determine its incidence. It is essential here to separate firmly what Locke believed to be the necessary obligations of all men under the divine law of nature from what he judged to be the reasons for action which any particular human being contingently happens to possess on a particular occasion. He had no doubt that under the divine law of nature all human agents had a clear obligation to keep their promises. Faith and the keeping of faith belong to men as men and not as members of society (*Two Treatises* II.14. 17–19). Promises and oaths 'tye the infinite Deity' himself (II.6.6). 'The Obligations of that Eternal Law . . . are so great, and so strong, in the case of *Promises*, that Omnipotency it self can be tyed by them. *Grants, Promises* and *Oaths* are Bonds that *hold the Almighty*' (II.195. 4–7). This can be so, in Locke's view, because it is legitimate to say that 'God himself cannot choose what is not good; the Freedom of the Almighty hinders not his being determined by what is best' (*Essay* II. xxi. 49 (1975:265)). Divine freedom, in this respect, is analogous to human freedom. It is not a curb upon, or diminution of, our freedom but a perfection of this that we are determined 'to desire, will, and act according to the last result of a fair *Examination*' (II. xxi. 47 (1975: 264)). In addition to the full divine law of nature with its panoply of infinitely punitive and rewarding sanctions in another life, Locke also attempts in the undated manuscript 'Morality' to develop an account of the obligatory force of promises which is purely terrestrial and naturalistic in structure.[3] Men have not made themselves nor any other man; and they find themselves at birth in a world which they have not fashioned. Hence they have, on the basis of their own attributes, no original and exclusive right to anything in the world. In this condition, they will inevitably be subject to want, rapine and force and will fail to attain the happiness which only plenty and security can make possible. In order to avoid this predicament, they have no choice but to determine each other's rights by compact. Once they have done so, they have established the duty of justice as the first and general rule of their happiness, since the making of compacts would be incoherent and point-less without the commitment to observe them: 'These compacts are to be kept or broken. If to be broken their making signifies noe thing if to be kept then Justice is established.' This naturalistic would-be demonstration is clearly at odds with the theory of property right set out in the *Second Treatise* – a point of some interest, since there is good reason to suppose it to have been written well after that work was completed. But in the present context what is more important is that the structure which it suggests for the obligation to keep promises is so weakly related to Locke's theory of the reasons for individual action. The claim that promise-breaking is irrational because it is literally self-contradictory was defended

[3] *Bodleian Ms Locke* c 28, ff.139–40. For an excellent discussion see Colman 1983:194–9.

notoriously some three decades later by William Wollaston in his *Religion of Nature Delineated* (1738:8–20) (and later still mocked unmercifully by David Hume (1911: II, 170–1n)). But the moral objection to breaking a promise is that it deceives others, not that it involves the assertion and denial of an identical proposition; and, of course, to deceive others it is necessary for a promise to cause them to attribute a particular meaning to it and to shape their expectations accordingly. To make a promise would signify nothing at all unless it signified a commitment in due course to keep it in practice. But to choose to keep a promise in due course is still to decide to act in a particular manner; and, given Locke's hedonic theory of the grounds or determinants of an agent's choice, it is entirely possible for any agent in practice to find that they possess more pressing motives or more immediately cogent reasons for breaking a past promise than they do for choosing to keep it (see Colman 1983). The signification which a promise necessarily possesses is the signification which enables it to play an important role in the deception of others. It is not a signification which necessarily in practice, on this account, gives the maker of the promise a *sufficient* reason or a *determining* motive to observe it.

How far then, in Locke's view, can men be trusted? This question has been a focus of considerable, and rather poorly articulated, controversy in the interpretation of his political theory. Commentators such as Leo Strauss (1953:202–51) and Richard Cox (1960) have seen the core of Locke's politics as the conviction that humans are as radically untrustworthy as Hobbes depicted them as being, and have insisted accordingly that Locke's conception of the state of nature is distinguishable from that of Hobbes only by the degree of evasion with which Locke elects initially to describe it. The state of nature is a state not of peace, but of war. But this interpretation simply mistakes an account of the structure of rights between men (in which the state of nature and the state of war are in fact by definition incompatible with one another (*Two Treatises* II. 19)) for a description of the practical character of social relations in the absence of legitimate governmental authority. The latter, Locke fully recognizes, are likely to be both hazardous and disagreeable, particularly after the attainment of any great measure of economic advance and consequent social and economic inequality. To the question 'How far can men be trusted?', Locke has no simpler and more readily applicable general answer to offer than does Niklas Luhmann. It depends on many different sorts of considerations: on the contingencies of individual disposition, of the prevailing culture of a particular community and of the practical structures of material interests which are at issue. If Locke had been obliged to construct a theory solely on the basis of judgements of practical prudence, he would have been hard put to it to proffer any firmer and more concrete direction[4] on the pragmatics of allocating individual trust than Luhmann (or indeed we ourselves) can readily muster.

But if human trustworthiness, like any other instance of weakly structured probability, can in practice only be assessed with a large margin of error, Locke does of course possess a conception of the nature of its determinants. It is not perhaps an entirely coherent conception, particularly in its understanding of the fundamental character of human agency, where he has been plausibly accused of vacillating between a robustly hedonist mechanical theory of motivation and a distinctly less determinate theory of reasons for action expressed in a misleadingly hedonic language (Jenkins 1983: ch. 7 (esp. 150–2); Colman 1983: ch. 8 (esp. 207)). (On this point, there seems little doubt that the most lasting impulse of his thought, reflected in the major amendments to his account of free agency, and in the treatment of personal identity, added in later editions of the *Essay*, was to secure at virtually any cost men's responsibility for their own actions (II. xxvii (esp. 26; 1975: 346–7); II. xxi. 44, 47–53, 56 etc.).) But whether expressed in the terminology of pleasure, desire or uneasiness, or in that of reason, the main determinants of human trustworthiness can be identified with some confidence.

There are four positive components. The first of these is the rational understanding, or the revelation, of God's requirements for his creatures, weakly enforced by prudential sanctions within this life but backed by overwhelming sanctions in the next (*Essay*, II. xxi. 70 (and see also 44, 65)). The moral content of this determinant is *ex hypothesi* perfect – the divine law of nature – but its immediate motivational incidence on particular human beings is regrettably fitful. The second component is the emotional impact of moral socialization within a particular family and community,[5] the law of reputation, enforced by men's desire for each other's approval and their aversion to each other's blame. (As an epistemic criterion for the true law of nature, the moral traditions of particular communities are irretrievably unreliable. But in practice their content does overlap to a considerable degree with the divine law of nature (Colman 1983: 171), and their motivational impact is reassuringly vigorous. Such trustworthiness as most human beings contrive to display in their interpersonal relations is in fact the product, in this manner, of their moral socialization.)[6] The third

---

[4] Locke, *Essay* IV. xiv (esp. 2.16–19): 'So in the greatest part of our Concernment, he has afforded us only the twilight, as I may so say, of *Probability*, suitable, I presume, to that state of Mediocrity and Probationership, he has been pleased to place us in here; . . .').

[5] Locke, *Essay* II. xxviii. 10–12 (1975: 353–7, esp. p. 357); *Some Thoughts Concerning Education* in Locke 1968b.

[6] Locke, of course, does not himself employ the term 'socialization'. But he gives an exceedingly penetrating account in the *Essay* and in *Some Thoughts Concerning Education* of what we now mean by the term.

component is the public law of particular political communities, backed by the coercive sanctions at the disposal of their rulers. (On all matters which are morally indifferent in communities where these rulers possess legitimate political authority, such laws constitute authoritative extensions of the divine law of nature. But the mere fact that something is the public law of a particular political society offers no guarantee that its subject matter falls within the class of indifferent things or that the rulers of this society possess legitimate political authority (Dunn 1969: Pt III). In civilized and economically developed countries, much human trustworthiness does in fact depend upon the existence of effective governmental power. But wealth is no guarantee of political legitimacy; and no constitutional form can ensure that the subject matter of public law is confined to the class of morally or religiously indifferent things. Even illegitimate political authorities may well make a real contribution to sustaining human trustworthiness in some domains of activity (and their subjects may even owe them duties of obedience because of their provision of these services).[7] But they themselves have no right to be obeyed; and their commands, as such, carry no necessary moral authority. Even the commands of a legitimate sovereign lose their authority when what they order is in breach of the divine law of nature.) The fourth and final positive component of human trustworthiness is not an external pressure upon men's wills, but an aspect of their motivation: what is sometimes referred to as their 'natural sociality'. Locke presents this both in the *Two Treatises* and in the *Essay* as a motive for men's entry into continuing social relations at all: 'God having made Man such a Creature, that, in his own Judgment, it was not good for him to be alone, put him under strong Obligations of Necessity, Convenience, and Inclination to drive him into *Society*, as well as fitted him with Understanding and Language to continue and enjoy it' (*Two Treatises* II. 77. 1–4; and see Locke 1954: 156). The God who gave men all things richly to enjoy (*Two Treatises* II. 31. 5–7; II. 34. 1–3) gave them also a judicious combination of practical compulsions and capacities to enter and sustain society and psychic inclinations to seek out and to enjoy it. What makes a relatively unforced human trustworthiness readily attainable under some conditions is that fact that human beings can and do take pleasure in each other's company. It is men's natural sociality which enables the law of reputation to have such a vivid impact upon their sentiments and causes them to care so keenly what other men feel about them.

To balance these positive components, the motivational pressures, external and internal, which promote human trustworthiness, there are also, of course, negative components, motivational pressures which

---

[7] For a general formulation of the duty see his Journal entry for 15 July 1678 (*Bodleian Ms Locke* f. 3,202, cited in Dunn 1969: 49n, and see Dunn 1980: ch. 3).

militate more or less decisively against it. Some of these are also external, most importantly the simple and unstartling recognition, expressed as early as the *Essays on the Law of Nature*,[8] that human material interests do conflict regularly and directly with each other. In conditions of limitless abundance, as Locke clearly acknowledges in the *Two Treatises* (II. 46, 48) and Hume later insists so effectively in the *Treatise of Human Nature* III. II. iii (1911: II, 199–200), the concepts of property rights in material objects and of justice would be otiose. But material scarcity implies the permanent possibility of acute conflicts of material interest.

It is quite clear from his discussion of the character which the state of nature would be likely to assume in practice in conditions of moderate economic progress and complexity, that Locke recognized the causal significance of this external and negative motivational pressure upon human trustworthiness. But in itself, as Hume's subsequent analysis brings out, scarcity serves merely to explain[9] men's invention of the institutional forms (ownership, promise-making and keeping, and the rules of justice) best calculated to minimize the threat which it poses. It has no determinate implications for how to conceive men's motivation in relation to these institutional forms; and it offers no basis for assessing the prospective punctiliousness with which they can be expected to observe these norms in practice.

The basis for such assessment in Locke's thinking is provided by his theory of human motivation and his conception of men's reasons for action. These two were not very successfully distinguished by Locke himself; and it cannot be said that their implications harmonize very successfully. The mechanical hedonist account of motivation, as initially elaborated even in the *Essay* itself, makes it very unclear how men can be genuinely responsible for their actions and has correspondingly pessimistic implications for the assessment of human trustworthiness. The revised account of the nature of the will and of human freedom, with its stress on the agent's capacity for rational suspension of practical choice to enable him or her to reconsider more soberly what is at stake, (*Essay* II. xxi. 47–53 etc.), is certainly less destructive of agent responsibility and offers more insight into how a human agent can in principle be worthy of trust and not simply dispositionally unalarming. But the revised account, for this very reason, is less well fitted to serve as a basis for the practical assessment of trustworthiness. Its implications are less pessimistic precisely because they are less clear and less determinate.

---

[8] Locke 1954: 204–15. This is why 'An Hobbist with his principle of self-preservation whereof him self is to be judge, will not easily admit a great many plain duties of morality' (*Bodleian Ms Locke*, ff. 2, 128).

[9] Some continue to doubt how far it does serve to *explain* these; cf. Elster 1982.

Because, on Locke's analysis, human beings are free agents, responsible for their own actions, they are in principle capable of taking responsibility for many aspects of their own beliefs. This consideration is central to the understanding of human trustworthiness because only human beings who do fully understand what is at stake in their choices can be *depended* upon to have sufficient reason to be consistently worthy of trust. As natural creatures, all men are 'liable to Errour, and most Men are in many Points, by Passion or Interest, under Temptation to it' (*Essay* IV. xx. 17 (1975:718)). Unless they anticipate a future life (as in Locke's view they have good reason to do), they are perfectly rational in pursuing whatever terrestrial pleasures happen to appeal to them (II. xxi. 55 (1975:269–70)). Some of the terrestrial pleasures which *do* happen to appeal to them can readily have highly deleterious consequences. 'Principles of Actions indeed there are lodged in Men's Appetites, but these are so far from being innate Moral Principles, that if they were left to their full swing, they would carry Men to the over-turning of all Morality' (I. iii. 13 (1975:75)). Locke's image for the cognitively appropriate mechanism for inhibiting *these* principles of action is quaintly archaic: 'a Pleasure tempting, and the Hand of the Almighty visibly held up, and prepared to take Vengeance' (I. iii. 13(1975:75)). But its archaism cannot simply be brushed aside. To be rationally and consistently trustworthy, for Locke, a human being must fear the wrath of God. It seems clear that his *Essay* was centrally motivated by the desire to show how human beings can take full responsibility for the content of their own beliefs and discharge this responsibility in an edifying manner (Passmore 1978; Dunn 1984a: ch.3). Given the key role of the Hand of the Almighty in securing an acceptable content for the outcome of men's rationally assessed motives, it is not surprising that the *Essay*'s implications for the epistemology of morals should have fallen so far short of Locke's hopes. Nor would it be surprising if, as I shall suggest is in fact the case, the political conclusions of the *Two Treatises* seem appreciably bleaker to those of us who cannot discern the Hand of the Almighty than they did to Locke himself.

The central premise of the *Two Treatises* is that men belong to their divine Creator and that their rights and duties in this earthly life derive from his ownership of them and from the purposes for which he fashioned them. The law of nature articulates these purposes as rationally intelligible authoritative commands. Its interpretation and enforcement within the natural world is left to human reason and human force. Every man or woman must judge rationally for themselves what its precepts are and how these bear upon their conduct; and every human being possesses the executive power of the law of nature, the right and duty to enforce these precepts when they have been flouted. This structure of rights, duties and powers is given by the character of the natural order, seen as a divinely created order which expresses in its entirety the purposes of its Creator. This is the proper understanding of what the state of nature is (*Two Treatises* II. ch. 2). But in itself it offers (and seeks to offer) no explanation whatever of why human beings for the most part within the real history of their societies find themselves subject to the additional coercive power of political authorities. To this question, 'Why does political power exist at all?', Locke gives two very different but in no sense incompatible answers. The first answer specifies what benign purposes such power can serve and is worked out with some tenacity in the *Second Treatise* as a whole. The second answer simply indicates the extremely prominent role in the history of political power of purposes which are in no sense benign. Even illegitimate political power can and will serve, intermittently, some of the benign purposes which political power is capable of serving; and even the most legitimate political power can always be diverted to wholly deplorable ends. But, *ex hypothesi*, the grounds for viewing legitimate political power with some measure of trust are far more substantial than those for viewing illegitimate political power in this light. In the latter case indeed, although some measure of trust is likely to be accorded if the power is used at all benignly in practice, *trust* as such is scarcely an appropriate attitude. Human beings are, and have to be, very trusting creatures. But illegitimate political power, even where in detail it deserves acceptance, cannot deserve trust. It cannot deserve trust because it is in no way reciprocal in character.

The more important analytical question for Locke, given the moral and legal coherence of the order of nature as such, is why political power can serve benign purposes, why human history contains instances of legitimate political power and why such power, while it sustains its own legitimacy, does deserve the trust of those over whom it is exercised. The answer to this question is simple enough. Human beings are not merely liable to error (cognitively fallible) in the interpretation of their rights and duties under the law of nature, they are also often 'by Passion or Interest, under Temptation to it' (*Essay* IV. xx. 17. 33–5). It is the inherent partiality of human practical judgement in the face of temptation which ensures that human beings will in practice often misinterpret the law of nature and abuse their own power to enforce this. The benign end which wholly legitimate political power is plainly able to serve is the institutionalized provision of clearer epistemic standards (known standing laws (*Two Treatises* II. 124.5–12; cf. II. 90, II. 131 etc.)) and less partial enforcement agencies for the structure of rights and duties specified in the law of nature. The need for such institutionalized provision becomes more pressing as human society develops in complexity and social scale and as the potential conflicts of immediate interest within it sharpen, as they plainly must with the genesis of massive disparities in economic entitlements. All men, rulers as much as ruled, legitimate rulers as well as illegitimate ones, are partial in their own case and liable to error in their judgements. But in practice they vary very widely indeed in the degree to which they succeed in controlling their impulse to partiality and in judging as reason prescribes that they should. The two opposite extremes which define this range of variation are reason and duty, God's way for man, and force, arbitrary power and personal pleasure, the way of beasts (II. II. 16–27; II. 172. 9–19), who cannot suspend the execution of their desires (*Essay* II. xxi. 56 (1975:270–1)) and must accordingly respond without internal check to the full swing of the principles of action lodged in their appetites.

When men confer power upon other men and establish a legitimate political society by doing so, they seek to provide against the inconveniences of the state of nature, the practical hazards posed by the general partiality of mankind. But they also expose themselves more acutely to the potential partiality of the particular human beings who always in practice constitute the holders of governmental power.[10] Political power is presented 'to the Governours, whom the Society hath set over it self, with this express or tacit Trust, That it shall be imployed for their good, and the preservation of their Property (*Two Treatises* II. 171. 1–5). The metaphor of a legal trust, which Locke employs at a number of points in the *Two Treatises* to express the nature of the relation between subject and sovereign in a legitimate polity, was not original to him (Gough 1950: ch.7); and it carries little or no distinctive weight in his argument. (To conceive of a legal trust as tacit represents at least as decisive an etiolation of the concept as with the more notorious instance of tacit consent.) But the more elaborated metaphor does serve to express more sharply the implications of his pervasive insistence on the centrality of the psychological and moral relation of trust to the benign working of political authority. For political power to serve the purposes for which men need it, it *has* to be subject to drastic and potentially destructive abuse. The legal concept of trust captures nicely three features on which Locke is anxious to insist: the clarity of a ruler's responsibility to serve the public good, the existence of a structure of rights external to the practical relation of ruling on which a sovereign's claim to authority must depend, and the inescapable asymmetry of power between ruler and ruled which precludes the latter from exercising direct and continuing control over the former.

In the chapter on Prerogative in the *Second Treatise* (*Two Treatises* II. ch. 14), Locke insists on the degree of this asymmetry. The power of a legitimate sovereign rests on the law. But in the English constitution at least, where the ruler holds not merely the executive and federative powers

[10] *Bodleian Ms Locke* c 28, f.85ʳ (quoted in Dunn 1969:148n1).

but also a share in the legislative power, it extends beyond into areas where the law is silent; and it can rightfully be exercised, where the public good requires it and the people acquiesce in its use, even against the direct letter of the law. Prerogative is '*the Power of doing publick good without a Rule*' (II. 166. 20–1). Discretion is intrinsic to its use. Indeed, whatever the laws prescribe, discretion must always be intrinsic to the use of that concentrated coercive power which all rulers derive from the accumulated executive powers of the law of nature which their subjects have surrendered to them. The prerogatives of the English monarch give legal status to the practical opportunities which no ruler can in practice be denied. But the status depends upon the use of this power to serve the public good. Should its possessor elect to follow his or her own whims, and to make force, the way of beasts, to be his rule of right, his subjects have no duty tamely to submit. Human beings must and do trust their rulers. They trust them on the whole far beyond the latters' deserts, and to the damage of their own interests. But in the last instance they retain (and indeed have no power to abandon) the right and duty to judge for themselves how far their trust has been deserved and where and when it has been betrayed. And if they do judge it to have been betrayed, they have every right to act in concert and seek to re-establish for themselves a form of sovereign power in which they can, once again, rationally place their trust. For Locke, political participation is a burden, not a pleasure or a privilege: something to be abandoned gratefully when one's community is fortunate enough to be ruled well (Locke 1976: IV, 148). But it is also, where the public safety is genuinely in danger (as, alas, it often is), both a duty and a right. Political virtue does not necessarily require an activist disposition. But it does require, in the last instance, a genuine commitment to the public good and a preparedness to make sacrifices on its behalf.

In the *Two Treatises* Locke expounds the political duty of trustworthiness for both rulers and ruled, and sets out clear limits on the duty of the ruled to act trustingly in the face of bitter experience. In doing so he vindicates the rights of all men to take political action in defence of their own interests. But he also stresses repeatedly their corresponding duty to judge for themselves, soberly and scrupulously, when and where and how to exercise this right. Prior to the question of what is to be done, there is the question of what is to be believed. This too, as John Passmore (1978) has insisted, is essentially an ethical question for Locke. Before men can discern how they should act, they must ascertain what they *should* believe. To learn how to act responsibly, it is first necessary to learn how to take full moral responsibility for the content of one's own beliefs. This is a puzzling and barely coherent conception in the eyes of many modern philosophers. The ethics of belief may play a minor interstitial role in modern epistemology – in parts of the philosophy of natural science, for example. But most of any person's beliefs at a particular time must surely be a matter of fate rather than choice. Yet, odd though Locke's conception may look to us, there is little doubt that it was this queasy project of *taking* responsibility for the content of one's beliefs to which the *Essay concerning Human Understanding* was principally directed. Credally, human judgement on the occasion of its occurrence is, in Locke's eyes, just as compulsive as human knowledge. But, unlike his more confidently offered candidates for knowledge, judgement is plainly an activity under a substantial measure of voluntary control and one which offers ample opportunity for the suspension of our more pressing desires, to permit a wider and less hasty consideration of just what is at stake in our actions (*Essay* IV. xiv. 2 (esp. lines 16–29); II. xxi. 47–71).

The *Essay* does in fact offer an elaborate analysis of the factors which enable men to assume a large measure of responsibility for the content of their own beliefs and judgements, and which therefore justify their being held responsible for these. But, especially in the case of specifically ethical beliefs, it is discouragingly undirective on the topic of what men have reason to do. One conclusion which it does draw, however, is the impossibility of supplanting, over most of the field of human belief, the discretionary condition of active judgement by the compulsive condition of knowledge. It is a decisive implication of Locke's epistemology that over much of the field of human belief there is no possibility in principle of escaping the need to rest one's beliefs on epistemically insufficient grounds. Credally, just as much as politically, therefore, men's existence requires them to put their trust in what may well in practice prove to betray them. All human life is an encounter with hazard; and the best that men can do in the face of these hazards is to meet them with, as Locke put it in 1659, 'virtue and honour'.[11]

In his last major work, *The Reasonableness of Christianity*, Locke sets out a clear and simple account of how for an English Christian in 1695 trust may be more confidently and securely disposed. There is no doubt that his answer to this question – the faith that Jesus was the Messiah and the promises attendant on this faith – lay behind and sustained his thinking throughout his intellectual life. What, above all, it sustained and rendered rational was the systematic scheme of good intentions which made an ethics of belief a plausible approach to epistemology and which enabled him to undertake his extraordinary intellectual odyssey.

It was this scheme of good intentions which made it possible for Locke to see human political society as a whole as the historical contrivance of a

---

[11] Locke 1976: I, 122. This places Locke in an intriguing relation to the trajectory sketched by Alasdair MacIntyre 1981.

creature, man, whose empirical characteristics ensured that he could never become particularly trustworthy; and yet for him to retain his own intellectual and moral nerve in the face of this vision.

In its political implications his view stands at the opposite extreme to modern functionalist social holism. So far from every array of productive forces, for example, being guaranteed in due course the capacity to engender a social apparatus capable of ensuring their continued expansion, for Locke nothing about human history or human society was or is guaranteed, except perhaps its starting point and its eventual destination. All the rest is made by the actions of individual human beings, every one of which is prospectively consequential, and the relations between which are wholly contingent in their impact. Men, not languages, or cultures or societies or productive forces, make human history. It is always human individuals, one by one, who are responsible for the sustaining and shaping of human societies. In contrast with the alienated modern conception of the context of political agency (Dunn 1980; 1983a) and the predominantly instrumental view of its character which dominate modern political thinking, Locke combines a radically individualist conception of both the human significance and the rationality of political agency with a wholly unalienated conception of its social context. Because his conception of political agency depends for its structure and stability on a personal relation between the individual human agent and the deity, it can scarcely be *adopted* as a basis for grounding modern political identities. But when held up against the more prominent candidates for such adoption in the political world in which *we* live our lives, it does bring out dramatically the devastating imaginative poverty and evasion which are characteristic of these (Dunn 1979; 1984b; 1980: ch. 9). If the synthesis of trust (the creation and sustaining of trust) remains, and will always remain, an indispensable human contrivance for coping with the freedom of other men, it is scarcely conducive either to virtue or to honour to have to make do with such deformed and superficial conceptions of how to trust one another or to be trustworthy, individually or politically. And now that the human race has acquired the power to destroy itself for ever, this is a theme which must surely be at the very heart of any philosophy which aspires to take *politics* at all seriously.

REFERENCES

Bayle, Pierre. 1911–12. *Pensées diverses sur la Comète*, ed. A. Prat and E. Cornély, 2 vols. Paris

Cohen, G. A. 1978. *Karl Marx's Theory of History*. Oxford: Clarendon Press

Cohen, G. A. 1982. 'Reply to Elster on Marxism, functionalism and game theory', *Theory and Society* 11(4):483–96

Colman, John. 1983. *John Locke's Moral Philosophy*. Edinburgh: Edinburgh University Press

Cox, Richard H. 1960. *Locke on War and Peace*. Oxford: Clarendon Press

Dunn, John. 1969. *The Political Thought of John Locke*. Cambridge: Cambridge University Press

Dunn, John. 1979. *Western Political Theory in the Face of the Future*. Cambridge: Cambridge University Press

Dunn, John. 1980. *Political Obligation in its Historical Context*. Cambridge: Cambridge University Press

Dunn, John. 1982. 'Understanding revolutions', *Ethics* 92(2):299–315

Dunn, John. 1983a. 'Social theory, social understanding and political action', in Christopher Lloyd (ed.), *Social Theory and Political Practice*. Oxford: Clarendon Press, 109–35

Dunn, John. 1983b. 'From applied theology to social analysis: the break between John Locke and the Scottish Enlightenment', in Istvan Hont and Michael Ignatieff (eds.), *Wealth and Virtue*. Cambridge: Cambridge University Press, 119–35

Dunn, John. 1984a. *Locke*. Oxford: Oxford University Press

Dunn, John. 1984b. 'Totalitarian democracy and the legacy of modern revolutions: explanation or indictment?', in *Totalitarian Democracy and After: Colloquium in Honour of Jacob Talmon*. Jerusalem: Israel Academy of Sciences

Elster, Jon. 1982. 'Marxism, functionalism and game theory: the case for methodological individualism', *Theory and Society* 11(4):453–82

Gough, J. W. 1950. *John Locke's Political Philosophy*. Oxford: Clarendon Press

Hume, David. 1903. *Essays Moral, Political and Literary*. London: Henry Frowde, World's Classics

Hume, David. 1911. *A Treatise of Human Nature*, 2 vols. London: J. M. Dent & Son

Jenkins, John. 1983. *Understanding Locke*. Edinburgh: Edinburgh University Press

Locke, John. 1954. *Essays on the Law of Nature*, ed. W. von Leyden. Oxford: Clarendon Press

Locke, John. 1960. *Two Treatises of Government*, ed. Peter Laslett. Cambridge: Cambridge University Press

Locke, John. 1967. *Two Tracts on Government*, ed. Philip Abrams. Cambridge: Cambridge University Press

Locke, John. 1968a. *Epistola de Tolerantia(A Letter on Toleration)*, ed. J. W. Gough and R. Klibansky. Oxford: Clarendon Press

Locke, John. 1968b. *The Educational Writings of John Locke*, ed. James L. Axtell. Cambridge: Cambridge University Press

Locke, John. 1975. *An Essay concerning Human Understanding*, ed. Peter H. Nidditch. Oxford: Clarendon Press

Locke, John. 1976–. *The Correspondence of John Locke*, ed. E. S. de Beer. Oxford: Clarendon Press

Luhmann, Niklas. 1979. *Trust and Power*, ed. T. Burns and G. Poggi. Chichester and New York: John Wiley

MacIntyre, Alasdair. 1981. *After Virtue*. London: Duckworth

Moore, Barrington, Jr. 1978. *Injustice: the Social Bases of Obedience and Revolt.* White Plains, NY: M. E. Sharpe

Passmore, John. 1978. 'Locke and the ethics of belief', *Proceedings of the British Academy* 64:185–208.

Strauss, Leo. 1953. *Natural Right and History.* Chicago: University of Chicago Press

Thompson, Martyn. 1977. 'Hume's critique of Locke and the "original contract"', *Il Pensiero Politico* 10(2):189–201

Williams, Bernard. 1981. *Moral Luck.* Cambridge: Cambridge University Press

Wollaston, William. 1738. *The Religion of Nature Delineated*, 6th edn. London

◁ ══ ▷

13

Berkeley and Hume:
a question of influence

MICHAEL AYERS

Introduction

'While until recently the tendency was to deny any influences [on Hume] other than Locke and Berkeley, the present tendency appears to be going the other way' (Laing 1932:69). The most interesting thing about that sentence is that it was written over fifty years ago. The question of Hume's relationship to Berkeley is involved in a rather curious situation in the historiography of philosophy. On the one hand, a certain view of the formative period of modern philosophy remains more or less frozen in lecture-courses, examination schedules and, no doubt, in the minds of some teachers and students. Philosophers are slotted into distinct traditions like animals into their species. On the other hand, something of an academic industry has grown up over many years which is devoted to the business of attacking just that 'standard' view. The assumption that Hume followed Berkeley in the 'British Empiricist' tradition has long been seen as one of its main points of weakness.[1]

One very good element in this critical reaction is a wider awareness of the intellectual promiscuity of the early modern period, of significant alliances which cut across the old superimposed categories, of radically disparate purposes which exist within them. Such connections often cross the boundary of what is regarded as centrally philosophical, into theology, physics, biology and so forth; and they may do so in ways which remind us that that boundary suffers from a certain fluctuation and indeterminacy. It may consequently even be that the discreteness of philosophy is in some

---

[1] The 'standard' view of Hume as the third British Empiricist is commonly taken to have its origins in Reid's reaction, expressed, for example, in his letter to Hume, 18 March 1763, quoted by Kemp Smith (1964:5f). An extreme version, making Locke and Berkeley the *only* significant influences on Hume, was advanced in the edition of Green and Grose (1882). It is ritually attacked by many writers, including Laing (1932:68), Kemp Smith (1964:7, 79f), Passmore (1980:84ff), Bracken (1977:230, 237), Loeb (1981:25–36 *et passim*), Norton (1982:4f, 11, 56). Yet even in his earliest article (1905:149f) Kemp Smith had stated that Green's thirty-year-old opinion was already generally rejected.

quarters now underestimated. Philosophical doctrine may stem in part, it is true, from external considerations, and sometimes from motives which are political or sectarian, social or institutional, rather than more purely intellectual. Yet the notion of a dialectic internal to 'philosophy' which by itself promotes change and growth is by no means without foundation. Certainly nothing has contributed remotely as much to the background conditions, including the language, in which recognizably philosophical doctrines have been advanced as other recognizably philosophical doctrines. The analysis of the broadly logical or internal relations between philosophical ideas and their antecedents will therefore always be the bread and butter of the historiography of philosophy. Such analysis is the most important prerequisite of all to the understanding of philosophical texts. But the present point is simply that it reveals a complex network of relationships rather than separate or opposing linear traditions. It is open to us, in tracing influence and movement, to pick any of a number of significant paths, noting the transformations and innovations which may affect ideas and doctrines as their individual proponents struggle for self-coherence. Alternatively we can make an individual the centre of attention, illuminating a text by reference to its multiple relationships. There is no longer a felt need to record the progress of the torches of 'Rationalism' and 'Empiricism' as they pass from hand to hand; or to present the growth and development of the New Philosophy as an act of preparation for Kant and Hegel.

A less attractive feature of the reaction has been a tendency on the part of some to see nothing good, 'interesting', or even true in the old way of looking at things. If Hume can be shown to have important connections with earlier sceptics or Pyrrhonists such as Bayle and Huet, then it is supposed that there cannot be similar, not to say stronger, connections with Berkeley.[2] If Berkeley can be pressed into service as a 'Cartesian' (Bracken 1974:15ff et passim) or a 'Continental Metaphysician' (Loeb 1981:320–6, 332–6), then he is, after all, in an entirely different regiment from Locke. Kemp Smith's unsubstantiated speculation that Hume's general philosophy is significantly indebted to the moral philosopher Hutcheson has survived as long as it has, one suspects, just because it is *not* the view that Hume was influenced by Berkeley. The anti-traditional stance has itself become a rather long-standing orthodoxy with a spurious air of innovation. Since Kemp Smith's critical study and Popkin's provocative question, the slenderest of considerations, the airiest of assertions, have been freely accepted and repeated provided that they are on the side of

---

[2] Cf. Popkin 1959b:542ff. This element in Popkin's argument is gently and properly criticized by Mossner (1959:995).

the view that Hume was no 'devoted student of Berkeley' (Passmore 1980:86).[3]

Some, it is true, felt that in asking 'Did Hume ever read Berkeley?' Popkin went too far (1959a; 1959b). Yet what is odd is that the evidence which emerged from that controversy has had so little effect on the interpretation of Hume. His direct references in letters and published works point unequivocally towards the conclusion that he took Berkeley, and his own relationship to Berkeley, very seriously indeed. Yet there simply has not been the close comparative analysis which one might have supposed would be stimulated by a judicious review of that evidence. To a remarkable extent recent commentators have simply looked elsewhere for Hume's inspiration, even when they do not explicitly endorse their predecessors' opinion that there is 'little trace of Berkeley in Hume's writings' (Popkin 1964:778; cf. Loeb 1981:34).

How the direct evidence has been discounted without scruple can be illustrated by the treatment accorded to Hume's striking acknowledgement to Berkeley in the *First Enquiry*. Kemp Smith typically manages to see that footnote, not as an expression of indebtedness, but as Hume's giving 'his reasons for not taking account of Berkeley' (1964:468; cf. 87).[4] This meaning is drawn from Hume's statement that

most of the writings of that very ingenious author form the best lessons of scepticism, which are to be found either among the ancient or the modern philosophers, Bayle not excepted ... That all his arguments, though otherwise intended, are, in reality, merely sceptical, appears from this, that they admit of no answer and produce no conviction. (1957:155)

Yet from a sceptic, even from a sceptic of a rather special sort, such comment would seem to be praise indeed. The sting in the tail hardly bears the construction which Kemp Smith and others place on it, since it entirely conforms to what Hume is prepared to say about his own sceptical reasoning. To put it mildly, it is improbable that Hume would have ranked Berkeley higher than Bayle without having read him carefully. It is hardly more likely that he would have set aside 'the best lessons of scepticism' in constructing his own. But before we can safely speculate (or moralize) about the reasons for such prejudices as Kemp Smith's, it is necessary to show, not just that it is probable that Hume made extensive use of Berkeley, but that it is certain that he did so.

---

[3] For further comment see Appendix below.
[4] For Popkin the passage is 'Hume's chastisement of Berkeley for his scepticism' (1959b:539)! Flew (1980:261) seems prepared to argue from the same passage that Hume had read only one of Berkeley's books, i.e. the *Principles*.

Space and time

An argument of Hume's which has plausibly been thought to owe something to Berkeley is the account of space and time in the *Treatise*. Hume claims to possess a 'system' with two 'intimately connected' parts or principles. The first is the principle that space and time are not infinitely divisible, being composed of spatially and temporally extensionless *minima*. The second is the doctrine that 'the ideas of space and time are . . . no separate or distinct ideas, but merely those of the manner or order, in which objects exist'. The connection between these principles emerges from the arguments for them. The first principle, as it applies to space, is supported by the argument that the impressions and ideas of extension, whether of sight or touch, are made up of *minima sensibilia*. If we continue to divide an impression or idea we eventually arrive at visible or tangible points which any attempt at further diminution would simply destroy. Since what is possible in the imagination is possible in reality, reality too could be composed of *minima*. And since other accounts of space lead to notorious absurdities, reality *must* be composed of *minima*, of the same type as *minima sensibilia*. But a visible or tangible point is not a mere mathematical point, it is something positive. Its content consists in colour or the corresponding tactual quality, which Hume here calls solidity. A visual line is thus composed of extensionless coloured points, and its extension is something second-order or relational, the 'manner or order' in which these points are disposed (1978:29–53).

The case for supposing Berkeley to have been an 'influence' in all this is fairly straightforward. He seems to have been the only philosopher previously to have proposed anything which comes at all near to either leg of Hume's system. He advances the first, or something exceedingly like it, in terms closely resembling Hume's: 'For, whatever may be said of extension in abstract, it is certain sensible extension is not infinitely divisible. There is a *Minimum Tangibile* and a *Minimum Visibile*, beyond which sense cannot perceive' (1967:191).[5] But he makes a further claim which can reasonably be taken to imply the second leg by the shortest of inferences. For he often tells us, in the *Essay towards a New Theory of Vision*, that that 'which I see is only light and colours. That which I feel is hard or soft, hot or cold, rough or smooth' (1967:212; cf. 223). It is, he says, a mistake to suppose that, beside these, there are other ideas common to both senses. Yet he does not want to deny that there are visible shapes and sizes or visible distances between points. He simply wants to give an

---

[5] Of course Berkeley rejects the notion of 'extension in abstract'. It is sometimes claimed (as Bracken 1977:228f) that Hume's *minima* differ from Berkeley's in being themselves unextended. Raynor (1980) points out that Hume follows Berkeley in this respect too.

account of these modes of visual extension which ties them to light and colour as he also wants to tie tangible extension to tactual qualities. In general, extension is not to be abstractible from secondary qualities. This second-order status of extension is hinted at in the *Theory of Vision Vindicated*, when he includes in the perceived variety of colours variety 'in their order and situation' (1967:266). Elsewhere he talks of 'that certain variety and *disposition* of colours which constitute the visible man' (1967:218). At the same time, the measurable *distance* between two visible points consists in 'the number of intermediate points' (1967:216). From all this it is a very short step to Hume's doctrine that perceived or imagined space is the 'manner or order' of the appearance of *minima sensibilia*. Something similar can be said about time, for Hume shares with Berkeley the inference from the premise that the idea of time derives from experienced succession, to the conclusion that duration without succession is impossible (Hume 1978:35–9; Berkeley 1964:83f).

In the *New Theory of Vision* Berkeley's purpose is not obviously related to infinite divisibility. Yet in the *Principles* he employs the same notion of *minima*, but not the expressions, in order to attack the conception of determinate external extension. All agree, he tells us, that 'any particular body . . . exhibits only a finite number of parts to sense' (1964:60); but the absurdities of infinite divisibility show more generally that 'no finite extension contains innumerable parts, or is infinitely divisible' (1964:98). The contrast is set up between finite, and so determinate, sensible extension and the supposedly infinite, and therefore indeterminate, external or abstract extension. The former makes sense, the latter does not (1964:98–101). Following Bayle, Berkeley explicitly links the issue of infinite divisibility to his critique of the distinction between primary and secondary qualities (1964:60): whatever is determinate is relative to sense, including size and motion (1964:45f). It helps to remember this connection (as I have tried briefly to show elsewhere) even in interpreting the arguments of the *First Dialogue*, where infinite divisibility is not explicitly mentioned (Ayers 1981:61–5). But for present purposes we need only notice that Hume may reasonably be supposed to have adapted the term *minima sensibilia* from the *New Theory*, while his employment of the notion more or less follows *The Principles*.

The fullest case *against* seeing Berkeley as a significant antecedent of Hume on space and time is advanced by Kemp Smith (1964:273–90). One argument Kemp Smith does not employ is the argument from differences between the two philosophers, since he finds it convenient to ignore Berkeley altogether. What he does is to ascribe the first part of Hume's system to his reflections on Bayle, and the second part to the influence of Hutcheson. The former claim need not detain us long. That Hume borrowed from Bayle is undeniable. As Kemp Smith says, he presents the puzzle of extension in just Bayle's terms, as a trilemma between infinite divisibility, a system of abstract points as conceived of by mathematicians, and a system of physical points or atoms (Bayle 1710:3078; 1730:540). Kemp Smith's account implies that Hume chooses a form of one of these three possibilities, although in the passage in question Hume presents his solution as in effect a fourth option, destroying the trilemma. Certainly his doctrine is something undreamed of by Bayle:

there is evidently a medium [betwixt the infinite divisibility of matter, and the non-entity of mathematical points], *viz*, the bestowing a colour or solidity on these points; and the absurdity of both the extremes is a demonstration of the truth and the reality of this medium. The system of physical points, which is another medium, is too absurd to need a refutation.   (Hume 1978:40)

But if Hume's proposal really is a fourth possibility, it cannot be *less* reasonable to suppose that it derived from Berkeley than to suppose that the original trilemma, with some of the destructive arguments, derived from Bayle. It is relevant to recall, of course, that Berkeley himself was evidently deeply affected by his reading of Bayle on infinite divisibility. Hume could hardly have read both and have failed to connect them.

Kemp Smith's efforts to find the origin of Hume's view of the idea of space in Hutcheson take roughly the following course. There are several, perhaps three, very short passages in which Hutcheson claims that there is a difference in kind between ideas of secondary qualities and the ideas of extension, figure, motion and rest (1728:3, 281f; 1742:33–6). Some perceptions, he says, are 'purely sensible, received each by its proper sense': i.e., 'tastes, smells, colours, sound, cold, heat, etc.'. Others accompany these 'sensations' or 'sensible qualities', e.g. the idea of duration and number, which are clearly not themselves 'sensible ideas' since they accompany all ideas whatsoever. But there are other members of the class of 'concomitant ideas' which 'are found accompanying the most different sensations, which yet are not to be perceived separately from some sensible quality'. These are extension, figure, motion and rest. All concomitant ideas, unlike the 'purely sensible', are 'reputed images of something external' (1728:3). The centre of Hutcheson's interest, of course, lies not with these ideas and the distinctions between them, but with the ideas of inner sense. Ideas of inner sense are for Hutcheson ideas which arise in a secondary way, after the reception of ideas of outer sense. They include the passions generally, and the aesthetic and moral sentiments in particular. Such sentiments are in some ways comparable to ideas of secondary qualities. Just as sensations of colour simply happen, without any intelligible connection with the primary qualities which cause them, so the moral and aesthetic sentiments simply happen, without any intelligible connection with the primary perceptions which regularly give rise to them. By this analogy Hutcheson answers the claim that, since moral objectivity requires that there is a rational way of deciding moral disagreements, ethics must at bottom be the business of reason rather than a matter of sentiment. He replies that, quite generally, defective judgements of sense, about secondary qualities as well as about primary qualities, can be corrected by other sensory judgements of the same kind, without recourse to reason.

Kemp Smith sees the claim that ideas of primary qualities are 'concomitant ideas' rather than pure sensations as being equivalent to the claim that they are not 'impressions'. This doctrine, that perceptions of primary qualities are ideas but not impressions, is believed by Kemp Smith to have been originally accepted by Hume himself, who is supposed to have abandoned it officially only as he came to adopt the usage of the terms 'impression' and 'idea' which is embodied in the principle that every simple idea is a copy of an impression. On Kemp Smith's view, the doctrine that space is the 'manner or order' in which coloured points are disposed remains in the *Treatise* as a relic of that earlier way of thinking.[6] It is, as Kemp Smith's chapter title boldly proclaims, 'Hume's version of Hutcheson's teaching that space and time are non-sensational'. For if Hume holds that extension is the manner in which simple impressions are ordered, then, Kemp Smith argues, he holds that it is not itself an impression. It may be 'given' or 'intuited' but it is not sensed. There is then a problem: why did Hume fail to realize that he had in effect allowed an exception to his fundamental principle, i.e. an idea which is not a copy of an impression? Kemp Smith's full answer remains obscure to me, but it seems in part to be that Hume had never really sorted out how his earlier, Hutchesonian distinction between impressions and ideas is related to his own later and official distinction. Moreover, despite his engaging in the discussion of space and time with a promise to employ the principle that ideas are copies of impressions, Hume's real aim, so Kemp Smith thinks, is to use his interpretation or elaboration of Hutcheson in order to supply a non-sceptical, rational solution of the antinomies of extension. The existence of such a solution is presumably supposed to constitute Hume's reason for not committing Euclid to the flames.

It does not seem that there is very much to be said for this story. Perhaps the careful comparison with Berkeley should be enough to make it implausible, but in any case there is little real resemblance between Hutcheson and Hume on the ideas of extension and its modes. In treating these ideas as perceptions which are not pure sensations, Hutcheson is

---

[6] Kemp Smith claims to find further remnants of the supposed earlier doctrine in *Treatise* II and III, but the passages in question seem each to have a clear enough point which is irrelevant to his interpretation (Kemp Smith 1964:49, 281–3).

simply trying to deal with the difference between the perception of primary qualities and the perception of secondary qualities. An earlier theory a little like his account is that of Malebranche, who distinguishes between *sentiments* and *idées*, the latter constituting independent objects of thought (namely ideas in the mind of God) which are distinct from such mere modifications of the mind as sensations. For Hutcheson, ideas of primary qualities do not, of course, *constitute* independent objects of thought, but they do represent external things as they are. Another, later theory reminiscent of Hutcheson is Reid's, which sharply distinguishes sensation from perception. Perception, for Reid, consists purely in conception and strong belief. We perceive primary qualities directly and distinctly, but secondary qualities only indirectly and obscurely, since we conceive of the latter only through the sensations which they cause. For Reid it is only by divine dispensation that perception involves sensation at all (1785:233). Hutcheson is less peculiar (as he is considerably briefer on the subject) than either Malebranche or Reid, but a further resemblance to both lies in the importance for his distinction of the point that primary qualities are perceived by more than one sense. It is, he says, *because* the ideas of 'Extention, figure, motion and rest . . . accompany the ideas of sight, or colours, and yet may be perceived without them, as in the ideas of touch', that they 'seem . . . to be more properly called ideas accompanying the sensations of sight and touch, than the sensations of either of these senses' (1728:3). Ideas of primary qualities are special because they are representations of reality abstractible from the sensations which accompany them, even though they are representations which never occur without some sensations or other.

All this could hardly be in greater contrast to the arguments of Berkeley, the underlying purpose of whose explanation of visual extension is to render it just as sense-relative as the colour from which it is inseparable. For Berkeley, of course, there are no ideas of two senses. The *last* conclusion that he would accept is that ideas of extension are 'non-sensational'. But is the same true of Hume? It certainly seems to be. For, as we have seen, the second branch of Hume's 'system' is the Berkeleyan principle that 'the ideas of space and time are . . . no separate or distinct ideas' (1978:39), a thought which conflicts sharply with Hutcheson's notion of concomitant but distinct ideas.

Yet, before deciding on this issue, we ought to consider one of the evident differences between Berkeley and Hume. Berkeley argues, in effect, that because light and colours differ in kind from tactual qualities, visual space, which is nothing but the disposition of light and colours, differs in kind from tactual space, the disposition of tactual qualities (1967:224f). The connection between the two, which explains why we talk as if they were not only specifically but numerically the same, consists in contingent associations. Hume, on the other hand, accepts that the idea of space is an idea of two senses. Yet this does not have for him the realist implications which it had for many other philosophers, including, as it seems, Hutcheson. He simply allows that, different as colour is from solidity, the 'impressions of touch are found to be similar to those of sight in the disposition of their parts'. He does not conclude that space is something which is in itself neither coloured nor tactually qualified, and which is the common object of sight and touch. On the contrary, he goes out of his way to remind us, with respect to this common idea of space, of the principle that all 'abstract ideas are really nothing but particular ones, consider'd in a certain light', which are able to represent quite different kinds of object provided only that there is one point of resemblance between them. In effect, he is offering a reductive explanation of ideas of two senses, with the implication that Berkeley need not have bothered paradoxically to deny their existence (Hume 1978:34). Yet even in this minor revision he seems to be following a lead supplied by Berkeley. For Berkeley himself draws a rather striking and meticulous distinction between the question whether there are individual objects common to sight and touch and a second question, which is supposed to remain when the first is answered negatively, whether the 'extension, figures, and motions perceived by sight are *specifically* distinct from the ideas of touch called by the same names': i.e., whether there is 'any such thing as one idea or kind of idea common to both senses' (1967:219–26). Moreover it is to Berkeley's own account of abstraction that Hume appeals in support of his dissenting answer to this second question.

Hume's acceptance that there are ideas of two senses is not his only difference from Berkeley which is such as actually to encourage us to suppose that he had Berkeley specifically in mind. Berkeley, as we have seen, is explicit that the determinate distance between two points in sensible space is determined by the number of sensible points between them. Hume bothers to argue, in pursuit of the conclusion that geometry is imprecise, that perceived points, although they exist, 'are so minute and so confounded with each other' that they are useless as a standard of equality, since we cannot count them (1978:45). The argument is, of course, a dangerous one for anyone who holds that there is nothing covert in an impression, but it is certainly not such as to locate Hume in a different philosophical world from Berkeley's. On the contrary, it reveals that that is the world which he inhabited.

Is it *important* that Hume's arguments about space owe little or, more probably, absolutely nothing to Hutcheson, and much to Berkeley? One way of approaching the question is to ask whether Kemp Smith's Hutchesonian Hume is significantly different from the Hume who emerges if we find Berkeleyan thoughts in his argument. Clearly there is a significant difference. For Kemp Smith, the supposed connection with Hutcheson helps to reveal what Hume is trying to do in the sections on space and time. On that view, Hume's purpose is not sceptical in any way. He 'follows Hutcheson in distinguishing, in a naively realistic manner, between space and time as apprehended by us and space and time as independently real'; and he rejects 'the sheerly sceptical conclusion' of Bayle, which he takes 'as a direct challenge to the defense of reason' (1964:283–6). So Hume is supposed to use realistic Hutcheson in order to solve sceptical Bayle's logical antinomies. Reason is thereby defended.

All this seems to be wild misrepresentation. It is true that in Book I Part ii, as often elsewhere in the *Treatise*, Hume readily refers to an external world as something within our experience. It is also in the discussion of space that there occurs the well-known passage in which he presents his 'specious and plausible' physiological speculation as to the cause in the brain of the principle that 'wherever there is a close relation betwixt two ideas, the mind is very apt to mistake them' (1978:60). But that this conception of a real world and real space is by no means as 'naive' as Kemp Smith proposes emerges from the argument itself. To see this, we should consider what really is the relation between Hume's argument and that of Bayle.

Bayle's discussion of infinite divisibility involves two unequal parts. Most of the argument is a straightforward defence of Zeno, and it is only in a final, fideist comment that, despite all, he expresses a preference for the natural human belief in the existence of extension and motion over the irrefutable deliverances of the intellect. The main argument is therefore not a sceptical attack on reason. It is an attack on extension, or Cartesian matter, through our idea of extension. For Bayle's Zeno, if reason draws antinomies from our idea of extension it has an easy way out: i.e. to deny that anything exists corresponding to a contradictory idea. The difficulties over infinite divisibility are thus 'proper for no other use than to make it appear that extension doth not exist anywhere but in our minds' (1710:3079b; 1730:541b). Bayle here rejects the view of those who 'shelter themselves in the nature of the subject, and allege, that our understandings being limited, none ought to be surprised that they cannot resolve what relates to infinity' (1710:3078a; 1730:540a). So Hume's supposed 'defense' of reason, his principle that 'Whatever *appears* impossible and contradictory upon the comparison of . . . ideas, must be *really* impossible and contradictory' (1978:29), is in effect already present in Bayle's argument. It is also present in Berkeley's, who, just like Bayle, pours scorn on the 'indolent scepticism' of those who think 'that proofs *a posteriori* [i.e., in this case, reductions to absurdity] are not to be admitted against propositions relating to infinity' (1964:100).

Before Hume, then, there were three relevant doctrines. First, the widely held view, to be found, for example, in the Port-Royal *Logic*, that there are contradictions, or at least difficulties, in our inadequate idea of extension, but of course not in infinitely divisible extension itself (Arnauld and Nicole 1965:296f; 1964:298f; cf. Malebranche 1980:203f; 1945:220f). Second, there is Bayle's argument that, since there are contradictions in our idea of extension, there can be no such thing as extension. Third, there is Berkeley's view that our *idea* of extension is free from contradictions, since perceived extension is not infinitely divisible; but that we tend also to have the confused and contradictory belief that there is an external extension, independent of sense-perception, which is infinitely divisible (1964:99f). Now of these three views, the one which Hume's view most resembles is Berkeley's, although he differs from Berkeley in taking for granted a belief in an 'external' or objective space which corresponds in all essential respects to our idea of space, i.e., which is not infinitely divisible. As with Berkeley, the philosophical or mathematical belief in infinite divisibility is put down to confusion, and a failure to grasp the nature of geometry. And, as with Berkeley, the premise that our idea of extension is free from the taint of infinite divisibility is established by an imagist or phenomenalist conception of an *idea*: in Hume's terms, by the principle that every idea is a copy of an impression.

How far does Hume's assumption of an external space take him from Berkeley? In some respects, not very far. The crucial element in Hume's position is that there is a conformity between the space we suppose to be external and our idea of it. He presents this conformity as a kind of truism:

For 'tis evident, that as no idea of quantity is infinitely divisible, there cannot be imagin'd a more glaring absurdity, than to endeavour to prove that, quantity itself admits of such a division; and to prove this by means of ideas, which are directly opposite in this particular.   (1978:52)

The same principle is employed in the curious argument in Part ii, Section 5, that we can have no idea of a vacuum. To have such an idea we should have to have an impression of sight not consisting of coloured points, or an impression of touch not consisting of solid ones. Here, however, he explicitly spells out the sceptical implications of the principle: 'my intention never was to penetrate into the nature . . . of bodies . . . For. . . such an enterprise is beyond the reach of human understanding, and . . . we can never pretend to know body otherwise than by those external properties, which discover themselves to the senses' (1978:64). So Kemp Smith is quite wrong to say that Hume distinguishes 'in a naively realist manner' between 'space and time as apprehended by us and space and time as independently real'. The main point of Hume's argument is that we ordinarily conceive of external space and time in a sense-relative way. In effect, what is 'independently real' cannot be thought about directly. Hence the objective and external space and time which we normally distinguish from this or that idea of them are still very much 'space and time as apprehended by us'. No doubt Hume differs from Berkeley in believing that there are things in themselves, i.e. some sort of unknown natural order behind phenomenal space and time, but he is like Berkeley in denying that we can conceive of a space or time which is sense-independent.

Hume's discussion of space, then, is not at all concerned with scepticism about reason, but with just the same general issues as Bayle and Berkeley have in mind, the problem of the external world. With respect to this problem, his position is sceptical, although his scepticism concerns essence rather than existence. That is made even more plain in Section 6, on the ideas of existence and external existence. The section may look like an irrelevant appendage, awkwardly linked to what has gone before. Yet here is spelt out the principle which the whole account of space and time has illustrated, that ' 'tis impossible for us so much as to conceive or form an idea of anything specifically different from ideas and impressions'. The best we can do towards thinking of external objects 'when suppos'd *specifically* different from our perceptions', i.e., as they are in themselves, 'is to form a relative idea of them, without pretending to comprehend the related objects'. 'Generally speaking', Hume continues, 'we do not suppose them specifically different; but only attribute to them different relations, connections and durations' (1978:67f). Thus the chapter on space and time has a primarily sceptical purpose, and leads naturally into the rather better known discussion, 'Of scepticism of the senses', a transition which Hume himself marks by an explicit forward reference to Part iv Section 2.

Scepticism of the senses

Is this later discussion as indebted to Berkeley as the earlier one? I believe that it is, although once again in order to give an accurate estimate of the relationship it is probably helpful to set both philosophers in a wider context and to examine other possibilities. Those who see Malebranche, rather than Berkeley, as the major influence on Hume's theory of perception might draw attention to Malebranche's conception of 'natural judgements' somehow embodied in sensations. These 'natural judgements' (which are immediate descendants of Descartes' 'teachings of nature') are held to be demonstrably flawed, and yet to be of practical value. The feeling that pain is in the hand, the appearance of colours on objects and so forth are false but useful. At the same time Malebranche, rather like Hume, offers to explain how false natural judgements can serve as the premises of philosophical theories, in particular of the Aristotelian doctrine of substantial forms. With the help of a fertile imagination, the errors of the senses give rise to 'all the other most general errors of school metaphysics' (Malebranche 1980:74f; 1945:81f). These broad resemblances between Malebranche and Hume are perhaps fairly unremarkable by themselves, if only because a conception of natural belief and the 'errors of the senses' is a general feature of Cartesian philosophy, while Descartes himself is not averse to offering insulting explanations of the errors, not only of the scholastics, but of materialism and atomism. Moreover, the structure of Malebranche's epistemology is thoroughly Cartesian in ways which differentiate him sharply from Hume. For example, he holds that sensations themselves do not err, but that we err when by a 'free judgement' we assent to the material for judgement supplied by sensation. It is this 'material for judgement' which Malebranche calls the 'natural judgement', although he warns us that it is not strictly a judgement at all, but a 'compound sensation' (1980:34; 1945:37f).

There is another line of Malebranche's thought, however, which might seem to bring him peculiarly close to Hume. First, he distinguishes between the sun and stars in the sky and the sun and stars which we immediately perceive. The two must be distinct, he holds, because it is self-evident that the soul cannot immediately perceive objects which are distant from it. He continues:

Now given that the stars immediately joined to the soul (which are the only stars it can see) are not in the heavens, it follows that everyone who sees the stars in the heavens and then voluntarily judges they are there performs two judgements, one of which is natural, the other free.   (1980:68; 1945:74)

In other words, when we accept our natural judgement, 'these same stars that are immediately seen are thought to be external to the soul and in the heavens'. Hume puts a very similar view when he claims that, for the vulgar, 'Those very sensations, which enter by the eye or ear, are with them the true objects' (1978:202). It might therefore seem reasonable to speculate that Hume took over this conception of the vulgar or natural belief from Malebranche, but rejected the notion that it could be corrected by reason, going on to give modern attempts to achieve such a corrected view of things-in-themselves broadly the same sort of insulting explanation as Malebranche reserves for Aristotelian doctrine. The distinction between the immediately perceived sun and the real sun is revealed as an irrational stratagem of the imagination, while the mechanical philosophy, so dear to Malebranche, is shown in its turn to be in nearly as bad a position as the grossly fanciful ancient philosophy. Consequently we have to fall back on our irrational, but practically useful, natural judgements, on action in place of theory, as sceptics had often recommended before Hume.

Such an interpretation of Hume's relationship to Malebranche is not groundless. The section, 'Of the ancient philosophy', for example, is strongly reminiscent of Malebranche's strictures on the fanciful errors of scholasticism. Nevertheless, as it stands, the interpretation exaggerates their relationship. That is not just because Hume's specific arguments are not those of Malebranche; or because, in his attack on realism, Hume never seems to have Malebranche's idiosyncratic position specifically in mind. An influence does not have to be total in order to be an influence. The point is rather that to relate Hume directly and solely to Malebranche in this way is to leave Berkeley out of account. For Berkeley's theory can also be seen as (among other things) a response to Malebranche, and we may reasonably assume that Hume recognized that relationship. No doubt he was fully aware of the affinity which exists between Descartes' and Malebranche's 'natural judgements' and his own notion of natural belief. But he could hardly have failed to realize that Berkeley's arguments constitute a considerable development of the notion that the vulgar draw no distinction between the immediate object of perception and the external or independent object; or that Berkeley already manages neatly to combine a partly critical attitude towards the vulgar view with a diagnosis of the causes of the errors of realist metaphysics. There is nothing in the resemblance between Hume and Malebranche to prevent us from supposing that Hume saw Berkeley's arguments as a significant advance towards the truth in these matters.

Berkeley's attitude towards the vulgar view of the sensible world has been the subject of some controversy, commentators disagreeing as to whether he is, either in fact or in intent, a defender of common sense. The dispute is an odd one, since he is so careful to explain his final estimate of the vulgar view: people ordinarily believe a mixture of truth and falsity. In its more formal or self-conscious exposition, this estimate is balanced by a similar estimate of philosophical realism. The thought that his own theory combines the truth in both sides of the opposition between the vulgar and the philosophical views is prominently employed in the summary which brings the *Three Dialogues* to an end.

I do not pretend to be a setter-up of *new notions*. My endeavours tend only to unite and place in a clearer light that truth, which was before shared between the vulgar and the philosophers: the former being of opinion, that, *those things they immediately perceive are the real things*; and the latter, that *the things immediately perceived, are ideas which exist only in the mind*. Which two notions put together do in effect constitute the substance of what I advance.   (1964:262)

Effectively the same thought is expressed, if less explicitly, early on in the *Principles*, but two later sections convey a more overt, and at the same time more discerning, response to realist doctrine. In Section 55f, Berkeley first dismisses the argument from universal consent for the existence of external things, and then offers to 'assign a cause of this prejudice'. His explanation follows Malebranche, except that externality is understood non-spatially: because ideas of sense are involuntary, people adopt the self-contradictory assumption that they exist 'independent of, and without the mind'. He continues:

But philosophers having plainly seen, that the immediate objects of perception do not exist without the mind, they in some degree corrected the mistake of the vulgar, but at the same time run into another which seems no less absurd, to wit that there are certain objects really existing without the mind, or having a subsistence distinct from being perceived, of which our ideas are only images or resemblances imprinted by those objects on the mind. And this notion of the philosophers owes its origin to the same cause with the former, namely their being conscious that they were not the authors of their own sensations . . . which therefore must have some cause, distinct from the minds on which they are imprinted.   (1964:64f)

The object of attack here is the distinction between the idea in the mind and the sensible quality which resembles it, a distinction which Berkeley apparently sees as constructed to satisfy a combination of insights, in the absence of the insight that the external cause of sensations is God. But that distinction is only a part of realist metaphysics. In Section 73 he offers a similar causal diagnosis of the belief in material substance. Again he starts from the vulgar view 'that colour, figure, motion, and the rest of the sensible qualities or accidents, did really exist without the mind'. This very belief made it seem 'needful to suppose some unthinkable *substratum* or *substance* wherein they did exist, since they could not be conceived to exist by themselves' (1964:72f). In other words, philosophers arrived at the notion of material substance because they recognized that sensible qualities are dependent, but did not get so far as to see that (being ideas) they are mind-dependent. The whole story allows, of course, for a combination of the previously explained resemblance-theory with this doctrine of an unthinking support. It is further developed in the same section, to account for the distinction between primary and secondary qualities. We may notice that Aristotelian doctrines play no role in the story. Berkeley was hardly interested in Malebranche's chief targets.

Berkeley's explanation of vulgar and philosophical errors constitute a central, structural element in his philosophy. A precise estimate of the weakness and strength of natural belief was, it is true, just as important to Cartesian philosophy. Yet even in the case of Malebranche, Cartesian explanations of rival philosophical doctrines seem little more than *ad hoc* polemics. Berkeley, on the other hand, saw the truth as revealed in the dialectical relationship between the vulgar view and philosophical views. The dialectic is externalized in the *Three Dialogues*. In the *First Dialogue*, for example, Hylas is introduced as a believer in material substance, but to begin with he is carefully portrayed as holding just the view characterized in the first part of *Principles* 1.73. For the philosophical belief in material substance is combined in Hylas with two supposedly vulgar beliefs: first, that 'sensible things are those only which are immediately perceived by the senses', and, second, that sensible things have 'a real absolute being, distinct from, and without any relation to their being perceived' (1964:175). Hylas is then gradually driven by Philonous, first to try to distinguish between primary and secondary qualities,[7] and then, near the end of the dialogue, to draw the philosophical distinction between immediately perceived ideas and mediately perceived qualities which resemble and give rise to them. Hylas lives out a version of Berkeley's explanation of vulgar and philosophical beliefs. Readers who have failed to grasp this careful dialectical structure may understandably be irritated and bewildered by what C. J. Warnock has denounced as the 'extraordinary assumption' involved in the early argument of the *First Dialogue* – i.e. the first component of the vulgar view, together with such implications as that 'Each visible object hath that colour which we see in it' (Berkeley 1964:183). To recognize the structure is to recognize the inappropriateness of Warnock's reaction.[8]

The course of Berkeley's dialectic is followed rather closely, *mutatis mutandis*, by Hume's argument in his three sections on scepticism of the senses, the ancient philosophy and the modern philosophy. *Treatise* 1.iv.2 begins with an analysis or explanation of the vulgar or primarily natural view, 'the doctrine of the independent existence of our sensible perceptions' (1978:187–210). This explanation is a lot more complicated than Berkeley's, and in a moment I shall consider why. Hume then moves on to the philosophical critique of the vulgar view, a critique which produces an uneasiness only resolved by the philosophical distinction between impressions and resembling sensible qualities (1978:210, 218). The explanation of the doctrine of substance is reserved for the section on ancient philosophy, a difference from Berkeley which is perhaps a manifestation of Hume's historical conscience, but which also enables him to append something corresponding to Malebranche's explanation of substantial forms and other Aristotelian principles. The section 'Of the

---

[7] An official diagnosis of the source of the allegedly bogus distinction is given (Berkeley 1964:191), but the course of Hylas' argument up to that point constitutes another such diagnosis more in accord with the argument employed by Hume.

[8] Warnock's reproof is significantly condescending: 'It is fortunately not necessary for us to examine these arguments in detail. It must be admitted that Berkeley handles them with much less than his usual ability' (1969:147).

modern philosophy' gives a similar treatment to the distinction between primary and secondary qualities (1978:225–31).

There are, of course, considerable differences of purpose from Berkeley. The true philosophy is not for Hume the neat combination of the elements of truth in each of the vulgar and the philosophical systems. It is rather the scepticism which arises when both systems are seen as the irrational and incoherent products of the imagination. The explanation of error is no longer an aspect of the process of sifting out truth, it is itself a part of the only substantive theory being advanced. That theory is a psychological theory of the imagination, a doctrine on quite a different level from either vulgar or philosophical views of the external world. The sources of Hume's theory of the imagination do not include very much of Berkeley, but consist in the conflicting attitudes to the imagination in the seventeenth century and the long-continuing dispute over the existence of a pure intellect. Hobbes brilliantly employed the notion of principles governing 'the consequence or train of imaginations' to explain both prudent expectation and rational science (1651:8–22). Cartesians, on the other hand, while allowing the imagination some utility as a stimulus to the intellect (e.g., in the visualization of geometrical figures), saw it as incapable of affording knowledge or scientific understanding. Similarly, the association of ideas may give rise to useful inclinations, but is liable to become a major source of error (Malebranche 1980:130–97; 1945:140–211). Locke, no friend of pure intellect but also no friend of unthinking belief, concurred in this derogatory estimate of association (1975:394–401). Hume could be said in a way to have combined Hobbesian and Cartesian viewpoints. Sense and imagination cover for him, as for Hobbes, the whole field of cognition, but except in a very limited area the product is not for Hume knowledge. It is rather belief which, in being at best unfounded and more generally absurd, fully satisfies (except in being involuntary) the Cartesian conception of error. Perhaps the only analogy with Berkeley in all this lies in Hume's readiness to see beliefs arising as ways of resolving tensions between opposite inclinations. Yet the irrelevance of Berkeley to Hume's associationism does not call into question the presence of a Berkeleyan framework in Hume's thinking about perception. It shows only that Hume has done something un-Berkeleyan within that framework.

The 'Berkeleyan framework' seems, indeed, to be much richer than I have so far proposed. For example, the discussion of the connection between continued existence and distinct or independent existence (Hume 1978:188) is reminiscent of what has come to be called the 'continuity argument' of the *Second* and *Third Dialogues* (Berkeley 1964:212–15, 230f). A second instance lies in Hume's point that 'our sight informs us not of distance or outness (so to speak) immediately and without a certain reasoning and experience' (1978:191). This is of course a Berkeleyan principle expressed in Berkeleyan language, although it is one that Berkeley himself introduces as agreed by all (Berkeley 1967:171).[9] More importantly, Hume interprets it in a Berkeleyan way for an immediate purpose close to Berkeley's own. Malebranche, who is sometimes thought to be the writer in Hume's mind, deals with the perception of distance in very different (and phenomenologically more plausible) terms. For him, the judgement of distance is immediate in the sense that it is a 'natural judgement' actually embodied in sensation or sense-perception. The postulation of antecedent 'reasoning' on the part of the soul is, he warns, a kind of fiction, introduced simply in order to elucidate the laws by which God produces the sensory perception of distance (1980:46f; 1945:52).

Evidence of another link with Berkeley lies in the overtones of Hume's characterization of the theory of the 'double existence of perceptions and objects'. Not to say anything more about the uneasiness which on Hume's account gives rise to the theory, the reason he gives why the postulated external sensible qualities are taken to resemble internal perceptions is because 'we can never conceive anything but perceptions, and therefore must make every thing resemble them' (1978:216). The Berkeleyan connections of this principle have been considered above under the topic of space and time. Even more significantly, the postulation of sensible qualities is described by Hume as the invention of 'a new set of perceptions', since it is 'impossible for us distinctly to conceive, objects to be in their nature any thing but exactly the same with perceptions' (1978:218). It is difficult not to be reminded, by the combination of these statements, of Berkeley's arguments for his principle that 'an idea can be like nothing but an idea' (1964:44). Moreover Berkeley himself had argued, in effect, that the only possible continuous and independent 'archetypes' of our intermittent ideas of sense must themselves be ideas, namely ideas in the mind of God.

Perhaps a more impressive indication of the place of Berkeley in Hume's thought consists in the recurrence of a certain pattern in Hume's argument which only appears if we relate it to Berkeley's. The first example of this pattern occurs when Hume expressly denies that the involuntariness of our impressions is a cause of our belief in their independence (1978:194). Here, of course, he departs from both Berkeley and Malebranche, and in effect from a long line of realists. Berkeley himself, in a passage in the *Third*

---

[9] Unsurprisingly, it has been held (Conroy 1969) that Hume owes the word 'outness', not to Berkeley, but to Thomas Taylor's translation of Malebranche. Yet Taylor uses the plural 'outnesses' to translate *des dehors*, while Hume and Berkeley share the phrase 'distance or outness' (Berkeley 1964:58). Dare one add that we can be sure that Hume read Berkeley with some care, whereas there is no particular reason to suppose that he had read Taylor? (Cf. Hall 1968; 1970; Wright 1983:77.)

Dialogue (1964:235) which might possibly have served as a hint to Hume, significantly qualifies his reliance on the criterion of involuntariness. For he has to fall back on the regularity and connectedness of 'real' or independent ideas of sense in order to distinguish them from 'lively and natural' dreams. Hume does not refer to dreams but points out that we do not regard pain as external, despite its involuntariness. Having dismissed the claims of sense and reason to be the source of our belief in the externality of objects, he offers the provisional explanation that it is the constancy and coherence of our impressions which produce the belief by acting on the imagination (1978:194–7).

The pattern which I have in mind is simply this. Having rejected a Berkeleyan explanation of a certain belief because that explanation is in conflict with his own general theory, Hume replaces it with another explanation which serves the same purpose. In this case, as it happens, the alternative is something equally reminiscent of Berkeley. But it seems clear enough that the Berkeleyan thought that what is not caused by my will must be independent of me is at odds with Hume's official account of ordinary causal reasoning, and so could not be admitted into his account of why we believe in independent objects.

At this point, however, Hume finds fault in turn with the proposal that constancy and coherence together determine which impressions are taken to be independent and continuous (1978:197f). They could do so only if they gave rise to a habit or custom 'of the same nature with our reasonings concerning causes and effects'. The problem is that there are no appropriately regular conjunctions of impressions or sensations. What regularity there is is such that 'the turning about of our head, or the shutting of our eyes is able to break it'. Why then should we 'bestow on [*scil.* external] objects a greater regularity than what is observ'd in our mere perceptions'? The explanation cannot be habit, for the habit would have to be 'a habit acquir'd by what was never present to the mind'. Roughly, Hume is pointing out that causal laws never hold (and are never supposed to hold) between our sensations or 'perceptions' as such, but are supposed to hold between items in the external world. The possible implications of this move for Hume's treatment of causality lie beyond our present concern, but it certainly refutes a view which only one philosopher, so far as I know, had ever adopted. It is Berkeley who seems entirely happy to talk as if our *ideas* occur 'in a regular train of series' according to 'the set rules or established methods . . . called the *Laws of Nature*' (1964:30, 36). Hume's point in effect demolishes the premise of Berkeley's attempt to give a theistic explanation of ideas of sense, but also constitutes something of a turning-point in his whole argument. For 'causal reasoning', although attributed by him to irrational habit, nevertheless retains a certain honorific status in his system, if only because induction seems intrinsically more reasonable than his theory can officially allow. It is therefore a moment of considerable significance when he insists that such 'reasoning' (as he freely calls it) makes only a limited contribution to our belief in the external world. Unsurprisingly, he proceeds to complete the explanation of that belief by means of principles of the imagination which are not only unreasonable but involve the allegedly incoherent notion of identity over time and through change. For Hume, the vulgar or natural view, quite as much as philosophical doctrine, involves an attempt by the mind to make itself easy in the face of 'a kind of contradiction' (1978:198–210).

The same general pattern appears again in the explanation of the beliefs of philosophers. Berkeley sees the philosophical recognition of the dependence of sensible things as essentially metaphysical, an intuitive glimpse of the ontological relationship between ideas and spiritual substances. But it is of the essence of Hume's enterprise that he can allow no such relationships. So once again he takes the trouble to deny Berkeley's explanation: i.e. to deny the principle that, as Berkeley puts it, the *esse* of sensible things is *percipi* or, as Hume prefers to say, 'the *appearance* of a perception in the mind and its *existence* [are] the same' (Hume 1978:206). He agrees that it can seem 'at first sight' a palpable contradiction to suppose a perception to exist without being present to the mind. But he argues that, since the mind itself is nothing but distinct perceptions extrinsically related, there is in fact no contradiction in the vulgar belief in the unperceived continuity of 'the very being which is intimately present to the mind'. This move, essential as it is to Hume's anti-metaphysical programme, leaves a gap to be filled, for he needs to find an alternative basis for the philosophers' insight that impressions are after all dependent on the perceiver. He finds it, very neatly, in familiar sceptical topics which he can present as further causal reasoning: i.e., in the so-called 'experiments' demonstrating that perceptions vary with variations in the perceiver (1978:210f). Thus Berkeley's conception of an *a priori* ontological dependence is replaced, as Hume's wider purposes demand, by an empirically ascertained causal dependence. Otherwise the argument follows Berkeley.

For Berkeley, as we have seen, the philosophers' intuition of the metaphysical dependence of 'sensible things' explains not only the distinction which they draw between mind-dependent ideas and external qualities, but their doctrine of material substance, the postulated 'unthinking support' of qualities perceived as themselves dependent. Consequently, in his own explanation of the philosophical notion of substance, Hume must once again look for an alternative to the Berkeleyan explanation. He finds it in other elements of the tradition: the 'substance, or original and first matter', is the unchanging substrate of qualitative change (1978:220). As such, it is a fiction of the imagination arrived at in order to reconcile the belief in identity with evident alteration. The associated notion of substance as simple and unitary, the distinction between form and matter, and the notion of the support of accidents and occult qualities, then receive separate and careful attention (1978:221–4). All these themes, of course, although originally Aristotelian, permeate seventeenth-century metaphysics.

Finally, in the section 'Of the modern philosophy' (1978:225–31), Hume attributes the mechanists' distinction between primary and secondary qualities (by contrast with the heated visions of ancient philosophy) to the most natural and healthy of the principles of the imagination, i.e. causal 'reasoning'. The presentation of this reasoning (1978:226f) is strongly reminiscent of the *First Dialogue*. The single argument brought to rebut it is an extended and elaborate exposition of the claim that primary qualities cannot be conceived in separation from secondary qualities. The emphasis Hume places on solidity may be somewhat un-Berkeleyan, yet it remains highly plausible that, as the *First Enquiry* acknowledges, 'This argument is drawn from Dr. Berkeley' (1957:155).

Conclusion

There are many other 'traces of Berkeley' in Book 1 of the *Treatise*. I have focussed on those which seem particularly relevant to Hume's statement that Berkeley unintentionally offers 'the best lessons of scepticism'. For I take it that this statement is Hume's considered acknowledgment of what he himself had chiefly drawn from Berkeley's arguments. On the one hand an analysis of the deep connections between their doctrines enables us to see clearly the sceptical significance of Hume's somewhat neglected and mysterious discussion of extension and infinite divisibility. On the other hand it supplies an indispensable key to some of the twists and turns of one of his most intricate and bewildering arguments. If the analysis is accepted, it can hardly be denied that the relationship between the two philosophers is important. Yet is that enough to resurrect the 'standard' view of 'British Empiricism'? I do not think so, but it ought to be enough to demolish the standard reaction to that view.

There are three things chiefly wrong with the 'standard view'. First, it is exclusive, underrating other connections. Second, it is relatively unconcerned with the overall *purposes* of the individuals Locke, Berkeley and Hume, and is still less concerned with the subtler features of those purposes. Finally, and perhaps most importantly, it is institutionalized. On the first two matters it is easily, indeed it is already, overthrown. It is the last matter, very likely, which accounts for the peculiarly long-drawn-out expression of hostility to the standard view. It is significant that one notable recent antagonist relies on an account of his own personal experience as a student and teacher, rather than on citations from the books and articles of leading contemporary historians of philosophy, in order to persuade us that the 'standard view' is a devil still needing to be exorcized (Loeb 1981:13–18).[10] But there are more ways, and more direct ways, of changing a syllabus than by flogging Popkin's dead cause in works on the history of ideas. We hear a good deal about the influence of institutions on the history of thought, but we need to be careful that a reaction to our own institutions does not distort our historical judgement. It would be a curious irony if, in the years to come, the reason why universities continue to offer courses on the 'Rationalists' and the 'British Empiricists' is to enable their professors to rehearse a set of bad standard arguments that such categories do not exist.

APPENDIX

Passmore (1980) begins his chapter on Hume 'the phenomenalist' with a judicious air, suggesting that the reaction against the Reid–Green interpretation may have gone too far, since it is 'still necessary to insist on the importance of the "theory of ideas" in Hume's philosophy'. His recognition of a relationship never descends from this level of generality, however, whereas he freely argues and speculates in some detail on the other side.

Somehow the issue is one which betrays the judgement even of very distinguished historians of philosophy. Passmore himself declares that 'Malebranche was very much more to Hume's taste' than Berkeley. For Hume 'does not conceal his high opinion of what he calls "The glory of Malebranche"'. Passmore's argument ends confidently: 'Probably he thought, as Reid did, that "Bishop Berkeley's arguments are found in [Malebranche] in their full force": hence Berkeley (on most matters) could be safely neglected.' Yet 'glory' simply means *fame*, and it is odd not to mention Hume's praise of Berkeley here. In Passmore's spirit of intuitive speculation, why not argue that 'Berkeley was more to Hume's taste than Malebranche. For "the glory of Malebranche is confined to his own nation, and to his own age," whereas Berkeley is, without qualification, "a great philosopher"'? Yet even such rules as this pastime possesses (truly, to borrow A. E. Housman's analogy, more like the rules of spitting than the rules of cricket) are surely transcended when a quotation from Reid (of all people) is employed with the implication that Hume must have been dissembling when he proposed Berkeley, and not Malebranche, as the 'very ingenious author' of 'the best lessons of scepticism'.

To take another example of special pleading, several writers are impressed by the supposedly impressive fact that Hume 'does not even bother to argue against

---

[10] Much of Loeb's discussion of the way in which Locke, Berkeley and Hume are institutionally conjoined is fair and sensible comment.

Berkeley at [some? any?] points where he disagrees with him' (Passmore 1980:87; cf. Popkin 1959b:543 and Loeb 1981:90, 360). Again there is no thought of what would happen if we applied this kind of argument generally. Where, for example, does Hume attack Malebranche on the point that we see all things in God? If the claim is that Hume *never* argues against a Berkeleyan doctrine, then (as we have seen) it is rather frequently and obviously falsified.

Another popular negative argument is that Berkeley is mentioned by name only three times in Hume's published works (Popkin 1959:536f; Flew 1980:260). In discussing Hume's direct references to any philosophers it should be evident that we are dealing with numbers too small to be statistically significant. Besides, for any such argument to have force we should need to consider possible special motives for Hume's choosing to name, or not to name, any particular author on any particular occasion. E.g., he presumably appeals to the names of Berkeley and Huet in *Letter from a Gentleman* (1967:21, 26, 30) because they are both churchmen of the highest reputation.

It is true that some interpretive arguments must take risks, and that vulnerable speculation has an honourable part to play. Extreme claims can sometimes help to break new ground. Popkin himself confessed later that he had originally written 'in fear and trembling' in case of the discovery of such firm contrary evidence as did in fact emerge (although that emotion was well enough disguised). What is odd, however, and surely so odd as to call for explanation, is that inconclusive and risky arguments are repeated long after they have been exposed as such, and even after they have been factually refuted (e.g. by the letter published in Popkin 1964. No weight can be placed on the letter of Morrisroe 1973 as long as it is unavailable to resolve any doubts about its authenticity which may be raised by phraseology or other considerations.) Years after it was established that Hume recommended Berkeley as propaedeutic to his own arguments, Loeb has claimed that Hume's failure to attack Berkeley's conception of spiritual substance raises the question 'Did Hume ever read Berkeley, and if so did he take him seriously?' (Loeb 1981:90, 360). Yet nothing short of evidence of forgery can now raise *that* question. The only justification for raking over the old controversy, even in the decent obscurity of an appendix, is to reiterate that point in the face of rhetoric like Loeb's. What is needed is a re-examination of Hume's arguments in the light of the strong direct evidence that he saw Berkeley as a source of important ideas having a certain definite relationship to his own. Popkin's intransigent question, 'Why is there so little trace of Berkeley in Hume's writings?' (1964:778) is based on no such re-examination. A more pertinent and historiographically more interesting question is why so many claims have been made about Hume's supposed independence of Berkeley without any close comparative analysis of their arguments. The attitude can be viciously self-supporting: 'In the absence of significant internal evidence entitling one to consider Hume as a development from Berkeley, I see no point in exploring the differences and similarities between Hume and Berkeley on abstract ideas' (Bracken 1974:38). How widespread it is can readily be discovered by pursuing the meagre references to Berkeley in the indexes of recent monographs and collections on Hume. Since the present essay was written, however, two works provide welcome evidence that analytical comparison of the two philosophers is at last ceasing to be unfashionable (Raynor 1983, Wright 1983).

REFERENCES

Arnauld, A., and Nicole, P. 1964. *The Art of Thinking: Port-Royal Logic*, translated by J. Dickoff and P. James. Indianapolis: Bobbs-Merrill

Arnauld, A., and Nicole, P. 1965. *La Logique ou l'Art de Penser*, edited by P. Clair and F. Girbal. Paris: Presses Universitaires de France (first published 1662)

Ayers, M. R. 1981. 'Berkeley's immaterialism and Kant's transcendental idealism', in *Idealism Past and Present*, edited by G. Vesey. Cambridge: Cambridge University Press, 51–69

Bayle, P. 1710. *An Historical and Critical Dictionary*, translated into English for J. Tonson. London

Bayle, P. 1730. *Dictionnaire Historique et Critique*, fourth edition, vol. IV. Amsterdam

Berkeley, G. 1964. *The Works of George Berkeley Bishop of Cloyne*, vol. II, edited by A. A. Luce. London: Nelson

Berkeley, G. 1967. *The Works of George Berkeley Bishop of Cloyne*, vol. I, edited by T. E. Jessop. London: Nelson

Bracken, H. M. 1974. *Berkeley*. London: Macmillan

Bracken, H. M. 1977. 'Bayle, Berkeley and Hume', *Eighteenth-Century Studies* 11:227–45

Conroy, G. P. 1969. 'Did Hume really follow Berkeley?', *Philosophy* 44:238–42

Flew, A. 1980. *Hume's Philosophy of Belief: A Study of his First Inquiry*. London: Routledge (first published 1961)

Green, T. H., and Grose, T. H. 1882. 'Preliminary Dissertation', *A Treatise of Human Nature*, by David Hume. London: Longman's (first published 1874)

Hall, R. 1968. 'Hume's actual use of Berkeley's *Principles*', *Philosophy* 43:278–80

Hall, R. 1970. 'Yes, Hume did use Berkeley', *Philosophy* 45:152–3

Hobbes, T. 1651. *Leviathan or the Matter Form and Power of a Commonwealth Ecclesiastical and Civil*. London (facsimile, Menston: Scolar Press: 1972)

Hume, D. 1957. *Enquiries concerning the Human Understanding and concerning the Principles of Morals*, edited by L. A. Selby-Bigge. Oxford: Oxford University Press (first published 1748–51)

Hume, D. 1967. *A Letter from a Gentleman to his friend in Edinburgh*, edited by E. C. Mossner and J. V. Price. Edinburgh: Edinburgh University Press (first published 1745)

Hume, D. 1978. *A Treatise of Human Nature*, edited by L. A. Selby-Bigge, second edition revised by P. H. Nidditch. Oxford: Oxford University Press (first published 1739–40)

Hutcheson, F. 1728. *An Essay on the Nature and Conduct of the Passions and Affections, with Illustrations on the Moral Sense*. London (facsimile, Menston: Scolar Press 1972)

Hutcheson, F. 1742. *Metaphysicae Synopsis: Ontologiam et Pneumatologiam Complectans*. Glasgow

Kemp Smith, N. 1905. 'The naturalism of Hume', *Mind* new series 14:149–73 and 335–47

Kemp Smith, N. 1964. *The Philosophy of David Hume: A Critical Study of its Origins and Central Doctrines*. London: Macmillan (first published 1941)

Laing, B. M. 1932. *David Hume*. London: Benn

Locke, J. 1975. *An Essay Concerning Human Understanding*, edited by P. H. Nidditch. Oxford: Oxford University Press (first published 1690)

Loeb, L. E. 1981. *From Descartes to Hume: Continental Metaphysics and the Development of Modern Philosophy*. Ithaca: Cornell University Press

Malebranche, N. 1945. *De la Recherche de la Vérité*, edited by G. Lewis, vol. I. Paris: J. Vrin (first published 1674–5)

Malebranche, N. 1980. *The Search after Truth*, translated by T. M. Lennon and P. J. Olscamp, with *Elucidations of the Search after Truth*, translated by T. M. Lennon. Columbus: Ohio State University Press

Morrisroe, M. 1973. 'Did Hume read Berkeley? A conclusive answer', *Philological Quarterly* 52:310–15

Mossner, E. C. 1959. 'Did Hume ever read Berkeley? A rejoinder to Professor Popkin', *Journal of Philosophy* 56:992–5

Norton, D. F. 1982. *David Hume: Common-Sense Moralist and Sceptical Metaphysician*. Princeton: Princeton University Press

Passmore, J. 1980. *Hume's Intentions*. London: Duckworth (first published 1952)

Popkin, R. H. 1959a. 'Review of Boas, *Dominant Themes of Modern Philosophy*', *Journal of Philosophy* 56:67–71

Popkin, R. H. 1959b. 'Did Hume ever read Berkeley?', *Journal of Philosophy* 56:535–45

Popkin, R. H. 1964. 'So, Hume did read Berkeley', *Journal of Philosophy* 61:773–8

Raynor, D. 1980. '"Minima Sensibilia" in Berkeley and Hume', *Dialogue* 19:196–9

Raynor, D. 1983. 'The role of imagination in Hume's philosophy', D. Phil. Thesis, University of Oxford

Reid, T. 1785. *Essays on the Intellectual Powers of Man*. Edinburgh (facsimile, Menston: Scolar Press, undated)

Warnock, G. J. 1969. *Berkeley*. Harmondsworth: Penguin Books (first published 1953)

Wright, J. P. 1983. *The Sceptical Realism of David Hume*. Manchester: Manchester University Press

◁ ═══ ▷

14

Frege: the early years

HANS SLUGA

I Introduction

I, Friedrich Ludwig Gottlob Frege, was born at Wismar on November 8, 1848. My father Alexander, who was principal of a girls' high school there, was taken from me by death in the year 1866. My mother Auguste, née Bialloblotzki, is still alive. I was educated in the Lutheran faith. After attending grammar school in my hometown for fifteen years I graduated from it at Easter 1869 and spent two years at Jena and five semesters at Göttingen on mathematical, physical, chemical, and philosophical studies. In Göttingen I received the Ph.D.   (Frege 1967:84)

This short statement, appended to Frege's *Habilitationsschrift* of 1874, is exceptional in his body of writing for its autobiographical character. Because of Frege's general reticence about himself and because he became famous only decades after his death we no longer possess much information about Frege's life. The statement I have quoted is therefore particularly significant since it draws our attention to Frege's intellectual development before he conceived of his philosophical projects.

My concern here is with that early period of Frege's development. I want to ask what mathematical, scientific, and philosophical ideas he was exposed to and how they shaped the conception and construction of his new logic.

In answering those questions I want to show that Frege developed a conception of the overall organization of human knowledge in the years preceding the *Begriffsschrift* and that his interest in logic and in the project of the reduction of arithmetic to logic was entirely motivated by that conception. Michael Dummett has argued that the whole of modern philosophy from Descartes onwards was dominated by the idea of the primacy of epistemology. According to him it was Frege and the early Wittgenstein who restored logic to the foundational place in philosophy (a place it had previously held within the medieval scholastic tradition). For that reason Frege marks for Dummett a deep discontinuity in the development of philosophy (Dummett 1973:xv; 1978:441).

Dummett is surely right in observing that in the last hundred years logic has regained an importance in philosophy which it has not had since the decline of scholastic philosophy. Dummett's picture of the course of modern philosophy is nevertheless in need of emendation and that for two reasons. The first is that logic was, of course, never forgotten during the period from Descartes to Frege and that there were philosophers within that period who ascribed to logic the role of first philosophy (e.g., Leibniz). While Frege and the early Wittgenstein were, probably, instrumental in promoting that view of logic their efforts must be seen in the context of a large development of which they were part, but which they did not originate by themselves. That development was the rapid mathematization of science in the nineteenth century – including the mathematization of logic.

The second reason for treating Dummett's account with caution is that the claim that logic is in some sense primary or foundational to the rest of philosophy is, of course, itself a claim about the nature of human knowledge, and thus in a wider sense an epistemological claim. Looked at in this way Frege's belief in the primacy of logic is not at all discontinuous with the modern tradition beginning with Descartes, but of a piece with it. It is in this sense that Richard Rorty has written: 'The kind of philosophy which stems from Russell and Frege is, like classical Husserlian phenomenology, simply one more attempt to put philosophy in the position which Kant wished it to have – that of judging other areas of culture on the basis of its special knowledge of the "foundations" of these areas' (Rorty 1979:8). Rorty's observation seems to me more correct here than Dummett's alternative.

In tracing the development of Frege's view of the overall structure of human knowledge in the period up to the *Begriffschrift* I hope to be able to show that his conception was, to some extent, the product of specific historical circumstances and that we should not unquestioningly adopt that conception as Dummett seems to do. Instead we must try to understand Frege's motivations for assigning philosophical primacy to logic, assess their validity, and, if necessary, form a different and more adequate picture of the organization of human knowledge and the place of logic in it.

II Frege in Jena

In the spring of 1869 Frege had enrolled as a student of mathematics at the University of Jena. That University was at the time, above all, a place with a distinguished past. At the turn of the eighteenth century it had been closely connected with the cultural centre at Weimar. Schiller, Fichte, Schelling, and Hegel had all taught at the University and its reputation had been very high. But because of financial problems it had failed to participate in the growth of science at other German universities and, as a consequence, had fallen behind. In 1869 it had fewer than 500 students and only eight chairs in the faculty of letters and science: five in the humanities, one in chemistry, one in biology, and one combining the three areas of mathematics, physics, and astronomy.

The holder of the latter chair was Karl Snell, a competent though unoriginal mathematician, whose main interest lay in philosophy, where he advanced anti-materialist and anti-evolutionary views of a spiritualist kind. There were nevertheless some outstanding members of the faculty, the most widely known being the biologist Ernst Häckel. He had come to Jena in 1865 already well-known as the most radical defender of Darwinian thought in Germany. At Jena he was known as a popular lecturer and a powerful force in the faculty. Nevertheless, there is no sign that Frege ever attended Häckel's lectures or had any other substantial contact with Häckel. But two other outstanding members of the faculty, the mathematician Ernst Abbe and the philosopher Kuno Fischer, were among his teachers.

Abbe was only eight years older than Frege, but already well-established in his career when Frege arrived in Jena in 1869. After studying mathematics at Jena and Göttingen, Abbe had received his doctorate at the age of twenty-one, and with Snell's support had quickly become an instructor at Jena. In 1871 he married one of Snell's daughters and, living in Snell's house, became part of the intellectual circle with which Snell had surrounded himself. Like his father-in-law Abbe had considerable philosophical interests, though unlike his father-in-law he never expressed them in print. As a student at Jena he had taken courses in the history of philosophy, in metaphysics, in logic and in aesthetics, the latter two given by Kuno Fischer. In Göttingen he is said to have worked with Hermann Lotze. In his Göttingen years he had also studied carefully the first edition of Fischer's book on Kant and had been deeply impressed by it.

Abbe's professional interests lay in the area of applied mathematics. That interest had brought him together with the University mechanical engineer Karl Zeiss, who was looking for someone who could provide better theoretical foundations for the construction of optical lenses. Abbe's collaboration with Zeiss led to his highly original work in optics and, in particular, the theory of the microscope. Zeiss and Abbe eventually became partners in a joint business enterprise which Abbe took over completely after Zeiss' death and, with unusual business acumen, turned into a world-famous optical instruments company; in a bold gesture, he also transformed the company into a foundation whose beneficiaries were the workers as well as the city and the University of Jena.

As a student at Jena Frege regularly attended Abbe's courses, hearing him on the theory of functions, on mechanics, on gravitation and electrodynamics, and also on experimental physics. Abbe in turn became Frege's faithful patron. After two years at Jena Frege went to study at the University of Göttingen, like Abbe before him, and worked there with some of Abbe's own former teachers. When he had obtained his PhD, Abbe called him back to Jena and got him appointed as a lecturer in mathematics. Later on he secured promotions for Frege and provided him with a regular salary out of funds of the Zeiss Foundation (Bynum 1972:3–8).

It is not easy to say what intellectual influence Abbe may have had on Frege's thought, since he never published anything that did not directly apply to the topic of mathematical optics. We can see some influence, perhaps, in Frege's consistently Kantian outlook; it is certainly visible in Frege's belief that scientific theories must be built on foundations of pure mathematics. Abbe's work in optics and the theory of the microscope had depended essentially on such a conviction. He had been convinced that the purely mathematical part of lens optics should be separated as sharply as possible from practical problems due to the quality of the glass employed and the process of lens grinding. It is also known that in his course on mechanics, which Frege attended, Abbe emphasized the need to separate the purely mathematical theory from questions of applied mechanics and that he considered the mathematical theory the foundation of the physical one. In Göttingen Abbe had studied the theory of functions with Bernard Riemann and it is said that in his own lectures on function theory (attended by Frege) he presented a further development of Riemann's own work in the field, but no notes are left of the Abbe lectures. Frege's interest in the theory of functions from the time of his *Habilitationsschrift* onwards and the fact that he subsequently built his logic around a generalized notion of function tie in very naturally with the interests of his teacher Abbe.

When Frege came to Jena in 1869 Kuno Fischer already had a national reputation as a dynamic and compelling lecturer on philosophical and literary topics. In 1872 Fischer was to receive a call to the University of Heidelberg, where he spent the rest of his academic year. Wilhelm Wundt, who was then at Heidelberg, wrote later in his memoirs:

When, after Zeller's departure, Kuno Fischer was called from Jena, the position of philosophy in the University underwent a complete transformation. In him a man had been appointed who could captivate the academic youth with his brilliant teaching and speaking talent and who, with his gift for the written and even more the spoken word, could create a newly awakening interest in philosophy in wider circles. Kuno Fischer was himself no outstanding philosopher, but he was an incomparable interpreter of the philosophers, particularly of German idealist philosophy from Kant onwards. (Wundt 1920:238f)

Fischer's fame rests today on a monumental history of modern philosophy on which he worked for more than fifty years. In 1869 he had just published, in two big volumes, the second edition of that part of his history which deals with Kant. Though some of its scholarship may be antiquated, the book is worth reading even today because of the clarity of its style and because of the convincing developmental picture of Kant which is drawn in it.

Fischer's book on Kant was also a strong re-affirmation of a long philosophical tradition at Jena (Wundt 1932). The University had long been a stronghold of Kantian ideas in Germany. Kant's philosophy had first been taught there around 1780. Early on, Jakob Friedrich Fries had combined Kant's thought with Lockean empiricism and had thereby initiated an important psychological and anthropological tradition of Kant interpretation. That tradition was to have a long life at Jena, and during Frege's student years was represented by the philosopher Carl Fortlage. From 1794, during Jena's philosophically most influential period, Fichte had taught at Jena for five years. His interpretation of Kant, more faithful than that of the psychological school to the master's own intentions, stressed the transcendental aspects of Kant's philosophy. Then in the period to 1819, Schelling, Hegel, and finally Oken all advanced metaphysical interpretations of Kant in their classes at Jena. With Fischer's arrival at Jena in 1856 interest in Kant's philosophy received a strong new impetus. In his own philosophical thinking (as it appears, for instance, in his book on logic) Fischer was greatly influenced by Hegel, but as a scholar he advanced once more the study of Kant's philosophy, moving beyond the psychological and the metaphysical interpretation of Kant once more to the transcendental one.

While he was a student at Jena, Frege took only one course in philosophy and that was Fischer's on Kant (Asser 1979:12). There is every reason to think that this was where the foundations of his understanding of Kant were laid, and we must therefore return to the question of what he may have learnt in that course.

III The Gaussian tradition

Before discussing the philosophical elements of Frege's thought it is important to examine his mathematical background, since his intellectual interests were at first predominantly mathematical.[1] During his student

---

[1] Paul Benacerraf has recently emphasized the mathematical and pragmatic elements in Frege's thought. My discussion owes much to his reflections. Cf. Benacerraf 1981.

years Frege enrolled in exactly two philosophy courses; all the others were in the fields of mathematics and natural science. In Göttingen, for instance, he took five courses in mathematics (three of them in geometry), five courses in physics (the majority in experimental physics), and only one course in philosophy (Bynum 1972; Asser 1979; Kratzsch 1979).

Frege's mathematical education was strongly rooted in the tradition of Carl Friedrich Gauss. Two of his teachers at Göttingen were directly linked to Gauss, who had spent many years at that University until his death in 1855 (Hall 1970). One of them was the physicist Wilhelm Weber, with whom Frege worked exclusively for a whole year in experimental physics. Weber had been Gauss' close friend and had collaborated with him in numerous scientific experiments (Wiederkehr 1976). The other was the mathematician Ernst Schering, who was to become Frege's dissertation supervisor. Schering was Gauss' official successor at the University observatory and the first editor of his collected works (Auerbach 1918). In addition Ernst Abbe, Frege's mentor, had also been a student of Weber and Schering as well as of Bernhard Riemann who, in turn, had been Gauss' student and had held Gauss' chair in mathematics before his death in 1866 (Auerbach 1918).

The Gaussian tradition was characterized by two main features: its emphasis on the need for greater precision in mathematics and its concern with the application of mathematics in science. Weber, Schering, and Abbe characteristically did all their work in applied mathematics and in mathematical physics. In contrast, the Gaussian tradition did not stress the need for a philosophical examination of mathematics. Gauss himself is said to have had very limited philosophical interests. Though he had admired Kant's *Critique*, he had completely rejected the Kantian claim that geometry and arithmetic are based on the *a priori* intuition of space and time. Instead he had considered geometrical truths empirical and arithmetical ones purely conceptual.

Gauss' emphasis on the logical rigour of the Greek mathematicians is reflected in Frege's own later writings. In the *Foundations of Arithmetic* he was to write:

After deserting for a time the old Euclidean standards of rigor, mathematics is now returning to them and even making efforts to go beyond them . . . In all directions these same ideals can be seen at work – rigor of proof, precise delimitation of extent of validity, and as a means to this, sharp definition of concepts.   (Frege 1884:1)

What we do not find in Frege's work is the interest in applied mathematics so characteristic of the Gaussian school. Given Frege's extensive training in experimental physics it is, in fact, surprising to find that he never pursued actual research in the natural sciences. Instead he developed an interest in the foundations of mathematics. The Gaussian concern with applied mathematics was nevertheless significant for this turn in Frege's thought. Given the fundamental role the Gaussian tradition assigned to mathematics in the sciences, it was natural for Frege to come to think of the question of the foundations of mathematics itself as basic to the understanding of the whole structure of human knowledge.

It is important to recall at this point that scientific experimentation was undergoing great change in the nineteenth century. It was extended to areas where it had not previously been used (i.e., the study of perception), new experimental techniques were being developed (using instruments made available by new technologies), and the use of mathematics was becoming more pervasive and more systematic in scientific research. We can see those tendencies clearly in the work of Weber. His reputation rests on his fame as an experimenter in the fields of magnetics and electrodynamics. He was particularly adept at inventing new measuring instruments, but at the same time his work involved a great deal of mathematics: the definition of suitable measuring units, the statistical description of measurements, and their correlation into mathematical equations expressing scientific laws.[2]

It is the idea that empirical science rests on foundations of pure mathematics, that empirical research involves the use of mathematical methods, which gives Frege's work on the foundations of mathematics its significance for him. He speaks in the *Foundations of Arithmetic* of 'the procedure of the sciences, with its objective standards' (1884:16) and interprets those standards as ultimately mathematical in character. Scientific laws are found by induction, but this induction is no mere habituation, as the empiricists maintain; scientific procedure 'will at times find a high probability established by a single confirmatory instance, while at others it will dismiss a thousand as almost worthless' (*ibid.*). Such a procedure can be explained only by assuming that induction is based on the theory of probability. 'But how probability theory could possibly be developed without presupposing arithmetical laws is beyond comprehension' (*ibid.*:16f). It follows then that the procedure of induction on which all empirical science relies 'can itself be justified only by general propositions of arithmetic' (*ibid.*).[3]

---

[2] The emergence of mathematical physics as a new discipline in the nineteenth century which must be separated from both the earlier experimentalist and the earlier mathematical tradition is discussed in Kuhn 1977. Kuhn refers to Wilhelm Weber's contribution to that process. We may conjecture that Weber's concern with the definition of measuring units has some bearing on Frege's later claim that the definition of unity is crucial to arithmetic. His later characterization of the real numbers as measuring numbers may also have suggested itself to him through Weber's work.

[3] Cf. Gauss' work on the theory of observational error and the theory of probability, briefly discussed in Hall 1970:73–83.

IV The faculty of intuition

Given Frege's predominantly mathematical and scientific training, it cannot surprise us that his philosophical interests developed slowly. Philosophical concerns are certainly marginal to his doctoral dissertation of 1873 and the *Habilitationsschrift* of 1874.

The former is devoted to a question arising out of analytic geometry. The equations with which we describe geometrical configurations yield at times imaginary rather than the expected real values. Thus, when we calculate the points at which a straight line lying outside a circle intersects that circle the analytic equations will determine those points as imaginary ones. Gauss had shown how complex numbers can be represented geometrically as points on a plane with a system of coordinates whose one axis represents real and whose other axis represents imaginary values. Frege's project in his dissertation was to find a general geometrical method for representing imaginary figures in real space. The problem had been attacked before him by Christian von Staudt (a student of Gauss), Otto Stolz, and Felix Klein (Staudt 1856–60; Stolz 1871; Klein 1872). Frege's attempt, while similar in motivation, is new in the details of its execution (which, however, will not concern us).

While most of the dissertation can be read as a piece of straightforward mathematics, there is at least one hint at a deeper philosophical motivation. That hint is found in the first, introductory sentence, which reads:

When one considers that the whole of geometry rests ultimately on axioms which derive their validity from the nature of our faculty of intuition (*Anschauungs-vermögen*), the question of the meaning of imaginary figures seem to be justified, since we ascribe to them properties that commonly contradict any intuition (*Anschauung*).   (Frege 1873:1)

The statement can be read as making the somewhat limited claim that geometry is based on intuition. That claim can be made to sound even more innocuous, if we translate *Anschauung* by 'visual perception' rather than by the Kantian term 'intuition'. The claim that geometry is based on perception or intuition is, of course, not uncontroversial, but it is a philosophically limited claim because it can be reconciled with both an empiricist interpretation of geometry such as John Stuart Mill's and an *a priori* interpretation such as Kant's.

Nevertheless, we are probably not too far off in taking that first sentence of the dissertation to imply a Kantian view of the nature of geometry (and, thus, a view in sharp contrast with Gauss'). Such a reading is suggested by Frege's use of the term *Anschauungsvermögen* which is a characteristically Kantian notion. In the *Critique of Pure Reason* Kant writes:

The faculty of sensible intuition (*Das sinnliche Anschauungsvermögen*) is strictly only a receptivity, a capacity of being affected in a certain manner with representations, the relation of which to one another is a pure intuition of space and time (mere forms of sensibility).   (Kant 1787:522)

The fact that Frege, like Kant, says that geometry rests on the nature of our faculty of intuition, rather than on our having particular intuitions, suggests that he considers geometry to have an *a priori* source and thus to consist of (synthetic) *a priori* propositions. But if such a Kantian view of geometry and of space is suggested by the introductory sentence of the dissertation, the assumption remains a mere hint without further consequences for the course of the argument within the dissertation. In so far as the essay has philosophical implications they remain condensed in the one occurrence of the Kantian term *Anschauungsvermögen*.

V Kuno Fischer's Kant

If the beginning of Frege's dissertation hints at a Kantian view of geometry, we must go back to his student years at Jena and to Kuno Fischer's course on Kant to find its roots. When Frege took that course, Fischer had just published the second edition of his book on Kant. From it we can see clearly what interpretation of Kant Frege became familiar with (Fischer 1869).

In this book Fischer argues that Kant's view on *mathematics* was crucial to his whole philosophy. 'The point where critical philosophy begins', he writes, 'is the right view of the scientific nature of mathematics' (*ibid.*:305). He considers it of particular importance that Kant rejected the Humean assumption that mathematical truths are analytic. Hume had argued that all necessary truths are trivial and express no real insight because they are all analytic. Kant had agreed with Hume that analytic or logical truths can never extend our knowledge. But he had also held that mathematical truths, though necessary, at the same time can extend our knowledge, for they can contain both novel and unexpected results. It is this which makes them so useful in the description of nature.

It was therefore important for Kant to show that mathematical truths could be necessary and nevertheless not analytic. He found the solution in the doctrine that they are synthetic *a priori*. Fischer writes:

With the insight that mathematical judgments are synthetic and at the same time *a priori* Kant separates himself once and for all from Hume and enters the course of critical thought ... Mathematics is the negative instance on which Kant brings scepticism to fall.   (*Ibid.*:308f)

As synthetic *a priori*, mathematics is for Kant grounded in the pure intuitions of space and time. Fischer shows how the doctrine includes the belief that space and time are not metaphysically real. They are rather forms of intuition and for that reason subjective. But Fischer is also clear that this doctrine of the subjectivity of space and time cannot be the whole story for Kant. Kant regarded geometry as an objective science. He had said that geometrical propositions express conditions of the possibility of experience and had asserted that 'the conditions of the possibility of experience in general are likewise conditions of the possibility of the objects of experience, and for this reason they have objective validity in a synthetic *a priori* judgment' (Kant 1787:197).[4]

Fischer emphasizes that Kant took space and time as in one sense subjective, but in another objective. He writes:

> Compared with the things in themselves space and time are, of course, subjective and ideal; but compared with the objects of possible experience or even with intuitive objects, they are objective and real . . . The first Kant calls the 'transcendental ideality' of space and time, the second their 'empirical reality'.
>
> (Fischer 1869:348)

The view of space and time as objectively valid is for Kant their view from science; it is only the philosophical, transcendental view that must conceive them as ultimately subjective. Kant's notion of objectivity does not then mean the same as metaphysical reality. It is rather a weaker notion, compatible with the idea of transcendental ideality. When calling things objective in this sense we are speaking only of an internal objectivity and reality, not of their objectivity and reality from the external, philosophical viewpoint.

If we want to understand Frege's philosophical outlook, it is essential that we should see this Kantian background to his thought. As his later writings reveal, he never abandoned the Kantian view of geometry. In the *Foundations of Arithmetic* he wrote, 'in calling the truths of geometry synthetic and *a priori* he [Kant] revealed their true nature' (Frege 1884:101f). And though he came to disagree with Kant's assessment of the status of arithmetical propositions (for reasons that require careful analysis), he was at pains to argue that the analyticity of arithmetic did not show arithmetical truths to be trivial tautologies. It is rather the case that analytic truths can sometimes extend our knowledge. Like the Kant of Fischer's book, Frege considered the question of the nature of mathematical truth essential for overcoming radical empiricism and scepticism.

---

[4] Michael Dummett has recently tried to drive a wedge between Frege's and Kant's views on geometry by claiming that for Kant space was merely subjective whereas Frege considered spatial intuitions to have both a subjective and an objective component (Dummett 1982a). My summary of Fischer's remarks on this topic should be sufficient to show that there is, in fact, no disagreement between Kant and Frege on this point.

In assessing Frege's later philosophical statements about the objectivity of not only mathematical truths, but of thoughts in general we must always keep in mind the fact that Frege learned his use of the objective–subjective distinction initially in the context of an examination of Kant's philosophy.

VI The concept of magnitude

The *Habilitationsschrift* which Frege completed in 1874, one year after his dissertation, is, like the earlier piece, concerned with purely mathematical matters. It begins with a restatement of the claim of the dissertation that geometry rests on intuition, but then departs sharply from the Kantian interpretation of the nature of arithmetic. Frege writes: 'The elements of all geometrical constructions are intuitions and geometry points to intuition as the source of its axioms. Since the object of arithmetic has no intuition, its principles can also not derive from intuition' (Frege 1874:50).

The object of arithmetic is defined by Frege in this context as the notion of magnitude (*Grössenbegriff*). He believes that intuition can illustrate for us what a magnitude is, but the concept itself is independent of intuition. It may have its origins there, but with the introduction of negative and imaginary magnitudes the intuitive notion of magnitude has been transcended. 'There remain only certain general properties of addition and those now become essential features of magnitude. In this way the concept has slowly separated itself from intuition and has become independent' (*ibid.*). The generality of the notion of magnitude shows that it is independent of intuition, and arithmetic, as based on that notion, is thus sharply separable from geometry.

Frege assumes that there are different kinds of magnitude (*Grössenarten*), some of which are perhaps even unknown to us. Every kind of magnitude is defined by means of an operation of addition and a notion of sameness of magnitude. 'There is such a close connection between the concepts of addition and magnitude that it is impossible to understand the one without the other' (*ibid.*:51). He says, somewhat loosely, that in a process of addition 'we replace a group of things by a single one of the same kind . . . A kind of magnitude – e.g., length – is therefore a property a group of things can share with an individual thing of the same kind independent of their arrangement' (*ibid.*). We can paraphrase his remark as saying that the operation of addition must satisfy the conditions of associativity and commutativity, i.e.,

$$(x + y) = (y + x)$$
$$\text{and } x + (y + z) = (x + y) + z$$

and furthermore for all x, y, and z such that

$$(x + y) = z$$

it must be the case that if x and y belong to a kind of magnitude, so does z.

It is worth pointing out that Frege's basic conception of the nature of arithmetic is here still thoroughly traditional. We can see that by citing briefly the beginning of Leonard Euler's *Elements of Algebras* of 1771:

Whatever is capable of increase or diminution, is called magnitude or quantity (*Grösse*) . . . It is evident, that the different kinds of magnitude must be so various, as to render it difficult to enumerate them: and this is the origin of the different branches of mathematics, each being employed on a particular kind of magnitude. Mathematics, in general, is the science of quantity . . .   (Euler 1771:1)

Euler goes on to say that magnitudes are generally expressible in numerical terms and that the first move must be to define addition for magnitudes and to determine when two magnitudes are the same.

The traditional nature of Frege's characterization of arithmetic deserves emphasis because it shows how far he still is from the thesis that arithmetical truths are logical truths. Arithmetic is for him in the *Habilitationsschrift* a conceptual science, but he makes no attempt to break the notion of magnitude itself down into more basic logical notions, nor does he give even a hint of the later logical analysis of the natural numbers.

His project is rather to define the notion of magnitude in such a way 'that it allows the most varied applications so that the largest possible area can be subjected to arithmetic' (Frege 1874:51). He believes that his characterization of it in terms of the notions of addition and equality performs that job adequately, that the whole 'content of arithmetic is contained in the stipulated qualities of magnitude' and that more specific kinds of magnitude 'such as natural number and angle' can be defined from this position (*ibid.*). But he does not elaborate on those claims.

Instead he sets out to show how the notion of magnitude can be applied to operations or functions (terms he uses indiscriminately at this point). Functions do not, of course, constitute one single area of magnitude 'but divide into infinitely many different ones' (*ibid.*:52). Frege is conscious of the difficulty of formulating such a theory in its most general terms. He restricts himself therefore to the simplest cases and their immediate consequences, 'apart from a few general sentences whose validity has been proved for all functions and systems of functions' (*ibid.*:83).

If we apply an operation repeatedly to its own result we can also regard the ultimate outcome as the result of an application of a single new operation. The order in which the original operations were applied is here obviously unimportant.

We can now look at arithmetical operations from this point of view. There are numerous examples of repetitions of the same operation in arithmetic. In this way addition leads to multiplication and multiplication to involution. All calculating by approximation consists in the repeated application of the same operation. Every recursive formula teaches one how through repetition of the same procedure we can get from the result for 1 to that for 2, 3 and so on. (*Ibid.*:52)

These passing remarks indicate a certain continuity of interest in Frege from the *Habilitationsschrift* to the *Begriffsschrift*. In the former he deals with sequences of operations and in the latter he states as a theorem the conditions under which we are entitled to say that a property belonging to one element in a sequence also belongs to another one. But apart from such hints at things to come the *Habilitationsschrift*, just like the dissertation, contains little of philosophical interest.

VII Lotze's logic

With the completion of the *Habilitationsschrift*, the path cleared for Frege's appointment as instructor of mathematics at Jena and Abbe saw to it that the appointment was made as quickly as possible. Back in Jena, Frege now joined the intellectual circle led by Snell and Abbe which met every Sunday afternoon at their house to discuss scientific, political, and above all philosophical issues (Auerbach 1918:138–41; 162f). Frege, who attended those meetings, was known even then as extremely introverted and quiet. Originally, there had been three such groups at Jena: a philosophical circle led by Fischer, a scientific one led by Häckel, and Snell's and Abbe's circle. With Fischer's departure the remaining members of his group (in particular Carl Fortlage) joined the latter of the two remaining circles. In Häckel's group naturalistic views predominated, fuelled by Häckel's own passionate advocacy of evolutionist monism; in the other, more traditional philosophical conceptions and, in particular, Kantian ideas prevailed.

In the winter semester of 1874–5 Frege announced his first course at Jena – a course on analytic geometry 'according to newer methods'. It was to be repeated several times before 1879. In the same period he also offered courses in algebra, analysis, Abelian integrals, and the theory of functions (Kratzsch 1979:537f).

In addition he had begun to think about arithmetic. In the preface to the *Begriffsschrift* he says that he had considered the question whether arithmetical judgments can be grounded in general logical laws alone or are dependent on experiential facts. He writes: 'My initial step was to attempt to reduce the concept of ordering in a sequence to that of *logical* consequence. To prevent anything intuitive from penetrating here unnoticed, I had to bend every effort to keep the chain of inferences free of gaps.' And that, he adds, led to the construction of his new logic (Frege 1879:5).

This turn of thought is surprising because there is no indication that

Frege had previously thought about the question whether arithmetic can be grounded in general logical laws alone, nor had there been any indication of an earlier independent interest in logic. In Jena Frege had heard Kuno Fischer on Kant's philosophy and in Göttingen he had heard Hermann Lotze on the philosophy of religion; but while both also taught courses in logic Frege had attended no such course.[5]

It is nevertheless plausible to assume that Frege's suddenly awakened interest in logic had something to do with his education in philosophy, for his interest in logic developed after the completion of his *Habilitationsschrift* in 1874 and it was in that very same year that Lotze had published his book on logic. Since Frege never mentions Lotze by name the claim that he was influenced by Lotze's work on logic must remain conjectural, but the claim is not just based on a superficial comparison of Lotze's and Frege's writings, as some of its critics have charged. There is, to begin with, decisive evidence that Frege knew Lotze's book. That fact is established by Frege's use of the term *Hilfsgedanke* in one set of notes; a term which was coined by Lotze and does not occur in other writings (Dummett 1981). While this fact is sufficient to establish Frege's familiarity with the text, it does not yet constitute strong evidence that Frege was substantially influenced by Lotze's ideas. That is provided through the testimony of the philosopher Bruno Bauch, for many years one of Frege's colleagues at Jena and one of his close associates, who characterized Frege's work as 'not independent of Lotze's' (cf. Sluga 1980:53). It was Bauch, too, who wrote a special essay on Lotze's logic as an introduction to Frege's late paper 'The thought'. The essay, which was published in the same volume of the journal in which Frege's piece appeared, emphasized four elements of Lotze's thought as most relevant to an understanding of Frege. They were Lotze's anti-psychologism, his distinction between an object of knowledge and its recognition, his reformulation of Platonism as an ontology-free theory, and his account of concepts as functions (cf. *ibid.*). Bauch's testimony on this point seems to me so substantial that no interpretation of Frege can ignore it. Those critics who have disputed Lotze's influence on Frege have just failed to take the available evidence seriously enough.

In fact, careful examination of the relevant texts establishes beyond doubt that Lotze's views on various topics are closely akin to some of Frege's characteristic convictions. Most important for Frege is, from the

---

[5] During Frege's student years at Göttingen Lotze taught his logic course three times (Lotze 1884b:104–13). While the philosophy of religion lies outside Frege's professional interests it was central to Lotze's own philosophy. The content of his lectures during Frege's student years is described in Schmidt-Japing 1925. A readable account of Lotze's life and work can be found in Stumpf 1918. Stumpf was a lecturer in philosophy at Göttingen during Frege's years there; the two later corresponded. Whether they knew each other in Göttingen is unknown.

start, Lotze's distinction between subjective mental acts and their objective contents. Lotze writes on this topic:

If we distinguish, as we have done, between the logical act of thinking, and the thought which it creates as its product, the former can claim only a *subjective* significance; it is purely and simply an inner movement of our minds, which is made necessary to us by reason of the constitution of our nature and of our place in the world, and through which we make that thought . . . an object of our consciousness. . . The thought itself on the other hand in which the process of thinking issues . . . has *objective* validity. (Lotze 1884a:492)

Frege begins the *Begriffsschrift* by distinguishing in a similar manner between subjective acts of assertion and their objective asserted content. It is the latter which he (as well as Lotze) believes to be the concern of logic.

Lotze's influence on Frege is also evident in the *Begriffsschrift* theory of judgment, in its theory of identity, in its characterization of concepts as functions, and in the terminology of idea (*Vorstellung*) and content (*Inhalt*). But of most immediate significance for Frege must have been Lotze's account of the relation of arithmetic to logic.

Since Kant, general philosophical opinion had held that arithmetical and geometrical propositions could not be derived from logic alone. Leibniz's views to the contrary had been dismissed as mistaken. Opinion was, however, divided between those who postulated with Kant a pure intuition as the basis of the two branches of mathematics and those who wanted to base them on experience. It was Lotze, as the first major philosopher of the nineteenth century, who reasserted the Leibnizian claim that mathematics really belongs together with logic. At the same time he agreed with Kant that mathematical propositions are no mere instances of the principle of identity. Additional principles are required to derive the mathematical truths. Those principles are known by pure intuition. Mathematics thus has an intuitive base and in this respect Kant had been right. But he had been mistaken in thinking that the truths of arithmetic are based on a pure intuition of space and time. They are based rather on an intuitive grasp of the realm of objective ideas. That realm is the concern of logic and, for this reason, arithmetic must be taken to belong properly to logic. Lotze's account of the nature of arithmetical truths evidently aims at a compromise between the Leibnizian and the Kantian conception (Sluga 1984).

Whatever the details of Lotze's position, it is clear that in some sense he subscribed to the claim that arithmetical propositions are grounded in general logical laws alone. That claim was close to the one Frege had made in his *Habilitationsschrift* when he had called arithmetic a conceptual science. But it went further in claiming that arithmetic was, in fact, a purely logical science.

Though Lotze claimed that arithmetic was really part of logic he never tried to show how that conclusion could be established in detail nor did he list the additional logical principles which he considered necessary for that task. It was Frege who set out to provide the necessary details. He was already convinced that mathematics (and, in particular, arithmetic) was basic to science. He now concluded that logic, in turn, was basic to arithmetic.

VIII Logic as an instrument

The *Begriffsschrift* begins with the question whether arithmetical propositions are ultimately grounded in the laws of logic or in facts of experience. (Though Frege seems to leave the answer open, we know which one he is inclined to give.) In order to answer the question, he says, he has found it necessary to depart from ordinary language and to construct 'a formula language of pure thought', based on the conception of the symbolism of arithmetic (Frege 1879:6). In the process of the construction of such a language certain reforms of logic itself have suggested themselves to him.

We can be sure that Frege's interest in logic after 1874 drew his attention first to the traditional theories. In the *Begriffsschrift* Frege reveals familiarity with (at least) some parts of the traditional theory of judgment. He discusses the distinction of categorical, hypothetical, and disjunctive judgments as well as that of assertoric, apodictic, and problematic ones (Frege 1879:13). He also mentions the traditional square of opposition (*ibid*.:28), the syllogistic forms Felapton, Fesapo (*ibid*.:52), and Barbara (*ibid*.:54), and such traditional logical principles as *duplex negatio affirmat* (*ibid*.:45). He also says that he initially conceived of his new logic in terms of the traditional subject–predicate analysis of judgments; a project he quickly abandoned (*ibid*.:13).

While Frege was familiar with some aspects of traditional logic he seems to have been unaware of the work of Hamilton, Boole, and Jevons when he began work on his own logic. The first discussions of the mathematical logic developed in England appeared only very late in Germany. It was in 1877, when Frege must have been well embarked on the construction of his own logic, that Ernst Schröder *Operationskreis des Logikkalkuls* was published (Schröder 1877). In the same year Alois Riehl reviewed the work of Boole and Jevons in an article in the *Vierteljahrsschrift für wissenschaftliche Philosophie* (Riehl 1877). The two pieces contained the first expositions in German of the new English logic. It is clear from Frege's writings immediately following the *Begriffsschrift* that he knew both of them by about 1880 (Frege 1881). Whether he was already familiar with them before the completion of the *Begriffsschrift* is less clear, but a passing remark in the preface of that work, stating that 'any effort to create an artificial similarity [of logic with arithmetic] by regarding a concept as the sum of its marks was entirely alien to my thought', suggests a criticism of the Boolean conception of logic (Frege 1879:6). If we compare Schröder's and Riehl's expositions of the new logic with that of the *Begriffsschrift* we discover, in any case, almost no common ground. There is, furthermore, no reason to think that by 1879 Frege knew of Boolean algebra independently of its description by Schröder and Riehl.

Frege seems also to have been unaware of Bolzano's *Wissenschaftslehre*[6] and of all the post-Boolean logicians he was the only one whose work appeared before Cantor's set-theoretical writings and thus remained uninfluenced by them. Frege's later hostility to set theory must be explained by the fact that by the time of the completion of the *Begriffsschrift* he had convinced himself that logic had to be primarily a theory of concepts rather than of classes.

However independent Frege's work may have been from that of Boole and Jevons, it shares with them the idea that progress in logic depends on tying logic to mathematics, that a reform of logic demands the use of mathematical notions and techniques in it. Beyond that point there are, of course, important differences between Frege and the Boolean logicians. The latter treated logic as a branch of mathematics, whereas Frege's aim was to show that arithmetic was only an extended logic. In spite of that disagreement Frege and the Booleans share common ground. The work of both is part of the larger process of the mathematization of science that occurred in the nineteenth century. Their disagreement is not over the question whether logic and mathematics are closely linked, but only over the question which of them demands priority.

Integral to that process was the concern of both Frege and the Booleans with appropriate systems of notation for the expression of logical relations. The philosophical tradition in logic, particularly in Germany, had put almost no emphasis on the idea that logic demands its own notation. Since Leibniz that idea had remained in recess. Lotze, for instance, in his book of 1874 explicitly discusses the idea of a 'logical language', but expresses

---

6 Bolzano's book was pretty much forgotten at that time. Lotze, who was widely read and to whom the work might have appealed, was unfamiliar with it. Husserl, who was influenced by it in his *Logische Untersuchungen*, got to know the work only because of a chance discovery in a second-hand book store (Schuhmann 1977:463).

    In the preface to the *Begriffsschrift* Frege refers to an essay by Trendelenburg on Leibniz's idea of a symbolic language (Frege 1879:6). I have described elsewhere what the content of that essay is and what ideas Frege may have taken from it (Sluga 1980:48–52). Given Frege's limited philosophical interests, there is a question why he should ever have got to know that essay, published by Trendelenburg in a volume entitled *Historische Beiträge zur Philosophie*. One possibility is that he discovered it because Fischer's book on Kant refers repeatedly to one of Trendelenburg's other essays in that volume. Another possibility is that Frege's attention was drawn to it because of a reference in Schröder 1877.

doubt about its realizability and usefulness (Lotze 1884a:205–7). He questions the possibility of a 'universal system of characterizing concepts (*Begriffscharakteristik*)', and adds that it 'derives only an apparent confirmation from the mathematician's language of signs and the symbols of chemistry' (*ibid.*).[7] In the second edition to his work, published in 1880, he adds a special note on Boolean algebra, once again expressing his doubts (*ibid.*:208–23).

It is precisely the sign systems of 'arithmetic, geometry, and chemistry' which Frege treats as partial realizations of a universal logical characteristic (Frege 1879:7). He thinks of such a system of notation initially very much in mathematical and instrumental terms. The influence of the Gaussian tradition, of Abbe and of Weber is clearly evident at this point in his conception of the new logic. The symbolism and the logic formulated in it are for Frege at this point an instrument 'invented for scientific purposes' (*ibid.*:6). He prides himself on having invented a *method* of investigation, a procedure by which certain scientific questions can be answered definitively, questions about how propositions follow from each other. He is confident that his notation 'can be successfully used wherever special value must be placed on the validity of proofs' (*ibid.*:7).

At the same time he is willing to grant that the new logic is an instrument with its own peculiar limitations. Ordinary language, he says, is like the human eye: versatile, but limited in its power of resolution. The new logic, on the other hand, is sharp in its resolution, but limited in the number of its applications. Referring back to the work of his teacher Abbe on the limitations of the optical microscope he writes: 'As soon as scientific goals demand great sharpness of resolution, the eye proves to be insufficient. The microscope, on the other hand, is perfectly suited to precisely such goals, but that is just why it is useless for all others' (*ibid.*:6).

IX The primacy of logic

Though Frege initially characterizes his new logic in purely instrumental terms, it is clear from the preface of the *Begriffsschrift* that he considers his work to have, at least potentially, a more general philosophical significance.

---

[7] It is worth noting that Lotze says that a system of signs as such would be of limited interest. 'The truth is that the usefulness of the signs rests here upon the fact that we already have unambiguous *rules* which enable us to determine what follows from the simplest combinations of magnitudes, and then being applied anew with the same freedom from ambiguity to the results thus obtained issue in these elegant and certain methods of solving problems' (Lotze 1884a:207). Frege was, of course, the first of the modern logicians who was careful in stating rules of inference and was clear about the distinction between logical truths and logical rules. He may in this respect have been influenced by Lotze's remarks.

Comparing his work to the Leibnizian project of a universal characteristic he says that Leibniz, probably, underestimated the difficulty of
constructing such a system of notation. But like Leibniz he conceives of his
notation as eventually applicable far beyond the confines of traditional
logic and the limited task of establishing that arithmetic is reducible to
logic. He speaks of the extension of his logic to the differential and integral
calculus and to geometry. 'The transition to the pure theory of motion and
then to mechanics and physics could follow at this point' (*ibid.*:7).
Chemistry, too, is to be integrated. Finally, an extension 'to fields that up
to now have lacked such a language' is envisaged (*ibid*). The application of
the new logic to philosophical problems is also considered, and it is argued
that the symbolism, 'further developed for these purposes', could help
philosophers to lay bare misconceptions due to the nature of our language.

In the decades before Frege there had been much activity in German
logic. Überweg lists 137 German works in his history of logic for the
century between 1781 (the date of Kant's first *Critique*) and 1879, and he
makes no claim to completeness (Überweg 1882). Much of that work had
been produced in the belief that traditional logic was in need of reform, a
reform that was not, however, meant to lead to a reconstruction of the
theory of inference itself, but to a re-examination of the philosophical
principles of the whole science. Following Kant, philosophers tended to
think that the traditional theory of concept, judgment, and inference was
essentially complete, but in need of new philosophical foundations.
German writers on logic in the period after Kant were characteristically
concerned with the development of 'philosophical logic' rather than of
'formal logic'. In his early book on logic Hermann Lotze could write in this
sense:

Logic should not be an enumeration of the laws of thought, but an explanation and
scientific presentation of their foundations and their relation to other mental
activities. In this way it might gain more influence on the development of actual
knowledge than could happen through [a preoccupation with] that abstract
formalism.   (Lotze 1843:5)

The question which German writers on logic asked most frequently was
that of the relation of their subject to other parts of human knowledge and,
in particular, its relations to other parts of philosophy. In reaction to both
the psychological and the metaphysical interpretations of the subject that
had dominated in the early parts of the century (and that were still
powerful in the later parts), a number of writers in the period immediately
preceding Frege set out to stress the independence of logic from either.

Lotze is again characteristic of this new development. In his early work
on logic (1843) he had already opposed both types of interpretation. He

had spoken there of two dominant misconceptions of the subject (pp. 7f). The first, he had said, tries to ground logic in a subjective necessity brought about by the construction of our minds; that interpretation puts undue weight on the 'subjective side of thinking' (p. 10). The second brings logic into close contact with metaphysics and gives a realistic account of the logical forms (p. 8). That view overemphasizes 'the supposedly objective, real meanings of the logical forms' (p. 10). Lotze's aim had been to steer a middle course between the two extremes.

He retains this same objective in the later work on logic (1874). He writes at the end of that work: 'I have maintained the opinion throughout that logic cannot derive any serious advantage from a discussion of the conditions under which thought as a psychical process comes about' (Lotze 1884a:467). At the same time he opposes the metaphysical interpretation of the logical forms which is often associated with the name of Plato (Sluga 1980:119). In the earlier book, Lotze had spoken of a dichotomy of the subjective and the objective, equating the latter with the metaphysically real. To keep logic free from the encroachment of psychology as well as from that of metaphysics had meant at that time to assign it a status somewhere between the realms of the subjective and the objective. In the later work Lotze assumes that a distinction must be drawn between reality and objectivity. There are now for him three realms. First, there is the realm of subjective mental states, next that of actual reality (*reale Wirklichkeit*), and finally a third realm of objectively valid ideas or contents, a *Reich der Inhalte* (p. 497), which is the concern of logical inquiry.[8] Lotze assumes, moreover, that a knowledge of actual reality is made possible only through the mediation of our knowledge of the realm of objective contents. His views thus assure (a) the objectivity of logic, (b) its independence from psychology, (c) its primacy over other knowledge, and therefore (d) its independence from metaphysics.

I have previously stressed that Frege's doctrine of objectivity cannot be fully understood unless we examine its relation to Fischer's (and Kant's) use of the subjective–objective distinction. That claim can now be supplemented by the further observation that his doctrine of objectivity must also be interpreted in the light of Lotze's views on the matter. Like Lotze

[8] Dummett has recently claimed that 'objectivity is not a key notion for Lotze' and that the term occurs substantially only once at the beginning of the 1884a book (Dummett 1982b:112n23). The present discussion should help to correct those claims. Dummett has also suggested that a set of Frege's notes known as '17 Key Sentences on Logic' were meant as a critical commentary on the Introduction of Lotze's book. They certainly show Frege's acquaintance with that book; whether they should be read as a critique of Lotze and whether they can be tied specifically to the Introduction of his book seems less clear. Since the notes were almost certainly written some time after the *Begriffsschrift* (the notion of truth plays an important role in them but does not occur in the *Begriffsschrift*) the text falls in any case outside the period with which I am here concerned.

he means to assure the objectivity of logic, its independence from psychology, as well as its primacy in the whole body of human knowledge and thereby its independence from metaphysics.

The idea that logic occupies such a place of primacy had been expressed forcefully a generation before Frege by Hermann Ulrici, who had begun his *Compendium of Logic* with the words:

Logic is the first, introductory, foundational discipline of the philosophical system as well as of all science; no other can precede it. For all proof, all justification, induction and deduction, explanation and exposition, as well as the resolution of all scientific problems and questions – even of the basic question of all inquiry, whether there is any knowledge at all – depend, as we will see, on the laws, norms, and forms of logic. (Quoted from Ulrici 1872:1)

It is in just that sense that Frege speaks in the preface of the *Begriffs-schrift*. He calls the logical laws there 'those laws upon which all knowledge rests' and again 'those laws of thought that transcend all particulars' (1879:5). Logic possesses for him the status of primacy within the body of human knowledge because we must use the laws of logic as well as those of arithmetic in order to gain knowledge from our subjective experiences. Arithmetic, in turn, he believed in those early years, rests on logic, and logic can occupy this place of primacy within our knowledge because of the generality of its laws.

While he later abandoned the claim of the reducibility of arithmetic to logic and, instead, set out to reduce it to geometry, he never abandoned the overall view of knowledge that made him assign primacy to our knowledge of logical and mathematical truths. In the late notes on 'Sources of knowledge in mathematics and the mathematical sciences' he wrote: 'Sense perceptions alone are of little use to us' (Frege 1924–5:287). Referring once more to Abbe's work on the limitations of the optical microscope he continued: 'Our knowledge of the refraction of light teaches us that many images produced by the microscope are thoroughly unreliable' (*ibid.*). And he concludes that 'for the knowledge of natural laws we also need those other sources of knowledge: the logical and the geometrical one' (*ibid.*).

X The limits of foundationalism

When Frege began his studies in 1869 he did not initially have any interest in logic nor did he initially concern himself with the question of the reducibility of arithmetic to logic. His initial concern was rather with natural science and pure mathematics. From it and from his (limited) work in philosophy he slowly came to form a picture of the overall structure of human knowledge, and it was that picture which made the study of logic and the question of the reducibility of arithmetic to logic important to him.

The conception of knowledge he formed in that early period was that of a linear or tree structure such that some part of it can be said to be either first or deepest or highest, depending on which metaphor we use. The part of knowledge which occupies such a place of primacy is then thought of as presupposed by all other knowledge and hence, in yet another metaphor, as the foundation of all the rest.

Frege's foundationalism assumes that *logic* is, in the required sense, first or deepest or highest knowledge. He thinks that logic plays that role because its laws are the most general laws and no knowledge can be derived without the use of general principles. Specific sense perceptions, he believes, are never sufficient for arriving at knowledge; we also need general principles for the assessment of those perceptions, principles of mathematics and of logic. Those principles cannot, in turn, derive their validity from perception since otherwise there would be a circle in our reasoning. They derive rather from another and separate source of knowledge. Because of the place Frege assigns to logic we can call his kind of foundationalism a logicist foundationalism. The term 'logicism' is generally used to characterize the doctrine, also held by Frege, that arithmetic is reducible to logic. I use it here in a wider sense which, though not the most common, is also not unknown in the literature (Wundt 1910).

Foundationalism is an ancient philosophical conception of knowledge. We can find it already in Aristotle's characterization of metaphysics as first philosophy. In the nineteenth century the issue of foundationalism was, however, cast in a new light because of the development of a number of new sciences and because of rapid growth in a number of old ones. In the course of that proliferation of knowledge various branches of science began to conceive of themselves as potentially capable of absorbing all the other sciences into themselves. As a result various forms of foundationalism were promoted by philosophers and philosophizing scientists. Psychologism considered psychology the fundamental science, materialism looked to physics and physiology as fundamental, historicism conceived of historical studies as basic, and so on.

Logicism (which itself has had a venerable history in philosophy) also gained new life in that period. And it gained that life because logic itself underwent a radical reconstitution and subsequently rapid growth in the nineteenth century. A number of reasons can be given for that development, but the most important is the redefinition of the relation of logic to mathematics. Traditional logic had practically no links to mathematics. The new logic of the nineteenth century came about through the introduction of mathematical concepts and techniques into logic, and was conceived as a tool for the analysis of mathematics.

Frege's work, like that of Boole and Jevons before him and that of

Russell after him, testifies to the fruitfulness of that procedure. His logic was made possible by the use of a generalized notion of function which he had taken from mathematics. Frege had studied the mathematical theory of functions with Abbe in Jena and with Schering in Göttingen, he had tried to construct a general theory of magnitude of functions in his *Habilitationsschrift*, and from the beginning of his own academic career had taught the theory of functions as a regular part of his teaching schedule. By introducing ideas taken from this work in mathematics into his logic he was able to transform the traditional theory of concept, judgment, and inference into an altogether new science, a science capable of dealing with the problems of the foundations of arithmetic.

In spite of the intense philosophical debate that arose in the course of the nineteenth century about which science should be regarded as the foundation of the rest of human knowledge, we can doubt whether the foundationalist view of knowledge (including the logicist view) is philosophically satisfactory. Foundationalism derives from a certain understanding of the structure of human knowledge. It sees that structure in architectonic terms – as a building grounded in the soil. But there may be better and more flexible ways of thinking about human knowledge. We can think of it, for instance, as a network that can be traced from different ends, as a city with many routes of access, or as a labyrinth with various entrances and exits.

The problem of foundationalism has always been that it has never produced a neutral criterion for determining what is deeper or less deep in human knowledge and what therefore should be counted as the foundation of the whole structure. The criteria that have been offered have characteristically been self-serving. They have been formulated in terms of that part of knowledge that the given argument is supposed to establish as foundational. Thus, logicists have characteristically argued that logic is surely foundational because it is concerned with rationality, inference, truth – concepts which clearly must be considered fundamental to all knowledge. But such an argument will not convince someone already committed to another form of foundationalism. It will not, for instance, convince the materialist who argues that surely physics and physiology must be foundational, because logical reasoning is a process that is ultimately physiological and physical in nature.

To say that foundationalism has no clear defence is not to say that it is without any value. But its value is that of an investigatory strategy and not that of a theoretical truth. When we consider a particular part of human knowledge as foundational to the rest we mean in practice that we are inclined to look at the rest of human knowledge from the perspective of that particular part. We mean to propose the concepts of our preferred area of knowledge as models for the understanding of all the rest. And such a strategy may (or may not) be fruitful. Foundationalism becomes dangerous only when we treat it as a deep theoretical truth. For we will then persist with it even if it provides no new insights. It has then become for us a stultifying dogma.

We can see that point clearly in the case of logicism. Frege's logicist foundationalism was, no doubt, a brilliantly successful investigatory strategy. It led him to the construction of a new logic, to new questions about the nature of mathematical truth and the meaning of mathematical terms, and to new semantic questions, distinctions, and theories. But after Frege logicism becomes a much less interesting doctrine. Today it can have a deadening touch.

Two considerations speak against logicism as a theoretical truth. The first concerns the ability of logic to solve problems, the second its ability to represent them. If we treat logicism as a strategy rather than as a truth, these considerations show what the promise and the limitations of that strategy are.

The first is that Frege invented his new logic to solve certain problems concerning the nature of arithmetic. He wanted to show that arithmetical truths could be derived from purely logical ones. That conclusion, in turn, was supposed to yield certain very general results about the nature of human knowledge. There is reason to think that Frege did not solve his problems and that they cannot be resolved in the way in which he set out to do so. Though his undertaking has thus, in one sense, turned out to be unsuccessful, it has nevertheless helped to clarify the questions that he tried to answer. His work has led to a clearer formulation of the issues; it has improved the representation of the problems; it has helped us to understand the alternatives we have in thinking about mathematics.

After Frege logicians and philosophers tried to show how logical methods could determine the meaning of scientific theories, decide the conflict between realism and nominalism, and settle philosophical quarrels about the notion of existence. In each case, we can see today, logic has advanced our understanding of the issues, but has failed to settle the questions.

That does not mean that logic is unable to solve any philosophical problems. The difficulty in deciding whether it can or cannot is that we have no clear criterion of what makes a problem philosophical. Is the question whether we can give a complete axiomatization of arithmetic a philosophical problem? If so, then Gödel's incompleteness theorem can be said to resolve it. But even so we can be sure that logic has not resolved many of the philosophical problems which philosophers and logicians had hoped it would solve. Its problem-solving ability is obviously limited.

Secondly, logical techniques have been found useful in representing issues in mathematics, in parts of natural science, and in some parts of philosophy. But the uses of such techniques are limited.

They are most successful in those areas of human knowledge where we operate with relatively sharp concepts. But many other areas of knowledge are of a different kind. Their concepts have no sharp definition and we do not know how to give them such definitions. That may be so because we fail to have a very good grasp of the phenomena to which those concepts are supposed to apply. When we talk of human relations, for instance, we deal with an area of human understanding that is not only extremely complex, but also quite imprecise. We cannot, for instance, say in very precise terms what it is for someone to be influenced in his thinking by someone else, though the notion of influence is clearly central to any account of the history of thought. In the area of social relations, we deal with phenomena that involve a large multiplicity of details which are extremely varied, extremely complex, and extremely resistant to verbal analysis. It comes, therefore, as no surprise that logical analysis and logical techniques of representation prove to be of little interest for the understanding of social relationships.

Logical techniques are useful for describing relatively simple formal structures; but they seem particularly well adapted to describing synchronic or timeless structures (such as the syntax of a language or a hierarchy of sets). They are not very well adapted to the description of temporal structures such as processes, activities, practices, actions, social and political developments. I do not mean to say that we could not use the machinery of logic and set theory to describe such temporal structures; but there is nothing in that machinery to make it specifically suited to that task.

Logic, no doubt, has its uses for solving some problems and clarifying others, but it is clearly not the foundation of the whole structure of knowledge, it is not primary to all other knowledge, and it does not provide us with a universal strategy of investigation.

There are human enterprises and cognitive pursuits where the consideration of logical structures is of little significance, where the consideration of other types of structural patterns may be more important, such as, for instance, that of temporal and evolving structures. Inquiry which is directed towards such enterprises and cognitive pursuits has profited little from the new logic. In some cases preoccupation with that logic has actually led to a decline in the quantity and quality of such inquiry. In philosophy that is clearly evident in the study of the history of philosophy and the philosophical study of history, the fields of ethics, aesthetics, and political philosophy, the philosophy of biology and the wide area of cultural philosophy – all of those fields came to be diminished by the preoccupation with the new logic rather than augmented by it. They have begun to flourish again in recent years only to the extent to which they have succeeded in freeing themselves from the domination of thinking in logical patterns.

Frege has certainly not left us a universal method of investigation. In that sense his logicism, his belief in the primacy of logic for all knowledge, has been misconceived. But when we think of his logicism not as a theoretical truth, but as an investigatory strategy we can, nevertheless, see how important and fruitful it was for him. Without his commitment to it he might never have constructed his logic. The same is true of the philosophy that has come after Frege. Without its commitment to logicism it might never have attained the standards of clarity and precision which are so characteristic of it.

But the temporary success of logicism as an investigatory strategy does not vindicate the claim that it is a theoretical and permanent truth. Logical models are indeed useful in philosophy, but they do not possess the significance logicism ascribes to them. They do not reveal to us the basic structure of thought, language, knowledge, or the world. After years of preoccupation with logical models, it may be important to look for other philosophical models, to look for other schemata for organizing our understanding. Logicism, if we let it rule our minds, would stop us from such a search. But to abandon logicism does not mean to abandon the achievements of modern logic. Frege's insights do not depend on the truth of logicism. We can be sure that his logic will remain as logicism fades away.

REFERENCES

Asser, G., et al. 1979. 'Gottlob Frege – Persönlichkeit und Werk', in Begriffsschrift – Jenaer Frege Konferenz. Jena: Fr. Schiller Universität, pp. 6–32
Auerbach, F. 1918. Ernst Abbe. Leipzig: Akad. Verlagsges.
Benacerraf, P. 1981. 'Frege: the last logicist', Midwest Studies in Philosophy 6:17–35
Bynum, T. W. 1972. 'On the life and work of Gottlob Frege', in G. Frege, Conceptual Notation and Related Articles, trans. and ed. T. W. Bynum. Oxford: Clarendon, pp. 1–54
Dummett, M. 1973. Frege. The Philosophy of Language. London: Duckworth
Dummett, M. 1978. Truth and Other Enigmas. London: Duckworth
Dummett, M. 1981. 'Frege's "Kernsätze zur Logik" ', Inquiry 24:439–54
Dummett, M. 1982a. 'Frege and Kant on geometry', Inquiry 25:1–21
Dummett, M. 1982b. 'Objectivity and reality in Lotze and Frege', Inquiry 25: 95–114
Euler, L. 1771. Elements of Algebra, transl. J. Hewlett. London: Longman, 1822
Fischer, K. 1869. Geschichte der neuern Philosophie, 2nd rev. edn. Heidelberg: Bassermann
Frege, G. 1873. 'Über eine geometrische Darstellung der imaginären Gebilde in der Ebene', in Frege 1967:1–49

Frege, G. 1874. 'Rechnungsmethoden, die sich auf eine Erweiterung des Grössenbegriffs gründen', in Frege 1967:50–84

Frege, G. 1879. *Begriffsschrift*, in J. V. Heijenoort, *From Frege to Gödel*. Cambridge, Mass.: Harvard, 1967, pp. 5–82

Frege, G. 1881. 'Booles rechnende Logik und die Begriffsschrift', in Frege 1969:9–52

Frege, G. 1884. *The Foundations of Arithmetic*, trans. J. Austin, 2nd edn. Oxford: Blackwell, 1959

Frege, G. 1924–5. 'Erkenntnisquellen der Mathematik und der mathemetischen Naturwissenschaften', in Frege 1969:286–94

Frege, G. 1967. *Kleine Schriften*, ed. I. Angelelli. Hildesheim: Olms

Frege, G. 1969. *Nachgelassene Schriften*, ed. H. Hermes *et al.* Hamburg: Meiner

Hall, T. 1970. *Carl Friedrich Gauss. A Biography*. Cambridge, Mass. and London: MIT Press

Kant, I. 1787. *Critique of Pure Reason*, 2nd edn, transl. N. Kemp Smith. London: Macmillan, 1963

Klein, F. 1872. 'Zur Interpretation der komplexen Elemente in der Geometrie', *Nachrichten v. d. kgl. Gesellschaft d. Wissenschaften*; repr. in F. Klein, *Gesammelte Math. Abhandlungen*, ed. R. Fricke and A. Ostrowski, vol. 1. Berlin: J. Springer, 1921, pp. 402–5

Kratzsch, I. 1979. 'Materialien zu Leben und Wirken Freges aus dem Besitz der Universitätsbibliothek Jena', in *Begriffsschrift – Jenär Frege Konferenz*. Jena: Fr. Schiller Universität, pp. 534–5

Kuhn, T. S. 1977. 'Mathematical versus experimental traditions in the development of physical science', in *The Essential Tension*. Chicago and London: Chicago University Press, pp. 31–65

Lotze, H. 1843. *Logik*. Leipzig: Weidmann

Lotze, H. 1880. *Logik*, 2nd edn. Leipzig: S. Hirzel. (Unchanged reprint of first edition with an additional note on Boolean algebra.)

Lotze, H. 1884a. *Logic*, transl. B. Bosanquet. Oxford: Clarendon (translation of Lotze 1880)

Lotze, H. 1884b. *Grundzüge der Aesthetik*. Leipzig: Hirzel

Riehl, A. 1877. 'Die englische Logik der Gegenwart', in *Vierteljahrsschrift für wissenschaftliche Philosophie* 1: 50–80

Rorty, R.1979. *Philosophy and the Mirror of Nature*. Princeton, NJ: Princeton University Press

Schmidt-Japing, J. W. 1925. *Lotzes Religionsphilosophie in ihrer Entwicklung*. Göttingen: Vandenhoeck

Schröder, E. 1877. *Der Operationskreis des Logikkalkuls*. Leipzig: Teubner

Schuhmann, K. 1977. *Husserl-Chronik*. Den Haag: Nijhoff

Sluga, H. 1980. *Gottlob Frege*. London: Routledge & Kegan Paul

Sluga, H. 1984. 'Semantic content and cognitive sense', *Synthèse*

von Staudt, C. 1856–60. *Beiträge zur Geometrie der Lage*, 3 vols. Nürnberg. F. Korn

Stolz, O. 1871. 'Die geometrische Bedeutung der komplexen Elemente in der analytischen Geometrie', *Mathematische Annalen* 4:416–41

Stumpf, C. 1918. 'Zum Gedächtnis Lotzes', *Kantstudien* 22:1–26

Überweg, F. 1882. *System der Logik und Geschichte der logischen Lehren*, 5th edn by J. B. Meyer. Bonn: Marcus

Ulrici, H. 1872. *Compendium der Logik*, 2nd edn. Leipzig: Weigel

Wiederkehr, K. H. 1976. *Wilhelm Eduard Weber*. Stuttgart: Wissenschaftl. Verlagsges

Wundt, M. 1932. *Die Philosophie an der Universität Jena*. Jena: Fischer

Wundt, W. 1910. 'Psychologismus und Logizismus', *Kleine Schriften*. Leipzig: Engelmann

Wundt, W. 1920. *Erlebtes und Erkanntes*. Stuttgart: A. Kröner

◁ ═══════════════════════════════════════ ▷

15

Moore's rejection of idealism

THOMAS BALDWIN

In his account of his philosophical development Russell wrote (1959:54): 'It was towards the end of 1898 that Moore and I rebelled against both Kant and Hegel. Moore led the way, but I followed closely in his footsteps.' I want here to describe the route Moore followed in this rebellion against idealism, and then to explore briefly his initial development of central themes arising out of it.

One of the founding myths of analytic philosophy is that Moore and Russell refuted their idealist predecessors by deploying robust common sense and a new logic. As with most myths, there is some truth to this one. On one occasion Moore does make an important point by means of an appeal to common sense, though much of his early philosophy is very far removed from common sense, which he was, indeed, initially inclined to reject (1899a:192). Likewise, Russell's work on infinity was of great importance in clearing away Kant's first antinomy (cf. Russell 1903:ch.52). Nonetheless, it is a myth that Moore and Russell refuted Kant, Hegel, and Bradley. No one now believes this to be true of Kant; Hegel is never seriously discussed by Moore and Russell; and though Bradley receives some attention from them, he is usually misunderstood or dismissed without much argument. Moore's famous paper 'The refutation of idealism' (1903a) contains no argument that an idealist need have been disturbed by. But once the myth of refutation is discarded, the question returns as to what sort of break with idealism was initiated by Moore. For there certainly was a break; as Russell put it, he and Moore 'rebelled'. I want to show here how Moore reacted against two of the central features of late-nineteenth-century idealism, subjectivism[1] and holism, and replaced them by an extreme realism and atomism. Moore combined these positions with

---

[1] Idealists such as Bradley would reject this characterization of their views. For they regarded themselves as occupying a position distinct from that of 'Subjective Idealists' such as Berkeley. Although there is a point to this protest, Bradley is nonetheless committed to a form of subjectivism: cf. 1897:146, 'Reality is sentient experience'.

a hostility to empiricism which he took over from the idealists, and the resulting combination is largely definitive of his early philosophy. This fact has a certain irony: for it turns out that Moore's early philosophy is defined by his response to the idealist philosophy against which he was reacting. Furthermore, since the same general themes of realism, atomism, and anti-empiricism persist throughout his philosophy (though I shall not show this here), his early dealings with idealism established a framework for all his philosophy. Moore certainly rejected idealism; but, as happens to some atheists, that which he rejected continued to shape his thoughts.

This is a feature of Moore's philosophy which is obviously not discernible when that philosophy is abstracted from its context and critically assessed as if it had been written today. Indeed this kind of critical assessment could barely be performed for Moore's early philosophy, since it is so immediately concerned with the task of exposing what Moore takes to be fallacies in the dominant idealist philosophy of the time. Thus one could not sensibly apply here the division of labour between 'historical' and 'philosophical' tasks with which Sainsbury prefixes his abstract discussion of Russell's philosophy (1979:9). However, to insist that Moore's philosophy can only be comprehended and assessed if one sets it in its context is not to imply that there is nothing novel in it. Moore's early philosophy includes a novel conception of propositions as both meanings and states of affairs which gives a new significance to logical analysis, and, by its unification of semantics and ontology, founds the project of analytic philosophy of language as ontology. There is perhaps here a modest moral for the study of the history of philosophy. Although I do not believe that this study can have a single methodology, since the questions to be raised concerning philosophers and their work are too various to be encompassed within anything worth calling a methodology, a simple analogy from the gestalt theory of perception, regularly employed to this effect by the phenomenologists (e.g. Merleau–Ponty 1945: 440ff), is instructive. On the gestalt theory, perception of a figure requires a ground from which the figure stands out; similarly, I suggest, critical appreciation of the work of a philosopher such as Moore requires a grasp of the context from which that work stands out. Figure/ground ambiguities are possible in the history of philosophy too: we can return to Bradley in the light of his treatment by Moore and Russell.

My aim, therefore, is to give a critical account of Moore's early philosophy by showing how that philosophy stands out against the idealist background. In undertaking this inquiry I shall draw on some of Moore's unpublished early papers which are now accessible, and it seems sensible to start with a brief description of the three works of this kind with which I shall be primarily concerned. Two of these are dissertations submitted in the annual competition for Prize Fellowships at Trinity College, Cambridge. The first was submitted in 1897 under the title 'The metaphysical basis for ethics', and part of this was soon published under the title 'Freedom' (1898a). That dissertation was unsuccessful in the competition; so a year later, in 1898, Moore submitted, this time successfully, a revised dissertation under the same title, which included most of the material from the previous dissertation, together with two new chapters, one of which forms the substance of his famous paper 'The nature of judgment' (1899a). These dissertations are crucial documents for my present purposes, for, as I shall show, in the first dissertation (1897) Moore's views are largely taken from the idealists whose work he then admired (especially Kant and Bradley); whereas in the second dissertation (1898b) he turned decisively against idealism. The third unpublished early work to which I shall refer is the text of a set of lectures on ethics, delivered late in 1898 (i.e. just after he had begun his Fellowship), and called 'The elements of ethics with a view to an appreciation of Kant's moral philosophy' (1898c). Moore contemplated publishing these lectures; but he wisely decided against this plan, although he did incorporate large chunks of them *verbatim* into *Principia Ethica* (1903b). The importance of these lectures is that they show how Moore begins to apply themes from his rejection of idealism to the construction of his ethical theory.

The predominant theme of Moore's youthful idealism, as propounded in his 1897 dissertation, is an opposition between reality and appearances; this is a distinction, he writes at this time, 'than which I know none more profound' (Apostles paper (unpublished mss 1897), 'What is it to be wicked?'). Moore understands the reality/appearance distinction in a roughly Kantian way, as a distinction between two worlds – a world of noumena, and one of phenomena; the distinction is founded upon his belief that Kant's first antinomy shows that time, and hence the world of phenomena, is inherently contradictory, and therefore unreal (1898a:195). It follows from this, Moore thinks, that one must reject 'the common point of view which takes the world of experience as ultimately real' (p. 194), i.e. empiricism. This rejection of empiricism, understood primarily as an ontological doctrine, is an aspect of Moore's early philosophy which, in a weaker form, as the claim that reality is not exclusively empirical, he retained long after he had abandoned the idealist doctrines which led him to it; but he always recognized that his anti-empiricism was initially stimulated by idealist criticism (cf. e.g. 1903b:110). His most famous application of this anti-empiricism is in ethics, in his ethical anti-naturalism, whose origins lie in this youthful idealism. For if one grants that ethics concerns the nature of ultimate reality, it follows that an empiricism which restricts itself to what exists in time, and is therefore unreal, cannot do justice to ethics. There is, therefore, Moore writes in the 1897 dissertation, a 'fallacy involved in all empirical definitions of the good', and this 'fallacy' is of course the first expression of the famous 'Naturalistic Fallacy' of *Principia Ethica*. It is worth noting that this 'fallacy' in empiricist ethics, as thus identified, owes nothing to Sidgwick, whom Moore was later to treat as the discoverer of the Naturalistic Fallacy, but everything to idealist philosophers whose work Sidgwick emphatically repudiated. I should add, however, that the 1897 dissertation also contains passages to the effect that there is a fallacy in supposing that goodness, the fundamental ethical concept, is definable at all, and this thought is rather closer to Sidgwick's position, though not a thought actually maintained by Sidgwick. This ambiguity concerning the identity of the Naturalistic Fallacy notoriously persists in *Principia Ethica* itself.

This early argument against empiricist, or naturalist, ethics requires the assumption that ethics concerns the ultimate timeless reality. Moore raises the question of the truth of this assumption at the end of 'Freedom' (1898a:204). His answer, extraordinary though it is that he should ever have given it, comes in the 1897 dissertation: 'that which is ultimately real appearing to us as the reason of whatever happens, is also necessarily "good", and alone absolutely good'. This claim, strongly reminiscent of Bradley (1897:ch.25), is the high water mark of Moore's youthful idealism; one year later it is rejected in the 1898 dissertation. This difference between the two dissertations is indicative of the fact that it is in the second dissertation that Moore commences his break with idealism. The break is not immediate and total. For example, Moore explicitly retains the crucial belief that Kant's first antinomy shows that time is unreal. But he now turns against the thought, which he had previously accepted, that there is a timeless noumenal reality which grounds, or provides a sufficient reason for, phenomenal existence. Yet Moore does not now embrace the empiricism he had previously rejected. For retaining the belief that time is unreal, and in conscious opposition both to empiricism, understood as an ontological doctrine about the sole reality of the temporal objects of experience, and idealism, similarly understood as an ontological doctrine about the sole reality of an atemporal supersensible world which grounds all phenomena, he introduces a realm of timeless beings which stand in no explanatory relationship to phenomena, and which can be apprehended as directly as any temporal phenomena. Natural numbers are, predictably, paradigm members of this realm. His ethical non-naturalism is therefore reformulated (in 1898c) to place ethical values within this realm of timeless being, with the result that ethical non-naturalism now stands opposed, not only to empiricist, or naturalist, ethics, but also to idealist, or metaphysical, ethics, as chapter IV of *Principia Ethica* makes clear.

Two questions now arise: first, when did Moore discard his belief in the unreality of time? Second, whether in discarding this belief, and thus accepting the reality of empirical existence, Moore undermined his ethical non-naturalism, and his general anti-empiricism? There is no straight-forward repudiation of Kant's first antinomy among Moore's early writings, but I myself think that he discarded his previous belief in the unreality of time pretty quickly, late in 1898 or early in 1899.[2] If this is right, it makes the second question all the more pressing: whether Moore has any good new arguments for his ethical non-naturalism, his 'Platonism' with respect to mathematical objects and universals, and for the conception of propositions as timeless objects of consciousness, all of which views he developed in the years immediately after 1898. Moore certainly has some new arguments for these positions: for example the 'open question' argument of *Principia Ethica* first occurs clearly in a review published in 1899 (1899b). The issue as to whether these arguments establish what Moore wants is, however, not easily decided, and I do not want to enter into it here. All I want to insist upon is that it was his belief in the unreality of time which initially prompted Moore to invoke a realm of timeless being; and thus that one of the characteristic features of Moore's early philosophy is inherited from the idealism against which that philosophy is directed with increasing passion.

In the 1898 dissertation Moore does not offer any serious argument against the hypothesis of a timeless noumenal reality which grounds temporal phenomena. He just says that he thinks that no good reason for such a hypothesis has ever been given. Insofar as he later addresses himself to this issue, he suggests that there is an insoluble problem as to how anything timeless could ground what is temporal (cf. e.g. 1903b:117–18), and this seems a fair point. It is, however, worth noting that Moore is typically rather unfair to many of those whom he criticizes on this issue, since he tends to ascribe a Kantian two-world reality/appearance distinction to philosophers such as Bradley and McTaggart whose reality/appearance distinction is not Kantian, but is rather the Hegelian complete/incomplete distinction. But what Moore does argue against in detail in his 1898 dissertation, and elsewhere, is Kant's view that the moral law expresses the rational structure of the Pure Will, and, more generally, Kant's view that *a priori* principles, whether theoretical or practical, are expressive of Pure Reason. Indeed the two chapters which constitute the

---

[2] Some of the articles written in 1899 for Baldwin's *Dictionary* (1902) clearly imply the reality of time (e.g. 'Change'); and the text of 'The nature of judgment' (1899a) does not easily accommodate a belief in the unreality of time. Although this article is certainly derived from a chapter in the 1898 dissertation in which this belief is explicitly propounded, the chapter from which it is taken survives only minus the parts used for the article, and the latter may, therefore, incorporate some modifications.

great part of the new material in his revised 1898 dissertation are primarily devoted to substantiating this criticism of Kant (though he is here developing points already briefly suggested in the 1897 dissertation). The essence of Moore's case against Kant is that Kant's account of the *a priori* is excessively psychological, and thus that the objections which Kant and other idealists raise against empiricist psychologism are equally valid against their own transcendental psychologism. So, in ethics, Moore writes (1903b:133), 'Kant's assertion of the "Autonomy of the Practical Reason" thus has the very opposite effect to that which he desired; it makes his Ethics ultimately and hopelessly "heteronomous" '.

I do not propose to discuss the justice of this familiar kind of criticism of Kant. It seems to me undeniable that there is a level of discourse in Kant, associated with his talk of a 'Copernican Revolution' (cf. Moore 1903b:133), which strongly suggests the views which Moore criticizes. It may be objected that Moore has failed to grasp the significance of Kant's transcendentalism; and though I think that this is correct, it seems to me a distinctive, and valuable, feature of Moore's philosophical style that he was always suspicious of transcendental moves in philosophy, be they Kant's or, later, Wittgenstein's. What I want instead to stress is that although Moore was emphatic in his rejection of Kant's 'Copernican Revolution', he also believed for some years that Kant had established some enormously important logical truths which needed to be liberated from the context of the transcendental philosophy – truths concerning, familiarly enough, geometry, arithmetic, substance and causality (1899a:190–2). This sounds like Strawson's 'austere' interpetation of Kant (1966:Pt 1); but there is an important difference between Moore's and Strawson's rational reconstructions of Kant. For Moore, Kant's important logical truths are of the form 'that *p* presupposes that *q*' (e.g. 'that this rose is red presupposes that there are permanent substances'), whereas for Strawson they are of the form 'that I can know that *p* presupposes that *q*' (e.g. 'that I can know that this rose is red presupposes that there are permanent substances'). Moore's principles are, therefore, separated from Strawson's by the principle 'that *p* presupposes that I can know that *p*'. Although Moore would, I think, have accepted this principle, he does not see any need for it, since his hostility to the 'Copernican Revolution' results in the view that all questions about the conditions for the possibility of knowledge belong to psychology and not philosophy. The result is that Moore's views about Kant's genuine insights, and his uses of Kant's terminology, are both far removed from Kant himself.

Moore retained his belief in these supposedly Kantian principles for a few years; for example, in 'The elements of ethics' (1898c), and elsewhere, he maintains that Kant proved the truth of determinism by showing that it is presupposed by the truth of any objective claim whatever. They disappear from his writings after 1901 when, I suppose, their intrinsic implausibility became apparent to him. His rejection of them may explain the puzzling absence from *Principia Ethica* of any discussion of free will, for his discussion of this topic in 'The elements of ethics' had been founded on the 'Kantian' argument for determinism. It is nonetheless important to grasp that Moore also, at least initially, conceived of his ethical theory as, in important respects, Kant's ethical theory minus his transcendental philosophy. He opens 'Freedom' (1898a) with the remark: 'The present paper is selected from a much longer essay on Kant's notion of Freedom [sc. his 1897 dissertation], which I hope in future to rearrange and enlarge into a treatise on the whole of his Ethical Philosophy'; and there is a sense in which *Principia Ethica* itself is the fulfilment of this project. This is most clearly seen in 'The elements of ethics' (1898c), whose full title ('The elements of ethics with a view to an appreciation of Kant's moral philosophy') explicitly adverts to this project, and which contains remarks such as that the Categorical Imperative is 'the opposite and refutation of the naturalistic argument' and 'amounts to the assertion that Good is good'. Admittedly, there is much in Moore's ethics that is not Kantian, especially his consequentialism, which of course comes from Sidgwick, and Moore does not pretend otherwise. But in important respects Moore's metaphysics of ethics, ethical non-naturalism, is Kant's metaphysics of ethics minus the latter's transcendental philosophy.

Moore's criticisms of Kant do not stop with his rejection of Kant's 'Copernican Revolution'. The anti-psychologism which, rightly or wrongly, he uses against Kant's conception of the *a priori* is a feature of a more general anti-subjectivism that is turned against other aspects of Kant's thought. As opposed to Kant's view that concepts are the work of the mind, Moore insists (1899a:179) that 'the concept is not a mental fact, nor any part of a mental fact'. And as opposed to the phenomenalism which he finds within Kant's account of objectivity, he insists not only on the separation of content from object in sensation, but also comes close to a denial that sensations have any content at all; thus he insists that pain is always an object of consciousness, and quite distinct from our consciousness of it (1903b:212). These claims are supported by a variety of arguments, more or less inconclusive, with which we need not concern ourselves. What is nonetheless to be noted is the presence, and persistence, of a realist hostility to subjectivity within Moore's philosophy. Although this is a theme which issues from his critical reflections on Kant's philosophy, it is obviously manifest in his stubborn insistence throughout his life that sense-data are not subjective, and in his less well known scepticism about the self (cf. e.g. 1914:174–5). I think that this anti-

subjectivism also helps to explain his inability to sympathize with Sidgwick's views about egoism. For if one believes that consciousness is just a
'transparent' awareness of independent objects (1903a:20), then it may
seem natural to suppose that there is no intrinsically subjective concept of
good – 'my good'; there is just the one objective concept of good. Moore, I
think, has this in mind when he writes (mss Feb. 1898) that 'the true good
requires one to do away with the distinction between the self and the
world'. This remark also provides an interesting point of contact between
Moore and his pupil Wittgenstein, who was likewise to reject the traditional conception of subjectivity (cf. *Tractatus* (1921) 5.63, 'I am my
world' etc.). The same theme recurs in the writings of Heidegger and
Sartre; there are, indeed, striking similarities between Moore's account of
consciousness in 'The refutation of idealism' and that propounded thirty
years later by Sartre in *The Transcendence of the Ego* (1936). These
similarities, and the shared theme of anti-subjectivism, should therefore
make one wary of Rorty's claim (1980: Pt 1) that analytic philosophy is
committed to having a 'theory of representation', and to conceiving the
mind as a 'Glassy Essence' that 'mirrors nature'. Moore manifestly rejects
these claims, but if he is not an analytic philosopher, then no one is.

I have so far concentrated on Moore's rejection of Kantian idealism. But
Moore was well aware that idealist philosophy had not stood still since
Kant. Moore's initial response to the Absolute Idealism of Bradley and
McTaggart was, however, considerably more favourable than was his
response to Kant. In the preface to the 1897 dissertation he writes 'It is to
Mr Bradley's *Principles of Logic* and *Appearance and Reality* that I chiefly
owe my conception of the fundamental problems of Metaphysics', and
there is a similar only slightly less warm passage in the preface to the 1898
dissertation, though of course this also contains the criticisms of Bradley's
views about ideas which later appeared in 'The nature of judgment'. But
Moore's attitude changed quickly. By 1900 he was abusing Hegel for
making self-contradiction respectable; and his 1903 paper 'The refutation
of idealism' (1903a) contains much sarcasm about the thesis of the spiritual
nature of reality which is clearly directed against Bradley.

Since Moore's oft-repeated charge against Absolute Idealism was that it
made contradiction respectable, one might expect him to concentrate his
fire upon the notion of the dialectic. In fact, however, it is to the notion of
an organic whole that he primarily directs his critical attention, beginning
with some knockabout abuse in 'The elements of ethics' (1898c; for some
characteristic abuse cf. 1903a:15–16 and 1903b:33–4). However, since we
have today rather lost touch with Absolute Idealism, thanks partly to
Moore, it is hard now to appreciate the significance of Moore's attack on
organic wholes. So I shall say a little about Absolute Idealism in order to

indicate where Moore makes contact with it, even though it is, I think, an internal feature of Absolute Idealism that it is extremely difficult to say anything brief about it which is neither misleading nor unfair.

The predominant feature of Absolute Idealism is an extreme commitment to holism. In some fashion, it is held, everything is so intimately connected with everything else that one cannot hope to understand any one aspect of the universe without a grasp of the ways in which this aspect relates to absolutely everything else. Already one can begin to see the point of the thoughts that the universe is an organic whole – a whole which is such that it is essential to each part that it be a part of that whole – and that all relations are internal – for it is because all relations are internal that the universe is an organic whole, though, equally, it is because facts, or judgments, are organic wholes that all relations are internal. But these thoughts provide only a crude characterization of Absolute Idealism. To get a little closer we can consider Bradley's late essay 'Relations' (1935). Bradley here distinguishes between three levels of consciousness: feeling (or immediate experience), judgment (or relational experience), and the Absolute, which somehow combines the inarticulate unity of feeling with the articulated detail of judgment. We have here something like the familiar Hegelian triad, in which the first two stages are 'transcended' in the last stage. Obviously many questions arise here – e.g. as to the kind of idealism required by the claim that the Absolute comprehends everything; but the aspect I want to concentrate on here is the account of judgment, and the degree to which it is misleading to attribute to Bradley the thesis that all relations are internal. This matters because although Moore and Russell both attributed this thesis to him, and argued that it was mistaken, Bradley protested that this involved a serious misunderstanding of his position (1935:642ff).

What should be clear from my brief sketch of Bradley's views is that it is indeed misleading just to characterize Bradley as holding that all relations are internal. For Bradley held that all relations (and not just external ones) are unreal, insofar as they are in some sense 'contradictory', and this is one reason why judgment is to be transcended by the Absolute. Nonetheless, there is some justification for the attitude of Moore and Russell to the thesis that all relations are internal. For although Bradley's most famous argument, which I discuss below, is an argument for the unreality of all relations, his emphatic rejection of external relations because they are external (cf. esp. 1897: appendix B; e.g. p. 579, 'Nothing in the world is external so except for our ignorance') is not matched by any similar rejection of internal relations because they are internal. And Bradley certainly does hold that there are essential connections between every aspect of reality; he writes (1897:457), 'There is nothing in the Absolute which is barely contingent or merely accessory.' Hence one might say that Bradley's view is that if, *per impossibile*, there could be any relations, they would all be internal; it is just that he also holds that the analysis of a judgment into a relation and its terms is mistaken, and, in this sense, that all relations are unreal.

One way of reformulating this point is to say that Bradley combines two kinds of holism – an essentialist holism which carries one up to the all-embracing Absolute, and a semantic holism, which is directed against the analysis of judgments. Many of Bradley's remarks about wholes are indeterminate between these two kinds of holism, and his views about relations are informed by both of them, as Moore himself noticed later (1919:277–8). Nonetheless, these two aspects of his holism can be separated, and in considering Moore's response to Bradley it is, I think, helpful to keep them apart.

Returning now to Moore's rejection of Absolute Idealism, the feature, as I mentioned, which Moore primarily singled out for criticism was the commitment to 'organic wholes', conceived of as wholes such that it is essential to any of their parts that they be parts of the wholes of which they are parts (cf. Bradley 1897:174; Moore 1903b:33–4). Given the essentialism of this conception, it is clear that it is essentialist holism that is here primarily at issue. Moore claimed that this very conception was incoherent (1903b:33–4), but his arguments to this effect are not persuasive. The set of even numbers is an uncontentious example of an organic whole in this essentialist sense. But what Moore's arguments point to is the danger of vicious circularity in explanations which involve organic wholes. For insofar as a whole is organic, it seems that the nature of its parts is to be explained by reference to the whole within which they belong; and yet it also seems natural to assume that the nature of any whole is to be explained by reference to its parts. Clearly, however, we cannot do both at once; and I think it was because Moore accepted, almost without thinking about it, the natural assumption that one should explain wholes by their parts (1903b:33) that he rejected the conception of an organic whole as incoherent. We are today less likely to accept without qualification Moore's natural assumption here, and to that extent likely to be more sympathetic to holism. But there is still a problem about the priorities of explanation within a holistic scheme, though this problem is eased if one operates only with a weaker holism which just introduces holistic constraints upon explanation, since this does not require the essentialism that is characteristic of a full commitment to organic wholes. It is only this weaker holism that one finds, for example, in the work of Davidson (cf. e.g. 1974).

Alongside Moore's criticisms of organic wholes run his criticisms of the thesis that all relations are internal. It is a misinterpretation of Moore to ascribe to him the view that all relations are external;[3] he just denied that all relations are internal, a claim which, I argued, could be ascribed to Bradley, albeit with due caution. Initially, as in the following passage (1899a:179), Moore just implies that there are external relations: concepts, he writes, 'may come into relation with a thinker; and in order that they may do anything, they must already be something. It is indifferent to their nature whether anybody thinks them or not. They are incapable of change; and the relation into which they enter with the knowing subject implies no action or reaction.' The atomism of Moore's critique of the holism of Absolute Idealism is nowhere more clearly expressed than in passages such as this. It is also characteristic of his thought that the denial of internal relations should arise through a denial of an internal relation between subject and object in knowledge. For this point connects directly with the criticisms of Kantian idealism which I have already discussed. Moore in fact says little directly on the topic of internal relations throughout the period of his disentanglement from idealism. His longest paper on the topic, 'External and internal relations', was written in 1919 and by that time Moore was more interested in developing modal logic (which he does with remarkable prescience) than in arguing against Absolute Idealism. Furthermore, although this paper contains some acute observations and arguments concerning internal relations, its central critical thesis, that upholders of the thesis that all relations are internal have been guilty of the simple modal fallacy of 'exporting' strict implication, is hard to accept. There is no evidence for this fallacy in the writings of Bradley. There is, however, a short paper from 1907 which is, I think, admirably expressive both of Moore's attitude to internal relations and of one of his character-istic methods of argument. Moore's paper was occasioned by Russell's review (1906) of Joachim's Bradleian book *The Nature of Truth* (1906). Russell had argued that Joachim was committed to the false 'dogma' that all relations are internal, but also that there was no way of showing to upholders of that dogma that it was mistaken without begging the question at issue. Moore responded by arguing that a method of proof was available: namely, by showing that the 'dogma' in question was inconsistent with something else which an upholder of it would not want to deny, in this case with such everyday contingencies as that he might not now be thinking about the things that he is thinking about. Hence, Moore implies, once we grasp that the thesis that all relations are internal rules out contingency, we will reject it.

This argument rests on an appeal to common sense similar to that employed by Moore in his later arguments against scepticism. It is open to the difficulty that an upholder of the claim in dispute can simply reject the

[3] This misinterpretation occurs in Passmore (1966:201).

common sense truism on the basis of which the disputed claim is to be rejected; and Joachim did just this in his reply to Moore (1907:414). It may seem, then, that Moore's argument achieves nothing non-question-begging, as Russell had predicted. But this is not wholly fair: for faced with a choice between a philosophical principle – that all relations are internal – and a common sense truism – that I might not be thinking about the things that I am thinking about – the burden of proof surely lies on upholders of the philosophical principle. And that is, in effect, Moore's point.

Perhaps this is not enough. Certainly Bradley attempts to discharge this burden, and neither Moore nor Russell do justice to the complexity of his thought. But it is hard to take essentialist holism seriously, and I want to turn now to semantic holism, which is what lies behind Bradley's argument for the unreality of all relations (1922:96; 1897:32–3). The core of this argument is that the judgment that aRb cannot be treated simply as the sum of the relation R and its terms a and b; for in the judgment that aRb the relation R is related in a specific way to a and b, and the nature of this relationship is not specified when the judgment is treated simply as the sum of these constituents, nor can it be specified by including a further relational constituent within the judgment. It follows from this argument that judgments cannot be treated as the sums of their constituents, and hence that relations can be at most abstracted aspects of complete judgments; and this is Bradley's reason for thinking that relations are unreal (where 'unreal' means incomplete). It is partly because he also thinks that judgments nonetheless present themselves to us as analysable into their constituents, insofar as it certainly seems to us that the meaning of a sentence is determined by the meaning of its constituent phrases, that he thinks that judgment is itself contradictory and therefore to be transcended within the Absolute. But we need not follow him here.

At this point we are back with the problem of explanatory priority which I mentioned before in connection with organic wholes, in this case that of the relative priority of word-meaning and sentence-meaning. Bradley's argument can be taken as a strong reason for insisting on the priority of sentence-meaning over word-meaning, in that there is no way of specifying the meaning of predicates except by reference to that of sentences in which they occur. It may be suggested that there are ways of getting round Bradley's argument by taking relations to be concepts in Frege's sense – i.e. essentially incomplete; but it is also arguable that Fregean concepts are derivative upon the thoughts expressed by whole sentences, and thus that this 'solution' to Bradley's problem simply concedes his conclusion.[4] It is notable that Russell, who grasped more

4 Cf. esp. Sluga 1980: ch.5.

clearly than Moore the impact of Bradley's argument, never invokes propositional functions to resolve the problem raised by Bradley – presumably because propositional functions are, at least in his early writings, abstracted aspects of propositions (cf. 1903:section 85). Yet undoubtedly, there is a price to be paid for embracing this Bradleian conclusion about the unanalysability of judgments, or, equivalently, the priority of sentence-meaning over word-meaning; for the familiar thought that the meaning of a sentence is determined by the meanings of its constituent phrases can now be given only a derivative status.

Since the issue raised here is a crucial one, it was a fateful moment for the early history of analytic philosophy when Moore and Russell rejected Bradley's argument for the unreality of relations. In thinking about the issues raised, they were doubtless not helped by its apparent connections with the thesis that all relations are internal, and with the merging of essentialist and semantic holism in Bradley's thought. But Moore, at any rate, was I think primarily guided by his natural assumption that the nature of a whole is to be explained by reference to its parts; in this case that the meaning of a sentence is determined in an ultimate fashion by the meanings of its constituent phrases. Moore showed himself less conscious than Russell of the difficulties of this position, but he was just as exposed to them. When he wrote (1899a:180) that 'a proposition is constituted by any number of concepts, together with a specific relation between them; and according to the nature of this relation the proposition may be either true or false', he is not only exposing himself to the objection that, on such a view, a proposition is, if true, necessarily true, and if false, necessarily false (a consequence actually embraced by Moore (*ibid.*:192), though his position could easily have been modified to avoid it, as it soon was); he is also exposed to Bradley's dilemma: is this 'specific relation' a constituent of the proposition or not? If it is, we have no proposition, but just a collection of concepts; if it is not, then the nature of the proposition is not determined by its constituents.

'The nature of judgment' (1899a), which is, as I mentioned, extracted, with perhaps further revision, from the 1898 dissertation, brings together most of the themes I have been discussing in a marvellously lucid fashion. Semantic atomism is manifest in the passage I have just cited; and despite his unnecessary commitment here to the view that propositions are, if true, necessarily true, the rejection of essentialist holism is manifest in a passage I cited before that concepts 'may come into relation with a thinker; and in order that they *may* do anything, they must already *be* something. It is indifferent to their nature whether anybody thinks them or not' (*ibid.*:179). This passage is also characteristic of Moore's anti-subjectivism, which reaches its climax in the final sentences of the paper in which he declares that the mind itself is just a complex proposition. And, finally, his ontological anti-empiricism, that is, his affirmation of a realm of timeless being, is manifest in his insistence that concepts are not to be explained 'in terms of some existent fact, whether mental or of any other nature' (*ibid.*:178).

The crucial doctrine of 'The nature of judgment' is, however, Moore's rejection of the correspondence theory of truth, and his insistence that truth and falsehood are 'immediate properties' of propositions, not dependent upon their relation to something else (*ibid.*:192). On this view reality simply comprises true propositions, and even ordinary material objects are somehow identified with true existential propositions. Moore was very excited by this latter thought: he wrote at this time to his friend Desmond MacCarthy (August 1898), 'I have arrived at a perfectly stagger-ing doctrine . . . An existent is nothing but a proposition: nothing *is* but concepts. There is my philosophy.' But it is not worth spending much time on this 'perfectly staggering doctrine', for Moore discarded it very soon. However, the claim that truth and falsehood are immediate properties of propositions is a central plank of the early philosophies of Moore and Russell, whose abandonment by them in 1910 (Moore 1953:ch.14; Russell 1910) is a clear sign of the end of those philosophies. It is, therefore, worth reflecting on this claim. In one way, it is just another instance of Moore's anti-subjectivism: propositions are the objects of consciousness, and since consciousness is a direct apprehension of objective reality, it follows that propositions must constitute that reality (though notice here a character-istic unhappiness about the status of false propositions; despite being objects of consciousness, they are not allowed to enter into reality). Thus propositions, on this account, are very much what we might regard as possible states of affairs; and there are obvious connections here with Wittgenstein's *Tractatus* (1921). There is also a connection with the development of consequentialist ethics: Moore is the first consequentialist to insist that what matters for ethical judgment is the value of 'states of affairs', a phrase he first uses in this connection in *Ethics* (1912:96), though he had written in *Principia Ethica* of 'states of things' with the same meaning (e.g. 1903b:183).

Once propositions are assigned their familiar role as the meanings of sentences, this realism concerning propositions entails that semantic doc-trines become ontological. Thus, given Moore's theory of truth in 'The nature of judgment', his semantic atomism turns into ontological atomism; and this identification of the semantic and ontological is the hallmark of the early philosophies of Moore and Russell. Since in 'The nature of judgment' Moore held, as we have seen, that propositions are somehow composed of concepts, this semantic doctrine leads to the ontological doctrine that concepts are the ultimate substances – 'nothing *is* but concepts', as he had expressed himself to MacCarthy (August 1898).

This ontological doctrine, however, leads Moore into self-contradiction. For concepts were initially held not to exist at all, but just to be (timelessly); this was Moore's anti-empiricism with respect to meaning. Yet the ontological doctrine, that concepts are the only substances, requires that some concepts should exist in time, as Moore explicitly acknowledges in 'The nature of judgment' (1899a:187). Moore therefore quickly changed his views in such a way that this problem no longer arises; in 1899 he radically modified his account of the constituents of propositions, replacing the concepts of 'The nature of judgment' with universals and particulars (cf. 1902, which was written in 1899), and insisting that whereas universals never exist in time, particulars can do so. Universals therefore seem to inherit his anti-empiricism about meaning, and particulars the ontological role of concepts as basic substances. But in truth there is not here any breach of the identity of semantics and ontology; for particulars can be meant, and universals enter into reality through their occurrence in true propositions. So it is only the general anti-empiricism about meaning with which Moore opens 'The nature of judgment' that is here discarded. Nonetheless, it is worth stressing that Moore changed his views in this way. For 'The nature of judgment' is by now well known, and there is a tendency to treat it as a blueprint for all of Moore's early philosophy.[5] Naturally, I do not deny that it was a crucial paper, as my frequent references to it demonstrate; but in assessing its significance one must realize that its theory of concepts was very quickly discarded. Indeed Moore drops the word 'concept' from his philosophical vocabulary for many years after 'The nature of judgment'. In *Principia Ethica* goodness, or good, is variously described as an 'object', 'idea', 'notion', 'property', and 'predicate' – but never as a 'concept'.

In the theory of universals and particulars which replaces the theory of concepts, nothing much needs to be said about universals, which are regarded in a conventionally Platonist fashion (1901:114); the particulars, however, are idiosyncratically Moorean. Moore treats almost every predicate as sortal, that is, as the distinctive characteristic of a sort of thing; and particulars are just instances of predicates of this kind, with the distinctive characteristic that the Identity of Indiscernibles does not apply to them (cf. 1901). Moore's standard examples of particulars are particular instances of a colour; his view is that particular colours of this kind can differ numerically even though they are exactly similar. It is a bare particular of this kind, a 'blue', which figures prominently in the argument of 'The

---

[5] E.g. Sluga 1980:176–7.

refutation of idealism' (1903a); and it is similarly bare particulars of this kind which lie behind the peculiar doctrine, characteristic in its blend of semantics and ontology, that most of a thing's properties are parts of it (1903b:41). For it is the particular instances of a thing's universal properties that are parts of 'the composite existents usually called "things" ' (1902:407).

It is not, I think, necessary to dwell on the defects of this strange atomist metaphysics, which was, incidentally, not wholly shared by Russell. Unfortunately, these Moorean particulars were to have a long future; for they are the prototypes of his sense-data – hence all those discussions as to whether sense-data are parts of material objects – and sense-data inherit many of their problems. What I do want to develop briefly, however, is the context for the problem which shattered Moore's confidence in his early atomist metaphysics. To set this up, one must grasp that these particulars do not even have to exist in time in order to be. For they can be constituents of wholly imaginary propositions as well as of true ones, and just as it makes no intrinsic difference to a proposition whether or not it is true, it makes no intrinsic difference to a particular whether or not it exists (1903b:206). This is not an accidental feature of Moore's views; it is required by his realist anti-empiricism with respect to propositions. For it is only because existence in time is never essential to particulars that Moore can hold that those propositions whose constituents include particulars that do exist in time do not themselves exist in time.

Yet this ontological generosity undermines Moore's 'refutation' of scepticism in 'The refutation of idealism'. Moore had here thought that he could use his anti-subjectivist account of consciousness as the awareness of independent objects as a refutation of scepticism. 'There is', he writes (1903a:27), 'therefore, no question of how we are to "get outside the circle of our own ideas and sensations". Merely to have a sensation is already to *be* outside that circle. It is to know something which is as truly and really *not* a part of *my* experience, as anything which I can ever know.' Once it is allowed, however, that the objects of sensation do not have to exist in order to be, or in order to be sensed (for that is his account of delusion – 1903b:197–8), it is apparent that the sceptical problem is back with a vengeance, now in the form of the question as to how we know that any objects of sense-experience exist, or are true. Moore's early philosophy provides no answer to this question, as he makes painfully clear in his 1905 paper 'The nature and reality of objects of perception' (cf. esp. pp. 95–6). From then on, therefore, Moore is engaged in a complex process of salvage and reconstruction, which never yields anything as putatively all-embracing as his early philosophy. Furthermore, he is forced to attend much more closely to issues of epistemology than he had previously done; he can no longer dismiss it as cognitive psychology. Yet throughout this long process he never really calls into doubt the triple themes of anti-empiricism, anti-subjectivism, and anti-holism which derive from his early encounter with idealism. And in that way, this early encounter established a theoretical framework out of which his thoughts never ventured.

REFERENCES

Bradley, F. H. 1897. *Appearance and Reality*, 2nd edition. London: Allen and Unwin

Bradley, F. H. 1922. *The Principles of Logic*, 2nd edition. London: Oxford University Press

Bradley, F. H. 1935. 'Relations', in Bradley, *Collected Essays.* Oxford: Clarendon

Davidson, D. 1974. 'Psychology as philosophy', reprinted in Davidson, *Essays on Actions and Events*. Oxford: Clarendon, 1980

Joachim, H. 1906. *The Nature of Truth*. Oxford: Clarendon

Joachim, H. 1907. 'A reply to Mr Moore', *Mind* 16:410–15

Merleau-Ponty, M. 1945. *Phenomenology of Perception*, trans. Smith. London: Routledge, 1962

Moore, G. E. 1897. Dissertation on 'The metaphysical basis of ethics', unpublished

Moore, G. E. 1898a. 'Freedom', *Mind* 7:179–204

Moore, G. E. 1898b. Revised dissertation on 'The metaphysical basis of ethics', unpublished

Moore, G. E. 1898c. 'The elements of ethics with a view to an appreciation of Kant's moral philosophy', unpublished lectures

Moore, G. E.1899a. 'The nature of judgment', *Mind* 8:176–93

Moore, G. E. 1899b. Review of F. Bon, *Uber das Sollen und das Gute* (Leipzig, 1898), *Mind* 8:20–2

Moore, G. E. 1901. 'Identity', *Proc. Aristotelian Society* 1:103–27

Moore, G. E. 1902. 'Quality', in J. Baldwin (ed.), *Dictionary of Philosophy and Psychology*. London: Macmillan

Moore, G. E. 1903a. 'The refutation of idealism', in Moore 1922

Moore, G. E. 1903b. *Principia Ethica*. Cambridge: Cambridge University Press

Moore, G. E. 1905. 'The nature and reality of objects of perception', in Moore 1922

Moore, G. E. 1907. 'Mr Joachim's "Nature of Truth" ', *Mind* 16:229–35

Moore, G. E. 1912. *Ethics*. London: Williams and Norgate

Moore, G. E. 1914. 'The status of sense-data', in Moore 1922

Moore, G. E. 1919. 'External and internal relations', in Moore 1922

Moore, G. E. 1922. *Philosophical Studies*. London: Routledge

Moore, G. E. 1953. *Some Main Problems of Philosophy*. London: Allen and Unwin

Passmore, J. 1966. *One Hundred Years of Philosophy*. London: Duckworth

Rorty, R. 1980. *Philosophy and the Mirror of Nature*. Oxford: Blackwell

Russell, B. A. W. 1903. *The Principles of Mathematics*. London: Allen and Unwin

Russell, B. A. W. 1906. Critical Review of Joachim 1906, *Mind* 15:528–33

Russell, B. A. W. 1910. 'On the nature of truth and falsehood', in Russell, *Philosophical Essays*. London: Allen and Unwin

Russell, B. A. W. 1959. *My Philosophical Development*. London: Allen and Unwin

Sainsbury, M. 1979. *Russell*. London: Routledge

Sartre, J.-P. 1936. *The Transcendence of the Ego*, transl. Williams and Kirkpatrick. New York: Octagon, 1972

Sluga, H. 1980. *Frege*. London: Routledge

Strawson, P. F. 1966. *The Bounds of Sense*. London: Methuen

Wittgenstein, L. 1921. *Tractatus Logico-Philosophicus*, transl. Pears and McGuiness. London: Routledge, 1961

◁ ═══ ▷

16

The nature of the proposition
and the revolt against idealism

PETER HYLTON

Writing in 1900, soon after his rejection of neo-Hegelianism, Russell made the following striking statement: 'That all sound philosophy should begin with an analysis of propositions is a truth too evident, perhaps, to demand a proof.'[1] What is remarkable about this statement is not just that Russell thinks the analysis of propositions to be of crucial philosophical importance, but that he thinks this fact is *obvious*. G. E. Moore was very closely associated with Russell at this time, and the first work that he published after rejecting idealism shows a similar concern with the nature of the proposition. It is called 'The nature of judgment'. In that article, and in the longer work from which it is drawn, Moore uses the notion of judgment as a point of attack against Bradley and Kant, and goes on to begin to articulate a metaphysics fundamentally opposed to that of Kant or Bradley or any other idealist.[2] So, at the moment when Russell and Moore rejected idealism the problem of the nature of the proposition was a central concern of theirs. In spite of what Russell says, it is I think not obvious why this should be so. What I want to do in the first part of this paper, then, is to sketch an explanation, in historical terms, of why this problem might have seemed to them, at that moment, a central and inescapable concern. In the second part of the paper I shall indicate how this explanation may shed some light on Russell's early views. Finally I shall talk very briefly about the point of the sort of historical enterprise that I have undertaken in this paper.

I begin with Russell's conception of the nature of the proposition in 1900 and immediately thereafter. This conception gives rise to a problem for

---

[1] Russell 1937a:8.
[2] Moore 1899. By 'the longer work from which it is drawn' I mean the 1898 version of Moore's Research Fellowship dissertation, 'The metaphysical basis of ethics'. Most of Chapter 2 of the dissertation is missing, but the internal evidence strongly suggests that the missing material was used in 'The nature of judgment'. I should like to thank the Librarian of Trinity College, Cambridge for allowing me access to Moore's two dissertations.

which Russell has no solution, and it is this unsolved problem that forms the chief theme of this paper. Russell took propositions to be abstract, non-linguistic entities. These entities are complex, i.e. made up of simpler entities which Russell calls *terms*. Because propositions are made up of simpler entities they must, according to Russell, be decomposable into those entities. (The validity of this process of decomposition, or analysis, as a philosophical method is a central claim of the new philosophy of Moore and Russell, and a point of sharp disagreement with their idealist precursors. It is important to note that Moore and Russell, at this period, thought of analysis as almost analogous to physical decomposition. It is not a matter of the definition of words, but of finding the parts of which things are in fact made up.)[3] Thus the proposition that Socrates is wise is seen as made up of two elements, one corresponding to 'Socrates' and one to 'wisdom'. (Russell sometimes suggests that there is a third element in a proposition of this form, corresponding to the copula 'is'; but his position on this seems to remain vague or agnostic – see *Principles of Mathematics*,[4] section 53.) Now granting all of this – and it is granting a lot – Russell still faces a difficulty about the nature of the proposition. In section 54 of *Principles* he says:

Consider, for example, the proposition 'A differs from B'. The constituents of this proposition, if we analyze it, appear to be only A, difference, B. Yet these constituents, thus placed side by side, do not reconstitute the proposition. The difference which occurs in the proposition actually relates A and B, whereas the difference after analysis is a notion which has no connection with A and B. It may be said that we ought, in the analysis, to mention the relations which difference has to A and B, relations expressed by *is* and *from* when we say 'A is different from B'. These relations consist in the fact that A is referent and B relatum with respect to difference. But 'A, referent, difference, relatum, B' is still merely a list of terms, not a proposition. A proposition, in fact, is essentially a unity, and when analysis has destroyed the unity, no enumeration of constituents will restore the proposition. The verb, when used as a verb, embodies the unity of the proposition, and is thus distinguishable from the verb considered as a term, though I do not know how to give a clear account of the precise nature of the distinction.

[3] This conception of analysis is manifest in Moore's discussion of the notion of definition, and of the sense in which good is indefinable (Moore 1903: section 8). After distinguishing two kinds of verbal definition, using the definition of 'horse' as an example, and saying of each that it is not what he means, Moore goes on to say: 'But (3) we may, when we define horse, mean something much more important. We may mean that a certain object, which we all of us know, is composed in a certain manner: that it has four legs, a head, a heart, a liver, etc., etc., all of them arranged in definite relations to one another. It is in this sense that I deny good to be definable. I say that it is not composed of any parts, which we can substitute for it in our minds when we are thinking of it. We might think just as clearly and correctly about a horse, if we thought of all its parts and their arrangement instead of thinking of the whole . . . but there is nothing whatsoever which we could so substitute for good; and that is what I mean, when I say that good is indefinable.'
[4] Russell 1937b. I shall cite this work in the text as *Principles*.

Without our accepting this as a definitive formulation, it will provide us with a useful way of getting at the unsolved problem which is posed by Russell's conception of the proposition, and which I shall sometimes refer to as the problem of the unity of the proposition.

I turn now to the task of sketching an explanation, in historical terms, of why this problem should have impressed Russell as a central one. Perhaps the first thing to do is simply to stress that the problem, or something recognizable as continuous with it, *has* a history; it did not spring fully formed from Moore's forehead in 1898. T. H. Green, in his Introduction to Hume's *Works*,[5] says that after Hume the nature of the proposition 'becomes the central question of philosophy, the answer to which must determine our theory of real existence just as much as of the mind' (Green 1894:185, section 224). So to a philosopher of the idealist tradition the question of the nature of the proposition was as central a question as it later was for Russell. How can we explain this?

I begin the attempt to answer this question by looking very briefly at a claim of Leibniz's. It is well known that Leibniz held that in every true proposition the subject-concept *includes* the predicate-concept. In his correspondence with Arnauld, for example, Leibniz says: 'I have given a decisive reason, which I take to have the force of a demonstration. It is that always, in every true affirmative proposition, whether necessary or contingent, universal or particular, the notion of the predicate is in some way included in that of the subject. *Praedicatum inest subjecto*; otherwise I do not know what truth is.'[6] It is, I think, correct to see this view as arising from what is in some sense the same concern as that which we have seen in Russell: how do the components of a proposition come together, what unifies them? In Leibnizian terminology, what is the relation between substance and attribute which makes it intelligible that a substance can *have* an attribute? Leibniz's answer has the form of a rejection of the question: nothing is required to unify the components of a proposition. They are already unified – the subject-concept contains the predicate-concept. The attribute is not something separate from the substance, whose relation to it may be problematic; it is already included in the substance. This answer connects with some of the most fundamental features of Leibniz's metaphysics. Since every substance contains its attributes, genuine relations are ruled out, as Russell emphasized in his book on Leibniz. According to Leibniz, then, the world is made up of completely self-contained substance – monads – among which there are no genuine interactions. Thus although Leibniz in some sense rejects the question, it is certainly not a rejection that denies all force to the question. On the

[5] Hume 1874. Green's Introductions are reprinted in Green 1894.
[6] Letter to Arnauld 4/14 July, 1686, translated in Loemker 1956:I, 517.

contrary, Leibniz seems to acknowledge that a central metaphysical issue is at stake: '*Praedicatum inest subjecto*; otherwise I do not know what truth is.'

Not surprisingly, we can see Kant as responding to these views of Leibniz's. And again, the response can be phrased in terms of the problem of the unity of the proposition. As against Leibniz's view that the problem of the unity of a proposition does not arise, Kant emphasizes the need for what he calls 'logical functions of unity in judgment'. These logical functions of unity are, so to speak, *ways in which* a judgment can be unified. For reasons which need not delay us here, Kant holds that there are exactly twelve such ways, twelve logical functions of unity in judgment. Now if we consider judgment not wholly abstractly, but rather as applied to sensible intuition, these twelve logical forms of unity in judgment become the twelve Kantian categories, as Kant makes clear in section 20 of the B Deduction (B. 143).[7]

The categories, Kant claims, are the only ways in which what he calls *synthesis* of the diverse elements given in sensible intuition can take place. This synthesis is the source of the unity and relatedness of these diverse elements. As Kant says at B.130, the combination or unity of diverse representations is not something that can be 'given through objects'; the unity of representations cannot be just a further representation on a level with the others. This unity is rather the product of synthesis, which is our own *act* of combining the various representations. This act of combination is the source of the unity of the manifold elements given in sensible intuition and this unity is necessary if the sensory manifold is even to be an object of awareness. Since, to repeat, this act of combination must take place in accordance with the categories, and the categories are derived directly from the functions of unity in judgment, it follows that 'The same function which gives unity to the various representations *in a judgment* also gives unity to the mere synthesis of representations *in an intuition*' (B.104–5). Experience for Kant is thus judgmental through and through. Even the simplest kind of experience, on Kant's account, involves bringing intuitions under concepts, and is therefore subject to categories.

I am not, of course, trying to summarize the Transcendental Deduction, but rather to extract from it a line of thought which is crucial for my purposes. We can see this line of thought as made up of two claims, and a conclusion from those claims. The first claim is that there are *conditions* on the unity of judgment, or synthesis: that it comes about only in certain definite ways, subject to certain constraints. The second claim is that

---

[7] I follow the usual practice of citing the second edition of Kant's *Kritik der reinen Vernunft* (1787) simply as 'B', followed by the page number of that edition. The translation used is Kant 1929.

experience is judgmental in character, and is therefore subject to the same conditions or constraints. The conclusion from these two claims is that the conditions of judgment are the conditions of possible experience, and thus also the conditions of any possibly experienceable world – conditions that must be satisfied by any world that we could possibly have experience of.

This Kantian conclusion is not the same as the claim which one might take as central to post-Kantian idealism, that these are necessary conditions of judgment, or a necessary structure to thought, which are also the necessary conditions or structure of reality as a whole. But the two are sufficiently close to make it comprehensible that Russell should have largely ignored the differences between them, and taken Kant to be an idealist. One point is worth making very briefly here about the differences between Kant and later idealists in this respect. The Kantian formulation refers to 'possible experience', or to 'a world that we could possibly have experience of', not simply to 'reality'. This is of course because of the Kantian distinction between phenomena and noumena, and the accompanying doctrine that the noumenal world, the world as it is in itself, is not an object of possible experience for finite beings. Kant's idealist successors, almost without exception, rejected the Kantian distinction and its accompanying doctrine that the noumenal world is beyond possible experience. They found the idea of a world beyond all possible experience to be incoherent. Reality, on this view, is not transcendent; it is not wholly beyond experience but is somehow immanent within it.

All of this has taken us a long way from Russell's worry about the unity of a proposition. Yet there is, I hope, enough continuity here to make it unsurprising that Russell and Moore should have taken the issue of the nature of judgment as a central metaphysical problem. The Kantian notion of synthesis can be thought of as providing a solution to a problem which structurally, at least, is very close to the Russellian problem. And given this Kantian move, the way is open, as I have tried to indicate, for an idealist metaphysics. If the necessary conditions of judgment are also necessary conditions of reality, or at least of the knowable world; and if judgment is in some sense our own act; then it is hard not to see the world as at least partially constituted by this act. Crucial to this account is the idea that the nature of the proposition is formed by what is in some sense a mental *act* – Kant emphasizes that synthesis is 'an act of spontaneity', which does something that could not be done by any representation which we received from objects (B.130). In the early stages of his reaction against idealism Russell opposes the view that sees propositions as in any sense formed by an act of the mind. The basic intuition behind this opposition can, I think, be expressed quite simply. The intuition is that what is true is true; it is true absolutely and objectively, and true regardless of any mental states or of the acts of any mind – it would be true even if there were no minds at all. But if a truth is to be true quite independently of any mind, then we must, it seems, oppose the view that says that propositions are constituted by acts of the mind, for this view makes the entities which are the bearers of truth or falsehood mind-dependent.

What I am taking as Russell's basic intuition here is one which, in some forms, is hard to deny. Hardly any philosopher, I think would want to say that I can take some arbitrary proposition and make it true or false by my acts or beliefs, or other mental acts; in some sense, almost any philosopher will agree that whether or not a proposition is true is independent of whether I happen to believe it. (I assume that we are not talking about propositions which are about me or my beliefs.) What is striking is not that Russell too wants to make these assertions, but that he interprets Kantianism in a way that makes it incompatible with them. In the Leibniz book he describes a view which he says 'constitutes a large part of Kant's Copernican Revolution' as the view 'that propositions may acquire truth by being believed' (1937a:14); and in the *Principles* he describes Kantianism, in a similar vein, as 'the belief that propositions which are believed solely because the mind is so made that we cannot help but believe them may yet be true in virtue of our belief' (1937b:450).

Now as interpretations of Kant such passages are quite misleading. Kant would of course deny that I can make something true by believing it; or that something which I cannot help believing must for that reason be true. Kant is not talking about mind in any sense of 'mind' in which you have one mind and I have another, perhaps quite different, mind; again, Kant is at pains to distinguish the empirical from the transcendental sense of such expressions as 'outside us' or 'independent of us'. Russell rides roughshod over such crucial Kantian distinctions. But this should not be seen as mere error on Russell's part; it is more interestingly the expression of a certain philosophical attitude. If asked, is this truth independent of the mind? a Kantian will presumably reply: in the ordinary sense, yes of course it is; but there is another sense of 'independent' and another sense of 'mind' in which . . . and so on. Russell, if I read him aright on this point, writes from a philosophical mood which is perhaps familiar, in which carefully drawn distinctions seem to be just equivocations, and all of one's opponent's subtlety looks like sophistry. The Kantian must say that terms such as 'objective' or 'independent of us' call for careful interpretation, and are perhaps ambiguous; Russell's position is that they have a perfectly clear sense to those unencumbered by a false theory. For Russell, the question: are there propositions which are true wholly independently of us and our beliefs? is not a subtle or ambiguous question, not a question which calls for a yes-in-one-sense-but-no-in-another-sense answer; the only possible answer is *yes* – full-voice, flat-out, no ifs, no buts. Anything less is tantamount to saying no. Russell, we may say, insists that there are naive senses of 'objective', 'independent of us' and 'true', and that these naive senses are all we need.

Russell's attack on Kantianism must, I think, be understood along these lines. But now, to avoid the Kantian position, Russell insists that the source of the unity of the proposition is in *no* sense a mental act or synthesis. A proposition, to put it another way, has to be something which we do not in any sense *make*; it has to be something objective in the most simple-minded sense, something *out there*. The tone of Russell's extreme naive realism about abstract objects can be seen in this passage from *Principles*: 'all knowledge must be recognition, on pain of being mere delusion. Arithmetic must be discovered in just the same sense in which Columbus discovered the West Indies, and we no more create numbers than he created the Indians' (1937b:451). This realism is hardly less marked in the case of propositions. Not only the entities which make up the propositions, but also, crucially, the propositions themselves, are out there, in Russell's version of some platonic heaven. Our relation to them is simply one of apprehension or recognition; the human mind, on this picture, is purely passive in judgment.

The most obvious problem raised by this way of thinking about propositions is the one with which we began the discussion: the problem of the unity of the proposition. Russell takes an extreme realist view both of the things which can be constituents of propositions – Socrates, wisdom, etc. – and of the propositions themselves – Socrates is wise, for example. Now in a case of this sort, the proposition is clearly made up from the entities in some way; but in *what* way? How do the entities combine to form the proposition? Russell admits that he has no answer to this question; but in fact the situation is worse than he suggests. The problem is in principle unsolvable within the metaphysical framework which he establishes.

It would require more space than I have at my disposal to argue this point with any care. Very roughly, the point is that according to Russell's early metaphysics everything – 'Whatever may be an object of thought, or may occur in a true or false proposition, or can be counted as *one*', as he says (*Principles*, section 47) – is a *term*, i.e. is independent and object-like. At bottom, we may say, he has only one ontological category, and it is that category which is most obviously exemplified by the subjects of subject-predicate propositions. It is this metaphysical vision that Russell relies upon to support the idea that philosophical analysis, as he understands it at this period, is a valid philosophical method (see p. 376 and n.3 above). An obvious contrast to the view that everything is object-like is Frege's distinction of concepts from objects; Russell's argument against this distinction is instructive. If the distinction were correct, Russell points out, concepts could not be logical subjects. In that case, he claims, we could not say anything about concepts, and nothing can be true or false of them. But the distinction cannot be drawn if we can say nothing about concepts, and if the distinction held, then there would be something true of concepts, namely that they are different from objects. So the distinction cannot be correct (see *Principles*, sections 49 and 481).[8] If everything is, so to speak, object-like, what *could* be the source of the unity of the proposition? Anything one might put forward as an answer would turn out to be just one more item in need of unification. One way to think of this is in the terms that Russell used in the passage I quoted from section 54 of *Principles* about the proposition 'A is different from B'. Russell's attitude there was that any component of the proposition would be – well, just one more component with the same status as the others. Only something with quite a different status, Russell implied, could play the role of unifying the components into a proposition. But Russell's metaphysics rules out the possibility of there being anything with this kind of different status. Russell's anti-Kantianism forbids an appeal to what is in any sense an *act* of unification or synthesis; and his metaphysics forbids any other kind of answer. The constraints within which Russell was working in the years immediately following his rejection of idealism make the problem of the unity of the proposition in principle unsolvable for him at that time.

Given the role which the issue of the nature of judgment plays in the idealist tradition, this fact ought to be a very serious embarrassment for Russell. We can see this more clearly if we talk about the issue of relations. Russell placed great weight on the reality and objectivity of relations. In *Principles*, for example, he argues that a refusal to accept the reality and externality of relations was responsible for many of the contradictions that philosophers had claimed to find both in mathematics and in space and time. Russell emphasizes relations in this way in large measure because the British idealists, much more than their German counterparts, had made

---

[8] For Frege's distinction between concepts and objects, see 'Über Begriff und Gegenstand' (1892), translated as 'On concept and object' in Frege 1952. It might be thought that Frege's notion of a concept embodies a solution to the problem of the unity of the proposition, but this opinion is mistaken both philosophically and textually. Concepts and objects can unite because concepts are, as Frege says, 'unsaturated' (*ungesattigt*); but this cannot be an explanation, for we have no understanding of this notion of unsaturatedness except in terms of the ability of concepts to unite with objects. It is, moreover, clear from Frege's writing that he did not hold that the idea of unsaturatedness has any explanatory power, for he intended that the notion of unsaturatedness, and thus also of a concept (and also, I believe, of an object), was to be understood in terms of the prior notion of a complete thought. As well as 'Concept and object', see Frege 1879:section 9, and Frege 1969:17–19, 273 (this last work is translated in Frege 1979, and the corresponding pages are 15–17, 253).

essential and explicit use of the notion – Bradley, I suppose, is notorious for having denied the reality of relations.[9] Bradley's metaphysics, however, is highly eccentric and atypical, so I shall talk instead about T. H. Green – much more nearly a nice normal British neo-Hegelian. Green, unlike Bradley, did not argue for the unreality of relations, but he did argue that they are mind-dependent. And since it is clear that it is not your mind or my mind that they depend upon, Green argued that there must be a single eternal mind, in which you and I partake, but which is independent of us.[10] (Nice normal British neo-Hegelianism tends to have a theological twist to it.) Now this is just the sort of view that Russell wants to reject by insisting upon the objectivity and independence of relations. But if one examines Green's arguments, it is clear that what is really moving him when he talks about relations is the problem of *unity* – in particular the problem of the unity of judgment and of fact. The issue is always how the *relatedness* of two things comes about. But this issue cannot be dealt with by Russell's tactic of just assuming that relations are among the things which there are in the world. For, as we saw in the case of 'A is different from B', assuming the abstract relation of *difference* is not a means of accounting for the relatedness of A and B. It would not, I think, have occurred to Green to distinguish the relation as such from the relation as actually relating, as the source of relatedness. But if one makes this distinction, as Russell did, it is clear that Green's concern is with the latter, with the possibility of relatedness, the way in which a relation actually *relates* its objects. And on this issue, as we have seen, no plausible line of reply is open to Russell in the early years of his anti-idealism. I think it is correct to say of the British idealists quite generally, as I said of Green, that their concern with relations is always a concern with the unity of the diverse and, in particular, with the unity of judgment. The fact that Russell has no coherent account of the unity of the proposition therefore seriously undermines his claim to have a refutation of the idealist view of relations.

Thus far I have been talking about Russell's views from the period 1900 to 1906. Sometime between 1906 and 1910, however, he comes to hold quite different views about the issues that I have been discussing. It is these new views, and Russell's reasons for preferring them to the old, that I shall now consider. My emphasis, once again, will be on the role played by the problem of the unity of the proposition.

The chief reason why Russell abandons his earlier view of the proposition has to do with the need to give an account of truth. We have seen that Russell unequivocally insists upon a straightforward view of truth: what is true is true absolutely and completely independently of us. Russell argues

---

[9] See especially Bradley 1930:ch.3.
[10] See, for example, Green 1883:section 51.

vehemently against the idea that truth could be a matter of degree, and against the view that it could depend upon the coherence of a number of beliefs with one another. Now the most natural view of truth, for someone with this sort of strong realist and objectivist attitude, is that it is based on some sort of correspondence between our judgments on the one hand and the reality that we judge about on the other hand. This sort of view of truth, however, is not available to one who holds the view of propositions which Russell held in the early years of this century. One way of seeing why this should be so is to emphasize the fact that Russell, in those early years, has no account of the unity of the proposition. Although he takes propositions as complex, i.e. as made up of other entities, he has no account of the way in which those entities unite to form the proposition. He treats judgment, therefore, as a relation between a person and a proposition, and in his account of this relation the composite character of the proposition plays no role. This fact is enough to rule out the view of truth as correspondence to reality as an option for Russell at this period. We cannot say that judgment is a relation between a person and a *fact*, because this threatens to make a false judgment into a relation between a person and nothing at all – whereas the same reality which makes our true judgments true also makes our false judgments false. The correspondence view of truth, in any form, thus requires that we see judgments as essentially composite or articulated. Judgments must be seen as having parts which correspond to parts of reality; only in this way can they be guaranteed a connection with reality which is independent of their truth. The correspondence view of truth is unavailable to Russell because he cannot, in this way, treat judgment as composite.

With the correspondence view of truth ruled out, it is no surprise to find Russell, in the early years of the century, treating truth and falsehood as simple properties – much as Moore had treated *good* in *Principia Ethica*, except that truth and falsehood are properties of propositions. According to this view, a true proposition is a complex that stands in a certain relation to the concept of *truth*; a false proposition is a complex which stands in that same relation to the concept of *falsehood*; and the concepts *truth* and *falsehood* are simple and indefinable. To say that truth is simple and indefinable, however, is to say that it is inexplicable, that we have no account of what it is for a proposition to be true, or of the way in which a true proposition differs from a false one. Russell's insistence on the objectivity and absoluteness of truth is at the heart of his opposition to idealism; but this insistence appears hollow in the face of his inability to tell us in what this truth which he so emphasizes consists. Since we have no account of *truth*, or of *falsehood*, or of the difference between them – they are simple and indefinable – we have no understanding of the difference between true propositions and false propositions. We can dramatize the difficulty that this created for Russell by showing that his inability to give an account of truth or of falsehood led him to two consequences which are very hard to accept. First, the fact that each proposition is either true or false, and that none is both, must be accepted as completely inexplicable, as a brute contingency. Second, and perhaps worse, if truth is indefinable and inexplicable then no connection is made between the truth of a proposition, on the one hand, and reality or fact on the other hand. If we cannot make this connection, and cannot say how truth differs from falsehood, then we cannot explain why our beliefs aim at truth rather than at falsehood. At one stage Russell realized, and accepted both of these consequences. In his article on Meinong (1904),[11] he says:

> It may be said – and this is, I believe, the correct view – that there is no problem at all in truth and falsehood; that some propositions are true and some false, just as some roses are red and some white . . . But this view *seems* to leave our preference for truth a mere unaccountable prejudice, and in no way to answer to the feeling of truth and falsehood.[12]

Then a page or so later:

> the analogy with red and white roses seems, in the end, to express the matter as nearly as possible. What is truth and what falsehood, we must merely apprehend, for both seem incapable of analysis. And as for the preference which most people – so long as they are not annoyed by instances – feel in favour of true propositions, this must be based, apparently, upon an ultimate ethical proposition: 'It is good to believe true propositions and bad to believe false ones.' This proposition, it is to be hoped, is true; but if not, there is no reason to think that we do ill in believing it.

Such a position is, I take it, evidently absurd. Even Russell, who had a White Queen-like talent for believing the impossible, came to find it so. In an article on the nature of truth written in 1906[13] he professes doubt about his view of propositions. When this article was reprinted in 1910 (in *Philosophical Essays*) the last section was replaced by a separate piece in which the doubt of the 1906 article is replaced by the firm opinion that his

---

[11] Russell 1904, reprinted in Russell 1973. The passages quoted in the text are from 1973:75–6.

[12] Compare Wittgenstein 1961b:6.111: 'All theories that make a proposition of logic appear to have content are false. One might think, for example, that the words "true" and "false" signified two properties among other properties, and then it would seem to be a remarkable fact that every proposition possessed one of these properties. On this theory it seems to be anything but obvious, just as, for instance, the proposition "All roses are either yellow or red", would not sound obvious even if it were true.'

[13] The original article was titled 'The nature of truth', and published in the *Proceedings of the Aristotelian Society*, 1906–7. In Russell 1910 the first two sections of that article are reprinted under the title 'The monistic theory of truth'. The third and last section of the original article is discarded, its place being taken by a separate essay entitled, 'On the nature of truth and falsehood'.

former views were wrong. Russell gives up the idea that there are propositions which are independent of our acts of judgment. Rather than conceiving of an act of judgment as the apprehension of a single entity entirely distinct from the act – a proposition – Russell now says that there are no such entities. He now takes judgment to be a relation between a person and various non-propositional entities which the person judging somehow unites so that a judgment is formed. This is the view which is known as the 'multiple-relation' view of judgment, because judgment no longer appears as a two-place relation (between a person and a proposition) but as a three-or-more-place relation (among the person and the various entities which, to use the language of the old theory, make up the proposition that is judged). It is important to note that the multiple-relation theory of judgment is not merely a theory about propositional attitudes, but also a theory about propositions. More accurately, a theory about propositional attitudes now has to carry much of the weight which was formerly carried by the theory of propositions. According to Russell's new view there are no propositions, and all apparent references to propositions have to be understood as being in fact references to mental acts of judgment or of understanding.

Now the most striking thing about this view, from the present perspective, is that it seems to accept just that feature of Kantianism which we saw Russell reject so vehemently: propositions become dependent for their existence (or pseudo-existence) upon mental acts. Russell's willingness to take this step must be seen in part as a result of a shift in his concerns. By 1910 the battle with idealism is, to his mind, long since over; Kantianism no longer poses the threat to him that it did in 1900. But this is only part of the explanation. More important is the fact that the step which Russell takes is not as large as it might appear. The crucial point here is that the mental act of unification which is involved in judgment imposes no constraints on what can be judged or, therefore, on what can be true. Unlike the Kantian notion of synthesis, Russell's appeal to a mental act of judgment imposes no limits or conditions upon what can be judged; so no general metaphysical consequences follow.

This un-Kantian feature of Russell's multiple-relation theory of judgment can be seen as leading to the downfall of that theory. In the case of the crude 1910 version of that theory which I outlined above, this point is relatively straightforward. Because the mental act which the theory of judgment involves remains purely formal and without the power to impose constraints on what is judged, that theory has the consequence that anything whatsoever can be judged. As far as Russell's theory is concerned, there is no reason why I cannot form a judgment from any selection of objects with which I am acquainted, and so judge, for example, that this table penholders the book.[14] Russell cannot say that what is judged must be a proposition, for his theory of judgment is not subservient to an independent theory of the proposition. The theory of judgment is, rather, intended to play the role of a theory of the proposition. Nor can Russell happily claim that the mental act of judgment itself imposes constraints upon what can be judged, for such a claim is a significant step towards a Kantian view of judgment. Russell's 1910 theory of judgment, therefore, does not explain why it is impossible to judge nonsense; it is thus quite inadequate to play the role that Russell intended it to play.

Given the inadequacy of the 1910 version of the multiple-relation theory of judgment, it is no surprise to find that Russell produced a more sophisticated version of that theory in 1913.[15] Central to the 1913 theory is the notion of logical form. It is still a mental act of judgment which unites objects so that a proposition is formed, but it is logical form which explains *how* these objects are united in the proposition. Logical form is, Russell says, 'the way in which the constituents are put together' ('Theory of knowledge', p. 183). To make a judgment, therefore, one must be acquainted not only with certain objects but also with the logical form which is the way in which those objects are united in the proposition formed by the judgment. If there is no such logical form for a given group of objects, then that group of objects cannot be united to form a proposition – the act of judgment, in such a case, cannot be carried out. Logical form is thus the source of the constraints on what can be judged. Russell identifies the logical form of a given proposition with a certain wholly abstract fact: that fact which is obtained if we replace all of the constituents of the proposition with existentially quantified variables. Thus the logical form of 'The book is on the table' is 'Something has some relation to something' $((\exists x)(\exists y)(\exists\varnothing)\ \varnothing xy)$. (Although we can best think of logical form by beginning with a proposition and replacing its constituents with variables, this process reflects only the order of our knowledge. The wholly abstract fact is prior to, and simpler than, the propositions of which it is the logical form; acquaintance with the abstract fact is a prerequisite of the act of judgment from which the less abstract propositions are formed. Relying upon the distinction between the logical and the psychological,

---

[14] See Wittgenstein 1961a:95, 103; and 1961b:5.5422. This criticism of Wittgenstein's seems to have been made not of Russell's 1910 theory but of his 1913 theory, which I discuss below.

[15] In a manuscript entitled 'The theory of knowledge'. This is the draft of a book which Russell never completed. Some portions of the book are published in the *Monist*, between January 1914 and April 1915; my references are all to unpublished material, and my citations are to the original manuscript pages. I should like to thank the Russell Archives, McMaster University, for making this material available to me, and for permission to quote passages from it. The completed portions of the book are soon to be published in Russell 1984.

Russell says that 'we need not be alarmed by this inversion of the psychological order' – 'Theory of knowledge', p. 244.) The obvious objection to make at this point is that our understanding of the proposition 'The book is on the table' is explained in terms of our understanding of the proposition 'Something has some relation to something', but that this latter understanding is left completely unexplained. Thus we seem to be left with a problem of exactly the same kind as that with which we began. In Russell's theory, however, the problems are not of the same kind. The understanding of wholly abstract propositions – those with no constituents other than variables – is different in kind from the understanding of all other propositions. In the case of wholly abstract propositions, understanding the proposition is identified with being acquainted with the corresponding fact. Understanding propositions cannot in general be explained in this way, for this would imply that every proposition which we can understand corresponds to a fact and is therefore true. For the special case of wholly abstract propositions, however, Russell is willing to accept this consequence: for propositions of this sort there is no duality of truth and falsehood; any such proposition must be true. Russell suggests that this fact is connected with the self-evidence of logical truth, but the part of the manuscript that was completed does not explore this connection.

Even from this brief sketch, it is clear that the 1913 version of the multiple-relation theory of judgment is much more complex than the 1910 version. The added complexity, however, is to no avail. The later theory succeeds no better than the earlier in reconciling Russell's atomistic and objective metaphysics with an explanation of the unity of the proposition. The failure of the theory can be brought out in two ways. The first, which seems to me the more straightforward, is to focus on the notion of logical form, and to show that Russell can offer no coherent account of logical forms. The second is to show that the 1913 theory is vulnerable to the same objection as the 1910 theory, i.e. that it cannot show why it is impossible to judge nonsense. This objection, although less clear-cut, is of greater historical interest because it seems to have played a large part in Wittgenstein's rejection of Russell's attempts to come up with a theory of judgment.[16] I shall briefly discuss both objections.

According to Russell's multiple-relation theory, a judgment is formed by a mental act of combination. This act is of course subjective – it is the act of the mind which judges. This view is, however, as far as Russell can go towards the idea that propositions are constituted by the mind; he holds

---

[16] See note 14. I do not mean to imply that this is Wittgenstein's only criticism of Russell's theory. In particular, Wittgenstein also attacks the view that one sentence's making sense can depend upon the truth of another sentence – the one which expresses the fact which is the logical form of the first sentence. See Pears 1977.

that not only the constituents of propositions but also the ways in which they are combined are objective. Russellian logical forms – unlike Kantian logical functions of unity in judgment – are thus objective and entirely independent of the mind. For Russell (and not for Russell alone), to conceive of something as objective in this strong sense is to conceive of it as an object. Russellian logical forms are objects ('Theory of knowledge', p. 181). This immediately suggests a difficulty. Logical forms must, in virtue of the role assigned to them, be wholly different in kind from other sorts of objects; what account can be given of this difference? Russell says that logical forms, although they are objects, 'cannot be regarded as "entities" ' (*ibid.*:181), but nowhere says how we are to think of them, or what the distinction between object and entity amounts to. This is not simply a matter of an unexplained notion, however: worse is to come. Russell argues that the logical form of a proposition is not itself a constituent of that proposition:

[The logical form] cannot be a new constituent, for if it were, there would have to be a new way in which it and the two other constituents are put together, and if we take this way as again a constituent, we find ourselves embarked on an endless regress.

It is obvious, in fact, that when *all* the constituents of a complex have been enumerated, there remains something which may be called the 'form' of the complex, which is the way in which the constituents are combined in the complex.

(*Ibid.*:183–4)

Yet in some propositions logical forms presumably *do* occur as constituents – in those propositions of 'The theory of knowledge' that discuss particular logical forms, for example. How this is possible – how we are able to talk about logical forms – is an issue that Russell never faces. The point, however, is very similar to that which he used as a reason for rejecting Fregean *Begriffe* (see p. 382 above). Whatever we can talk about, whatever there can be truths about, must presumably be capable of occurring in propositions. It is therefore absurd to suppose that there are objects which cannot occur in propositions.[17] Yet Russell's logical forms appear, at least, to be objects of just this kind.

The second objection to the 1913 theory of judgment is that it, like the 1910 theory, does not show that it is impossible to judge nonsense. If the theory were to show this, it would have to show that some groups of objects can, while other groups cannot, be combined in the way indicated by a given logical form. Because the logical form here is an object, distinct

[17] This issue is more complicated than appears from the text. It would be more nearly accurate to say that the supposition that there are objects which cannot appear in propositions is one that is absurd unless some kind of explanation of this fact is given for the particular kind of objects in question. In particular, this explanation would have to show that it is nevertheless possible for us to talk about such objects. Russell attempts no such explanation for logical forms, and it is not apparent that any such explanation is possible in that case.

from the group of objects which can or cannot be combined, the issue is one of the relation between the logical form on the one hand and the group of objects on the other. There must be a relation which a logical form has to those groups of objects which can be combined in the way represented by that logical form, and which it fails to have to groups of objects which cannot be combined in this way. If we are to have an explanation of the fact that certain groups of objects can be combined into propositions, while others cannot, we must have an explanation of the fact that this relation holds in certain cases and not in others. But it is quite mysterious what such an explanation might look like, and what facts it might appeal to. The point can be put like this. Given Russell's conception of an object, the potentiality, or lack of potentiality, which two objects have for combining into a proposition cannot be explained simply in terms of features of those objects: we have to invoke the notion of logical form. But if the potential for combination which the objects have cannot be explained in terms of features of those objects, then neither can the fact that the pair of objects stands in the appropriate relation to a logical form. The introduction of logical forms, or of further objects, is simply irrelevant to the task of explaining why certain groups of objects can be combined to form propositions, while other groups cannot. The 1913 theory is thus no better able to explain this than was the 1910 theory.

The objection of the previous paragraph is, as I have said, Wittgenstein's – although the method of explaining and arguing for it is not. Wittgenstein's criticisms had a devastating effect on Russell. Writing to Lady Ottoline Morrell in May 1913 he said:

I showed him [Wittgenstein] a crucial part of what I have been writing. He said it was all wrong, not realizing the difficulties – that he had tried my view and knew it wouldn't work. I couldn't understand his objection – in fact he was very inarticulate – but I feel in my bones that he must be right, and that he has seen something I missed.[18]

By the end of the summer Russell had abandoned 'The theory of knowledge', and the book was never completed. Three years later, writing to Lady Ottoline Morrell about that period, he wrote: 'His [Wittgenstein's] criticism . . . was an event of first-rate importance in my life, and affected everything I have done since. I saw he was right, and I saw that I could not hope ever again to do fundamental work in philosophy.'[19] There is, I think, a sense of 'fundamental' on which this assessment is correct. For further insight into the issues that I have been discussing we must look not to any work of Russell's but to Wittgenstein's *Tractatus*. There we see the issue of the nature of the proposition resolved, and with it questions about the

[18] Russell to Lady Ottoline Morrell, 28 May 1913. Quoted in Clark 1976:204.
[19] Russell to Lady Ottoline Morrell, 1916 (exact date unknown). Quoted in Russell 1968:57.

nature of truth and of the status of logic. The metaphysical price for this resolution, however, is no lower for Wittgenstein than it was for the idealists. And indeed, one might well be struck by the way in which the *Tractatus* not only contains ideas which are familiar from our discussion of Russell's work, but also resurrects certain idealist themes. The idea of logical form, and more particularly, the idea that the logical form of a proposition is a *fact*, are clearly Russellian ideas which Wittgenstein transforms; again, the idea that logical form is something about which we cannot speak is an idea strongly suggested by Russell's work, although Russell himself would not have accepted it. Doctrines familiar to idealism are interwoven with these Russellian ideas. The unspeakability of logical form goes along with a distinction between the transcendental and the empirical standpoints: the transcendental standpoint is that of the unspeakable truths and the superlative facts which make possible the ordinary facts and truths of the empirical standpoint. Again, there is a sense in which the logical form of which the *Tractatus* speaks is one, a single and indivisible whole. While still atomistic on the empirical level, the *Tractatus* revives a kind of monism at the transcendental level. Most obvious of all, perhaps, is the idea of a necessary structure to thought or language which is also the necessary structure of the world. That it is language, rather than thought, which bears the metaphysical weight in the *Tractatus* is a fact which, from a sufficiently distant perspective, might seem less significant than the revival of the fundamental Kantian idea of a necessary structure of the (knowable) world.

I want now, in the rest of this paper, to stand back and reflect upon the kind of enterprise that I have been engaged in so far. I began by asking why Russell, at the turn of the century, should have held the nature of the proposition to be a central philosophical issue. I went on to sketch a partial answer to this question in terms of the idealist background to Russell's thought, and to indicate some of the further ramifications which the issue of the nature of the proposition had in Russell's work early in this century. I shall now raise a question about my original question: what is one doing in asking such a question, and in offering the kind of answer that I have sketched?

It might be held that there is a straightforward philosophical problem about the nature of the proposition, a problem which can perfectly well be understood independently of the historical background against which it arises. If one holds this view of the matter, then one will naturally think that the question: why was Russell concerned with this problem? is simply a question about *Russell* – what features of his mind or his historical position led him to focus on this problem? The question with which I began the paper will thus seem to be a purely historical or even psychological question, interesting enough in its way, no doubt, but not relevant to the substantive philosophical issue of the nature of the proposition, or to any other substantive philosophical issue. Now I hope that the main body of this paper has done something to make this attitude unappealing. In particular, I hope to have made it plausible that asking *why* Russell was interested in the nature of the proposition is inseparable from asking what exactly it was that he was interested in when he was interested in the nature of the proposition; or asking, what is the issue of the nature of the proposition, as Russell understood it? To understand the question, 'What is a proposition?', as Russell asked it, one must have some idea of the context of the question – why it arises, what purpose the answer is to serve, the constraints within which this answer is to be sought, and so on. It is from such things that the question gets its life and its force.

The claim that I am making is a claim about what it is to understand Russell's concern with the nature of the proposition. Understanding here demands that we recapture Russell's presuppositions and motives, that we see what general views he takes for granted, or wishes to advance, or wishes to oppose; and that we see how he interpreted these views and how he connected them with one another and with other views. To identify the problems at stake, and the arguments being put forward, we have to articulate the framework within which the problems arise and the arguments operate. In particular, we have to see how the historical context gives rise to this framework. A claim of this sort, about what is involved in understanding something, is also a claim about the nature of the thing that is to be understood. Although I spoke of Russell's question on the one hand, and of the context of that question on the other, I do not mean to suggest that these can be thought of as separate and independent items. My claim is, on the contrary, that Russell's question is that question which it is only in virtue of its context. The context is, if you like, partially constitutive of the question.

The complexity and context-dependence which, I have claimed, hold of Russell's problem of the nature of the proposition are, I think characteristic of many philosophical views or problems. I have not, of course, substantiated this general view here; at most I have sketched a single illustration. I shall, nevertheless, say something about the interest which I take this view to have. In particular, I shall say something about the difference that this view makes to our understanding of the relation between philosophy and its history. A crucial part of understanding this relation is, I take it, to explain why the study of the history of philosophy should be thought of as being itself a philosophical activity. One answer to this which is, I think, quite widely accepted, is that there are certain philosophical problems which we are concerned to solve, and that studying classic philosophical texts helps us to find solutions to them. This is the sort of view that John Mackie, for example, advances in the introduction to his book on Locke.[20] The 'main aim' of the book, he says there, 'is not to expound Locke's views, or to study their relations with those of his contemporaries or near contemporaries, but to work towards solutions of the problems themselves'. The philosophical problems here are taken as given. The emphasis is on solving these problems and, in this enterprise, we enlist the help of Locke, or Russell, or Kant, or of anyone whose work we find useful. Studying the history of philosophy, insofar as this is a philosophical activity, is, on this view of the matter, a cooperative endeavour aimed at solving philosophical problems. Seeing things in this way makes the historical aspect of the history of philosophy – the fact that the texts that we study were written at specific moments in the past – irrelevant to its philosophical uses. The cooperative endeavour would go forward in the same way whenever the works had been written.

I wish to propose a rather different way of thinking about the relation of philosophy to its history, which is suggested by the view of philosophical understanding which I have been discussing. The emphasis here is not so much on solving philosophical problems as on gaining a deeper understanding of what a given problem is, why it arises, what gives it its force, why it grips us or fails to grip us. The main body of the paper suggested the way in which an appeal to its historical background might give us a deeper understanding of Russell's problem of the nature of the proposition. But the real interest and philosophical point of these ideas emerges when we think of their application not to others but to ourselves and our own philosophical activity. Where do the problems that grip us come from? What gives them their force, and why do they grip us? To confront questions of this sort is to attempt to understand our own philosophical position in terms of our philosophical history. Our own philosophy no more takes place in an historical vacuum than did Russell's, and like Russell's, our own philosophical position is in part to be understood in terms of its historical context. Self-understanding, on this view, is one of the motives to a study of the history of philosophy.

It may, however, be questioned whether this view of the history of philosophy as a search for historical self-understanding does justice to the philosophical importance that I wish to claim for it. Similar historical enterprises have been undertaken for a variety of subjects, including the more prestigious sciences; yet the practitioners of those sciences do not seem to find this historical knowledge of any relevance to their scientific work. An examination of episodes in the history of physics, say, can teach

[20] Mackie 1976:2.

us something about what physics is. But the sort of thing we can learn here seems to be of interest to philosophers of physics but not, in their professional capacity, to physicists themselves.[21] Why is philosophy not like this? We cannot answer this question by appealing to the fact that a philosopher of physics is not a physicist, whereas a 'philosopher of philosophy' (if there were any) would be a philosopher. One objection to this answer is that it appeals to institutional arrangements and departmental boundaries without considering their rationale; it thereby simply fails to meet the question. A second objection is that the answer suggests that an interest in the nature of philosophy is, or ought to be, the concern of a number of specialists within philosophy, rather as the philosophy of physics is; this picture clearly misrepresents the matter. A more nearly satisfactory answer involves substantive and controversial claims. In particular, I wish to claim that the nature of philosophy is something which is always liable to arise in the course of ordinary philosophical argument. Philosophy is a subject for which the meaningfulness of its terms and the correctness of its procedures is always an issue; the distinction between philosophy and metaphilosophy is therefore not a useful one, because meta-level issues constantly arise within the practice of the subject.[22] These claims are claims about the nature of philosophy, and are to be established not by direct argument but by the accumulated weight of examples which bear it out; in other words, these claims are to be established historically. We are thus in a curious, but not paradoxical, position. I argued that one reason for a philosophical interest in the history of philosophy is that we learn from it something about the nature of philosophy. But the claim that what we can learn in this way is relevant to the practice of philosophy is itself one that must itself be established historically. The weakness of this position is that it will do nothing to persuade those who hold that the lessons of the past do not apply because we have, at last, found the true method and made philosophy a science – which I take to mean, among other things, that it can safely proceed in a relative ignorance of its own history and without worries as to its nature. To those who are capable of believing this there is nothing that can be briefly said, except perhaps to observe that their idea, that philosophy has broken with its past and become a science, is itself one that has a long history. Mark Twain observed that giving up smoking was easy, he had done it a hundred times; the same might be said of philosophy's attempts to repudiate its past and establish

---

[21] Compare Kuhn 1977:120: 'Among the areas to which the history of science relates, the one least likely to be significantly affected is scientific research itself.'

[22] Compare Cavell 1969:xviii: 'I would regard this fact – that philosophy is one of its own normal topics – as in turn defining for the subject . . .' The Foreword to this book has been a recurrent source of inspiration and instruction to me in my attempts to think about the nature of philosophy, and its relation to its history.

itself on a new, and scientific, footing. This does not, of course, show that the latest attempt will not be successful, but it does suggest that the appropriate attitude is a sceptical one.

I claimed that the nature of philosophy is always liable to become an issue in ordinary philosophical argument; and I said that this claim could only be established historically. Short of doing this historical work, however, there are ways of thinking about the claim which may be helpful. One such way, which I shall call the negative way, can best be approached through the most pessimistic attitude towards philosophy. The pessimist contrasts philosophy with the most obviously successful sciences – especially physics. As philosophers have long insisted, physics is successful in ways in which philosophy is not. In the light of this contrast, the pessimist goes on, there is every reason why philosophers should question the meaningfulness of philosophical terms and the correctness of philosophical procedures, for the (relative) failure of philosophy gives reason to think that those terms are meaningless, and those procedures incorrect. On this pessimistic view, philosophy is and ought to be a self-reflective subject because it is at best an open question whether this subject has any claims to be regarded as a branch of knowledge at all. Some of the ideas on which this pessimistic view is based must be accepted. First, philosophy is not a science, not a technical subject; if it is thought of as a science it will certainly appear as a most unsuccessful one. Secondly, the terms in which the past is subjected to philosophical criticism, and a new philosophical doctrine advanced, are specific to that new philosophy. (To adapt an idiom of Kuhn's, we may say there is no 'normal philosophy'.)[23] A less pessimistic attitude towards these same facts would emphasize the idea that in philosophy we seek to question the fundamental presuppositions of various kinds of human knowledge and activity. A subject of this sort must inevitably be concerned with its own fundamental presuppositions; and once these are at stake they will clearly play a special role, for to question them is implicitly to question all the other philosophical conclusions that we may have reached.

A second, and positive, way of thinking about the self-reflective character of philosophy appeals to the connection between philosophy and self-knowledge. Thought of in this way, philosophical criticism is directed, in the first instance, not against the ignorance of others but against the confusions to which one is oneself constantly vulnerable. What one can hope to gain from philosophy is not, primarily, positive doctrine but rather a clearer mind and a deeper insight into one's position in the world. If these Socratic ideas appeal to us at all, then it will seem unsurprising that the philosophical enterprise should itself be subject to philosophical examina-

[23] Kuhn 1962.

tion and criticism. If, indeed, we accept that philosophy has to do peculiarly with self-knowledge, we might well find it obvious from the start that the history of philosophy is a part of philosophy itself. One way in which we can understand our own philosophical position is historically, by seeing how it has developed through time. At this point it becomes clear that thinking about Russell and his break with idealism does more than provide us with an example of an interesting philosophical moment. Russell's break with idealism is a decisive point in the development of what is sometimes called the analytic tradition in twentieth-century philosophy. Many of us are in some more or less remote sense the heirs of Russell, as also perhaps of Frege and the young Wittgenstein. Here I include those who find the approach of these authors deeply misguided, and who struggle to free themselves from it and to develop alternatives; as the example of Russell and idealism itself shows, a philosophical position must be understood in terms of what it is most fundamentally reacting against, as well as of the positive aim that it hopes to achieve. In studying Russell's break with idealism we are, therefore, studying a crucial moment in the historical background to our own philosophical period. My subject in this paper has been an issue in the history of philosophy, but my ulterior aim has been philosophical self-knowledge. What I hope I have conveyed in these concluding remarks is the idea that philosophical self-knowledge and an understanding of our own philosophical history are intimately connected.[24]

REFERENCES

Bradley, F. H. 1930. *Appearance and Reality*. Oxford: Oxford University Press. 1st edition 1893, 2nd edition, with Appendix, 1897

Cavell, Stanley. 1969. *Must We Mean What We Say?* New York: Scribners

Clark, Ronald W. 1976. *The Life of Bertrand Russell*. New York: Knopf

Frege, G. 1879. *Begriffsschrift*. Halle: L. Nebert

Frege, G. 1952. *Translations from the Philosophical Writings of Gottlob Frege*, ed. Peter Geach and Max Black. Oxford: Blackwells

Frege, G. 1969. *Nachgelasseneschriften*, ed. H. Hermes *et al.* Hamburg: Felix Meiner Verlag

Frege, G. 1979. *Posthumous Writings*, ed. H. Hermes *et al.* Oxford: Blackwells

Green, T. H. 1883. *Prolegomena to Ethics*, ed. A. C. Bradley. Oxford: Oxford University Press

[24] Versions of this paper were read at the University of Pennsylvania, the University of California at Berkeley and the University of Chicago, as well as Johns Hopkins University. I should like to thank the audiences at each of these institutions for their comments. I have also benefited from discussions with Stefan Collini, Christine Korsgaard, Dan Lloyd, Susan Neiman, Hubert Schwyzer and, especially, Burton Dreben about earlier drafts. Part of the work on this paper was supported by the American Council of Learned Societies, under a programme made possible in part by the National Endowment for the Humanities.

Green, T. H. 1894. *The Works of Thomas Hill Green*, vol. I, ed. R. L. Nettleship. London: Longmans, Green, and Co. 1st edition 1885

Hume, D. 1874. *Works*, ed. T. H. Grose and T. H. Green. London: Longmans

Kant, I. 1929. *Critique of Pure Reason*, trans. N. Kemp Smith. London: Macmillan

Kuhn, T. S. 1962. *The Structure of Scientific Revolutions*. Chicago: Chicago University Press. Enlarged edition 1970

Kuhn, T. S. 1977. *The Essential Tension*. Chicago: Chicago University Press

Loemker, L. E. (ed.). 1956. *Leibniz: Philosophical Papers and Letters*. Chicago: Chicago University Press

Mackie, J. L. 1976. *Problems from Locke*. Oxford: Oxford University Press

Moore, G. E. 1899. 'The nature of judgment', *Mind* 8: 176–93

Moore, G. E. 1903. *Principia Ethica*. Cambridge: Cambridge University Press

Pears, David. 1977. 'The relation between Wittgenstein's picture theory of propositions and Russell's theories of judgment', *Philosophical Review* 86:177–96

Russell, B. 1904. 'Meinong's theory of complexes and assumptions', *Mind* n.s. 13:204–19, 336–54, 509–24

Russell, B. 1910. *Philosophical Essays*. London: George Allen & Unwin. Revised edition 1966

Russell, B. 1937a. *The Philosophy of Leibniz*. London: George Allen & Unwin. 1st edition 1900

Russell, B. 1937b. *The Principles of Mathematics*. London: George Allen & Unwin. 1st edition 1903

Russell, B. 1968. *Autobiography*, vol. II. London: George Allen & Unwin

Russell, B. 1973. *Essays in Analysis*, ed. D. Lackey. New York: Brazillier

Russell, B. 1984. *Collected Papers*, vol. VII. London: George Allen & Unwin (forthcoming)

Wittgenstein, L. 1961a. *Notebooks 1914–16*. Chicago. Rev. edn 1979

Wittgenstein, L. 1961b. *Tractatus Logico-Philosophicus*, published with a translation by D. F. Pears and B. F. McGuiness. London. 1st edn 1921

INDEX